Stockholm

Graeme Cornwallis

LONELY PLANET PUBLICATIONS
Melbourne • Oakland • London • Paris

Stockholm
1st edition – September 2001

Published by
Lonely Planet Publications Pty Ltd ABN 36 005 607 983
90 Maribyrnong St, Footscray, Victoria 3011, Australia

Lonely Planet offices
Australia Locked Bag 1, Footscray, Victoria 3011
USA 150 Linden St, Oakland, CA 94607
UK 10a Spring Place, London NW5 3BH
France 1 rue du Dahomey, 75011 Paris

Photographs
Many of the images in this guide are available for licensing from
Lonely Planet Images.
email: lpi@lonelyplanet.com.au
Web site: www.lonelyplanetimages.com

Front cover photograph
Statue by the waterfront, Stockholm (Lee Foster; image digitally
modified by Lonely Planet)

ISBN 1 74059 011 2

text & maps © Lonely Planet Publications Pty Ltd 2001
photos © photographers as indicated 2001

Printed by Craft Print International Ltd, Singapore

Contents – Text

2 Contents – Text

Contents – Maps

FACTS ABOUT STOCKHOLM

WALKING TOURS

THINGS TO SEE & DO

EXCURSIONS

COLOUR MAP SECTION   see back pages

The Author

GRAEME CORNWALLIS

Born and raised in Edinburgh, Graeme later wandered around Scotland before coming to rest in Glasgow. While studying astronomy at Glasgow University, he developed a passion for peaks – particularly the Scottish Munros – and eventually bagged all 284 summits over 3000ft in Scotland at least once. Graeme has travelled extensively throughout Scandinavia and he has a detailed knowledge of Sweden. He has also travelled widely in Asia, North and South America and the Pacific. Mountaineering successes include trips to the Bolivian Andes, Norway and Arctic Greenland; Graeme has also scaled Kebnekaise, the highest peak in Sweden. When he's not hiking, climbing, travelling or writing, Graeme teaches mathematics and physics at home in Glasgow.

FROM THE AUTHOR

Thanks are due to all the people who helped this book become reality. In particular, I'd like to thank the following: Margaret Cornwallis in Glasgow, for reading and checking the text; Fran Hooker, from St Louis, for companionship and good humour during the research period; Emelie Klein and Ann-Charlotte Carlsson at the Swedish Travel & Tourism Council in London, for their invaluable assistance with a variety of queries; Magnus Welin in Stockholm, for interesting chats and help with several complex issues; and Lars, Catarina and Anders Liljegren for a fantastic Christmas, advice on the glossary and a great pub crawl in Södermalm.

The staff at *af Chapman*, notably Sara, Hanna, Helena, Kirsi, Peter and Lena, allowed access to their detailed background knowledge on almost every aspect of the city. Åsa Ivarsson at Svenska Turistföreningen helped with a range of STF questions. Valuable conversations and coffee were provided by Christer Andersson and Mårten Skånman at alltomstockholm.se. Sylvie Kjellin, Charlotta Lorentz and Fanny Löfgren at SIS provided useful contacts and vast amounts of tourist-oriented material. Thomas Carlhed at the Swedish Institute helped with background information on the city, its people and culture. Camilla Sundelin at the Stadshotell in Sala helped out while the tourist office was closed.

Skansen was made all the more interesting by lively Marita Wikander. Stephen Fried at Fjärilshuset provided an insight into expat life for a Brit in Stockholm. Thanks to Britt Reuter-Hörnstedt and friends for their advice on the Shopping chapter. Last, but not least, thanks to Erik Stenfors, Peter Stenfors and Anita Andersson for another glimpse into Stockholm family life.

This Book

FROM THE PUBLISHER

This 1st edition of *Stockholm* was produced in Lonely Planet's Melbourne office. The mapping and design were coordinated by the *yerba*-sipping Agustín Poó y Balbontin and the book was edited by coffee-sipping Elizabeth Swan. They were assisted by the dynamic editing duo of Melanie Dankel and Darren O'Connell, and the fantastic mapping team of Yvonne Bischofberger, Csanád Csutoros, Cris Gibcus, Sally Morgan and Ray Thomson. Emma Koch compiled the Language chapter and answered all our Swedish-language queries *(tak!)*, Daniel New designed the beautiful cover, Birgit Jordan created the climate chart and Barbara Dombrowski in LPI supplied the colour slides. Matt King coordinated the illustrations, which were drawn by Kelli Hamblett (KH) and Mick Weldon (MW). A big *tak* to Mark Germanchis for his quick Quark assistance during layout, to Darren for last-minute map referencing, and to Graeme Cornwallis for his FTP patience and cheeriness!

Foreword

ABOUT LONELY PLANET GUIDEBOOKS

The story begins with a classic travel adventure: Tony and Maureen Wheeler's 1972 journey across Europe and Asia to Australia. Useful information about the overland trail did not exist at that time, so Tony and Maureen published the first Lonely Planet guidebook to meet a growing need.

From a kitchen table, then from a tiny office in Melbourne (Australia), Lonely Planet has become the largest independent travel publisher in the world, an international company with offices in Melbourne, Oakland (USA), London (UK) and Paris (France).

Today Lonely Planet guidebooks cover the globe. There is an ever-growing list of books and there's information in a variety of forms and media. Some things haven't changed. The main aim is still to help make it possible for adventurous travellers to get out there – to explore and better understand the world.

At Lonely Planet we believe travellers can make a positive contribution to the countries they visit – if they respect their host communities and spend their money wisely. Since 1986 a percentage of the income from each book has been donated to aid projects and human rights campaigns.

Updates Lonely Planet thoroughly updates each guidebook as often as possible. This usually means there are around two years between editions, although for more unusual or more stable destinations the gap can be longer. Check the imprint page (following the colour map at the beginning of the book) for publication dates.

Between editions up-to-date information is available in two free newsletters – the paper *Planet Talk* and email *Comet* (to subscribe, contact any Lonely Planet office) – and on our Web site at www.lonelyplanet.com. The *Upgrades* section of the Web site covers a number of important and volatile destinations and is regularly updated by Lonely Planet authors. *Scoop* covers news and current affairs relevant to travellers. And, lastly, the *Thorn Tree* bulletin board and *Postcards* section of the site carry unverified, but fascinating, reports from travellers.

Correspondence The process of creating new editions begins with the letters, postcards and emails received from travellers. This correspondence often includes suggestions, criticisms and comments about the current editions. Interesting excerpts are immediately passed on via newsletters and the Web site, and everything goes to our authors to be verified when they're researching on the road. We're keen to get more feedback from organisations or individuals who represent communities visited by travellers.

Lonely Planet gathers information for everyone who's curious about the planet – and especially for those who explore it first-hand. Through guidebooks, phrasebooks, activity guides, maps, literature, newsletters, image library, TV series and Web site we act as an information exchange for a worldwide community of travellers.

Research Authors aim to gather sufficient practical information to enable travellers to make informed choices and to make the mechanics of a journey run smoothly. They also research historical and cultural background to help enrich the travel experience and allow travellers to understand and respond appropriately to cultural and environmental issues.

Authors don't stay in every hotel because that would mean spending a couple of months in each medium-sized city and, no, they don't eat at every restaurant because that would mean stretching belts beyond capacity. They do visit hotels and restaurants to check standards and prices, but feedback based on readers' direct experiences can be very helpful.

Many of our authors work undercover, others aren't so secretive. None of them accept freebies in exchange for positive write-ups. And none of our guidebooks contain any advertising.

Production Authors submit their raw manuscripts and maps to offices in Australia, USA, UK or France. Editors and cartographers – all experienced travellers themselves – then begin the process of assembling the pieces. When the book finally hits the shops, some things are already out of date, we start getting feedback from readers and the process begins again ...

WARNING & REQUEST

Things change – prices go up, schedules change, good places go bad and bad places go bankrupt – nothing stays the same. So, if you find things better or worse, recently opened or long since closed, please tell us and help make the next edition even more accurate and useful. We genuinely value all the feedback we receive. A well travelled team reads and acknowledges every letter, postcard and email and ensures that every morsel of information finds its way to the appropriate authors, editors and cartographers for verification.

Everyone who writes to us will find their name in the next edition of the appropriate guidebook. They will also receive the latest issue of *Planet Talk*, our quarterly printed newsletter, or *Comet*, our monthly email newsletter. Subscriptions to both newsletters are free. The very best contributions will be rewarded with a free guidebook.

Excerpts from your correspondence may appear in new editions of Lonely Planet guidebooks, the Lonely Planet Web site, *Planet Talk* or *Comet*, so please let us know if you *don't* want your letter published or your name acknowledged.

Send all correspondence to the Lonely Planet office closest to you:

Australia: Locked Bag 1, Footscray, Victoria 3011
USA: 150 Linden St, Oakland, CA 94607
UK: 10A Spring Place, London NW5 3BH
France: 1 rue du Dahomey, 75011 Paris

Or email us at: talk2us@lonelyplanet.com.au

For news, views and updates see our Web site: www.lonelyplanet.com

HOW TO USE A LONELY PLANET GUIDEBOOK

The best way to use a Lonely Planet guidebook is any way you choose. At Lonely Planet we believe the most memorable travel experiences are often those that are unexpected, and the finest discoveries are those you make yourself. Guidebooks are not intended to be used as if they provide a detailed set of infallible instructions!

Contents All Lonely Planet guidebooks follow roughly the same format. The Facts about the Destination chapters or sections give background information ranging from history to weather. Facts for the Visitor gives practical information on issues like visas and health. Getting There & Away gives a brief starting point for researching travel to and from the destination. Getting Around gives an overview of the transport options when you arrive.

The peculiar demands of each destination determine how subsequent chapters are broken up, but some things remain constant. We always start with background, then proceed to sights, places to stay, places to eat, entertainment, getting there and away, and getting around information – in that order.

Heading Hierarchy Lonely Planet headings are used in a strict hierarchical structure that can be visualised as a set of Russian dolls. Each heading (and its following text) is encompassed by any preceding heading that is higher on the hierarchical ladder.

Entry Points We do not assume guidebooks will be read from beginning to end, but that people will dip into them. The traditional entry points are the list of contents and the index. In addition, however, some books have a complete list of maps and an index map illustrating map coverage.

There may also be a colour map that shows highlights. These highlights are dealt with in greater detail in the Facts for the Visitor chapter, along with planning questions and suggested itineraries. Each chapter covering a geographical region usually begins with a locator map and another list of highlights. Once you find something of interest in a list of highlights, turn to the index.

Maps Maps play a crucial role in Lonely Planet guidebooks and include a huge amount of information. A legend is printed on the back page. We seek to have complete consistency between maps and text, and to have every important place in the text captured on a map. Map key numbers usually start in the top left corner. Map, grid and key item references are indicated where appropriate throughout the text.

Although inclusion in a guidebook usually implies a recommendation we cannot list every good place. Exclusion does not necessarily imply criticism. In fact there are a number of reasons why we might exclude a place – sometimes it is simply inappropriate to encourage an influx of travellers.

Introduction

Stockholm is, without doubt, one of the most beautiful national capitals in the world and the particularly attractive buildings in Gamla Stan (Old Town) draw tourists throughout the year. Gamla Stan and some neighbouring areas are built on islands, so there are many channels and extensive areas of open water. There are few other world capitals where you can swim or fish safely in the city centre. Stockholm is also famous for the 24,000 rocky islands of its *skärgård* (archipelago), which protect the urban islands from the open seas.

The city waterways are utilised by all manner of craft, from yachts to ferries and luxury cruise liners. Stockholm's ideal situation for trade and maritime connections, where Lake Mälaren empties into the Baltic Sea, allows freighters loaded with goods to berth near the city centre. However, parts of the city are industrialised and some particularly bleak suburbs seem inspired by Kafkaesque and Stalinist baroque.

Around 1.6 million people live in Greater Stockholm and over 15% of them are immigrants, including many people from the Middle East. This lively, international city has suburban schools where over 100 different languages are spoken. Many of the Swedish people living in Stockholm have actually come from other parts of the country, creating a remarkably cosmopolitan place.

Stockholm is best seen from the water but you'll also enjoy seeing the parklands of Djurgården or the alleys of Gamla Stan on foot. Many of the 50-plus museums contain world-class treasures and you can see a selection of what Sweden has to offer at the Skansen open-air museum. Stockholm is a royal capital, with 10 royal castles in and around the city, including Kungliga Slottet (the largest palace in the world still in use), and the World Heritage-listed Kina Slott and Slottsteater at Drottningholm. There are also less well-known, off-the-beaten-track attractions, which are worth making the effort to discover. Don't miss the churches, with their ornate interiors and wonderful works of art.

There's a good range of budget accommodation on offer, including hostels in quaint, old ships and one in a former prison. Although the hostels aren't really inexpensive, they are all clean and comfortable. Top-end hotels offer sumptuous lodging but they're competing on service and luxury, so prices tend to be high. There's a definite shortage of beds in the middle price range and you're advised to make reservations well in advance, since finding a bed at any budget in Stockholm can be difficult in the height of summer and at weekends all year round.

Visitors can enjoy a wide range of international cuisine in the ethnic restaurants, from Polish to Japanese. Standards in the finer restaurants are usually outstanding and prices are often surprisingly reasonable.

Stockholm has an exciting nightlife scene and is known for its particularly good live jazz clubs. Nightclubs stay open until 5am at weekends, so night owls can always find some action. There are also some excellent pubs offering beer at very affordable prices.

When people think of Stockholm, three things usually come to mind – cold weather, winter darkness and high prices. While it's true that winters are long and cold here, there's nothing to beat a crisp, sunny day with deep snow. In summer, the weather is often very warm and the sun can shine for over 20 hours a day. Since Sweden joined the European Union and the krona settled at a reasonable level, many prices in Stockholm now have parity with the rest of Western Europe and you can enjoy much of what the city offers and have a great time on any budget.

Facts about Stockholm

HISTORY
Early Settlement

Around 8000 BC, at the end of the last glacial period of the Ice Age, most of what is now east-central Sweden lay under water. Freed of its burden of ice, the land rose, islands appeared, and humans had arrived by 6000 BC. Remains of early Stone Age settlements have been found at Tullinge, about 15km south-west of the centre of modern Stockholm.

The area remained lightly populated until medieval times. In the 11th century, a jetty was built in Strömmen and, by the following century, the first defensive towers were constructed on Stadsholmen (now also called Gamla Stan), a strategically placed island where the fresh water from Lake Mälaren enters the sea. The oldest buildings in Greater Stockholm (the churches at Bromma and Spånga) were consecrated in the late 12th century, not long after the full conversion of Sweden to Christianity.

Medieval Stockholm

Although Swedish Viking political power had been centred around northern Mälaren and Sigtuna for centuries, it was forced to move to the lake's outlet when rising land made navigation between the sea and lake impractical for large boats. Around 1250, a town charter was granted and a trade treaty was signed with the Hanseatic port of Lübeck. In 1252, Sweden's most important chieftain, Birger Jarl, ordered the strengthening of the defences on Stadsholmen and work began on the powerful Tre Kronor castle. Around the same time, locks were built on either side of Stadsholmen to control trade, using timber stocks arranged as a fence or boom. It's thought that Stockholm, meaning 'tree-trunk islet', is named after this boom.

By the 1270s, Franciscan monks had established a monastery on the islet Riddarholmen. The first mention of St Nicolai kyrka (consecrated as the cathedral Storkyrkan

in 1306) dates from 1279 and, in the 1280s, the Klara nunnery was set up in Norrmalm. When King Magnus Ladulås was buried in St Nicolai kyrka in 1290, the town had around 2000 residents.

The oldest surviving Stockholm seal (1296) shows a defensive wall, which ran around Gamla Stan's plateau, but the next seal (from 1326) shows a much stronger wall with towers and gatehouses. In 1301, Helge-andshuset, a combined hospital, chapel and cemetery, opened on Helgeandsholmen (which was connected to Norrmalm and Stadsholmen by wooden bridges). Tre Kronor castle now had a 25m-high round tower and six rectangular castellated towers linked by a curtain wall. The oldest street in Stockholm, Köpmannagatan, was first mentioned in 1323.

In 1350, the arrival of the Black Death killed around a third of the Swedish population. Around this time, growing German influence in Stockholm's affairs was curbed on the king's authority. The town council first used the Head of St Erik seal in 1376 – and it's still used today. In the 1380s, a new town wall was built around Stadsholmen, with large towers at the northern and southern entrances; it was further strengthened in the 1430s. Stockholm was besieged by the Danish Queen Margareta (also known as Margrethe) Valdemarsdotter from 1391 to 1395 and, in 1397, the crowns of Sweden, Norway and Denmark amalgamated under the Union of Kalmar and a governor directed Swedish affairs from the castle.

There were several serious fires in Stockholm during medieval times, but the worst occurred in 1407, when only stone buildings such as the castle remained standing and many people died. By the late 15th century, the population was around 6000 and Stockholm had become a significant commercial centre. The shipping of copper and iron to continental Europe was a lucrative trade dominated by German merchants. However, wealth was leaving along with the goods and the city's infrastructure entered a long period of decline.

In 1471, the Danish king Christian I besieged Stockholm while attempting to quell the rebellious Sten Sture the Elder, but his 5000-strong army was routed by the Swedes just outside the city walls at the Battle of Brunkenberg (the fighting took place between what is now Vasagatan, Kungsgatan and Sergels Torg). Even after the Danish retreat to Copenhagen, trouble between unionists and separatists continued. Things escalated in 1520 when city burghers, bishops and nobility agreed to meet the Danish king Christian II in Stockholm, and the king then arrested them all at a banquet. After a quick trial, the Swedes were found guilty of burning down the archbishop's castle near Sigtuna, and 82 men were beheaded the following day at Stortorget (the main square by Tre Kronor castle). This ghastly event became known as the Stockholm Blood Bath; heavy rain caused rivers of blood from the bodies to pour down the steep alleys descending from the square.

The Renaissance

A major rebellion followed the Blood Bath and, after a two-year siege, Gustav Vasa finally entered the city in 1523. The new king then ruled the city with a heavy hand – the role of commerce dwindled and the Catholic Church was extinguished entirely in 1527, but royal power grew and the city revolved around the court. The king ordered the reconstruction of Tre Kronor castle and defensive towers were also built on Riddarholmen – Birger Jarls Torn and the southern tower of Wrangelska palats are now the only parts of the medieval fortifications left above ground. The monasteries were closed and demolished.

The famous *Vädersolstavlan* painting shows a city built mostly of brick and wood, with steeples, windmills, a curtain wall, and castellated towers and gatehouses. Both Norrmalm and Södermalm (north and south of Gamla Stan, respectively) also had houses, and the population of the city stood at around 8000. The painting also shows an extraordinary atmospheric phenomenon, which startled the people on 20 April 1535 (there's a 17th-century copy of the painting in Storkyrkan).

Gustav's son Erik XIV (and later kings) racked up taxation on the burghers to fund wars, but some did well from arms manufacture and the city's importance as a military headquarters increased. By the end of the 16th century, Stockholm's population was 9000 and the city had steadily spread onto Norrmalm and Södermalm. Norrmalm was given town status in 1602, but it was withdrawn in 1635.

In 1625, western parts of Gamla Stan were gutted by fire and rebuilding took place on a grid pattern. The first town engineer, Anders Torstensson, planned the street grids in Norrmalm and Södermalm; Drottninggatan (Queen Street) was named after Queen Kristina. Stockholm was proclaimed capital of Sweden in 1634. By 1650, the city had a typical Renaissance plan and was an important European capital, supported by an expanding Swedish empire; the population soared from 15,000 in 1635 to 60,000 in 1685. Paper money was issued as early as 1645, but the first central bank had to wait until 1680.

Rising & Falling Fortunes

Famine wiped out 100,000 people across Sweden during the harsh winter of 1696–7 and starving hordes descended on the capital. Apart from the new north wing, the old royal castle (Tre Kronor) burned down, also in 1697. In 1711, plague arrived – the death rate soared to 1200 per day and a quarter of the population died. After a series of spectacular military defeats, loss of foreign possessions, and the death of King Karl XII in Norway (1718), the country (and Stockholm) went into decline. The Russian attacks in 1719 and the one-sided peace treaty of 1721 finished off Sweden's military adventures.

Work on building the Kungliga Slott (new Royal Palace) on the ruins of Tre Kronor began in 1727, but it wasn't completed until 1754. The Swedish Academy of Sciences was founded in 1739 and the observatory was opened in 1753. Throughout the 18th century, there was industrial awakening – distilleries, breweries, porcelain works and glass factories commenced operations – and the invention of the tiled stove in 1767 revolutionised domestic heating. In 1752, the first modern hospital (Serafimer-lasarettet) opened. Several fires burnt out sections of Norrmalm and Södermalm, notably in 1751 and 1759.

In 1772, King Gustav III curtailed the powers of the Riksdag (parliament) and, seven years later, he assumed the role of absolute monarch. During his reign, Swedish science, architecture and arts blossomed, allowing the creation of institutions and fine buildings such as the Opera House (1782). In 1792, three years after the French Revolution, several members of the Riksdag plotted to assassinate the king and Jacob Johan Anckarström shot him in the back while at a masked ball in the Opera House. The king died 13 days later and Anckarström was executed for regicide.

A period of stagnation followed the death of the king, but parliamentary rule was restored. By 1810, Stockholm's population was around 65,000, but it was decreasing due to lack of confidence in the capital. Conditions for ordinary people were extremely basic, with little running water, no sewage system, and frequent epidemics. Promised 19th-century reforms never arrived and bloody street riots weren't unusual.

Industrialisation & Expansion

By the mid-19th century, the industrial revolution finally arrived, with the construction of factories, mills, a gasworks and waterworks. The long-awaited sewage system was begun in 1863. Also in the 1860s, railways were opened and, in 1871, the northern and southern lines were connected via Centralstationen (Stockholm's central train station) and Riddarsholmen. The city rapidly industrialised and expanded – by 1880 the population stood at 168,000 and 10 years later it was 245,000.

Further town planning starting in the 1860s created many of the wide avenues and apartment blocks still to be seen today, although a by-law in 1876 laid down strict requirements for street widths and building heights. In the 1880s, Östermalm was laid out and Strandvägen was completed by 1897 (also the year in which Stockholm hosted the ambitious Art & Industry Exhibition in Djurgården). The 1890s also saw the arrival of various public utilities, including an electricity works in 1892. Other substantial buildings from this era include Operan (the new Opera House), the central post office (Map 6, D4, #110), Riksdagshuset Östra (the original parliament building; Map 7, A3, #10) and Rosenbad (government offices; Map 6, G5, #162).

In 1904, the city purchased land outside its borders, which was later used for the huge suburban expansion. Three years later, socialist power continued to grow and the conservative government was pressured into giving the vote to all men aged over 24. The government hoped this would stem socialist influence, but it continued to gain power and a general strike was called in 1909 to force major changes to workers' rights and salaries. Sweden declared itself neutral in 1912, just before the outbreak of WWI, and in that same year the summer Olympics were held in Stockholm at the newly built stadium in Östermalm. In 1915, there were 364,000 people living in Stockholm and Norrmalm continued its development as a business district with the opening of the NK department store (Map 6, D6, #94). The construction of Kungsgatan, which was cut through the Brunkebergsåsen ridge, was completed in the 1920s.

However, Sweden was in crisis from 1914 to 1917 due to WWI blockades and, in 1917, starving Stockholmers rioted in Gustav Adolfs torg. In 1923, the Stadshuset (city hall; Map 6, G2, #140) was opened and instantly became a symbol of the city. The 1930 Stockholm Exhibition, which lasted over four months and attracted 1.5 million visitors, featured the new functionalist styles which came to dominate the city during the long years of socialist rule. Only two years later, the Social Democrats took power in parliament and started to implement *folkhemmet* (the welfare state).

THE GROWTH OF STOCKHOLM

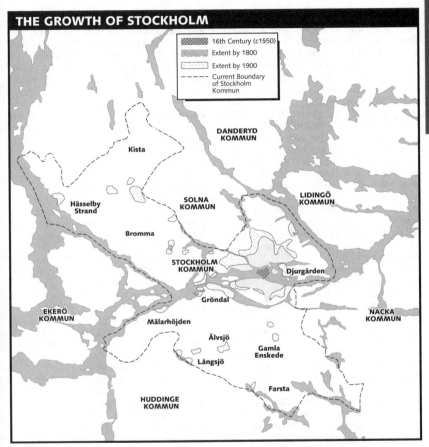

16th Century (c1550)
Extent by 1800
Extent by 1900
Current Boundary of Stockholm Kommun

DANDERYD KOMMUN

Kista

Hässelby Strand

SOLNA KOMMUN

LIDINGÖ KOMMUN

Bromma

STOCKHOLM KOMMUN

Djurgården

EKERÖ KOMMUN

Gröndal

NACKA KOMMUN

Mälarhöjden

Älvsjö

Gamla Enskede

Långsjö

Farsta

HUDDINGE KOMMUN

However, the Great Depression arrived and the country dropped into economic crisis.

Modern Stockholm

Although Swedish neutrality in WWII was ambiguous, the country became a safe haven for refugees from Finland, Norway, Denmark and the Baltic states, and thousands of Jews settled in Stockholm during the war, escaping persecution and death.

In the 1930s, many bridges and blocks of flats were built. The city council decided to construct the subway in 1941 and the first line (Slussen to Hökarängen) was opened in 1950. In the 1950s, new suburbs were constructed next to these subway lines, creating a radial pattern still in evidence today. The suburban centres each had services, office buildings, churches, a school and sporting facilities but the people were packed into ghastly Stalinist-style blocks of flats.

Meanwhile, the city centre (in Norrmalm) was also being 'developed' and large sections resembled the worst of bombed-out Europe as older buildings were demolished in a frenzy, which continued for years. The five towers of the Hötorgscity business complex, between Sergels Torg and

Hötorget, were completed by 1965. Well north of the city, Arlanda airport was completed in 1966, although it was in use from 1960. The ugly bridge, Centralbron (Map 6, G4), is another 1960s monstrosity. Construction on Essingeleden, the E4 motorway, lasted from 1966 right into the 1970s. North of the city, Stockholm University (Map 2, B6, #20) was built in the Frescati suburb, from 1968 to 1971. By 1971, Stockholm's population was 744,911.

Further expansions of the city on to virgin land included Bredäng (1962), Skärholmen (1964) and Rinkeby. In the 10 years from 1965, the national government ordered a massive construction program to ease the housing shortage – but these mostly grim and characterless blocks of flats lacked any aesthetic appeal, and most were built with a total lack of consideration for the future residents.

By 1971, people were fed up with government indifference and when the authorities planned to cut down healthy elm trees, mass protests took place in Kungsträdgården. The government backed down, but public anger increased, with frequent protests at the horrific scale of continuing demolitions around the city. However, after the 1973 oil crisis, which dampened the economy and slowed construction, things quietened down.

On 24 April 1975, West German terrorists affiliated with the Bader-Meinhof group attacked the West German embassy in Stockholm and murdered the military attache. The building blew up and two terrorists were killed. Two years later, a related group planned to kidnap the Swedish foreign minister for use in a 'prisoner exchange', but the police uncovered the plot and arrested the organisers, including Norbert Kröcher, who was deported to West Germany and spent over 20 years in jail.

In 1977, the business and shopping complex at Kista Centrum was opened; this area has since developed into the Swedish equivalent of Silicon Valley, dominated by Ericsson Radio Systems and IBM since the 1980s. Housing complexes were built in Kista, Skarpnäck and other suburbs throughout the 1980s.

The bungled police inquiry into the 1986 assassination of Prime Minister Olof Palme shook ordinary Swedes' confidence in their country, its institutions and its leaders. Although there have been many theories about the still unsolved killing, which happened in Sveavägen, it seems likely that foreign intervention lay behind the murder. Certainly, the fortunes of the Social Democrats took a turn for the worse, and subsequent corruption and scandals, including the arms manufacturer Bofors, seriously damaged the government.

Redevelopment of Hötorgscity, Kungsgatan, Stureplan and central parts of Södermalm took place during the late 1980s and the 1990s. Also at this time, economic revival took off as credit laws were relaxed. Building and property investment caused rents to soar and Stockholm became ridiculously expensive. Once that bubble burst due to the 1990s world recession, the devalued krona actually helped Stockholm – Swedish tourism grew, and foreign tourists arrived in ever-increasing numbers. The easing of licensing restrictions on bars and restaurants, such as hours during which alcohol could be sold, type of alcohol sold and age of clientele, caused a huge increase in the number of licensed premises.

In 1995, Sweden joined the European Union (EU) and the economy recovered, partly due to an austerity program and swingeing cuts to the welfare state. Stockholm was the Cultural Capital of Europe in 1998 and there was a record number of visitors to the city. Although Stockholm placed a bid for the 2004 summer Olympics, Athens was chosen instead. In 2000, the new metro link, Tvärbanan, opened and connected western parts of the city using the first nonradial line. The current population of 743,703 (1 January 2000) is expected to rise to 773,645 by 2005.

GEOGRAPHY & GEOLOGY

The geography and geology of the Stockholm area are inextricably linked. The nearly two billion year-old gneiss and granite bedrock is part of the Baltic shield. For much of its history, this rock has been eroded but there were also periods of faulting in the north-west to south-east direction. Rivers further eroded these fault planes, creating many of the valleys typical of the area. More recent east-to-west faulting has created high escarpments, including the northern side of Södermalm and the southern side of Djurgården.

In the last two million years, there were several periods of glaciation lasting around 100,000 years each, and the area was covered with an ice sheet up to 1km thick. The ice moved in a south-easterly direction smoothing out the landscape as it went. When it melted about 10,000 years ago, vast amounts of rock debris were dumped as moraines and also as ridges called eskers. The most prominent esker is Brunkebergsåsen, which lies just east of Vasagatan.

After the end of the last glaciation, the land was 100m lower than it is today but, freed of the weight of ice, it steadily rose out of the Yoldia Sea. By around AD 600, the water level was only about 10m higher than today, but the channels from Mälaren became unnavigable in the 12th century when Mälaren became a lake.

Stockholm is built on the mainland and many islands, ranging from 8km-long Lidingö to 50m-wide Strömsborg. To the west, Mälaren initially contains many extensive islands separated by relatively narrow channels, but there's more open water towards Västerås. To the east lies the archipelago, with large islands and narrow fjords gradually giving way to the small rocky islets typical of its outer reaches. North and south of the city the land is generally under 100m, but it's not particularly flat, with many narrow lakes in the valleys.

CLIMATE

Stockholm has a cool temperate climate, with precipitation in all seasons. The land masses of southern Sweden, Denmark and the UK shield the city from the worst effects of Atlantic low pressure systems and their moisture-laden south-westerly winds, hence yearly precipitation totals are moderate. High-pressure systems over Russia bring more stable and sunny conditions

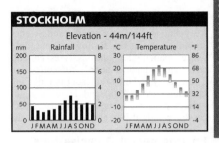

with warm weather in summer, and cold weather in winter.

The long-term average temperature for January to March is -2°C and for July and August it's 16°C. In summer, it can be hot and humid, with temperatures of around 30°C not unknown. However, in January or February, overnight lows of -20°C are possible. During long cold spells, the lakes freeze (allowing excellent skating) but the sea only freezes around once or twice every 10 years.

ECOLOGY & ENVIRONMENT

Ecological consciousness among Swedes is high and is reflected in their concern for native animals, clean water and renewable resources. Although concern for the environment has only become common since the 1970s, Sweden and Stockholm now have good records when it comes to environmental policies. Industrial and agricultural waste is highly regulated, sewage disposal is advanced and efficient, greenhouse gas emissions are only about 1% of the level in the USA, recycling is popular, there's little rubbish in waterways and on streets, and general tidiness takes a high priority in both urban and rural environments.

Stockholm takes pride in the fact that you can swim and fish for trout and salmon in the waters by the city centre. The city also has the world's first national city park, Ekoparken, which stretches 14km from the Fjäderholmarna islands to the northern suburbs.

For general environmental details on Sweden, check the Swedenvironment Web site at **W** www.swedenvironmen.environ.se. See also Environmental Organisations later in this section.

Recycling

Recycling is extremely popular and Swedes strongly support the sorting of household waste – paper, glass, plastics, tyres, car batteries and organic matter – for collection. The country is the world leader in recycling aluminium cans (86%), and the recycling of glass and paper, though not quite so successful, stands at 59% and 50% respectively.

Environmental Organisations

Naturvårdsverket (the Swedish Environmental Protection Agency; ☎ 08-698 1000, fax 202925, ⓔ natur@environ.se) is at Blekholmsterrassen 36, SE-10648 Stockholm. It has a highly informative Web site at ⓦ www.internat.environ.se/index.php3, which includes details on national parks.

Svenska Naturskyddsföreningen (the Swedish Society for Nature Conservation; ☎ 702 6500, fax 702 0855, ⓔ info@snf.se), Box 4625, SE-11691 Stockholm, has a Web site at ⓦ www.snf.se/english.cfm. It has around 175,000 members and has successfully protected endangered species, including peregrine falcons.

FLORA & FAUNA

Stockholm is surrounded by rural forest and there are also several extensive parks within the city boundaries. Hagaparken, north of the city centre, looks like an English park, with deciduous woodland and open grassy areas.

Native woodland consists of pine *(furu* or *tall)*, Norway spruce *(gran)* and deciduous species such as elm *(alm)*, linden *(lind)*, oak *(ek)*, beech *(bok)*, birch *(björk)* and horse chestnut *(hästkastanj)*. On forest floors, you'll find mosses and fungi, including edible mushrooms. Tyresta National Park, just 20km south-east of the city centre, includes virgin pine forest – some trees are nearly 400 years old.

Sweden has a wide variety of land mammals and you may see anything from the diminutive mouse *(mus)* to a full-grown bull elk *(älg)*. Rural woodlands are home to hedgehogs *(igelkott)*, squirrels *(ekorre)*, roe deer *(rådjur)* and owls *(ugle)*. Although only rarely seen in recent times, lynx *(lodjur)* have been observed as close as the suburb Täby, bears *(björn)* have approached within 50km of the city and in May 2001, there was a wolf *(varg)* sighting in central Stockholm. Mallards *(gräsand)*, swans *(svan)*, sparrows *(sparv)*, pigeons *(duva)*, crows *(kråka)*, blackbirds *(koltrast)*, starlings *(stare)* and great tits *(talgoxe)* are regular visitors to city streets, waterways and parks. Bats *(fladdermus)* and geese *(gås)* are mainly found in rural areas.

Free fishing is possible from the bridges and quaysides in central Stockholm. Catches may include pike *(gädda)*, perch *(abborre)*, salmon *(lax)* or sea trout *(havöring)*. Crayfish *(kräfta)* may be found in small rivers, roach *(mört)* live in lakes, and herring *(strömming)* exist in fair numbers in the archipelago.

National Parks

Tyresta National Park, 20km south-east of the city centre, has lakes and marshes that support a variety of bird life. No other European city has a national park so close to the city centre and the silence in the ancient forests is a welcome escape from the city bustle. Tiny Ängsö National Park, on an island 54km due north-east of central Stockholm, is known for its traditional archipelago scenery, spring flora and bird life.

National parks are established by Naturvårdsverket (the Swedish Environmental Protection Agency; for contact details see Environmental Organisations); however, they're managed by local government, both at county and municipal level. The agency provides national park information for visitors in Swedish and English in the form of pamphlets, an excellent book *Nationalparkerna i Sverige* (National Parks in Sweden; Skr312), and its Web site is at ⓦ www.internat.environ.se/index.php3.

GOVERNMENT & POLITICS
Government

The city council consists of a mayor (who heads the Finance Department and chairs the Council of Mayors and Stockholm City Executive Board meetings) along with seven vice mayors and 92 ordinary council members. All 101 members of the city council are elected by the people of Stockholm, who are aged 18 or over, once every four years. The council members then elect a mayor (currently Carl Cederschiöld) and the vice mayors.

The city council has responsibility for standards and equality of municipal services, by-laws and appropriate expenditure of tax revenue. It determines the rate of local income tax and the level of any fees to be charged, and also approves the budget and accounts from each of its committees and corporations.

The 13-member City Executive Board drafts items of business for the twice-monthly city council meetings. At these meetings, the council deals with resolutions referred to it by the district councils or the committees, who actually run most of the city's affairs. Public attendance at council meetings is extremely low and averages only 1.5 people!

Currently, the city has 18 district councils (slimmed down from 24 in 1999), most with 13 members and 13 deputies, all of whom are appointed by the city council. Each district has a full-time director who is responsible for implementation of decisions – interestingly, most city council decisions are made at this level.

In 1999, most of the city's expenditure of Skr28 billion was spent on: care for the elderly (27%); schools (21%); pre-school day care (14%); other education funding (10%); social benefits (9%); after-school day care (5%); the social services committee (5%); streets, parks and housing (4%); and culture and sport (3%).

The entire city administration employs around 51,500 people. More information about the city council can be found on the Internet at **W** www.stockholm.se.

The county of Stockholm consists of the city and 25 other *kommun* (municipalities). The low-key *landsting* (county council), elected by popular vote at the same time as the city council elections, has responsibility for regional public transport and health care. It raises income tax to pay for its expenses and owns and appoints the board members of Storstockholms lokaltrafik (SL;

the regional transport network). For more details, visit **W** www.sll.se/international /default.asp on the Internet.

Politics

At the last election in September 1998, the turnout was 76.2% and the people elected a city council with a right-wing majority. The right-wing Moderate Party got the most seats (35), followed by the left-wing Social Democratic Party (29 seats), the Left Party (13 seats), the right-of-centre Liberal Party (nine seats), the right-wing Christian Democratic Party (six seats), the leftist Green Party (six seats) and the centrist Stockholm Party (three seats).

The main issues stirring up the electorate include traffic reduction, high taxation (currently 28.94% on taxable income) and restoration of acceptable standards of kindergarten care (this had been slashed by the austerity program after the 1990s economic crisis). Plans to alleviate congestion by building a highway through Ekoparken have created controversy, but no decision has been forthcoming.

ECONOMY

Stockholm was founded to control trade in the Baltic region and, despite the economic crisis of the early 1990s, the city remains the strongest trading centre in the region. In fact, Stockholm is a leading European economic area and only 13 out of 200 EU regions have a higher per capita Gross Domestic Product.

From 1985 to 1996, the Stockholm Gross Regional Product increased by 25%, rather more than the Swedish national average of 13%. In this time, the public sector share of the economy has decreased (unlike in other parts of Sweden).

Unemployment in the county of Stockholm was 3.6% in February 2000, which compares well with the national figure of 6.8%. Since the end of the economic crisis (in 1994), the county of Stockholm has accounted for around 90% of the increase in the Swedish employment figures. The following figures refer to the percentage of the total workforce in each industry in the county of Stockholm: banking, insurance and other financial services (25.3%); trade and communications (20%); medical care and social welfare (15.1%); personal and cultural services (12.7%); energy production and manufacturing (8.6%); education and research (8.5%); public administration (6.1%); construction (3.2%); and agriculture and fishing (0.2%).

The average Stockholmer earns Skr180,000 (US$17,885) per annum and around 80% of the workforce is in the service sector. The largest employers (1998 figures), in descending order, are: the city council (51,500), the postal service (6540), Ericsson Radio Systems (4120), the Telia telecommunications company (3570), Skandinaviska Enskilde Banken (3470), Stockholm University (3450), Ericsson Telecom (2940) and the Konsum group of cooperative supermarkets (2890). Tourism employs around 62,000 people. In 1999, the turnover of the tourist industry was Skr12.7 billion in the county of Stockholm, or Skr7.9 billion in the city alone.

The private sector is larger in Stockholm than elsewhere in Sweden. Several Swedish companies have their head offices and research and development units located in the capital but production units may be elsewhere in the country, or abroad. One fifth of companies are at least half foreign-owned. Of the total industrial production, 35% is exported but the share of exports from the high-technology industries is 70%.

More than 150,000 companies operate in Stockholm, but 98% are small companies with fewer than 20 employees and most are single person companies, with no employees. Of private sector employment, small companies account for 35%, medium-sized account for 22% and large (over 200 employees) account for 43%.

In 1997, Stockholm was the leading region for new companies in Sweden, with nearly 10,000 in the city, one third of the Swedish total.

The Ports of Stockholm container terminal, the largest in the Baltic region, had a freight turnover of 7.5 million tons and a financial turnover of Skr469 million, both in 1999. A total of 15,295 ships were registered entering port.

Inflation is low and the official figure for 2000 is 1.7%.

POPULATION & PEOPLE

The official population of Stockholm on 1 January 2000 was 743,703, but the population of Greater Stockholm (which includes 22 municipalities within 'commuting' distance, such as the satellite cities of Solna, Sollentuna, Täby and Södertälje) was 1,643,366. Around 20% of the population are under 20 years and a further 17% is aged over 65. The birth rate is 1%.

Population movements into the city exceed those leaving, creating a net increase of 7590 in 1999. The most common family unit is a single parent with one child, but over half the population lives alone.

Most of Stockholm's population is considered to be of Nordic stock. These people are thought to have descended from Central and northern European tribes who migrated northward after the end of the last Ice Age around 10,000 years ago and are the indigenous peoples of southern and central Scandinavia.

There are also 75,188 foreigners from 80 nationalities living in Stockholm, but many more people of foreign extraction now have Swedish citizenship. The largest single group is the Finns, who number 13,703 and form 18% of the total. The next four largest groups are Iraqis, Somalis, Turks and Iranians – including many Kurds who fled from fighting in Kurdistan and settled in Sweden before tightening of the previously liberal immigration laws in the late 1990s. There are also 2337 Brits and 2233 Americans in the city.

EDUCATION

From the age of six or seven, every child in Stockholm faces nine years of compulsory *grundskolan* (comprehensive school) education. The performance of 14-year-olds (compared with other industrialised nations) is good in reading, below average in mathematics and average in science. Depending on interest and ability, almost all pupils then move on to the three-year *gymnasieskolan* (upper secondary school) where they can study academic courses specifically designed for university entrance, or take a variety of vocational courses. Within Europe, Sweden has one of the lowest rates of school leavers departing without a certificate.

The universities and a variety of other higher education institutions attract around one third of young Swedes within five years of their completion of gymnasieskolan, but most students study short courses rather than complete a three-year degree. Stockholm University, founded in 1878, is located north of the city centre at Frescati. Another important educational establishment is Kungliga Tekniska Högskolan, the Royal Technical College.

Education, books and lunches in the municipality-run schools are provided free of charge. Teaching at the mainly state-run higher education institutions is free and students can obtain loans on very good terms. A basic student grant, dependent on parental income for students under 20, is available to all and is usually worth around Skr1500 per month.

ARTS

For many years, the arts were best represented by literature, but in more recent times modern music has risen in significance and some well-known pop groups have emerged from obscurity to international stardom.

Dance

Ballet is quite popular in Stockholm and the Royal Swedish Ballet, founded in the capital by King Gustav III in 1773 (the fourth oldest ballet company in the world), now contains 75 dancers. The company has a good reputation for the quality of its productions, including classical and modern ballets. In Stockholm, there's the Dansens Hus (House of Dance), the Dansmuseet (Dance Museum), the Kulturhuset (Stockholm Cultural Centre, the principal venue for guest appearances in the capital) and the Dance Centre, which arranges festivals and encourages people to get involved.

Folk dancing goes hand-in-hand with folk music and the best time to enjoy this is in rural areas (or at Skansen) during Midsummer, when music and dancing last until well after midnight.

Music

Music is popular in Stockholm and is highlighted by the fact that Swedes buy more recorded music per capita than any other nationality. Events range from regular choral and organ concerts in churches to live jazz or rock bands in pubs. Some Swedish pop groups are well known internationally.

Classical Although Sweden has never produced a classical composer to match Norway's Edvard Grieg, there has been no shortage of contenders.

One of the earliest was the serious Franz Berwald (1796–1868), who wrote chamber music, operas and four symphonies, but wasn't fully appreciated as one of Sweden's finest composers until the 20th century. Berwaldhallen, the concert hall just east of the city centre, is named after him. Wilhelm Stenhamrar (1871–1927) was a fine composer of symphonic, vocal and chamber music, but his work has appealed more to musical experts than the people at large.

The Wagnerian Wilhelm Peterson-Berger (1867–1942) composed musical dramas with a strong flavour of Swedish folk culture. Peterson-Berger's opera *Arnljot* became the Swedish national opera but he's better known for his lyrical piano miniatures.

Hugo Alfvén (1872–1960), one of Sweden's greatest symphonists, also conducted several tours abroad as leader of a men's choir. One of his finest works, *Svensk rapsodi nr 1, Midsommarvaka*, completed in 1903, was influenced by a wedding in the Stockholm archipelago.

Opera flourished after the opening of the Royal Opera House in Stockholm (1782) and, since 1922, other venues have appeared, including the Drottningholm Court Theatre and Folkoperan, which brings the audience into close contact with the singers.

Folk Interest in Swedish folk music really took off in the 1970s and 1980s, assisted by the Falun Folk Music Festival (in Dalarna), and it's considered by some to be the fastest growing area in Swedish music, with folk rock and other avant-garde variants becoming increasingly popular. Traditional Swedish folk music revolves around the triple-beat *polska*, originally a Polish dance. Instruments played include the fiddle, accordion, harp, violin and (more rarely) the bagpipes. Although most folk events take place in rural areas, folk music and dancing can also be experienced in Stockholm.

Ethnic minority folk music includes a wide range of styles brought in by immigrants from around the world. Stallet is the principal venue in Stockholm.

For information on folk performances in Stockholm, see the Entertainment chapter.

Jazz Between the 1930s and 1960s, jazz was all the rave and Sweden produced a series of artists who excelled in the guitar, saxophone and clarinet, although early musicians were heavily influenced by American jazz. In the late 1930s, the Swing Swingers released a series of excellent records but, during WWII, Sweden was virtually cut off from the outside world and home-grown jazz expanded rapidly. Many excellent soloists appeared on the scene, including the trumpeter Rolf Ericson (1922–97), the saxophonist Carl-Henrik Norin (1920–67) and the clarinettist Putte Wickman (1924–).

In the 1950s, the leading Swedish jazz musician was Lars Gullin (1928–76), who excelled as a baritone sax, travelled abroad and cooperated closely with visiting American musicians. His career was tragically curtailed due to drug abuse. Bernt Rosengren (1937–), a tenor saxophonist, was the main star of the 1960s, but the pianist Jan Johansson (1931–68) succeeded in blending jazz and folk in a peculiar Swedish fashion.

The rise of jazz-rock during the 1970s and 1980s, and a good selection of young vocalists in the 1990s has ensured the place of jazz as an important music genre. There are three excellent jazz clubs in Stockholm – the Glenn Miller Café, Stampen and Jazz-club Fasching – and you should be able to catch a live performance on most evenings (but Sunday is relatively quiet).

Pop & Rock After the Beatles visited Sweden in 1963, the pop scene exploded in their wake and over 100 new bands were formed in a few weeks, many of them in Stockholm. Initially, groups were just imitations of British or American bands and styles, including the bizarrely named Ola & the Janglers and the space-age Spotniks, who became internationally renowned.

By the 1970s, a more distinctive Swedish pop tradition was growing. ABBA is the best-known Swedish pop group from this time (see the boxed text 'Mamma Mia, Here We Go Again...'), but its blatant commercialism caused controversy in Sweden. In the late 1970s, anarchic punk groups such as Ebba Grön arose to challenge the accepted order and, in 1986, the pop-rock group Europe, originally from the Stockholm suburb Upplands Väsby, achieved a number one hit around the world with *The Final Countdown*. Since 1986, the more mainstream pop duo Roxette and groups such as the Cardigans and Ace of Base have held international attention. In recent years, the extreme 'death metal' scene in Stockholm has developed an immense audience with a vast number of bands.

Teddy Bears Sthlm started off as a hard-rock band but it has now softened up and offers an alternative mix of rock, pop and rap. It's quite popular, with a number of Swedish Top 10 hits, and plays at occasional rock concerts in Stockholm.

Cheiron was one of the most successful contemporary music studios in the world – big names such as Britney Spears and The Backstreet Boys made recordings here – but it has now closed.

The pop and rock music industry has expanded to form one of Sweden's most successful exports and, in 1997, the country was the third-largest exporter of popular music in the world (after the US and Britain).

Mamma Mia, Here We Go Again...

During the 1970s the Swedish group ABBA, consisting of two couples, was founded and became one of the most successful popular music acts of the decade. The individual members were all show business veterans in their native Sweden, before the band was launched.

ABBA, an acronym of the names Agnetha, Björn, Benny and Anni-Frid, was used by its manager Stig Anderson for convenience, but when a newspaper competition came up with the same result, the decision was made and ABBA was born. There was already a Swedish canned fish company with the same name, but when Anderson asked it if it would mind lending its name to a popular music group, fortunately it didn't object.

ABBA won the Eurovision Song Contest in 1974 with *Waterloo*, topping the charts in several countries and reaching the top five in several others, including the USA. It went from success to success – ABBA toured the world, made a film and recorded many hit records. ABBA's last year together was 1982, but in 1992 the compilation album *ABBA Gold* became the group's biggest seller ever, topping charts the world over. Despite this revival success, no reunion is on the cards.

On 6 April 1999, 25 years to the day after winning the Eurovision Song Contest, Benny Andersson and Björn Ulvaeus' new musical, *MAMMA MIA!*, featuring 27 of ABBA's legendary songs, received its world premiere at London's Prince Edward Theatre.

Literature

The best-known members of Sweden's artistic community have been writers, chiefly the influential dramatist and author August Strindberg (1849–1912) and the widely translated children's writer Astrid Lindgren (1907–). Strindberg's *Röda Rummet* (The Red Room) was completed in 1879 and is considered by many as the first modern Swedish novel. Lindgren's well-known fantasy characters, especially Pippi Longstocking and her pet monkey Herr Nilsson, have an enduring fascination for children. Lindgren's book *Pippi Longstocking* was first published in English in 1950. For more details on these two writers, see the boxed texts later in this book.

Selma Lagerlöf (1858–1940) was also an early literary giant. Two of her best-known works are *Gösta Berling's Saga* (1891) and *Nils Holgerssons underbara resa genom Sverige* (The Wonderful Adventures of Nils; 1906–07); the latter was very popular in schools and has great character portrayals. Lagerlöf hailed from Mårbacka in Varmland (west-central Sweden), but she studied at the Royal Women's Superior Training Academy in Stockholm, graduating as a teacher in 1882. Despite her opposition to the Swedish establishment, Lagerlöf became the Nobel Laureate in Literature in 1909 'in appreciation of the lofty idealism, vivid imagination and spiritual perception that characterises her writings'. This accolade has also been awarded to five other Swedes (two jointly) in the years since.

During WWII, some Swedish writers bravely opposed the Nazis, including Eyvind Johnson (1900–76) with his *Krilon* trilogy, completed in 1943, and the famous poet, novelist and painter Karin Boye (1900–41), whose novel *Kallocain* was published in 1940. Johnson was the joint Nobel Laureate in Literature in 1974 and he spent his later years in Stockholm. Despite her talents, Boye was an unhappy woman and she committed suicide in 1941.

The social critic Karl Ivar Lo-Johansson (1901–90) wrote for over 50 years, mainly about ordinary people and landless peasants, and he won the Nordic Council Literary prize in 1979.

Twentieth-century Swedish poetry tended to dwell on political and social issues such as the Vietnam War, apartheid in Southern Africa, and social conditioning at home. Some of the better-known poets from the Stockholm area include Karin Boye (see earlier) and Katarina Frostenson (1953–), whose haunting poems strike some of the most basic chords within human nature. Frostenson has also written several fine avant-garde dramas and her works have been performed by the Royal Dramatic Theatre in Stockholm.

However, to the Swedish soul, the Gustavian balladry of Carl Michael Bellman is perhaps dearest. Bellman was born in Stockholm in 1740 and completed one of his best-known writings, *Fredmans Epistlar* (Fredman's Epistles), when he was only 30. Greek themes, with references to drunken revelry and Bacchus, the Greek and Roman god of wine, are strong features in this work. Evert Taube (1890–1976), sailor, author, composer and painter, is known as Bellman's modern successor. Part of Riddarholmen is now named Evert Taubes Terrass in his honour, and you'll also find a statue of him there.

More recently, the immensely popular troubadour Cornelis Vreeswijk (1937–87) wrote both amusing and serious lyrics and sang in perfect Swedish, although he was born in the Netherlands.

Architecture

While Greater Stockholm contains faceless office blocks and flats dating from the 1960s and 1970s, there's a wide variety of architectural gems around the city, in the surrounding towns and in the countryside. The finest examples include churches, palaces and many large public buildings from the 18th century onwards. Recently, as in many European cities, restoration of older buildings has become popular.

Early Structures Apart from the Iron Age and Viking Age stone ship settings and graves such as those at Anundshög (near Västerås) and Gamla Uppsala, little survives from the early periods in east-central Sweden.

Romanesque & Gothic Examples of Romanesque church architecture in east-central Sweden, primarily constructed in sandstone and limestone and characterised by archways and barrel-vaulted ceilings, include the substantial ruins of St Olaf and St Per in Sigtuna.

Mariakyrkan in Sigtuna (completed in 1237) and Uppsala cathedral, which was consecrated in 1435, feature Gothic styles from the 13th and 14th centuries, mainly in brick rather than stone. Part of the church Riddarholmskyrkan (Map 7, C2, #7) in Stockholm can also be described as Baltic brick Gothic.

Renaissance, Baroque & Rococo During and after the Reformation, monasteries and churches were plundered by the crown and wonderful royal palaces and castles were constructed (or rebuilt) instead. One such example is Gustav Vasa's Gripsholm Slott, 50km west of Stockholm, which has one of the best Renaissance interiors in Sweden. Part of the exterior of St Jakobs kyrka (Map 6, E7, #174), in central Stockholm, also features Renaissance styles.

Magnificently ornate baroque architecture arrived in Sweden (mainly from Italy) during the 1640s while Queen Kristina held the throne. The church Hedvig Eleonora kyrka, on Storgatan, has an octagonal baroque interior and Storkyrkan cathedral (Map 7, B4, #31) has a baroque exterior and tower. Riddarhuset (House of Nobility; Map 7, B2, #7) is a large Dutch-style baroque building constructed from brick and sandstone. Drottningholms Slott, just west of Stockholm, designed by the court architect Nicodemus Tessin the Elder and completed in the 1690s, is now on Unesco's World Heritage List. Nicodemus Tessin the Younger designed the vast 'new' Kungliga Slottet (Royal Palace) in Stockholm after the previous palace was gutted by fire in 1697, but it wasn't completed until 1754. The exterior is baroque but most of the interior is 18th-century rococo.

Highly ornamented, asymmetrical rococo designs of mainly French origin are prevalent in many other grandiose 18th-century buildings, including the exterior of Arvfurstens palats (also called Princess Sofia Albertinas palace; Map 6, F6, #165).

Neoclassical, Neogothic & Neo-Renaissance Towards the end of the 18th century, neoclassical designs became quite popular, especially with the king, Gustav III. A particularly good example of the king's interests can be seen at Gustav IIIs Paviljong, in Hagaparken (Map 2, B5). Generaltullstyrelsen, the former customs building on Skeppsbron at Tullgränd, has a typical neoclassical facade with cornices and hollow cast-iron columns, but it's not open to the general public.

Architecture of the 19th century known as the Carl Johan style clearly reflects that particular king's French neoclassical interests, including Skeppsholmskyrkan (no longer used as a church and closed to the public).

Later in the century, neogothic and neo-Renaissance architectural designs also appeared, including Johannes kyrka (brick-built neogothic) on Johannesgatan and Kungliga biblioteket (neo-Renaissance; Map 6, A7, #41). The Norra Latin City Conference Center (1876; Map 6, B3, #17), on Norra Bantorget, is an extraordinary Florentine neo-Renaissance building; the four-storey central tower has an oval staircase and the stunning interior includes murals by many leading Swedish artists.

Grand neoclassical architecture continued to appear in Stockholm until the 1920s. Some of the finest later examples include Konserthuset (1923–26; partly Art Deco; Map 6, C4, #101) and the art gallery Liljevalchs konsthall (1916; Map 4, G6, #101).

Neobaroque The Italian-style neobaroque church Gustaf Vasa kyrka (1906; Map 3, C5, #9) dominates Odenplan with its 60m-high cupola. Some of the finest baroque sculpture in Sweden (much older than the church) can also be seen inside.

Other examples of neobaroque architecture in Stockholm include most of Operan (the Opera House; Map 6, F6, #168) and the original (eastern) part of the parliament building Riksdagshuset (Map 7, A3, #10).

National Romanticism, Rhenish-Romanesque & Art Nouveau The late 19th century and early 20th century saw a rise in national romanticism, a particularly Swedish style mainly using wood and brick. The style produced such wonders as Stockholm's Rådhus (law courts; 1916), which resembles the castle Vadstena Slott, and the Stadshuset (Map 6, G2, #140), completed in 1923. Also built in national romantic style are Nordiska museet (1907; partly neo-Renaissance; Map 4, F6, #94), Stadion (Map 4, C4, #42) (the national Stadium; completed for the 1912 summer Olympic games and reminiscent of the medieval wall around Visby) and Kungliga Tekniska Högskolan (Royal Technical College; 1914–50).

There are comparatively few examples of Rhenish-Romanesque architecture in the Stockholm area, but Sofia kyrka (1906; Map 5, C8, #51) on Södermalm is the most prominent, with heavy facades in granite and sandstone.

Many of the excellent Art Nouveau buildings lying east of Nybroplan were built in the early 20th century. The finest of these is Dramatiska teatern (1908; Map 6, D8, #75), with its magnificent marble facade. The odd-looking Kungsholms församlingshus (parish social centre), on Kungsholmen, has a granite basement and limestone upper parts. The Rörstrandsgatan apartment buildings, 600m west of St Eriksplan, also feature Art Nouveau styles.

Functionalism From the 1930s to the 1980s, functionalism and the so-called international style took over, with their emphasis on steel, concrete and glass. Flat roofs and huge windows, hopelessly inadequate in Sweden, were eventually abandoned by architects. Although some buildings from this period are quite attractive, ghastly ranks of apartment blocks are an unpleasant reminder of the unacceptable face of Swedish socialism – conformity.

The best examples include the student centre Kårhus KTH (1928–30), Stockholm's first functionalist building. Another interesting building from this period is the Bromma airport control tower (1936). The Unesco World Heritage-listed Skogskyrkogården (Map 2, F7) is actually a graveyard, but it features high-quality functionalist and vernacular neoclassical styles. You'll also see other examples of functionalist styles in the Gärdet area of the city.

Neo-Modernism The latest styles in glass and chrome can be seen at the Channel 5 TV headquarters at Rådmansgatan 42. Other ultra-modern buildings include the Nordic Light Hotel (2001; Map 6, D3, #127) near Centralstationen and, in central Södermalm, the extraordinary semicircular Bofills Båge (1992; Map 5, C6, #30), which also has classical influences.

Painting

Interest in 19th- and 20th-century Swedish art has risen in recent years and sales at auctions have fetched extraordinarily high sums of money. There are substantial art collections at several art galleries and museums in the city. Although some of Sweden's most significant painters lived outside Stockholm, their works are displayed in galleries and public buildings throughout the city, so they're all mentioned here.

Carl Larsson (1853–1919), Nils Kreuger (1858–1930) and other painters were leaders of an artistic revolution in the 1880s. Some of the best 19th-century oil paintings were painted by Larsson in a warm Art Nouveau style. Anders Zorn's nudes and portraits of famous Swedes, and August Strindberg's surprisingly modern landscapes, have also come to the attention of the art world lately. The nature paintings of Bruno Liljefors (1860–1939) are well regarded and consequently sell for high prices at auction. The vivid Stockholm landscapes by Eugène Jansson (1862–1915) indicate influence from the Norwegian, Edvard Munch. The royal prince, Prince Eugene (1865–1947), lived and worked in an isolated mansion on Djurgården and produced many fine paintings.

Although there was an initially cautious approach to cubism, some artists embraced the concepts of surrealist and abstract art, albeit with their own Swedish style, such as the rather bizarre 'dreamland' paintings of Stellan Mörner (1896–1979). Otto Carlsund (1897–1948) was the driving force behind early abstract art in Sweden, which strongly impinged on the public conscience during the Stockholm exhibition of 1930 but didn't really become established until after WWII.

Olle Baertling's post-war geometrical styles still sell well at auction.

Considerably more radical art movements in the 1960s and 1970s were influenced by diverse sources including far left-wing politics, popular culture, minimalism and pop art. The intriguing paintings by Jan Håfström (1937–) remind observers how close many Swedes are to nature, and the vaguely disturbing *Will you be profitable, my little one?* by Peter Tillberg is clearly an attack on 1970s society and schooling. Peter Dahl, Norwegian-born but living in Stockholm, is noted for his paintings of Bellman ballads.

More recently, women artists have become increasingly significant. The photographer Annica Karlsson Rixon (1962–) is known for her provocative images and Maria Lindberg (1958–) is known for her outrageously humorous paintings and drawings.

The modern art scene has developed with a renewed interest in paint. Society and the environment continue to play an important role in inspiring many Swedish artists but, even more so than before, the future lies with the broad spectrum of international influence.

Sculpture

Stockholm is noted for its excellent street sculpture, which is often in bronze. The leading sculptors active in the 20th century were Carl Milles (1875–1955), who lived on the island Lidingö, and Carl Eldh (1873–1954), who had his studio in a superb location near Brunnsviken. There are various other works by sculptors around the city, including *Systarna* at Mosebacke torg, *Little Elephant Dreaming* at Greta Garbos torg, and the superb *Non Violence* (a revolver with a knotted barrel) on Sergelgatan.

Cinema

Sweden led the way in the silent films of the 1920s with such masterpieces as *Körkarlen* (The Phantom Carriage), adapted from a novel by Selma Lagerlöf and directed by Mauritz Stiller. However, the 'Golden Age' was short-lived, as Stiller and others (including the actress Greta Garbo, who also

Ingmar Bergman

The great film director and screenplay-writer, Ingmar Bergman, one of the major international successes in Swedish cinema, was born in Uppsala in 1918. He's also known at home for his theatre direction.

Bergman's first professional job was the film *Hets* (1944), but his arty psychological style wasn't initially popular with conservative producers or critics. However, after *Smiles of a Summer Night* received international acclaim in 1955, appreciation of Bergman's films became more widespread. The disturbing *Through a Glass, Darkly* and *Winter Light* (both 1962), and *The Silence* (1963), which investigates loneliness and loss of faith, are typical examples of his outlook. His last job as director, *Fanny and Alexander*, was released as long ago as 1982, but Bergman has since continued to write screenplays, including *Sunday's Children* (1993), which was directed by his son, Daniel Bergman.

worked in the PUB department store) emigrated to Hollywood.

After WWII, Swedish film makers produced more artistic movies which went down well with foreign audiences at film festivals throughout Europe. The highly acclaimed Ingmar Bergman directed many excellent films from the late 1940s up to 1982 (see the boxed text 'Ingmar Bergman'). Many of Astrid Lindgren's children's books were made into films which were (and still are) shown worldwide, and the actress Ingrid Bergman won Academy Awards for her roles in several films.

However, as in many other countries, the growing power of television in the 1960s caused cinema audiences to dwindle. Government intervention to save the industry caused increasing politicisation, but failed to halt the decline. By the 1990s, the trend had reversed and film making was rejuvenated with new blood and new styles, including close cooperation with television (terrestrial, satellite and cable) and video.

The latest in the long line of Swedish actresses (including Maud Adams, Britt Eckland, Mary Stavin and Christina Wayborn) who have starred as leading ladies in James Bond movies is Izabella Scorupco, in *Golden-eye*. Scorupco was actually born in Poland, but her family moved to a Stockholm suburb when she was eight.

Sweden has been incorrectly branded as a major source of blue movies, but compared to many other countries, little porn is produced in the country. Sweden actually has the world's oldest film censorship board (formed in 1911) and it can ban, cut, and set minimum ages for any film screened in the country.

Theatre

After King Gustav III founded the Royal Theatre in Stockholm in 1773, interest in theatre and opera blossomed. With the arrival of Social Democracy, theatres were built in functional style in Stockholm and other towns around the country, particularly from the 1920s to the 1950s, to encourage an appreciation among ordinary people. Currently, about 30% of government funding for the arts goes to the theatre, but there's still a struggle in the face of intense competition from other pursuits. Diversification into forms other than the spoken word includes mime, dance and music.

Indigenous Crafts

Local crafts vary from ornate weaving, sewing and woodcarving by individuals, which are displayed at village fairs, to the more industrial linen and glassware production, seen in the touristy souvenir shops in the city. Sami arts and crafts come from the far north of Sweden and there's a recommended outlet in Gamla Stan (see the Shopping chapter). Craftwork is often high quality, but prices also tend to be high.

SOCIETY & CONDUCT

Swedes are generally serious people but they're well known for boisterous drinking sessions, especially when they travel to countries where booze is cheaper. Many travellers, and many Swedes themselves, have noted that people in Stockholm can be stand-offish and even downright rude. While the majority of drivers are sensible and courteous, the rest includes maniacs who drive at speeds up to double the speed limit. Pedestrians and cyclists are urged to be extra careful on city streets – near-misses are frighteningly frequent.

The well-dressed, good-looking Swede perfectly complements the dynamic image of the country. However, other Scandinavians resent Sweden's quietly assumed superiority. If Sweden plays, say, Italy in a sports event, Norwegians and Finns will back the Italians.

Although Stockholm is a large city, rural connections are still strong and the summer cottage is almost *de rigueur* – there are thousands of second homes in the archipelago. Many people exercise their right of common access to the *allemansrätten* (countryside) especially during the berry- and mushroom-picking seasons in summer. (See the boxed text 'The Right of Public Access' in the Excursions chapter.)

Traditional Culture

To mark the end of winter, Valborgsmässoafton (Walpurgis Night) on 30 April is celebrated with choral singing and huge bonfires and upper-secondary-school graduates are often seen wearing distinctive white caps. These festivities have developed from a mixture of traditional bonfires on the eve of May Day. The following day is traditionally a workers' marching day.

Nationaldag (National Day) is on 6 June, but (surprisingly) it is not an official holiday. This is one of several days in the year when the distinctive Swedish flag (blue, with a yellow cross) is unfurled and hauled aloft at countless flagpoles around the country. Midsummer poles, although an imported concept from Europe, are central to the extensive Swedish Midsummer's Eve festivities. For more details on all festivals, see Public Holidays & Special Events in the Facts for the Visitor chapter.

Styles of traditional folk dress, known as *folkdräkt*, vary around the country and may be different in adjacent communities. The national version, which can be used everywhere, was designed in the 20th century. Women wear a white hat, yellow skirt, and a blue sleeveless vest with white flowers on top of a white blouse. Men wear a simpler costume of knee-length trousers (breeches), white shirt, vest and wide-brimmed hat. Folkdräkt comes out of the cupboard on national day, and for Midsummer, weddings, feasts, birthdays and church visits.

Dos & Don'ts

Most Swedes of Caucasian race have few customs that differ from those of other Europeans, North Americans or Australasians. There are of course the ethnic minority immigrants with Islamic and other customs.

Queuing by number is a favourite Swedish pastime and you'll have to do this in shops, government offices, some Systembolaget stores, police stations, post offices etc. Don't miss your turn, or you'll have to go back to the end of the queue!

The traditional handshake is used liberally in both business and social circles when greeting friends or meeting strangers. In the latter case, customary introductions will include your full names.

If you're an informal guest in a Swedish home, particularly in the countryside, it's not uncommon to remove your shoes before entering the living area. It's customary to present your host with a small gift of sweets or flowers and avoid sipping your drink before he or she makes the toast, *skål*, which you should answer in return. This traditional ritual is most frequently accompanied by direct eye contact with whoever offered the toast, symbolising respect and absence of guile. Don't toast the hostess if there are more than eight people at the table.

Treatment of Animals

Animals are generally well treated in Sweden and protected species such as bears and lynx live in areas remarkably close to Stockholm.

Svenska Djurskyddsföreningen (the Swedish Society for the Protection of Animals; ☎ 08-783 0368) can be contacted in Stockholm at Erik Dahlbergsgatan 28. Förbundet djurens rätt (☎ 08-555 91400), the antivivisection society, is at Box 2005, SE-12502 Älvsjö.

RELIGION

In 1523 at Storkyrkan, shortly after Gustav Vasa captured Stockholm, Master Olof preached the gospel in Swedish for the first time. Just four years later, the Reformation arrived and religion became heavily influenced by the German Protestant reformer Martin Luther, who viewed the scriptures as the sole authority of God and advocated that only by grace can humankind be saved from its savage nature. Nunneries and monasteries were demolished and the Catholic church was stripped of its wealth.

Since 1994, citizens don't legally acquire a religion at birth but voluntarily become members of a faith. Although the vast majority of the population are officially members of the Church of Sweden, a denomination of Protestant Evangelical Lutheranism headed by the Archbishop of Uppsala, less than 10% of the population regularly attend church. Complete separation of church and state took place on 1 January 2000 and Evangelical Lutheranism is no longer the official state religion.

Other religious groups represented in Sweden include several Christian denominations and sects (given here in descending order of numerical significance): Roman Catholics; the Orthodox Churches of the Finns, Greeks, Russians and Serbs; Pentecostals; the Mission Covenant Church of Sweden; Jehovah's Witnesses; the Salvation Army; Baptists; Estonian Lutheran Evangelists; Methodists; and Seventh-Day Adventists. The city also has over 50,000 Muslims and around 9000 Jews.

LANGUAGE

Swedish is a Germanic language, belonging to the Nordic branch, and is the first language of almost all people in Stockholm. Swedes, Danes and Norwegians can make themselves mutually understood. Most Swedes speak English as a second language but some people of foreign origin don't speak English at all.

Since English and Swedish share common roots and the Old Norse language left sprinklings of words in Anglo-Saxon, you'll find many similarities between the two languages. The pronunciations differ, however, and there are sounds in Swedish that aren't found in English: try repeating the correct pronunciation of 'Yxsmedsgränd'. Also, there are three extra letters at the end of the Swedish alphabet, namely å, ä and ö.

If you learn some common Swedish phrases, your attempts will be greatly appreciated by the Swedes, who aren't used to foreigners speaking Swedish. Mastering the language isn't easy but you'll get somewhere with it if you stay in the country for at least a year.

For pronunciation guidelines and useful words and phrases, see the Language chapter at the back of the book. For more extensive coverage of Swedish, see Lonely Planet's *Scandinavian Europe phrasebook*.

STOCKHOLM
KEY OF HONOUR

Facts for the Visitor

WHEN TO GO

Despite its northern location in Europe, Sweden isn't as cold as you might expect. Stockholm is at its best during summer and autumn (late May to September), but visitors to rural areas may wish to avoid the peak of the mosquito season (June and July). For more details, see Climate in the Facts about Sweden chapter.

Due to Stockholm's high latitude, daylight hours are long in summer, but you'll have to travel north of the Arctic Circle to experience the true 'midnight sun'. Stockholm has an average of about nine hours of sunshine daily from May to July and warm weather isn't uncommon. Winter days can be sunny and crisp but dull, bleak weather is common and there's less than six hours of daylight during the winter solstice.

However, deciding when to go should also be influenced by the following factors: from mid-June to mid-August, most hotels offer discounts of up to 40%, seasonal museums, youth hostels and camping grounds are open; and boats to the archipelago and rural buses are more frequent.

From December to March, winter sports are possible if there's enough snow, but there are no ski resorts near Stockholm. Most city museums, attractions, restaurants, pubs and clubs are open in winter, and there are relatively few tourists. However, the lack of daylight from November to February makes excursions to the archipelago rather pointless. Museums usually have very short opening hours from September to May (such places are clearly run for the benefit of the staff), allowing little time for whistle-stop tourists to see much of interest. However, with a little time, you can experience all that Stockholm has to offer at any time of year.

ORIENTATION

Stockholm is centred on the islands, but the modern business and shopping hub (Normalm) is focused on the ugly Sergels Torg.

This area has Centralstationen (the central train station) to the west and the popular park Kungsträdgården to the east. Subway entrances link Sergels Torg and Centralstationen with each other and the *tunnelbana* or T (metro) station T-Centralen.

The triangular island Stadsholmen and neighbouring islets (Riddarholmen and Helgeandholmen) accommodate Gamla Stan (Old Town) and Kungliga Slottet (new Royal Palace) – they're separated from Norrmalm by the narrow channels of Norrström. These islands and the mainland are interconnected with several bridges.

On the western and southern sides of Stadsholmen, the main bridge Centralbron and the chaotic Slussen interchange connect the southern part of the city, Södermalm, and its spine, Götgatan. From Södermalm, you'll see the southern landmark of the giant golf ball dome of the Stockholm Globe Arena, although you'll cross water again at Skanstull before reaching it. Most southern areas of the city are of little interest and consist of industrial areas and bleak housing schemes, which gradually merge with the forest. The Tyresta National Park lies just south-east of the suburbs.

To the east of Gamla Stan is the pleasant island of Skeppsholmen and its little neighbour, Kastellholmen. Further west along Strandvägen and past the berths at Nybroviken you can cross the bridge to Djurgården, with the impressive Vasamuseet, Nordiska museet, and Skansen on top of the hill.

Extensive parks run north from Djurgården, into Ladugårdsgärdet, and reappear (after a break) in Norra Djurgården, where you'll find the university. East of Norra Djurgården there's the tiny islet Tranholmen, the large island of Lidingö, and a series of fjords that lead towards Vaxholm and beyond to the archipelago. Another large area of parkland, north of the city centre, is located around the lakes Brunnsviken and Edsviken and includes Hagaparken and

Ulriksdal. These peaceful oases are surrounded by busy industrial suburbs such as Solna, Sundbyberg, Sollentuna and Danderyd. The E18 motorway cuts through these suburbs on its way from Norrtälje to Västerås.

Mälaren, the lake lying west of Gamla Stan, contains a host of other islands. The E4 motorway crosses Stora Essingen, Lilla Essingen and Kungsholmen on its way north to Uppsala; yet another series of bridges connects Långholmen with the western tip of Södermalm and the southern side of Kungsholmen. West from Kungsholmen, roads and bridges lead to the fairly rural Mälaren islands of Lovön, Ekerön, Färingsö and Adelsön.

MAPS

The maps in this book are sufficient for most purposes. However, the tourist office sells a range of rather expensive thematic maps, including *Cykelkarta Storstockholm* (Greater Stockholm cycle map, with eight routes; Skr195), *Nationalstadsparken* (the National City Park; Skr79), *Stockholms skärgård* (an excellent archipelago map; Skr125) and *Stockholm Trafikkarta* (motorist's map; Skr80). There's also the rather good *Gamla Stan karta* (Skr25), the 3-D *Gamla Stan Old Town City Map* (Skr5), the 1:10,000 scale *Stora Stockholmskartan* (covering the city, some suburbs and parts of the archipelago; Skr65) and the Storstockholms Lokaltrafik (SL) transport maps of the city and Stockholm county (Skr42 each).

The *What's On – Stockholm* tourist booklet, available free from tourist offices and hotels, has two basic map pages but the folded *Stockholms officiella turistkarta* (Skr15, from the tourist office) covers a larger area and is easier to read. Other free maps include the easy-to-use *Besökskartan*, the *Welcome to Stockholm Map* and *Your Free Guide/Map*. All of these can be found at the tourist office but *Besökskartan* can also be obtained at other tourist-related businesses such as Waxholmsbolaget (Map 6, F8, #196) and AVIS (Map 6, F4, #157 or Map 5, D6, #78).

If you're heading for the suburbs and you need a detailed map, visit the Kartbutiken map shop at Kungsgatan 74. The best available street atlas, *Atlas över Storstockholm* (Kartförlaget; Skr195), covers all of Greater Stockholm. Kartbutiken also sells some of the maps mentioned earlier in this section and it's usually considerably cheaper than elsewhere.

Several reasonable maps can also be bought abroad, including the 1:15,000 *Euro-City Map*.

RESPONSIBLE TOURISM

Since they're in residential areas, public recycling facilities in Stockholm aren't particularly easy to find, but there are some of the so-called 'igloos' for recycling glass, cans and paper on Krukmakargatan near Torkel Knutssonsgatan, in Södermalm. Newspapers can be recycled at any metro station. For tourists, STF hostels and other accommodation options offer environmentally friendly rubbish collection policies where you sort out your rubbish by type, eg, paper, cans and glass.

Supermarkets give refunds when you return plastic soft-drink bottles. The amount depends on the size of the bottle, but it's typically around Skr2.

TOURIST OFFICES
Local Tourist Offices

The main tourist office and Excursion Shop of the Stockholm Information Service (☎ 789 2490, fax 789 2491, @ info@stoinfo.se) is on the ground floor of Sverigehuset (Sweden House) (Map 6, D6, #180) at Hamngatan 27, by Kungsträdgården. Here you can book hotel rooms, theatre and concert tickets, and packages for such things as boat trips to the archipelago. There's also an Internet terminal where you can search the tourist office Web site (free) or check your email (Skr15/25 for 10/20 minutes). The office is open 8am to 7pm on weekdays and 9am to 5pm on weekends from June to August; the rest of the year it's open 9am to 6pm (9am to 3pm on weekends in May and September, 10am to 3pm on weekends from October to April). Telephone inquiries are only answered during office hours.

In the same building as the tourist office is a Forex currency exchange office and a travel agency specialising in the Finnish province of Åland. Upstairs you'll find the Sweden Bookshop, with information in English about Swedish life and culture provided by the Swedish Institute.

Perhaps more convenient for arriving travellers is Hotellcentralen (☎ 789 2490, fax 791 8666, e hotels@stoinfo.se) at Centralstationen. It's open 7am to 9pm daily May to September (9am to 6pm daily October to April). In addition to tourist information, you can reserve hotel rooms and hostel beds, buy both the Stockholm Package and Stockholm Card, book sightseeing tours and buy maps, books and souvenirs.

Both tourist offices charge Skr50 plus 10% deposit for hotel reservations and Skr20 for hostel, chalet or camping reservations. Outside the city, fees rise to Skr60/30/25 for hotel/chalet and camping/hostel reservations. Hotellcentralen is good at finding last-minute accommodation, but don't bank on it! Many publications and leaflets are free, including the useful booklets *What's On – Stockholm* (issued monthly in summer, every two months at other times), *Hotels & Youth Hostels in Stockholm* (annually) and *Stockholm Restaurangguide* (twice yearly).

The head office of the Swedish Travel & Tourism Council (☎ 08-725 5500, fax 725 5531, e info@visit-sweden.com), Box 3030, SE-10361 Stockholm, can provide general information on Sweden.

The other tourist offices in the city have all been closed.

Tourist Offices Abroad

Swedish tourist offices abroad include:

Australia (☎ 026-270 2700, fax 270 2755, e sweden@netinfo.com.au) Embassy of Sweden, 5 Turrana St, Yarralumla, ACT 2600

Denmark (☎ 33 30 13 70, fax 33 30 13 77, e info@swetourism.dk) Sveriges Rejse- og Turistråd, Skindergade 38, DK-1159 Copenhagen K

Finland (☎ 09-686 46260, fax 686 46299, e info@swetourism.fi) Oy Ruotsin Matkailuneuvosto, Meritullintori 3A, FI-00170 Helsinki

France (☎ 01 53 43 26 27, fax 01 53 43 26 24, e servinfo@suede-tourisme.fr) Office Suédois du Tourisme et des Voyages, 18 Boulevarde Malesherbes, F-75008 Paris

Germany (☎ 040-32 55 13 55, fax 32 55 13 33, e info@swetourism.de) Schweden-Werbung für Reisen und Touristik, Lilienstrasse 19, DE-20095 Hamburg

Netherlands (☎ 0900 2025200, fax 0172-460877, e zweden@werelds.com) Zweden Informatie Centrum, Postbus 350, NL-2400 AJ Alphen aan den Rijn

Norway (☎ 23 11 52 15, fax 23 11 52 18, e info@swetourism.no) Sveriges Reise- og Turistråd, Postboks 1668 Vika, NO-0120 Oslo 1

UK (☎ 020-7870 5600, fax 7724 5872, e info@swetourism.org.uk) Swedish Travel & Tourism Council, 11 Montagu Place, London, W1H 2AL

USA (☎ 212-885 9700, fax 885 9710, e info@gosweden.org) Danish & Swedish Tourist Board, 655 Third Ave, New York, NY 10017-5617

Other Information Sources

The telephone service Svar om Stockholm (☎ 567 85678), which is sponsored by the newspaper *Dagens Nyheter*, can answer a wide range of queries about goods and services in the city. If they don't know the answer, they're good at finding out and calling back.

TRAVEL AGENCIES

Travel agencies can be found in the Yellow Pages under *resebyråer*, but most of them are only for package tours. However, the following places are recommended for independent travel:

Kilroy Travels (Map 6, B6, #33) (☎ 0771-545769) Kungsgatan 4A. This place caters for youth travel (up to age 25) and students (up to age 33). Open 10am to 6pm weekdays only.

Nyman & Schultz (Map 5, C5, #28) (☎ 429 5000) Magnus Ladulåsgatan 5. This agency sells tickets for all major airlines and is also the agent for American Express.

Rese Varuhuset (Map 6, C5, #98) (☎ 587 25000) Sveavägen 20. A very flexible agency. Open 9am to 6pm weekdays only.

STA Travel (Map 6, B5, #27) (☎ 545 26666) Kungsgatan 30. A popular student travel association. Open 10am to 6pm weekdays only.

DOCUMENTS
Passport
Your passport must be valid for the intended length of your stay in Sweden. If it's about to expire, renew it before you leave home, as it can be time-consuming to do so on the road. Carry your passport at all times and guard it carefully.

Visas
A visa is a stamp in your passport or a separate piece of paper permitting you to enter the country in question and stay for a specified period of time.

Citizens of the European Union (EU) countries can enter Sweden with a valid passport or national identification card and stay up to three months, but nationals of Nordic countries (Denmark, Norway, Finland and Iceland) can stay and work in Sweden for an indefinite period. If you're not from a Nordic country and you want to stay more than three months and up to five years, you'll need to apply for a free *uppehållstillstånd* (residence permit) on arrival in Sweden. For an application form, contact the Swedish immigration office (☎ 08-470 9700, fax 470 9930), Solnavägen 96, Box 507, SE-16929 Solna, or the Swedish Migration Board (Migrationsverket; ☎ 011-156000, fax 108155, e migrationsverket@ migrationsverket.se), Tegelängsgatan 19A, SE-60170 Norrköping.

Citizens of other countries can also enter Sweden with a valid passport or national identification card and stay up to three months. However, 90-day tourist visas, which cost Skr250 and must be obtained from your nearest Swedish embassy before entering Sweden (allow two months for processing), are required by nationals of many Asian and African countries (including South Africa), Croatia, Serbia and Montenegro, Bosnia-Hercegovina, Bulgaria, Colombia and Guyana. Visa extensions aren't easily obtainable. Non-EU citizens can also obtain residence permits, which are valid between six months and permanent residency. You must apply for these before entering Sweden and you'll be interviewed by consular officials at your nearest

Swedish embassy – allow up to eight months for this process. Normally you'll have to be married or cohabiting with a permanent resident of Sweden and you may have to send in your passport to get it stamped. Extensions to six- or 12-month residence permits are available from the Swedish immigration office in Solna (see earlier in this section).

Foreign students are granted residence permits if they have comprehensive health insurance, can prove acceptance by a Swedish educational institution and are able to guarantee that they can support themselves financially.

For current visa details, check the Internet at W www.swedish-embassy.org.uk.

Travel Insurance
You should seriously consider taking out travel insurance that covers not only medical expenses, personal liability, theft or luggage loss but also cancellation or delays in your travel arrangements (due to illness, ticket loss, industrial action etc). Get your insurance as early as possible, as late purchase may preclude coverage of industrial action that may have been in force before you bought the policy.

A standard insurer may offer better deals than companies selling only travel insurance. Note that some policies specifically exclude 'dangerous activities' such as motorcycling, skiing, rock climbing, scuba diving or even hiking. Also check whether the policy covers ambulances and an emergency flight home.

Paying for airline tickets with a credit card often provides limited travel accident insurance, and you may be able to reclaim the payment if the operator doesn't deliver. A policy that pays doctors or hospitals directly may be preferable to one where you pay on the spot and claim later. If you have to claim later, make sure you keep all documentation. Some policies ask you to phone (reverse charges) an emergency number so an immediate assessment of the problem can be made.

In Sweden, EU citizens pay a fee for all medical treatment (including emergency admissions), but showing an E111 form will make matters much easier. You should make inquiries about the E111 at your social security office, travel agency or local post office well in advance. Travel insurance is still advisable, however; it allows treatment flexibility and will also cover ambulance and repatriation costs.

Driving Licence & Permits

Short-term visitors can hire or drive their own car using their own driving licence. Ask the automobile association in your home country for a *Lettre de Recommendation* (Letter of Introduction), which entitles you to services offered by affiliated organisations in Sweden, usually free of charge. Services include touring maps and information, help with breakdowns, technical and legal advice etc. For more details, see the Getting Around chapter.

Hostel & Student Cards

A Hostelling International (HI) card will give you reasonable discounts on Svenska Turistföreningen (STF) hostel rates. You can join the STF at hostels and many tourist offices while in Sweden (adults over 26 Skr260, 16 to 25 year olds Skr100, children under 16 free, and families Skr340) or you can get an HI card for Skr175.

The most useful student card is the International Student Identity Card (ISIC), a plastic ID-style card with your photograph, which provides discounts on numerous forms of transport (including airlines, international ferries and local public transport) as well as on admission to museums, sights, theatres and cinemas. Children under 16 and seniors normally receive similar discounts.

Other Documents & Cards

Stockholm Card The Stockholm Card covers all transport and almost all sightseeing needs – it's available at tourist offices, camping grounds, hostels and SL Centers, and costs Skr199/398/498 for 24/48/72 hours. A maximum of two children (Skr49/98/147 for each child) can accompany each adult. The card covers entry to 70 museums

and attractions (16 are open in summer only), city parking in metered spaces, sightseeing by boat (April to September) and travel on public transport (including the Katarinahissen lift, but excluding local ferries, some city buses and airport buses). To get maximum value, use two 24-hour cards over three days (with a rest day in between) and be sure to note opening hours: Skansen remains open until late, whereas royal palaces are only open until 3pm or 4pm.

Students and seniors get discounted admission to most museums and sights without the card, so you'll need to work out if it's cheaper for you to just get a transport pass and pay admission charges separately.

Stockholm Package This cut-price package basically includes a hotel room and the Stockholm Card. It costs from Skr455 to Skr1630 per person per night, depending on the standard of accommodation, when you stay, and whether a single supplement is required. Up to four children under six years old stay for free when sleeping in extra beds in their parents' room (Skr75 per child aged seven to 17). Travel agencies in other Scandinavian capitals or major Swedish cities can help with arrangements. Otherwise, contact Hotellcentralen in Stockholm (see the Local Tourist Offices section earlier in this chapter).

Copies

While the risk of theft in Sweden is low, it's wise to carry photocopies of the first few pages of your passport and any other essential documents, such as air tickets, insurance policies, driver's licence, serial numbers of travellers cheques and your prescription for spectacle or contact lenses.

It's also a good idea to store details of your vital travel documents in Lonely Planet's free online Travel Vault in case you lose your photocopies (or can't be bothered with them). Your own password-protected Travel Vault is accessible online from anywhere in the world – you can create it at Ⓦ www.ekno.lonelyplanet.com.

oot, toot! Kids enjoying a mini-train ride in a Stockholm park.

Royal guard, Gamla Stan

wedish seagulls squawking their goodbyes to seafaring tourists atop one of Stockholm's many boats

Stockholm in spring

Kungsträdgården – one of Stockholm's most popular parks

Skansen's mountain railway

The numerous festivals of Stockholm always attract huge crowds.

Magnificent pyrotechnic displays ensure that some of the city's festivals finish with a bang.

Gröna Lund Tivoli – terrifying and delighting people since 1883

A patriotic pin cushion

EMBASSIES & CONSULATES
Swedish Embassies & Consulates

The following are some of the Swedish embassies around the world:

Australia (☎ 026-270 2700, fax 270 2755, e ambassaden.canberra@foreign.ministry.se) 5 Turrana St, Yarralumla, ACT 2600

Canada (☎ 613-241 8553, fax 241 2277, e ambassaden.ottawa@foreign.ministry.se) 377 Dalhousie St, Ottawa, Ontario, K1N 9N8

Denmark (☎ 33 36 03 70, fax 33 36 03 95, e ambassaden.kopenhamn@foreign.ministry .se) Sankt Annæ Plads 15A, DK-1250 Copenhagen K

Finland (☎ 09-687 7660, fax 655285, e ambassaden.helsingfors@foreign.ministry.se) Pohjoisesplanadi 7B, FI-00170 Helsinki

France (☎ 01 44 18 88 00, fax 01 44 18 88 40, e ambassaden.paris@foreign.ministry.se) 17 rue Barbet-de-Jouy, F-75007 Paris

Germany (☎ 030-505060, fax 5050 6789, e ambassaden.berlin@foreign.ministry.se) Rauchstrasse 1, DE-10787 Berlin

Ireland (☎ 01-671 5822, fax 679 6718, e ambassaden.dublin@foreign.ministry.se) Sun Alliance House, 13-17 Dawson St, Dublin 2

Netherlands (☎ 070-412 0200, fax 412 0211, e ambassaden.haag@foreign.ministry.se) Burg van Karnebeeklaan 6A, NL-2509 LP Den Haag

New Zealand (☎ 04-499 9895, fax 499 1464, e sweden@xtra.co.nz) Consulate-General, Vogel Bldg, 13th floor, Aitken St, PO Box 12538, Wellington

Norway (☎ 24 11 42 00, fax 22 55 15 96, e ambassaden.oslo@foreign.ministry.se) Nobelsgate 16, NO-0244 Oslo

UK (☎ 020-7917 6400, fax 7724 4174, e embassy@swednet.org.uk) 11 Montagu Place, London, W1H 2AL

USA (☎ 202-467 2600, fax 467 2699, e ambassaden.washington@foreign.ministry.se) 1501 M St, NW, Suite 900, Washington DC 20005-1702

Embassies & Consulates in Sweden

Although the following diplomatic missions are located in Stockholm, some of the neighbouring countries also have consulates located in Gothenburg, Malmö and Helsingborg. Citizens of New Zealand should contact the nearest embassy of New Zealand

(☎ 31-70 346 9324), Carnegielaan 10-IV, The Hague, Netherlands.

Australia (Map 6, D5, #107) (☎ 08-613 2900, fax 247414, e info@austemb.se) Block 5, Sergels Torg 12

Canada (Map 6, F4, #159) (☎ 08-453 3000, fax 242491) 7th floor, Tegelbacken 4

Denmark (Map 6, F6, #170) (☎ 08-406 7500, fax 791 7220) Jakobs Torg 1

Finland (Map 6, E6, #175) (☎ 08-676 6700, fax 207497) 6th floor, Jakobsgatan 6

France (Map 6, D4, #45) (☎ 08-459 5300, fax 459 5321) Kommendörsgatan 13

Germany (Map 4, E7, #71) (☎ 08-670 1500, fax 670 1572) Skarpögatan 9

Ireland (Map 4, D5, #50) (☎ 08-661 8005, fax 660 1353) Östermalmsgatan 97

Netherlands (Map 7, F4, #102) (☎ 08-247180) Götgatan 16A

Norway (Map 4, E7, #73) (☎ 08-665 6340, fax 782 9899) Skarpögatan 4

Poland (Map 2, B4, #12) (☎ 08-764 4800, fax 983522) Consulate-General, Prästgårdsgatan 5, Sundbyberg

UK (Map 4, E7, #73) (☎ 08-671 3000, fax 662 9989, e britishembassy@telia.com) Skarpögatan 6-8

USA (Map 4, E7, #70) (☎ 08-783 5300, fax 665 3303, e webmaster@usemb.se) Dag Hammarskjölds väg 31

CUSTOMS

Duty-free goods can only be purchased when travelling from non-EU countries and Åland. The duty-free allowances (and duty-paid allowances within the EU) are: 1L of spirits (over 22% alcohol content by volume) or 3L of fortified wine (15% to 22% alcohol by volume); 26L of wine (3.5% to 15% alcohol by volume); 32L of strong beer (over 3.5% alcohol by volume); 400 cigarettes, 150 cigarillos, 75 cigars, or 400g of smoking tobacco. Tobacco products and alcoholic drinks can only be brought into Sweden duty-free if you're over 18 and 20 years, respectively.

Sweden has strict drug laws and you may be searched on arrival, especially if coming from Denmark. Mobile phones, live plants and animal products (meat, dairy etc) – from outside the EU – and all animals, syringes and weapons must be declared to customs on arrival.

For current customs regulations, ask at your nearest Swedish tourist office or contact Tullverket (Customs; ☎ 0771-520520, fax 08-208012, ⓔ info@tullverket.se), Box 12854, SE-11298 Stockholm. The rules for importing cats and dogs are posted on the Web site at ⓦ www.environ.se (search for The Public Access) or contact the National Board of Agriculture (☎ 036-155000), SE-55182 Jönköping.

MONEY
Currency

The Swedish *krona* (plural: *kronor*) is usually represented as Skr (preceding the amount) in northern Europe (and throughout this book) and SEK (preceding the amount) in international money markets, but within Sweden it's just kr (after the amount). One Swedish krona equals 100 *öre*. Coins come in denominations of 50 öre and Skr1, Skr5 and Skr10, while notes are in denominations of Skr20, Skr50, Skr100, Skr500, Skr1000 and Skr10,000.

At the time of writing, Sweden wasn't participating in the European single currency, or euro.

Exchange Rates

The following currencies convert at these approximate rates:

country	unit		krona
Australia	A$1	=	Skr5.16
Canada	C$1	=	Skr6.59
Denmark	Dkr1	=	Skr1.22
euro	€1	=	Skr9.16
Finland	Fmk1	=	Skr1.54
France	1FF	=	Skr1.39
Germany	DM1	=	Skr4.68
Japan	¥100	=	Skr8.42
Netherlands	f1	=	Skr4.16
New Zealand	NZ$1	=	Skr4.18
Norway	Nkr1	=	Skr1.13
Poland	zloty1	=	Skr2.51
UK	UK£1	=	Skr14.71
USA	US$1	=	Skr10.20

Exchanging Money

Changing money is easy in Stockholm. There are reliable exchange offices at major transport terminals and banks, and post offices also exchange major foreign currencies. Forex exchange offices usually offer the best exchange rates and low fees – Skr15 per travellers cheque and Skr20 for changing cash. X-Change offices don't charge a fee when you buy currency. Changing money at banks costs up to Skr60 per transaction. Eurocheques aren't accepted anywhere.

Exchange offices and banks include the following:

American Express (Map 5, C5, #28) (☎ 411 0540) Norrlandsgatan 21.

Exchange Center (Map 6, B4, #24) (☎ 411 2926) Sveavägen 23. No commissions. This outfit arranges Western Union money transfers. Open 9.30am to 7pm weekdays and 10am to 3pm Saturday.

Forex (Map 6, F3, #146) (☎ 411 6734) Centralstationen, main Vasagatan entrance. Open 7am to 9pm daily.

Forex (Map 6, E2, #138) (☎ 214280) Cityterminalen, the city bus terminal. Open 7am to 8pm weekdays and 8am to 5pm weekends.

Forex (Map 6, F4, #148) (☎ 104990) Vasagatan 14. Open 8am to 7pm weekdays and 9am to 3pm Saturday.

Forex (Map 6, D6, #180) (☎ 200389) Sverigehuset, Hamngatan 27. Open 8am to 6pm weekdays, 9am to 3pm Saturday and 10am to 3pm Sunday.

Forex (Map 5, D7, #76) (☎ 644 2250) Götgatan 94. Open 8am to 7pm weekdays and 9am to 3pm Saturday.

Forex (☎ 593 62271) Arlanda airport, terminal No 2. Open 6am to 10.30pm daily.

FöreningsSparbanken (Map 6, D6, #178) Hamngatan 31. Open 10am to 4pm Monday to Wednesday, 10am to 6pm Thursday and 10am to 3pm Friday.

Handelsbanken (Map 6, F7, #194) Kungsträdgårdsgatan 2. Open 9.30am to 3pm weekdays.

Handelsbanken (Map 5, B3, #11) Hornsgatan 140. Open 9.30am to 3pm weekdays.

Nordbanken (Map 6, D7, #93) Hamngatan 12. Open 10am to 4pm weekdays.

X-Change (Map 6, B5, #27) (☎ 506 10700) Kungsgatan 30. Open 8am to 7pm weekdays and 9am to 4pm Saturday.

X-Change (☎ 797 8557) Arlanda airport, terminal No 5. Open 5.30am to 8.30pm daily.

Cash You can use cash (Swedish kronor) to pay for almost everything. One major exception is car rental, where using your credit card is compulsory and 'extras' can be added to your bill without a further signature (see Car & Motorcycle in the Getting Around chapter).

Travellers Cheques Exchange offices, banks and post offices exchange major international brands of travellers cheques. However, Eurocheques aren't accepted anywhere.

Forex exchange offices are generally the best bet. Post offices have generally similar exchange rates to Forex, but charge a fee of Skr50 per transaction. Banks charge Skr40 to Skr50 per transaction for changing cheques. You're advised to shop around and compare exchange rates and fees.

ATMs With an ATM card from your home bank, Swedish ATMs will allow access to cash in your account. 'Bankomat' ATMs and the ForeningsSparbanken 'Automat' ATMs, found adjacent to many banks and around busy public places such as shopping centres, accept Visa, MasterCard, Plus and Cirrus format bank cards, and Electron and Maestro debit cards. Note that using credit cards at ATMs isn't recommended because you'll be charged interest immediately.

Credit & Debit Cards Visa, Eurocard, MasterCard, American Express and Diners Club cards are widely accepted. Apart from car rental, you're better off using a credit card since exchange rates are better and transaction fees are avoided. Credit cards can be used to buy train tickets but are not accepted on domestic ferries apart from sailings to Gotland. Electronic debit cards can be used in many shops.

If your card is lost or stolen in Sweden, report it to the appropriate agency:

American Express (☎ 020 795155) Open 8am to 5pm weekdays
Diners Club (☎ 146878) Open 24 hours
Eurocard/MasterCard (☎ 146767) Open 24 hours
Visa (☎ 020 793146) For non-Swedish Visa cards only. Open 24 hours.

Costs

Stockholm is fairly expensive and you can easily spend your money quickly, so it pays to plan your trip carefully. It's worth remembering that you have to pay for a wide range of things such as parking, tap water in some restaurants, and public toilets. Avoid a la carte restaurants in the evening if you want to keep prices down – go for pizzas, burgers, or supermarket food instead.

If you stay in commercial camping grounds and prepare your own meals, you can squeak by on around Skr150 per person per day. Staying in hostels, making your own breakfast, eating the daily special at lunchtime in a restaurant, and picking up supermarket items for dinner, will probably cost you Skr240 per day. During the low-price summer period, if you stay in a mid-range hotel (which usually includes a huge buffet breakfast), eat a daily special for lunch and have an evening meal at a moderately priced restaurant, you can expect to spend Skr500 per person per day if you're doubling up and Skr800 if you're travelling alone.

Day trips, museums, entertainment, alcohol, snacks and so on will further erode most careful budgets, but the city sells a 'tourist card' (called the Stockholm Card) that offers substantial savings on admission costs, parking and local transport. Reasonably priced hotel packages are also available. See Other Documents & Cards earlier in this chapter.

Petrol costs around Skr9.50 per litre but it's usually cheaper at automatic pumps, where you pay directly by credit or debit card (you don't pay the staff).

Tipping & Bargaining

Service charges and tips are usually included in restaurant bills and taxi fares, but there's no problem if you want to reward good service with a tip. Tipping in restaurants that charge cloakroom fees (or admission fees) isn't recommended. Bargaining isn't customary, but you can get 'walk-in' prices at some hotels and *stugby* (chalet parks). Sale prices in shops are advertised with the word *rea*; for discounts or special offers look for *lågpris*, *extrapris*, *rabatt* or *fynd*.

Taxes & Refunds

Value-added tax or *mervärdeskatt* (VAT, equivalent to sales tax in the USA), locally known as MOMS, is normally included in marked prices for goods and services, including books, food, transport, meals and accommodation. The amount varies but it can be as high as 25%.

At shops with the sign 'Tax Free Shopping', non-EU citizens making single purchases of goods exceeding Skr200 (including MOMS) are eligible for a VAT refund of 15% to 18% of the purchase price. Show your passport and ask the shop for a Global Refund Cheque. Upon departing the country (and prior to check-in), you should present the cheque along with your unopened purchases (within three months) to get export validation. You can then cash your cheque at any of the 78 European refund points listed in the *Tax Free Shopping Guide to Sweden*, which is available free from tourist offices.

Some shops are part of the tax-free shopping system but don't display a sign, so it's always wise to ask.

POST & COMMUNICATIONS
Post

The longest opening hours are offered by the post office at Centralstationen (Map 4, F1), which is open 7am to 10pm weekdays and 10am to 7pm weekends; it also has a fax service (fax 102584). The central post office (Map 6, D4, #110) is at Drottninggatan 53, SE-10110 Stockholm, and is open 8am to 6.30pm weekdays and 10am to 2pm on Saturday; pick up poste-restante mail here.

Other useful post offices (open 9am to 6pm weekdays and 10am to 1pm Saturday) include those at Hornsgatan 150B (Map 5, B3, #9) in Södermalm, Stora Nygatan 10-12 (Map 7, C3, #26) in Gamla Stan and Hantverkargatan 27 (Map 3, F5, #59) on Kungsholmen.

Stamps can also be bought at Pressbyrån newsagents, tobacconists and bookshops. Use the blue postboxes for local mail (within Stockholm) and the yellow postboxes for everywhere else.

If you're sending anything valuable, contact Federal Express (☎ 0200 252252) at Kabelgatan 5-6, Arlanda. It offers a free pick-up service on weekdays only.

Postal Rates Sweden has an efficient postal service. Postcards and letters weighing up to 20g cost Skr5 within Sweden (Skr4.50 2nd class), Skr6 to other Nordic and Baltic countries (Skr5 2nd class), Skr7 to elsewhere in Europe and Skr8 to the rest of the world (Skr6 and Skr7 2nd class, respectively).

Airmail to Europe/beyond costs Skr60/75 for small parcels (50g) or Skr200/240 for 2kg, with other price-weight combinations in between. It takes one or two days within Europe, but around a week to reach most parts of North America, even longer to Australia and New Zealand. Better-value *ekonomibrev* (economy post) surface rates are about 20% cheaper (Skr128/168 for 2kg, Europe/beyond), but you'll need to allow at least a month for delivery.

For current postal rates, contact customer services (toll-free within Sweden on ☎ 020 232221or ☎ kundtjanst@posten.se).

Addresses Stockholm's address system usually numbers buildings rather than individual doorways, so there may be several doors with the same street address. Always use the correct five digit postal code in front of the city or town name when sending mail to or within Sweden.

Telephone

Sweden is an expensive place to use telephones and you can rack up a substantial bill due to failed calls, so-called toll-free numbers, listening to recorded messages informing that the number you dialled has been changed, and speaking to answering machines! It's all very frustrating but don't even think of complaining to the main phone company (Telia) – it's virtually impossible to contact by phone.

Telia Butik (phoneshops) exist primarily to sell telephones but the staff can usually help with other inquiries; the most central phoneshop (Map 6, B5, #26) (☎ 475 1770) is at Kungsgatan 36.

For directory assistance, charged at Skr11.25 per minute, dial ☎ 118118 (numbers within Sweden) or ☎ 118119 (international).

Tones Tones are similar to those used throughout the EU. Short tones separated by long pauses mean that the number is ringing, but short equal on-and-off tones mean that the number is engaged. Sometimes a recorded message (in Swedish) tells you the number is engaged. If you've dialled incorrectly or the number has been changed, another recorded message will inform you about the problem.

Phonecards & Costs Almost all public phones in Sweden are cardphones, but most also take credit cards (although it's not advisable to use a credit card in a cardphone since charges are very high).

Telefonkort (phonecards) cost Skr35, Skr60 and Skr100 (giving 30, 60 and 120 units, respectively) and can be bought from Telia Phoneshops, tobacconists, kiosks, newsagents, and Expert and On Off electronic goods shops. At the time of writing, if you're using a 120-unit phonecard, calls to the USA will cost Skr8.65 per minute (10am to 10pm Monday to Saturday) or Skr6.65 at other times. Other options, such as Telia Travel Cards and Telia Budget Call, offer better value for international calls, but Lonely Planet's eKno (see later in this section) is better still.

All calls within Sweden (including local calls) cost a minimum of three units, which is expensive compared to most other European countries and is nearly six times the connection charge from a private phone. Telia rates from public phones are around two units (Skr1.67) per minute from 8am to 6pm on weekdays. National calls are 50% cheaper between 6pm and 8am, and on weekends. Phone calls from hotel rooms, after the owners have added their fee, are little short of extortionate.

eKno Communication Service Lonely Planet's eKno global communication service provides low-cost international calls (for local calls you're usually better off with a local phonecard) and charges around 25% less than the 120-unit Telia phonecard. eKno also offers free messaging services, email, travel information and an online travel vault, where you can securely store all your important documents. The eKno service works from private and public phones but note that the ☎ 0200 access number will take three units from your phonecard in a public phone. At the time of writing, a call to the USA costs US$0.47 per minute with eKno. You can join online at ⊠ www.ekno.lonelyplanet.com, where you will find the local-access numbers for the 24-hour customer-service centre. Once you have joined, always check the eKno Web site for the latest access numbers for each country and updates on new features.

Phone Books In addition to the Yellow Pages, which are also on the Internet at ⊠ www.gulasidorna.se, Telia phone books have purple (information in English), green (community services), blue (regional services, including health and medical care) and pink (businesses) pages. In Stockholm, the green, blue and pink pages are in a separate phone book, called *Företag* (the business directory). Local 'Din Del' phone books are easier to use.

Note that the letters å, ä and ö are placed at the end of the Swedish alphabet.

Phone Codes Calls to Sweden from abroad require the access code, the country code (46), the area code and telephone number, omitting the initial zero in the area code. For international calls from Sweden, dial ☎ 00 followed by the country code, the area code (usually omitting the initial zero) and the telephone number.

Most Swedish phone numbers have area codes followed by varying numbers of digits. Numbers beginning ☎ 020 or ☎ 0200 are toll-free (but aren't toll-free from public cardphones). You can't call Swedish ☎ 020 or ☎ 0200 numbers from outside the country. Numbers beginning with ☎ 010, ☎ 073 and ☎ 070 are mobile codes.

The area code for Greater Stockholm is ☎ 08.

Home Country Direct You can dial your home operator using the home country direct scheme and reverse the charges or run up the bill on your home phone company credit card, but there may be other options. This is usually an expensive way to make a call.

Remembering that these numbers aren't free if dialled from public phones, you can contact home operators on the following numbers:

country	phone	company
Australia	☎ 020 799061	Telstra
	☎ 020 799161	Optus
Canada	☎ 020 799015	
Ireland	☎ 020 799353	
New Zealand	☎ 020 799064	
UK	☎ 020 795144	British Telecom
	☎ 020 799044	NTL, Cable & Wireless
USA	☎ 020 795611	AT&T
	☎ 020 795922	MCI
	☎ 020 799011	Sprint

Mobile Phones In Stockholm, the Telia Mobiltel GSM system even has coverage in the subway. In remoter areas, Telia offers NMT 450. For details, call ☎ 90350. Comviq and Telia prepaid mobile phonecards can be bought at Pressbyrån newsagents but are only valid in Sweden. Your mobile may be locked onto your local network in your home country, so you must ask your home network for advice before taking your mobile phone abroad. If compatible, your phone will program automatically into the local network.

The Telia network charges Skr2.70 per minute for national calls from 8am to 6pm on weekdays (Skr1.50 at other times); calls made to other networks are a little bit more expensive.

Calls from your mobile may be routed internationally (even for local calls within Sweden) so prepare yourself for a substantial bill.

If you want to buy a mobile phone, expect to pay between Skr1000 and Skr2000. Rental isn't an option.

Fax

Faxes can be received at most hotels for free and you can send a fax for a moderate charge. The post office in Centralstationen offers a fax service with a flat fee of Skr25, plus Skr10 per page to numbers within Sweden, Skr25 per page to Europe, and Skr50 per page to the rest of the world. To receive a fax costs Skr10, regardless of the number of pages. The incoming fax number at this post office is ☎ 102584.

Email & Internet Access

Email and Internet services are popular in Sweden, and most tourism-oriented businesses now have email access. Internet cafes typically charge Skr1 per online minute. If you're going to use Internet cafes, arrange your email through Hotmail, Lonely Planet's eKno or a similar Web-based service.

Most public libraries offer free Internet and email access but there may be long queues at busy times and any bookable slots may be reserved well in advance. Take care to determine that you're allowed to use email before you start surfing, otherwise you may be removed from the premises! Several other libraries and government information offices in the city only offer Internet access for research purposes but the rules may not be posted.

If you're bringing a laptop and hope to access your home Internet or email accounts, you'll need a telephone adapter. Since three types of telephone jacks are used in Sweden, universal access will require three types of adapter. Duplex adapters allow a telephone to be connected in parallel with your modem, so you can dial manually or get an operator connection. A good source of information on adapters is Tele-Adapt (Ⓦ www.teleadapt.com). You'll also need a reputable 'global' modem, or you can by a local PC-card modem in Stockholm if you're going to stay a long time.

AOLnet has modem access numbers throughout Sweden; the number for Stockholm is ☎ 506 28996. The baud rate is 33.6kB/second and there's a US$3.95 surcharge per connection. Contact AOL for details. Visit W www.aol.com on the Internet and click on 'AOL Access Numbers'.

Compuserve's modem access number in Stockholm is ☎ 566 12000, which gives Internet access at 57.6kB/second (US ISDN) or 64kB/second (international ISDN), but there's a US$5 per hour surcharge. Instructions can be found on Compuserve's Web site (W www.compuserve.com) – click on 'Access Numbers', enter Stockholm and follow the links.

The following places offer public Internet access:

Internationella Bibliotek (Map 4, C1, #18) (☎ 508 31288) Odengatan 59. Metro: T-Odenplan. This annexe of the city library offers free walk-in 10-, 15- and 30-minute Internet slots and email is accessible. In the downstairs section, one 30-minute PC has Microsoft Word loaded and it also has a scanner and a floppy disk drive (handy for downloading or uploading lengthy text items). There are also 60-minute bookable slots available upstairs (Skr15); for reservations call ☎ 508 31289. Printouts cost Skr2 per page. Opening hours are 10am to 8.30pm Monday to Thursday, 10am to 6pm Friday and noon to 4pm on weekends. From 29 May to 20 August, it's open 10am to 7pm weekdays (closing 6pm on Friday) and noon to 4pm on Saturday. The 10-minute computers are available from 9am on weekdays year-round. There are other computers (both PC and Mac) in the main library building, nearby on Sveavägen 73; ask which ones allow private email.

Medborgarplatsen Bibliotek (Map 5, B7, #32) (☎ 508 12690) Medborgarplatsen 4. Metro: T-Medborgarplatsen. There are three email-accessible PCs here, with booking of free 60-minute slots available up to one week ahead. Two PCs offer short-term Internet access (snabb Internet). Printouts cost Skr2 per page. Open 11am to 7pm Monday to Thursday, 11am to 5pm Friday and 11am to 3pm Saturday.

Hornstull Biblioteket (Map 5, B2, #8) (☎ 508 40652) Hornsbruksgatan 25. Metro: T-Hornstull. This place has four computers with free Internet access, but email costs Skr10 for 30 minutes and printing is Skr2 per page. Bookings can be made 24 hours in advance. Open 11am to 7pm Monday and Tuesday, 10am to 6pm Wednesday, 10am to 5pm Thursday and 11am to 3pm Saturday.

Access IT (Map 6, D5, #154) (☎ 508 31489) basement, Kulturhuset, Sergels Torg. Metro: T-Centralen. Currently, there are 26 walk-in PCs and a ticket-machine queueing system. Charges are Skr1 per minute for up to 20 minutes, but only Skr20 per 30 minutes. Printouts cost Skr2 per page. Ask the staff about downloading onto disk. Open 10am to 7pm Tuesday to Friday and 11am to 5pm weekends.

Good Food (Map 6, D5, #106) (☎ 213180) Sergelgatan. Metro: T-Hötorget. This coffee shop and deli has five terminals offering access for Skr1 per minute (minimum five minutes). Printouts and floppy-disk use aren't possible. Open 8am to 8pm weekdays and 10am to 6pm weekends.

Skeppsholmen Hostel (Map 7, C7, #44) (☎ 463 2266) Flaggmansvägen 8. Metro: T-Kungsträdgården, or take bus No 65. Internet and email access costs Skr15 per 15 minutes, but printouts and disk use aren't possible. The facility is available 24 hours for guests but also 7am to midnight daily for nonguests.

Sverigehuset (Map 6, D6, #180) (☎ 789 2490) Hamngatan 27. Metro: T-Kungsträdgården. The tourist office offers more expensive Internet and email access at Skr15/25 for 10/20 minutes. Printing costs Skr3 per page. For opening hours, see Tourist Offices earlier in this chapter.

DIGITAL RESOURCES

The Internet is a rich resource for travellers. You can research your trip, hunt down bargain air fares, book hotels, check on weather conditions or chat with locals and other travellers about the best places to visit (or avoid!). Swedish-language Web sites may have a UK flag or some other place to click so you can get information in English.

A great place to start your Web explorations is the Lonely Planet Web site (W www.lonelyplanet.com), where you'll find summaries on travelling to most destinations, postcards from other travellers and the Thorn Tree bulletin board, where you can ask questions before you go or give advice on your return. You can also find travel news and updates on many of our most popular books, and the subWWWay section has many useful links to elsewhere on the Internet.

The Stockholm Information Service (W www.stockholmtown.com) manages the main tourist information Web site, but you may find the site short of detail. Alternatively, there is information for tourists (also in English) at W www.alltomstockholm .se/Stockholm/Tourist_Time/. This site is part of the much larger Swedish-language Web site at W www.alltomstockholm.se, which is definitely the best information source about Stockholm. There's a plan to include instructions in English to assist navigation around the Swedish pages.

Details of the main city museums, including the temporary exhibitions and events, are on the Internet at W www.stockholmsmuseer.com. Although this site is only in Swedish, there are links to museum homepages and some have information in English.

For archipelago information in English, go to the Archipelago Foundation Internet pages at W www.skargardsstiftelsen.se. You'll find *Stockholmskartan*, an excellent street map of the city, at W www.map.stockholm.se/kartago – use the zoom-in button repeatedly to get the best resolution. The text is in Swedish but it's easy to navigate through this site.

Details of restaurants (with up-to-date menus, but only in Swedish) are found at W www.kvartersmenyn.com and W www.lunchinfo.com. The former has lunch menus only, but the latter (a much more extensive site) covers both lunch and dinner, despite its name.

Yellow Pages directories of business phone numbers can be found on the Internet at W www.gulasidorna.se and W www.bizbook.se.

BOOKS
Guidebooks

One of the finest guidebooks in English about the city is *Close to Stockholm*, by Magdalena Koroty ska and Karin Winter (1998), an unusual picture book covering most of Stockholm, with hand-painted panoramas. It includes a detailed and well-researched guide to 160 buildings worth visiting.

Another unusual book, *The Stockholm Time Walk* by Michael Tongue (1996), suggests a walking tour past 50 points of interest, mostly in Gamla Stan but also in some neighbouring parts of Norrmalm and Södermalm. The book contains text and photos of these areas as they were around 100 years ago as well as clear maps of the route today.

Cultural Walking Tours, by Elena Siré and Sten Leijonhufvud (1998), covers 10 walking tours that explore the city's architectural and historical heritage. Although aimed at the disabled, this handy little book is also useful for other visitors.

An essential guide for architecture buffs is *The Complete Guide to Architecture in Stockholm*, by Olof Hultin et al (1998), which describes 400 buildings from the earliest times up to the present, using colour photos, detailed text and maps.

History

Stockholm's Annual Rings, by Magnus Andersson (1998), is an ambitious and detailed text regarding the development of the city over the centuries, with a strong architectural slant. Unfortunately, the translation into English is rather poor and the book is inordinately expensive.

General

The interesting collection of articles about life in modern Stockholm in *Stockholm*, by Ingmarie Froman (1997), includes a gazetteer but, unfortunately, it's already dated. *I Love Stockholm*, by Teddy Brunius et al (1998), is a collection of essays by local artists, writers and other cultural figures. *The Soul of Stockholm*, by Erland Josephson et al (1999), is a fine photobook with essays by local experts in a range of fields. The large format coffee-table book *Stockholm Horizons*, by Jeppe Wikström (1996), has over 800 photos, from panoramas to close-up detail.

If you're interested in Swedish festivals, try *Maypoles, Crayfish and Lucia – Swedish Holidays and Traditions*, by Jan-Öjvind Swahn (1997).

For an interesting and accurate guide to cultural behaviour, try *Culture Shock! – Sweden: A Guide to Customs and Etiquette*, by Charlotte Rosen Svensson (1998). *Smörgåsbord* by Kerstin Törngren (1996) details 20 recipes for the classic Swedish buffet, including herring, *gravad lax* (marinated salmon) and meat balls.

NEWSPAPERS & MAGAZINES

The *International Herald-Tribune*, *The Guardian in Europe*, London dailies, and English-language magazines, such as *Time*, *Newsweek* and *The Economist*, are sold at major transport terminals, Press Stop, Pressbyrån, and at tobacconists. The reading room at Internationella Bibliotek (Map 4, C1, #18) (International Library; ☎ 508 31288), Odengatan 59, has reasonably recent copies of many European newspapers, including London's *The Times* and *The Observer*. Sweden doesn't publish many specialist magazines, but a wide variety of astronomically priced English-language imports is available from Press Stop and Pressbyrån newsagents.

There are eight daily newspapers in Stockholm, but they're only published in Swedish. The main morning papers are the right-of-centre *Svenska Dagbladet* and the more moderate *Dagens Nyheter*, which appeals to a broader range of readers. Both papers have an events listing every Friday; the best is *På Stan*, which comes with Dagens Nyheter. The most significant afternoon tabloids are the sensationalist *Aftonbladet* and *Expressen*.

Useful Publications

The free *What's On – Stockholm* is published by Stockholm Information Service monthly in summer (bimonthly during the rest of the year) and can be found in hotels and tourist offices; it covers restaurants, museums and events. The department store Nordiska Kompaniet (NK) produces the free annual *Essential Guide to Stockholm*, covering restaurants, museums and other sights. You'll find it at the tourist office and in NK.

If you read Swedish, the aforementioned weekly events guide *På Stan* and the monthly *Nöjesguiden* entertainment guide (with sections on cafes, restaurants and pubs) are very useful. *QX* is a free Swedish-language tabloid, issued monthly, which concentrates on gay issues and can be found at RFSL (see the Gay & Lesbian Travellers section later in this chapter), gay nightclubs, and some stores and restaurants. It has details of bars and clubs, some events, lifestyle articles, restaurants and cafes.

RADIO & TV
Radio

The BBC World Service broadcasts to Sweden on short wave at 9410kHz from 7am to 10am and 4pm to 11pm daily. Channel P6 (Radio Sweden domestic), with programming in English, German, Samish, Latvian, Russian and Finnish, is at 89.6FM in Greater Stockholm and 1179kHz throughout the rest of the country. For current program lists, check the Internet at Ⓦ www .sr.se/rs/schedule or contact Radio Sweden (☎ 784 7288, fax 667 3701, Ⓔ info@ rs.sr.se), SE-10510 Stockholm.

National Swedish Radio *Riksradio* channel P2 (96.2FM) is good for classical music and opera. Radio Stockholm (103.3FM) has hourly news, traffic reports and discussion programs. For pop and rock music, try channel P3 (99.3FM in Stockholm but variable around the country) and local commercial stations such as Rockklassiker (106.7FM).

TV

The national TV channels TV1 and TV2 don't have advertising, but aren't particularly interesting to foreigners. TV3 and TV5 are commercial satellite or cable channels (not available nationally) with a lot of English-language shows and films. The commercial channel TV4 has good-quality broadcasting in Swedish and English. Foreign-made programs and films are always shown in their original language, with Swedish subtitles. Hotels may also have Euro News, BBC World, Sky News, ABC, NBC, CNN or EuroSport, all in English.

VIDEO SYSTEMS

When buying videos, remember that Sweden (like most of Europe and the UK) uses the PAL system, which is very expensive to convert to NTSC or SECAM.

PHOTOGRAPHY & VIDEO
Film & Equipment

Although print and slide films are readily available in towns and cities, prices are fairly high, so you may want to bring your own film and develop your slides back home.

Expert, a chain of electrical goods shops, usually sells a wide range of film, including slide film. One-hour print developing costs Skr107/143 for 24/36 exposures. If you can wait three days, the price drops to Skr69/89. Kodachrome 64 costs Skr149, including processing, and Fuji Sensia ISO 50 costs Skr83 without processing. Expert charges Skr39/75 for colour-slide developing, without/with frames. A twin pack of 90-minute 8mm video camera film costs Skr99. See also Photography in the Shopping chapter.

Camera equipment can be bought or repaired at Expert, but repairs will require sending your equipment away. Equipment isn't cheap but there is a wide range available.

Technical Tips
The clear northern light and glare from water, ice and snow may require use of a UV filter (or skylight filter) and a lens shade. ISO 100 film is sufficient for most purposes. In winter, most cameras don't work below -20°C.

Restrictions
Photography and video is prohibited at many museums and churches, mainly to protect fragile artwork. Don't take photos of military establishments and note that some specially widened sections of major highways fall into this category.

Photographing People
It's wise to ask permission first when someone is the main subject of a photograph.

TIME
Time in Sweden is one hour ahead of GMT/UTC, the same as Norway, Denmark and most of Western Europe. When it's noon in Sweden, it's 11am in London, 1pm in Helsinki, 6am in New York and Toronto, 3am in Los Angeles, 9pm in Sydney and 11pm in Auckland. Sweden observes daylight-saving time – the clocks go forward an hour at 2am on the last Sunday in March and back an hour at 2am on the last Sunday in October. Timetables and business hours are quoted using the 24-hour clock, but dates are often given by week number (1 to 52).

When telling the time, note that in Swedish the use of 'half' means *half before* rather than half past. Always double check which time is required – otherwise, you may be an hour late!

ELECTRICITY
Electricity in Sweden is supplied at 220V AC, 50Hz, and round continental-style two-pin plugs are standard. Equipment set for a different voltage or cycle will not function correctly in Sweden. You're advised to obtain a suitable adapter in advance.

WEIGHTS & MEASURES
Sweden uses the metric system; to convert between metric and imperial units, see the table at the back of the book. Some shops quote prices followed by '/hg', which means per 100g. Decimals are separated from whole numbers by a comma, and thousands are indicated by points. You'll commonly hear the word *mil* (mile) which equals 10km.

LAUNDRY
The coin-operated laundry is virtually nonexistent in Sweden. Many hostels and camping grounds have laundry facilities costing around Skr30 or Skr40 for wash and dry, and most hotels offer a laundry service. It's best to carry soap powder or a bar of clothes soap for doing your own laundry in basins.

A handy self-service laundry in the city area near the T-Odenplan metro station is Tvättomaten (Map 3, C5, #11) (☎ 346480) at Västmannagatan 61B, which charges Skr62 per machine load (maximum 5kg) for wash and dry. It's open 8.30am to 6.30pm on weekdays and 9.30am to 3pm on Saturday (last orders are accepted two hours before closing). In Södermalm, try Elittvätten (Map 5, C7, #73) (☎ 642 6941), Gotlandsgatan 59, which charges Skr60 per 5kg load for wash and dry (including soap powder). It's open 10am to 6pm on weekdays (closing at 7pm on Thursday).

TOILETS
Public toilets in parks, shopping centres, libraries, and bus or train stations aren't free

in Sweden. Toilets in restaurants are for the patrons only. Except at Centralstationen (where there's an attendant), pay-toilets are coin operated, and cost Skr5. You'll even have to pay at the main tourist office at Sverigehuset! However, there are free gents' urinals at the following locations: in the basement at Centralstationen (signposted 'urinoar', but it's fairly revolting); by Tegnérlunden Park; in Kungsträdgården, opposite Arsenalsgatan; and in the basement of Kungliga biblioteket (the National Library of Sweden).

LEFT LUGGAGE

There are four sizes of *förvaringsboxar* (left-luggage boxes) in the basement at Centralstationen, costing Skr20/30/50/70 (paid in multiples of Skr5 and/or Skr10 only) for every 24-hour period. The largest are clearly designed for skis! The change machines accept banknotes or you can pay an attendant. Four types of lockers at Cityterminalen (city bus station) cost Skr10/15/20/30 per 24 hours and they accept Skr5 and Skr10 pieces. The small Skr10 lockers are at the far northern end of the bus station. Similar facilities are available at Arlanda airport, and the terminals of Silja Line and Viking Line.

HEALTH

The health care system in Sweden is absurdly complicated and expensive, but it's very modern and almost all doctors speak English. There's no general practitioner system in Sweden so, for nonemergencies, you're advised to go to the local hospital or visit the local *apotek* (pharmacy). The central 24-hour pharmacy, CW Scheele (Map 6, E3, #133) (☎ 454 8130), is at Klarabergsgatan 64. *Hälso och sjukvård* (health and medical care) is listed in the blue pages of the pink-cover business phone book (Företag); you'll find your nearest suburban *vårdcentral* (medical centre) there. You can also contact the 24-hour medical hotline on ☎ 463 9100 or the medications hotline ☎ 020 667766 (toll free). The general emergency number, including the ambulance, is ☎ 112.

Dental treatment is definitely for the wealthy, since an hour's treatment costs around Skr700. Look for *tandläkare* (dentist) in the phone book, or visit the drop-in surgery at St Eriks Ögonsjukhus (Map 3, E4, #38) (☎ 654 1117), Polhemsgatan 48, open 7.45am to 8.30pm daily.

EU citizens with an E111 form are charged Skr120 to consult a doctor and up to Skr300 for a visit to casualty. Hospital stays cost Skr80 per day (free if you're under 16). Non-EU citizens must have adequate travel health insurance or be prepared to face astronomically high bills – an x-ray for a broken ankle costs Skr2000!

Immunisations aren't necessary for travel to Sweden, unless you've been travelling somewhere where yellow fever is prevalent. Ensure that your normal childhood vaccines (against measles, mumps, rubella, diphtheria, tetanus and polio) are up-to-date. You may also want to have a hepatitis vaccination, as exposure can occur anywhere.

You're unlikely to encounter serious health problems in Stockholm, but stomach upsets are possible. Occasionally, cooked meats displayed on buffet tables may cause problems. You should also take care with shellfish (cooked mussels that haven't opened properly aren't safe to eat), unidentified berries and mushrooms. Tap water is safe to drink in Stockholm, but drinking from rural streams may be unwise due to agriculture, old mine workings and wild animals. The clearest-looking stream water may contain giardia and other parasites.

Hospitals

The following hospitals have 24-hour accident and emergency (casualty) service:

Danderyds sjukhus (Map 2, A5, #5) (☎ 655 5000) Danderyd. Metro: T-Danderyds sjukhus.
Karolinska sjukhuset (Map 3, A3, #1) (☎ 517 70000) Haga. Take bus No 52 from Sergels Torg.
St Eriks Ögonsjukhus (Map 3, E4, #39) (☎ 672 3000) Fleminggatan 22, Kungsholmen. This hospital specialises in the treatment of eyes. Catch bus No 59 at Sergels Torg.
St Görans sjukhus (Map 3, E2, #43) (☎ 587 01000) Sankt Göransplan 1, Kungsholmen. Take bus No 52 from Sergels Torg.

Södersjukhuset (Map 5, D5, #27) (☎ 616 1000) Ringvägen 52, Södermalm. The most convenient hospital for the city centre. Catch bus No 43 in Regeringsgatan.

WOMEN TRAVELLERS

Sexual equality is emphasised in Sweden and there should be no question of discrimination. Kvinnojouren (☎ 760 9611), based in Stockholm, is the national organisation that deals with violence against women. Local centres are listed in the green pages of telephone directories or on the Internet at W www.gulasidorna.se.

Pregnant women with health emergencies should contact the nearest *mödravård-central* (maternity hospital) in the blue pages of the pink-cover business telephone directory (listed by municipality).

Some Stockholm taxi firms offer discounts to women at night, so be sure to ask when booking.

Recommended reading for first-time women travellers is the *Handbook for Women Travellers*, by Maggie and Gemma Moss, published by Piatkus Books but now out of print. *Going Solo*, by Merrin White, is also useful, but it's hard to find and is unobtainable in the USA.

There are several good Web sites for women travellers, including those at W www.passionfruit.com and W www .journeywoman.com, and the women travellers page on the Lonely Planet Web site's Thorn Tree (W thorntree.lonelyplanet.com).

GAY & LESBIAN TRAVELLERS

Sweden is a fairly liberal country and, along with several neighbouring countries, allows gay and lesbian couples to form 'registered partnerships' that grant marriage rights except access to church weddings, adoption and artificial insemination. Even so, take note that homosexual couples are discreet in public.

Up-to-date details of gay restaurants, bars, cafes, discos, nightclubs and culture (movies and theatre) are listed on the Internet at W www.qx.se/english/ and also in the associated free monthly tabloid newspaper *QX* (see Useful Publications earlier). Lesbians should check the tourist information

(for clubs, bars, coffee shops and restaurants) on the Web site W www.corky.nu. More general information for gay and lesbian travellers is posted on the Internet at W thorntree.lonelyplanet.com.

Stockholm Pride is a four-day event in late July/early August, mainly based in Pride Park, Tantolunden (Södermalm). The program includes art, debate, health, literature, music, spirituality and sport. There are song contests, transvestite drag shows, mud wrestling, film showings and (of course) a parade. For full details, check the Web site at W www.stockholmpride.org or contact RFSL.

Gay bars, nightclubs and other venues in Stockholm are mentioned in the Entertainment chapter, but ask at RFSL for up-to-date information.

Organisations

Riksförbundet för Sexuellt Likaberättigande The national organisation for gay and lesbian rights is commonly called RFSL (☎ 736 0213, e forbund@rfsl.se), Box 350, SE-10126 Stockholm. It's based at Stockholm's Gay-Hus (Map 4, C1, #23), Sveavägen 57, where there's also a bookshop, restaurant and nightclub.

Riksförbundet för hivpositiva The national society for people with HIV is also called just RFHP (☎ 714 5410, fax 714 0425, e info@ rfhp.a.se), Gotlandsgatan 72, SE-11638 Stockholm. It maintains a Web site at W www .rfhp.a.se, which is well worth reading and presents a new light on 'liberal Sweden'.

DISABLED TRAVELLERS

Stockholm is reasonably well set up for people with disabilities – there are many special transport services with adapted facilities, ranging from trains to taxis, but always contact the operator in advance. Some SL buses are wheelchair accessible and Taxi 020 (☎ 789 2496 9am to 5pm weekdays, ☎ 632 9070 at other times) offers taxi tours for disabled people. Public toilets, some hotel rooms and a few museums have facilities for the disabled, street crossings may have ramps for wheelchairs and audio signals for the visually impaired, and even grocery stores may be wheelchair accessible.

You may want to contact your national support organisation and try to speak with its 'travel officer', if there is one. These organisations often have complete libraries devoted to travel, and can put you in touch with tour companies that specialise in disabled travel.

Organisations

For further information on facilities for the disabled in Stockholm, contact Information-savdelning, De Handikappades Riksförbund (☎ 685 8000, fax 645 6541, ℮ info@dhr.se, Ⓦ www.dhr.se), Katrinebergsvägen 6, 5 tr, SE-10074 Stockholm.

The UK-based Royal Association for Disability & Rehabilitation (RADAR; ☎ 020-7250 3222), 12 City Forum, 250 City Rd, London EC1V 8AF, UK, can supply general advice for disabled travellers in Sweden.

In the USA, contact the Society for Accessible Travel and Hospitality (☎ 212-447 7284, fax 725 8253, ℮ sathtravel@aol.com), 347 5th Ave, Suite 610, New York, NY 10016. Special Interest Travel has a section for the disabled on its Web site at Ⓦ www.sitravel.com. In Canada, try the Web site at Ⓦ www.cta-otc.gc.ca/eng/toc.htm and click on 'Accessible Transportation'.

SENIOR TRAVELLERS

Seniors over 65 normally get discounts on entry to museums and other sights, cinema and theatre tickets, and air tickets and other transport. No special card is required, but show your passport if asked for proof of age. A few hotels, including the Radisson SAS chain, have senior discount schemes. At the time of writing, there are no organisations of particular interest to senior travellers in Stockholm.

In your home country, you may already be entitled to all sorts of interesting travel packages and discounts (eg, on car rental) through organisations and travel agencies that cater to senior travellers. Start hunting at your local senior citizens advice bureau or larger seniors' organisations such as the American Association of Retired Persons (AARP; Ⓦ www.aarp.org) in the USA or Age Concern England (Ⓦ www.ace.org.uk) in the UK.

STOCKHOLM FOR CHILDREN

Successful travel with young children requires planning and effort. If the kids have helped to work out where you're going, chances are they'll still be interested when you arrive. Ask your nearest Swedish tourist office for the brochure *Sweden for Children*. Lonely Planet's *Travel with Children* is also a useful source of information.

Public transport offers reduced rates for children. SL buses, commuter trains and the metro are free to those aged under six, and there's a roughly 40% discount for kids and teenagers from six to 17 inclusive. Some public toilets have nappy-changing facilities, eg, the toilet in the basement at Centralstationen. Breastfeeding in public is rare but is unlikely to cause offence.

To join the city-run day care centres, you'll need to stay over six months; contact Stadshuset (Map 6, G2, #140) (city hall; ☎ 508 29058) for details. An after-school and pre-school day care centre is Montes-soriförskolan Krokodilen (☎ 805880), Grönviksvägen 107, SE-16776 Bromma. Home-care service, including cleaning, laundry etc, is offered by Ansvar Hemservice (☎ 555 24112, fax 555 24110), Vretensvägen 13, SE-17154 Solna. Some hotels and companies (if you're in Stockholm on business) can also assist with childcare.

Many attractions and museums in Stockholm have sections set up specifically for the younger set, usually with toys, hands-on displays and activities. Admission is usually free for young children up to about seven years of age and half-price (or substantially discounted) for those up to 16 or so.

Stockholms Miniatyrmuseum (Map 4, C1, #17) includes mechanical models, dolls and dolls' houses; there are also lots of traditional toys and a daily children's theatre at Leksaksmuseet (Map 7, G2, #98). Skansen (Map 4, F7) has a mini zoo (with baby animals), a childrens' circus performed by kids, puppet shows and animal feeding time. The Aquaria Vattenmuseum (Map 4, G6, #100) and Fjärils & Fågelhuset (Map 2, B5, #16) will generally interest children. There is a section for children at the Post museum (Map 7, C3, #65), and several

Astrid & Pippi

Astrid Lindgren was born in 1907. Upon leaving school she went to Stockholm and trained to be a secretary, got a job in an office, married and had two children.

In 1941, when Lindgren's daughter Karin was ill, she wanted to be told a story. Lindgren asked her if she'd like to hear about a little girl called Pippi Longstocking. Pippi was a hit with Karin and her friends and the story was told over and over again.

In 1944, Lindgren sprained her ankle and, to pass the time, started writing down the Pippi stories in shorthand. She sent a copy to a publisher but it was rejected. However, she had written a second book, which she sent to another publisher and this won second prize in a girls' story competition. The next year, the same publisher organised a children's book competition and Lindgren entered a revised Pippi manuscript, which won first prize. In 1946, her publisher announced a new competition for detective stories for young people and she entered *Bill Bergson Master Detective*, and this won a shared first prize.

Lindgren's impressive output includes picture books, plays and songs and her books have been translated into more than 50 languages. She has worked in radio, television and films, was head of the Children's Book Department at her publishers for four years and has received numerous honours and awards from around the world. Lindgren still resides in Stockholm.

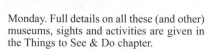

sections at Sjöhistoriska Museet (Map 4, E8, #74). Junibacken (Map 4, F5, #95), based on the children's books by Astrid Lindgren, is designed entirely for young children (under 10) and Tom Tits Experiment in Södertälje (see Excursions chapter) introduces kids to science.

Older children may be fascinated by Tekniska Museet & Teknorama Science Centre (Map 4, E9, #75), which has mechanical models, a mine display and sections on the history of electricity and chemistry. Naturhistoriska Museet and Cosmonova (Map 2, B6, #19) have interactive displays and exciting IMAX films, respectively. Kids enjoy walking through the displays at Medeltidsmuseet (Map 7, A4, #11), and the interactive 'Childrens Playworld' at Nordiska museet (Map 4, F6, #94) includes a farm with a log cabin, stables and a barn. At Musikmuseet (Map 6, C9, #76), there's a music workshop and regular children's activities. There are also activities at Kulturhuset (Map 6, D5, #154), daily except

Monday. Full details on all these (and other) museums, sights and activities are given in the Things to See & Do chapter.

There is also a film festival for children in early April (see Special Events later in this chapter), but films may not be in English.

In Stockholm, there are several public parks with play areas for kids; some restaurants and hotels also have play areas. Hotels and other accommodation options often have 'family rooms' which accommodate up to two adults and two to four children for little more than the price of a regular double. Scandic hotels have an eat-all-you-like children's menu (age under 14) for only Skr39.

Car rental firms hire out children's safety seats at a nominal cost, but it's essential that you book them in advance. Highchairs and cots (cribs) are standard in many restaurants and hotels. Swedish supermarkets offer a relatively wide choice of baby food, infant formulas, soy and cow's milk, disposable nappies (diapers) etc.

LIBRARIES

Many museums, cultural centres and institutes in Stockholm have private libraries, which are open on request.

Of more general interest is the city library, Stadsbiblioteket (Map 4, C1, #14) (☎ 508 31100) at Sveavägen 73, which is open 10am to 8.30pm Monday to Thursday, 10am to 6pm Friday and noon to 4pm on weekends. From 29 May to 20 August, it's open 10am to 7pm weekdays (closing 6pm on Friday) and noon to 4pm on Saturday. Once you've got your free library card, you can borrow a total of up to 50 books from any of the public libraries in Stockholm. Most of the public libraries have a few books in English and they can be found in the free leaflet *Välkommen till biblioteken!* (available from all public libraries), in the Yellow Pages under the heading 'Bibliotek' or on the Internet at **W** www.gulasidorna.se (enter Stadsbibliotek and choose 'Stockholm').

The nearby Internationella Bibliotek (Map 4, C1, #18) (☎ 508 31288), Odengatan 59, keeps the same opening hours and also stocks a wide range of non-Swedish newspapers, journals and magazines for reference purposes, but you can walk in and browse.

Kulturhuset (Map 6, D5, #154) on Sergels Torg has a free reading room (☎ 508 31470) with international periodicals and newspapers as well as books in various languages. It's open 10am to 7pm Tuesday to Friday and 11am to 5pm on weekends.

Kungliga biblioteket (Map 6, A7, #41) (☎ 463 4000), Humlegården, is the National Library of Sweden and it obtains a copy of everything published in Swedish. It's open 9am to 8pm weekdays (closing at 7pm on Friday) and 10am to 5pm on Saturday. The library Web site (**W** www.kb.se) has pages in English.

UNIVERSITIES

Stockholm Universitet (Map 2, B6, #20) was founded as a private institution (Stockholm College) as late as 1878; up until then, students went to Uppsala or Lund. Degrees weren't granted until 1904. When the college was taken over by the state in 1960, it was given university status. Initially, there were three faculties (Natural Sciences, Humanities and Law) but, in 1964, Social Sciences was added.

After moving to new premises in 1970, most of the university is located 3.5km due north of the city centre in the Frescati district (Metro: T-Universitetet). It's now the largest university in Sweden, with 33,000 undergraduate students, 1700 postgraduate students, 3450 permanent employees, around 80 departments, 800 courses and some 25 study programs.

You can find the university on the Internet at **W** www.su.se, which has information in English about courses for prospective international students. Fees are generally very small – you may only have to pay for the Student Union and other societies (Skr400) and health insurance (Skr750). However, there are no scholarships (so you'll have to pay all your expenses) and the university doesn't provide student accommodation – but it can provide contacts. You can contact Stockholm Universitet on ☎ 162000, fax 159522, at SE-10691 Stockholm.

CULTURAL CENTRES

You'll find the following cultural centres in Stockholm:

British Council (☎ 663 6004, **e** info@britishcouncil.se) Skarpögatan 6-8. The British Council organises English-language teaching and educational and cultural exchanges. You should go to the British Council Information Centre (Map 6, C3, #116), Klara Norra Kyrkogatan 29, open 2pm to 5pm Monday to Wednesday. Web site: **W** www.britishcouncil.se

Finlandsinstitutet (Map 6, A6, #38) (☎ 545 21200, fax 545 21210, **e** info@finlandskulturist.se) Snickarbacken 2-4. The library (☎ 545 21209) and reading room are open noon to 6pm Tuesday to Thursday and 11am to 3pm Friday and Saturday.

Goethe-Institutet (Map 4, E6, #64) (☎ 459 1200, **e** goethe@swipnet.se) Linnégatan 76. The library (☎ 459 1205, **e** goethe.bibl@swipnet.se) at this German cultural institute is open 1pm to 6pm Monday to Thursday. Web site: **W** www.goethe.de/stockholm (German and Swedish only)

Italienka Kulturinstitutet (Map 4, E7, #72) (☎ 660 3359, fax 660 6180) Gärdesgatan 14. Open by appointment only.

Judiska Biblioteket (Map 6, E8, #187) (☎ 679 2934) Wahrendorffsgatan 3. Located at the main synagogue, this Jewish library is open by arrangement only.

Kurdiska Biblioteket (Map 7, A8, #49) (☎ 679 8803) Slupskjulsvägen 26. The Kurdish library is open by arrangement only.

Polska Biblioteket i Stockholm (Map 4, C4, #48) (☎ 661 6359) Östermalmsgatan 75. The Polish library; open by appointment only.

Polska Institutet (Map 4, C3, #40) (☎ 210894) Villagatan 2. Open by appointment only.

DANGERS & ANNOYANCES

Stockholm is one of the safest cities in Europe and mugging is very rare. Some parts of the city aren't particularly safe late at night; take particular care in areas such as Sergels Torg, Medborgarplatsen (Södermalm) and Fridhemsplan (Kungsholmen), especially when the bars empty, any time after 1am. The suburb of Rinkeby also has a poor reputation at night. Pickpocketing is becoming a problem, especially in crowded places such as Drottninggatan, Centralstationen and the major museums. You should steer clear of night buses on weekends. The neo-Nazi demonstration in Kungsträdgården on 30 November should also be given a wide berth.

The most irritating things about Stockholm include discrimination at some nightclubs (there are usually different age limits for men and women and you may be selected for admission while queueing outside in the cold) and over-zealous issuing of parking tickets to hired or foreign-registered cars. The general feeling that the city and some of the people in it are determined to drain your wallet is actually quite pervasive!

In rural areas, mosquitoes are a problem from June to early August and elk are a serious motoring hazard especially at dawn or dusk. Ice (particularly on road bridges in country areas, on steep city pavements and at the top of subway stairs) can be deadly from October to April – too many people are having serious accidents.

EMERGENCIES

The toll-free emergency number for the fire service, police and ambulance is ☎ 112.

The police have 24-hour stations at Torkel Knutssonsgatan 20 (Map 5, B5, #22) (☎ 401 0300), Södermalm, and Kungsholmsgatan 37 (Map 3, F4, #51) (☎ 401 0000), Kungsholmen. There's also a police office by the (upstairs) Kungsbron entrance to Centralstationen; it's open 9am to 5pm weekdays.

The 24-hour pharmacy is CW Scheele (Map 6, E3, #133) (☎ 454 8130), Klarabergsgatan 64. Hospitals are listed in the earlier Health section. There's also a 24-hour medical hotline on ☎ 463 9100 and a medications hotline on ☎ 020 667766 (toll free).

The nearest thing to a rape crisis centre is Kvinnojouren (☎ 760 9611), the national organisation that deals with violence against women.

In the case of vehicle breakdowns and towing, contact Larmtjänst (☎ 020 910040).

LEGAL MATTERS

The police in Stockholm are generally friendly and helpful. The chances of being stopped by the police if you haven't been up to something are actually extremely small. However, in case of arrest, the police can hold someone for up to four days without charge. There may also be a restriction on phone calls if the matter is considered serious enough. The police also have the right to name an *advokat* (attorney), although the criminal justice court may appoint one. The police keep a list of attorneys, and bills for so-called public attorneys may be partly paid for by the state. The proportion of the bill to be paid may depend on the client's country of origin.

Parking is always a problem in Sweden and a typical fine amounts to Skr700. Although suburban areas have free street parking at night (5pm to 9am daily), you can be fined for parking during street-cleaning night and this varies from place to place. Fines have been issued in dubious circumstances and readers are advised to bring up these matters with any appropriate authority.

Sweden isn't liberal when it comes to illegal drugs – don't even think of bringing even a tiny amount into the country with you.

BUSINESS HOURS

Businesses and government offices are open 8.30am or 9am to 5pm on weekdays, although they can close at 3pm in summer. Banks usually open at 9.30am and close at 3pm, weekdays only, but on Thursday some branches stay open until 6pm. Some city branches open 9am to 5pm or 6pm every weekday.

Normal shopping hours are 9am to 6pm weekdays and 9am to between 1pm and 4pm on Saturday. City department stores stay open later on weekdays (usually until 7pm) and are usually open on Sunday (noon to 4pm, but NK is open 10am to 5pm). NK keeps shorter hours in June and July. Shops often close early on the afternoon before a public holiday. Some supermarkets stay open until 10pm and some inner-city 7-Eleven stores are open 24 hours. Systembolaget (the state-owned alcohol store; W www.systembolaget.se) is usually open 10am to 6pm (closing on Thursday and Friday at 7pm) on weekdays and 10am to 2pm or 3pm on Saturday. Some stores are open slightly later on weekdays. Lunch in restaurants often begins as early as 11am and is over by 2pm. McDonald's always has the best opening hours, with some outlets open until 3am on weekends. The McDonald's on Vasagatan is open 24 hours.

Most museums have short opening hours (even in July) and tourist offices outside the city may close at 4pm or not open at all on weekends. Opening hours are given in this book, whenever possible.

PUBLIC HOLIDAYS & SPECIAL EVENTS
Public Holidays

There's a concentration of public holidays in spring and early summer. Midsummer brings life almost to a halt for three days – attractions and restaurants may be closed and transport and other services are reduced (even on Midsummer's Eve). Some hotels, restaurants and tourist attractions are closed or have shorter opening hours between Christmas and New Year. It's also not uncommon for restaurants and hotels to close for several weeks between Midsummer and early August. Sweden celebrates Christmas on 24 December.

Public holidays (remember, many businesses will close early the day before and all day after) are:

Nyårsdag (New Year's Day) 1 January
Trettondedag Jul (Epiphany) 6 January
Långfredag, Annandag påsk (Easter) March/April – Good Friday to Easter Monday
Första Maj (Labour Day) 1 May
Kristi Himmelsfärds dag (Ascension Day) May/June
Annandag Pingst (Whit Monday) late May or early June
Midsommardag (Midsummer's Day) first Friday after 21 June
Alla Helgons dag (All Saints' Day) late October/early November – on a Saturday
Julafton (Christmas Eve) 24 December
Juldag (Christmas Day) 25 December
Annandag Jul (Boxing Day) 26 December
Nyårsafton (New Year's Eve) 31 December

Special Events

Many festivals and events are held throughout the year, varying from free to rather expensive. As well as the following listed events, there are others that aren't held annually and may only take place once. Current special events are listed in the tourist office publication *What's On – Stockholm*.

January

Stockholm Antiques Fair – third weekend in January. Over 200 exhibitors selling antiques, curios, fine art, interior decor and design. For information, contact Stockholmsmässan (☎ 749 4100, fax 992044), Mässvägen 1, SE-12580 Älvsjö.
Web site: W www.stofair.se

February

Sweden Hockey Games – second week of February. An ice hockey tournament with eight leading teams from around the world; tickets cost from around Skr200 to Skr300. Get details from Globen (☎ 725 1000).
Web site: W www.globen.se

Stockholm Furniture Fair – usually the second weekend in February, but only open to the public on Sunday. Features the latest in Scandinavian home furnishings, including lighting and textiles. Admission costs Skr80 but seminars are free. Contact Stockholmsmässan (for contact details, see earlier).

Globen Gala – third Thursday in February. For details on this indoor athletics competition, call ☎ 667 1930.

Vikingarännet – third or fourth Sunday in February. This immensely popular 80km-long ice-skating race from Uppsala to Stockholm is open to everyone but fees are steep at Skr525. For details, contact Vikingarännet (☎ 556 31245, fax 549012, ⓔ kansliet@vikingarannet.com). Web site: Ⓦ www.vikingarannet.com

March

Winter Sports Week – week nine, always early March. Winter sports and events in Kungsträdgården, including the ice-skating rink, a cross-country ski track, dog sledging, reindeer, Sami huts, winter camping and music. For details, call ☎ 555 10090 or ask at the tourist office.

Stockholm Art Fair – second weekend in March. This fair includes painting, sculpture, graphic design, photography and video. For details and admission fees, contact Sollentuna mässan (☎ 506 65000, fax 506 65225). Web site: Ⓦ www.sollfair.se

April

Stockholm Filmfestival Junior – first week in April (five or six days). This film festival for children takes place in various cinemas around the city. For details, call ☎ 677 5000 or check the Web site at Ⓦ www.filmfestivalen.se shortly before the festival.

Cirkus Princessan – from late April to late May, once daily (twice on each of Saturday and Sunday). The world's only all-female circus gala, with ringside seats for Skr495 and stalls for Skr395. For more detailed information, contact Bronett (☎ 660 0200, fax 660 0955, ⓔ cirkus@bronett.com). Web site: Ⓦ www.bronett.se

Valborgsmässoafton – 30 April. This event, Walpurgis Night, celebrates the arrival of spring with bonfires, fireworks and choral singing. Upper secondary school-leavers, with their white caps, are a common sight in the city at this time. The best place to see it is Skansen (Map 4, F7) (☎ 442 8000, fax 442 8282, ⓔ info@skansen.se); tickets cost Skr50/20 adult/child on top of regular admission fees. Web site: Ⓦ www.skansen.se

May

Bellmansfestivalen – one day in mid-May. This day is celebrated by a free picnic in Hagaparken, with a singing troubadour dressed as Carl Michael Bellman (and lots of other people in 17th-century clothes). Ask at the tourist office for details.

Drakfesten – one day in mid-May. For details on this free kite-flying festival in one of the Gärdet area's parks, ask at the tourist office.

Planket – one weekend in mid-May. A free festival arranged by photography students at Vitabergsparken, near Sofia kyrka.

Skärgårdsmarknad – one or two days on the last weekend in May. Traders from the archipelago come to sell herring, lamb and other foods. Ask at the tourist office for this year's time and location (usually Gälarvarvet, near Nordiska museet).

Elitloppet – last weekend in May. This trotting competition involving the finest Swedish horses takes place at Solvalla travbana (racetrack) in Sundbyberg. For details, call ☎ 635 9000.

Tjejtrampet – last Sunday in May. This 51km-long event starts in the Gärdet area and claims to be the world's biggest women's bicycle race. Contact the organisers (☎ 450 2610, fax 664 3815, ⓔ kansliet@tjejtrampet.com).

Restaurangernas Dag – from late May to early June. This five-day food festival is based in tents on Kungsträdgården (Map 6, E7) and it includes music, circus events etc.

June

Gärdes Loppet – first Sunday in June. This event takes place in Södra Djurgården and includes a parade, a race and a classic car exhibition. For further information, contact the tourist office.

Skärgårdsbåtens dag – first Wednesday in June. Sail to Vaxholm from central Stockholm in a typical archipelago boat. For information, call ☎ 662 8902.

Nationaldag – 6 June (Gustav Vasa was elected King of Sweden on 6 June 1523). The national day isn't a public holiday, possibly because patriotic feelings don't generally run high in Sweden. The main celebration, in the presence of the royal family, takes place on the Solliden stage (Map 4, G7, #83) at Skansen and is transmitted live on TV. Admission is free after 3pm, but you'll still have to pay the regular Skansen admission fee. For details, call Skansen (☎ 442 8000, fax 442 8282, ⓔ info@skansen.se). Web site: Ⓦ www.skansen.se

Stockholm Marathon – second Saturday in June. Around 13,000 people enjoy one of the finest marathon circuits in the world. Participants must be over 17 years and the fee is steep at Skr455. The deadline for entries is 20 April. For information, contact Stockholm Marathon (☎ 667 1930, fax 664 3822, e info@marathon.se).
Web site: W www.marathon.se

La Mayonnaise Open – third week in June. This is the largest boule competition in northern Europe and it takes place on Långholmen. There are tournaments for everybody, from beginners to the best players. Side tournaments for beginners have fees from Skr10 to Skr100. For information, contact La Mayonnaise (☎ 714 0420, fax 720 3921, e info@lamayonnaise.com).
Web site: W web.lamayonnaise.com

Slottsgala – third week in June. On this day various concerts are held in the grounds at Ulriksdal Slott, including classical and contemporary music. Tickets are very expensive and range from Skr300 to Skr895. Book via BiljettDirekt on ☎ 077 170 7070 in Sweden only.

Eken Cup – third weekend in June. These handball competitions for teams in every category are played on 35 grass fields in the central city area. Registration forms and fees are posted on the Internet at W www.ekencup.org.

Midsommar – first Friday after 21 June. Raising the Midsummer pole and dancing around it are traditional activities on Midsummer's Eve, mainly in towns and villages in the countryside. Skansen (Map 4, F7) (☎ 442 8000, fax 442 8282, e info@skansen.se) is the best place to see the activities in the city, with around 30,000 visitors on Midsummer's Eve. However, folk costumes, music, dancing, pickled herring washed down with *snaps*, strawberries and cream, and beer drinking, are common in rural areas around the city. Activities continue for two more days at Skansen and tickets to the Friday celebration cost Skr60/30 adult/child on top of regular admission fees.
Web site: W www.skansen.se

July

Stockholm Summer Games – first week in July. This sports competition for young people at Stadion (Stockholm's Olympic stadium) features all the main track and field events. For details, contact Östermalms IP (☎ 222160), Fiskartorpsvägen 2, SE-11433 Stockholm.
Web site: W www.summergames.se

DN Galan – mid-July, various dates. Track and field events at Stadion; tickets cost between Skr170 and Skr510. For details, contact DN Galan (☎ 141241, fax 108390, e info@dngalan.com).
Web site: W www.dngalan.com

Stockholm Jazz Festival – third week in July. This highly regarded (but expensive) festival features Swedish and international jazz artistes playing on Skeppsholmen. Tickets range from Skr240 (one day) to Skr990 (six days), with discounts for under 18s (free for under 12). For tickets, contact Biljett Direkt (☎ 077 170 7070) or Ticnet (W www.ticnet.se) at Sverigehuset. You can also email inquiries (e info@stockholmjazz.com).
Web site: W www.stockholmjazz.com

Skoklosterspelen – third week in July. An excellent medieval event at Skokloster (see the Excursions chapter) with 350 performances, including tournaments, theatre, music and weightlifting. Admission ranges from Skr30 to Skr90. Information is posted on the Internet at W www.skokloster.se (click on The Skokloster Pageant in the English pages). You can email inquiries (e info@skoklosterspelen.com).

August

Stockholm Pride – first week in August. For details, see Gay & Lesbian Travellers earlier in this chapter.

Strindbergsfestivalen – one week in August. Events of this festival, including poetry readings and discussions, are held in Tegnérlunden Park. Also on offer are seminars and excursions to Strindberg sites around Stockholm with a guide (this is expensive), with some tours in English. For details, contact Strindbergsmuseet (☎ 411 5354) or the tourist office.

KSSS City Match – fourth week in August. This regatta, organised by the Royal Swedish Yacht Club, is great to watch (free) and takes place in Riddarfjärden. For details, contact KSSS (☎ 717 0365, fax 717 3034, e ksss@ksss.se).
Web site: W www.ksss.se

Tjejmilen – last Sunday in August. This is the largest women's running race in northern Europe with around 26,000 participants and a 10km route in the Gärdet area. Fees are Skr195 to Skr255. For details, contact Tjejmilen (☎ 667 1930, fax 664 3822, e info@tjejmilen.se).

September

Stockholm Beer Festival – third and last weekends in September. This festival includes exhibitions, beer and whisky schools, and a vote on which is the best out of around 500 varieties of beer. It takes place at Nacka Strand Mäss & konferenscenter but contact Stockholm Beer Festival (☎ 662 9494, fax 662 9455, e marianne.wallberg@stockholmbeer.se).
Web site: W www.stockholmbeer.se

Great Crowns of Fire

Luciadagen (the Lucia festival) on 13 December has nothing to do with the Italian myth of St Lucia of Syracuse, but it's connected with restrictions after the Reformation and appears to be related to traditions from western Sweden. The festival has become popular throughout the country since the 1930s and it's now a major part of the Christmas celebrations, particularly at churches.

The main feature of this peculiar tradition is a procession of carol-singing children in white gowns led by Miss Lucia, who wears a crown of candles. Most Lucias these days are 'electric Lucias', due to the obvious fire risk! Miss Lucia visits schools, workplaces and private homes, usually in the afternoon, and serves coffee, buns called *Luciakatten* and gingerbread. Adult Swedes also enjoy their favourite Christmas drink, *glögg*, which is a spicy mulled wine.

October

Hem & Villa – first weekend in October. This exhibition of homes and interior design attracts around 50,000 visitors annually. Admission costs around Skr80. Contact Stockholmsmässan (☎ 749 4100, fax 992044), Mässvägen 1, SE-12580 Älvsjö.
Web site: ⓦ www.stofair.se

Lidingöloppet – first weekend in October. This is the world's largest cross-country race, with around 25,000 participants, including juniors (from age seven) to veteran class. The length ranges from 5.6km to 30km, and there are two women-only races. Junior fees start at Skr75, adults from Skr200 to Skr475 (cheaper if you register before 30 June). Obtain details from Lidingöloppet (☎ 765 2615, ⓔ run@lidingoloppet.se).
Web site: ⓦ www.lidingoloppet.se

If...Stockholm Open – last weekend in October. You'll see some of Sweden's best tennis players at this competition. For details, call ☎ 450 2625.
Web site: ⓦ www.stockholmopen.se

Poetry Festival – last weekend in October. Held at Dramatiska teatern (the Royal Dramatic Theatre) in Nybroplan, this festival offers poetry, theatre, music and dance. For more details, you can email inquiries (ⓔ tidskriften@00tal.com) or contact ☎ 612 1049.
Web site: ⓦ www.00tal.com

November

Stockholm International Filmfestival – third week in November. Over 150 films from around 40 countries are screened at various city cinemas during this 10-day festival. Contact ☎ 677 5000 or ⓔ info@cinema.se for details.
Web site: ⓦ www.filmfestivalen.se

December

Luciadagen – 13 December. For a description of events, see the boxed text 'Great Crowns of Fire'. You can see this festival at churches in Stockholm or at Skansen (Map 4, F7) (☎ 442 8000, ⓔ info@skansen.se); admission costs Skr30/20 adult/child on top of regular Skansen fees.
Web site: ⓦ www.skansen.se

Nyårsafton – 31 December. The Swedish New Year's Eve celebrations include traditional singing transmitted live on TV from the Solliden stage (Map 4, G7, #83) at Skansen followed by magnificent fireworks displays at Skansen and in the city centre.

DOING BUSINESS

If you're thinking of setting up a business in Stockholm, contact Näringslivskontoret (Trade & Industry Administration; ☎ 508 28000, fax 508 28090, ⓔ info@snk .stockholm.se, ⓦ www.snk.stockholm.se) at Stadshuset (Map 6, G2, #140).

For trade contacts, get in touch with the Utrikesdepartement (Map 6, F6, #165) (Ministry of Foreign Affairs; ☎ 405 1000, fax 723 1176, ⓔ registrator@foreign.ministry .se, ⓦ www.utrikes.regeringen.se/inenglish /index.htm), Gustav Adolfs Torg 1, SE-10339 Stockholm. This department deals with international development cooperation and international trade.

Another Web site worth a look is at ⓦ www.chamber.se, which is maintained by the Stockholm Chamber of Commerce.

Business Services

Most luxury hotels offer business facilities to their guests, but they're rather expensive.

Another good option, but not necessarily cheaper, is City Office (Map 6, D2, #131) (☎ 506 36200, fax 544 75090, ⒠ ingela.nordstrom@cityoffice.se, ⓦ www.cityoffice.se), World Trade Center, Klarabergsviadukten 70, Box 70396, SE-10724 Stockholm. City Office offers 90 fully furnished offices with reception (including telephone switchboard service, 8am to 5.30pm on weekdays), secretarial staff, garage facilities, conference rooms, and access to administrative support, including translation and other office staff. City Office can advise on how to set up a business bank account and which banks are most suitable.

Offices are available for day hire or for longer periods from City Office. Charges include furniture, electricity, heating, daily cleaning, phone, personal phone answering service, reception service, mail service, and access to kitchenettes and a cafeteria. Charges depend on the office size, which range from nine to 35 sq metres. As well as the City Office facilities, the World Trade Center has exhibition halls, banks, restaurants, hotels and a fitness centre.

Basic translation services are offered online free at ⓦ www.foreignword.com but you can get better service with the purchase of WordTran or by subscribing to InterTran (US$10 per month). Both are available from the aforementioned Web site but, at the time of writing, only Swedish-to-English translation is possible. Another company, Twenty-first Century Translation (☎ 08-560 32442, ⒠ kschuber@algonet.se, ⓦ www.swedishenglishtranslation.com), Gustavavägen 133, SE-17831 Ekerö, offers high-quality business-standard translation.

WORK

Most foreigners require a work permit in advance for paid employment in Sweden. Non-EU citizens need to apply for a work permit (and a residence permit for stays over three months), enclosing confirmation of the job offer from the prospective employer on either form AMS PF 1704 or form AMS PF 1707, a completed form (SIV 1040.U, available from Swedish diplomatic posts), a passport photo and passport. Processing of the permit takes one to three months and this must be done before entry to Sweden. There's no fee, except for returning your passport by post, if necessary. EU citizens only need to apply for a residence permit within three months of arrival if they find work, then they can remain in Sweden for the duration of their employment (or up to five years). For the latest details, check the Web site at ⓦ www.swedish-embassy.org.uk under Consular Affairs and Work Permits.

Unemployment is still fairly high and work permits are only granted if there's a shortage of Swedes with certain skills (eg, technical manufacturing areas). Speaking Swedish fluently is essential for most jobs. No one is looking for builders or people with social services or care skills, and service work opportunities are minimal. Go to the local branch of Arbetsförmedlingen (the employment office), which may be able to help, and it will have some literature in English. Arbetsförmedlingen's Web site (ⓦ www.ams.se) has information in English, including: starting a business in Sweden; working, studying and living in Sweden; details of unemployment insurance; and job vacancies listed by region or profession.

Students enrolled in Sweden can take summer jobs, but such work isn't offered to travelling students.

FACTS FOR THE VISITOR

Getting There & Away

Your first step when heading for Stockholm is to get to Europe and, in these days of airline competition, you'll find plenty of deals to European 'gateway' cities, particularly London, Paris, Frankfurt, Berlin and Copenhagen. Very few travellers approach Sweden from the east, via Russia, although the Trans-Siberian and Trans-Mongolian routes offer adventurous options – see Lonely Planet's *Russia, Ukraine & Belarus* guide for details.

AIR

You're unlikely to find an inexpensive direct flight to Sweden from outside Europe, but many European airlines will sell an inexpensive flight to Stockholm via their hub. Budget deals from the UK are offered to Nyköping Skavsta airport by Ryanair and to Stockholm's Arlanda airport by Scandinavian Airlines System (SAS).

Remember to reconfirm your onward or return bookings by the specified time – at least 72 hours before departure on international flights. Otherwise, there's a risk that you'll turn up at the airport only to find that you've missed your flight because it was rescheduled, or that you've been reclassified as a 'no show' and 'bumped' (see the Air Travel Glossary later in this chapter).

Departure Tax

Sweden levies a departure tax of Skr95. Check that it's included in the price of your airline ticket.

Other Parts of Sweden

Most of Sweden's domestic airlines use Stockholm Arlanda airport as a hub. SAS (☎ 020 727000) has daily domestic flights which serve the country from Malmö in the south to Kiruna in the north, but Skyways (Stockholm ☎ 08-509 05050) has more destinations. Malmö Aviation (☎ 020 550010) flies to Gothenburg and Malmö from Stockholm's Bromma airport. Note that cabin

luggage is limited to 8kg per person with SAS and Malmö Aviation, but only 5kg with Skyways.

Flying is expensive, but substantial discounts are available, such as return tickets booked at least seven days in advance or low-price tickets for accompanying family members, youths (under 26), students (with Swedish college ID) and seniors (over 65). SAS offers stand-by tickets for travellers under 25; currently these cost Skr240 per flight (from Stockholm). Malmö Aviation's stand-by tickets are available to under 25s for Skr200.

If you're flying into Sweden from abroad with SAS, you can purchase 'Visit Scandinavia Airpass' flight coupons (up to a maximum of eight) for US$75 per flight, except for Stockholm-Kiruna, which is US$125 per flight.

Air Travel Glossary

Alliances Many of the world's leading airlines are now intimately involved with each other, sharing everything from reservations systems and check-in to aircraft and frequent-flyer schemes. Opponents say that alliances restrict competition. Whatever the arguments, there is no doubt that big alliances are the way of the future.

Courier Fares Businesses often need to send urgent documents or freight securely and quickly. Courier companies hire people to accompany the package through customs and, in return, offer a discount ticket which is sometimes a bargain. However, you may have to surrender all your baggage allowance and take only carry-on luggage.

Fares Airlines traditionally offer 1st class (coded F), business class (coded J) and economy class (coded Y) tickets. These days there are so many promotional and discounted fares available that few passengers pay full fare.

Lost Tickets If you lose your airline ticket, an airline will usually treat it like a travellers cheque and, after inquiries, issue you with another one. Legally, however, an airline is entitled to treat it like cash and if you lose it then it's gone forever. Take very good care of your tickets.

Onward Tickets An entry requirement for many countries is that you have a ticket out of the country. If you're unsure of your next move, the easiest solution is to buy the cheapest onward ticket to a neighbouring country or a ticket from a reliable airline which can later be refunded if you do not use it.

Open-Jaw Tickets These are return tickets where you fly out to one place but return from another. If available, this can save you backtracking to your arrival point.

Overbooking Since every flight has some passengers who fail to show up, airlines often book more passengers than they have seats. Usually excess passengers make up for the no-shows, but occasionally somebody gets 'bumped' onto the next available flight. Guess who it is most likely to be? The passengers who check in late. If you do get 'bumped', you are normally offered some form of compensation.

Reconfirmation Some airlines require you to reconfirm your flight at least 72 hours prior to departure. Check your travel documents to see if this is the case

Restrictions Discounted tickets often have various restrictions on them – such as needing to be paid for in advance and incurring a penalty to be altered or cancelled. Others are restrictions on the minimum and maximum period you must be away.

Round-the-World Tickets RTW tickets give you a limited period (usually a year) in which to circumnavigate the globe. You can go anywhere the carrying airlines go, as long as you don't backtrack. The number of stopovers or total number of separate flights is decided before you set off and they usually cost a bit more than a basic return flight.

Ticketless Travel Airlines are gradually waking up to the realisation that paper tickets are unnecessary encumbrances. On simple one-way or return trips, reservations details can be held on computer and the passenger merely shows ID to claim their seat.

Transferred Tickets Airline tickets cannot be transferred from one person to another. Travellers sometimes try to sell the return half of their ticket, but officials can ask you to prove that you are the person named on the ticket. On an international flight, tickets are compared with passports.

The UK & Ireland

If you're looking for a cheap way into or out of Scandinavia, London is Europe's major centre for discounted fares. In fact, you can now find air fares from London that beat surface alternatives in terms of cost.

Currently, one of the best deals between the UK and Stockholm is with Ryanair (UK ☎ 0870 156 9569, Sweden ☎ 0911-233688, W www.ryanair.com), which flies two or three times daily between London Stansted and Nyköping Skavsta airport. Return fares start at UK£60 return (plus taxes). The Skavsta-Stockholm bus service meets all flights (Skr150 return, 80 minutes). Discounted tickets for travellers with Ryanair are often available for surface transport to/from airports in the UK and Sweden. It's worth noting that Ryanair is a budget airline and it doesn't guarantee connections, even with its own flights. Delays of five hours aren't unknown; if you miss a Ryanair connection, you'll be charged UK£25 for the privilege of getting a seat on a later flight! You can also fly twice daily from Stansted to Västerås (from UK£79 return, plus taxes); connecting buses (Skr12) run from the airport to the city centre. Flights from Prestwick or Dublin require changing planes in Stansted.

SAS (UK ☎ 0845 607 27727, Sweden ☎ 020 727000, W www.scandinavian.net), short for Scandinavian Airlines System, flies from Stansted and Heathrow to Stockholm Arlanda; other flights, from Edinburgh and Gatwick, require changing planes in Copenhagen. Return fares start at around UK£95 including taxes, but you have to buy at least three days in advance, stay one Saturday night minimum and 30 days maximum. The timetable is reliable. Direct SAS flights between Dublin and Stockholm began in March 2001.

British Airways (UK ☎ 0345 222111, Sweden ☎ 0200 770098, W www.british airways.com) flies up to eight times daily from London's Heathrow and Gatwick airports to Stockholm Arlanda; typical return fares start at around UK£100 (including tax). Finnair (UK ☎ 0207-408 1222, Dublin ☎ 01-844 6565, Sweden ☎ 020 781100, W www.finnair.com) has once- or twice-daily flights from both Manchester and Dublin to Stockholm Arlanda.

Maersk runs a British Airways franchise route from Birmingham to Stockholm with flights up to twice daily (no Saturday flights); return fares start at UK£152.90. Call British Airways on ☎ 0345 222111 (UK only) for current details. Skyways (UK ☎ 0161-489 3000, Stockholm ☎ 08-509 05050) flies once or twice daily from Manchester to Stockholm.

Airline ticket discounters are known as bucket shops in the UK. Despite the somewhat disreputable name, there's nothing under-the-counter about them. Discount air travel is big business in London. Advertisements for many travel agencies appear in the travel pages of the weekend broadsheets, such as the *Independent* on Saturday and the *Sunday Times*. Look out for the free magazines, such as *TNT*, which are widely available in London – start by looking outside the main train and underground stations.

For students or travellers under 26, popular travel agencies in the UK include STA Travel (☎ 0870 160 0599, W www.sta-travel.co.uk), which has an office at 86 Old Brompton Rd, London, SW7 3LQ, and other offices in London and Manchester. Usit Campus (☎ 0870 240 1010, W www.usit-campus.com), 52 Grosvenor Gardens, London, SW1W 0AG, has branches throughout the UK and also one in Ireland (☎ 01-602 1600) at 19-21 Alston Quay, O'Connell Bridge, Dublin 2. Both of these agencies sell tickets to all travellers but cater especially to young people and students.

Charter flights can work out as a cheaper alternative to scheduled flights, especially if you do not qualify for the under-26 and student discounts. British Airways offers courier flights through the Travel Shop (☎ 020-7606 3910), 101 Cheapside, London, EC2V 6DT.

Travellers pay a departure tax of UK£10 when flying from Britain to another European Union (EU) country, normally quoted in the ticket price.

Other recommended travel agencies include:

Bridge the World (☎ 0870 444 7434,
  ⓔ sales@bridgetheworld.com) 4 Regent
  Place, London, W1R 5FB
  Web site: ⓦ www.bridgetheworld.com
Flightbookers (☎ 020-7757 2626 or ☎ 0870
  010 7000) 34-42 Woburn Place, London,
  WC1H 0TA
  Web site: ⓦ www.ebookers.com
Trailfinders (☎ 020-7937 1234) 215 Kensing-
  ton High St, London, W8 6BD
  Web site:ⓦ www.trailfinders.com/onestop.htm

Continental Europe & Scandinavia

Although London is the discount travel capital of Europe, there are several other cities
where you'll find a range of good deals.
Generally, there's not much variation in air
fare prices for departures from the main
European cities. All the major airlines are
usually offering some sort of deal and travel
agencies generally have a number of special
offers, so shop around.

You can fly directly to Stockholm with
Finnair from Helsinki (up to 14 flights per
day), Turku, Vasa and Tampere. Finnair and
SAS also fly directly to a range of other
European destinations, including Barcelona,
Brussels, Copenhagen, Luxembourg, Oslo,
St Petersburg and Tallinn. The Swedish airline Skyways (Stockholm ☎ 08-509 05050,
ⓦ www.skyways.se) has flights from
Västerås to Oslo (twice each weekday),
from Stockholm to Vasa (two to four daily)
in Finland, and from Stockholm to Bergen
(twice each weekday) in Norway.

Many travel agencies in Europe have ties
with STA Travel, where you'll find inexpensive tickets that may be altered once
without charge. STA and other discount
outlets in important transport hubs include:

Alternativ Tours (☎ 030-881 2089, ⓔ info@
  alternativ-tours.de) Wilmersdorferstrasse 94,
  D-10629 Berlin
Kilroy Travels
  Berlin: (☎ 030-310 0040, ⓔ germany.sales@
  kilroytravels.de) Hardenbergstrasse 9,
  D-10623 Berlin
  Web site: ⓦ www.kilroytravels.com
  Amsterdam: (☎ 020-524 5100, ⓔ netherlands
  .sales@kilroytravels.de) Singel 413-415,
  NL-1012 WP Amsterdam
  Web site: ⓦ www.kilroytravels.com
NBBS Reizen (☎ 020-624 0989) Rokin 66,
  Amsterdam
OTU Voyages (☎ 01-40 29 12 12, ⓔ paris
  .bernanos@out.fr) 39 Ave Georges Bernanos
  (5e), Paris
SSR Travel (☎ 01-297 1111, ⓔ info@ssr.ch)
  Ankerstrasse 112, 8026 Zürich
  Web site: ⓦ www.ssr.ch
STA Travel (☎ 069-703035, ⓔ frankfurt.uni@
  statravel.de) Bockenheimer Landstrasse 133,
  D-60325 Frankfurt

The USA

The North Atlantic is the world's busiest
long-haul air corridor and flight options are
bewildering. Larger newspapers such as
The New York Times, *Chicago Tribune*, *San
Francisco Chronicle* and *Los Angeles Times*
all produce weekly travel sections in which
you'll find any number of travel agency ads
for air fares to Europe.

Thanks to the large ethnic Swedish population in Minnesota, Wisconsin, North
Dakota (and Manitoba in Canada), you may
find small local agencies in those areas specialising in travel to Scandinavia and offering good-value charter flights. Check local
telephone directories and newspapers.
Otherwise, you should be able to fly return
from New York or Boston to Copenhagen,
Oslo or Stockholm for around US$500 in
the low season and US$1000 in the high
season. With most tickets you can usually
travel 'open jaw', allowing you to land in
one city (Copenhagen, for example) and
return from another (such as Stockholm) at
no extra cost.

Icelandair (☎ 800 223 5500, ⓔ america@
icelandair.is) flies from New York, Boston,
Baltimore-Washington, Minneapolis and
Orlando via Reykjavík to many European
destinations including Oslo, Stockholm,
and Copenhagen. It often offers some of
the best deals and on all of its transatlantic
flights it allows a free three-day stopover
in Reykjavík – making it a great way to
spend a few days in Iceland. Return fares
start at around US$445, plus tax (mini-
mum one Saturday night, and maximum
stay 30 days).

On the other hand, if you're planning on flying within Sweden (or around Scandinavian and Baltic Europe), SAS (☎ 800 221 2350, W www.flysas.com) has some interesting regional discounts available to passengers who fly on its transatlantic flights (see Other Parts of Sweden earlier in this chapter). SAS charges from US$450 return (plus tax) for seats from New York Newark to Stockholm Arlanda, with a minimum of one Saturday night, maximum stay 30 days and seven days advance purchase. SAS also flies from Chicago to Stockholm, with return fares from US$490 plus tax. The other airlines flying direct to the USA are American Airlines (Stockholm-Chicago) and Delta Air Lines (Stockholm–New York JFK).

Airhitch (☎ 800 326 2009 or ☎ 310-394 4215, W www.airhitch.org), 2641 Broadway, 3rd Floor, New York, NY 10025, specialises in stand-by tickets to Europe for US$165 one way from the east coast and $233 one way from the west coast, but the destinations are by region (not a specific city or country), so you'll need a flexible schedule. You must be able to fly at any time within a set period, usually five to seven days.

If you're interested in courier flights, you can join the International Association of Air Travel Couriers (IAATC). The membership fee of US$45 (US$50 outside the USA and Canada) gets members a bimonthly update of air-courier offerings (the *Shoestring Traveler* newsletter) and access to daily courier updates on the Internet. For more information, contact IAATC (☎ 561-582 8320, fax 561-582 1581, e iaatc@courier.org, W www.courier.org). However, be aware that joining this organisation doesn't guarantee that you'll get a courier flight.

Discount Travel Agencies Discount travel agencies in the USA are known as consolidators. San Francisco is the ticket consolidator capital of the USA, although some good deals can also be found in Los Angeles, New York and other big cities.

Consolidators can be found through the *Yellow Pages* or the major daily newspapers. *The New York Times*, *Los Angeles Times*, *Chicago Tribune* and *The San Francisco Examiner* all produce weekly travel sections in which you will find a number of travel agency ads.

Council Travel, America's largest student travel organisation, has around 60 offices in the USA; its head office (☎ 800 226 8624, W www.counciltravel.com) is at 205 E 42nd St, New York, NY 10017. Call for the office nearest you. STA Travel (☎ 800 781 4040, W www.statravelgroup.com) has offices in Boston, Chicago, Miami, New York, Philadelphia, San Francisco and other major cities. Call for office locations.

Other travel agencies include:

Air-Tech (☎ 212-219 7000, e fly@airtech .com) Suite 204, 588 Broadway, New York, NY 10012-5405
Web site: W www.airtech.com
Cheap Tickets, Inc (☎ 888 922 8849)
Web site: W www.cheaptickets.com
Educational Travel Centre (☎ 800 747 5551) 438 N Frances St, Madison, WI 53703-1084
Web site: W www.edtrav.com
High Adventure Travel (☎ 800 350 0612 or ☎ 415-912 5600, e travel@airtreks.com) 4th floor, Suite 400, 442 Post St, San Francisco, CA 94102
Web site: W www.highadv.com
Interworld Travel (☎ 800 331 4456, e mayra@interworldtravel.com) 800 S Douglas Rd, Suite 140, Coral Gables, FL 33134-3125
Web site: W www.interworldtravel.com

Canada

Scan budget travel agency ads in the *Globe & Mail*, *Toronto Star* and *Vancouver Sun*.

Icelandair (☎ 800 223 5500) has low-cost flights from Halifax in Nova Scotia to Oslo, Stockholm and Copenhagen via Reykjavík, three days every week. Travel CUTS (Ontario only ☎ 800 667 2887, otherwise ☎ 416-614 2887, W www.travelcuts.com) is Canada's national student travel agency and has offices in all major cities.

For courier flights, get in touch with FB On Board Courier Services in Montreal (☎ 514-631 7925).

Australia & New Zealand

There's a large difference between low- and high-season fares and, unlike transatlantic flights, where prices rise and fall gradually on either side of the high season, the changes are more sudden. Book well ahead if you intend to fly close to the crossover dates around April/May and September. One-way flights cost around two-thirds of return flights.

The main players in the discount game in Australasia are Flight Centre (☎ 1300-362 665, W www.flightcentre.com.au) and STA Travel (☎ 1300-360 960, W www.statravel .com.au). STA is represented in most cities as well as on university campuses. New Zealand residents can call STA on ☎ 0800 874 773.

It still doesn't hurt to check the travel agency ads in the *Yellow Pages* and ring around. The Saturday travel sections of *The Sydney Morning Herald* and Melbourne's *The Age* newspapers have many ads offering cheap fares to Europe, but don't be surprised if they happen to be 'sold out' when you contact the agencies – they're usually low-season fares on obscure airlines with conditions attached.

From the east coast of Australia, there are a number of airlines with some good deals on fares to Stockholm. Generally, the best deals to Stockholm require a couple of stopovers on the way, usually Singapore or Bangkok and another European city. In the low season, expect to pay around A$1550 for a return fare with Lufthansa/ Singapore Airlines or Thai Airways International. Finnair/Gulf Air and Singapore Airlines have high season return fares starting from A$2050. Fares from the west coast of Australia are a couple of hundred dollars cheaper. From New Zealand, Thai Airways International has some of the best deals for travel to Stockholm. Low-season return fares start from NZ$2129/2559 in low/high season.

Airline Offices

Airline offices in Stockholm can be found under *flygbolag* or *flygföretag* in the Yellow Pages. Several airlines share the same address, while others don't have street addresses and can only be contacted by phone at the appropriate airport desk.

Aer Lingus (Map 6, B6, #90) (☎ 411 5262) Kungsgatan 19
Aeroflot (Map 6, B4, #23) (☎ 217007) 2nd floor, Sveavägen 31
Air Baltic (☎ 020 727555) c/o SAS, Stureplan 8
Air France (☎ 519 99990)
Alitalia (Map 6, B6, #90) (☎ 796 9400) Kungsgatan 19
American Airlines (☎ 791 5999) Kanalvägen 10A, SE-19461 Upplands Väsby
Austrian Airlines (☎ 0200 727373) c/o SAS, Stureplan 8
Britannia Airways (☎ 509 10000) Kanalvägen 10C, SE-19426 Upplands Väsby
British Airways (Map 6, D7, #181) (☎ 0200 770092) Hamngatan 11
Delta Air Lines (Map 4, D6, #61) (☎ 587 69101) Karlavägen 108
Emirates Airlines (☎ 651 2850) Sankt Göransgatan 84
Estonian Air (☎ 597 85105) Arlanda airport
Finnair (Map 6, D7, #92) (☎ 020 781100) 4th floor, Norrmalmstorg 1
Icelandair (Map 4, D1, #21) (☎ 690 9800) Kungstensgatan 38
KLM – Royal Dutch Airlines (☎ 587 99757) Vretenvägen 8, SE-17154 Solna
Lithuanian Airlines (☎ 593 60905) Arlanda airport
LOT Polish Airlines (Map 6, C3, #121) (☎ 243490) Kungsgatan 66
Lufthansa Airlines (☎ 020 727555) c/o SAS, Stureplan 8
Pulkovo Air Contact a travel agency
Ryanair (☎ 0911-233688) Nyköping Skavsta airport and Västerås airport
Sabena (Map 4, C8, #56) (☎ 587 70450) Tegeluddsvägen 64
SAS (Map 6, B7, #45) (☎ 020 727555) Stureplan 8
Skyways (☎ 509 05050) c/o SAS, Stureplan 8
Swissair (Map 4, C8, #56) (☎ 587 70445) Tegeluddsvägen 64
Thai Airways International (Map 6, C3, #121) (☎ 598 83600) Kungsgatan 66

BUS
Other Parts of Sweden

You can travel by bus in Sweden on national long-distance routes between towns and cities or by using one of the 23 *länstrafik* networks for more remote places. The main destinations from Stockholm, with daily bus service, are Uppsala, Gothenburg (Göteborg), Västerås and Malmö.

Swebus Express (☎ 0200 218218) has the largest 'national network' of express buses,

GETTING THERE & AWAY

but it only serves the southern half of the country. Fares for 'long' journeys are 30% cheaper if you travel between Monday and Thursday (autumn to spring). Svenska Buss (☎ 020 676767) and the cheaper Säfflebussen (☎ 020 160 0600) also connect many southern towns and cities with Stockholm. North of Gävle, connections with Stockholm are provided by several smaller operators, including Ybuss (☎ 060-171960) from Sundsvall, Östersund and Umeå. Only Swebus doesn't require seat reservations – it always guarantees a seat.

Young people (maximum age varies from 20 with Ybuss to 25 with Säfflebussen and Swebus Express) and seniors (over 65) receive a 30% discount, but student concessions require a CSN or SFS Swedish student card.

Neighbouring Countries

Säfflebussen (☎ 020 160 0600) runs buses two or three times daily from Stockholm to Oslo via Karlstad (Nkr300/210 weekends/weekdays, seven hours).

Swebus Express (☎ 0200 218218) in cooperation with Nor-Way Bussekspress (Oslo ☎ 82 05 43 00) runs buses three to five times daily (including a night bus) along the same route (Nkr345/240 weekends/weekdays).

Tapanis Buss (☎ 0922-12955 or ☎ 08-153300, ✉ info@tapanis.se) runs express coaches from Tornio (Finland) to Stockholm twice weekly via the E4 highway (Fmk310, 15 hours).

Eurolines (☎ 020 987377, 🔲 www .eurolines.se) runs buses four to six days per week from Stockholm to Copenhagen (Dkr375, 9½ hours). It's represented in Stockholm by Busstop (☎ 08-440 8570) at Cityterminalen.

Twice weekly (Tuesday and Friday southbound, Thursday and Sunday northbound), Eurolines buses connect Stockholm with Berlin (DM180, 17 hours), via Copenhagen and Rostock (Germany). Eurolines buses also connect with London (via Hamburg, and Amsterdam on some routes) but it's cheaper to fly, it takes up to 35½ hours and the trip is arduous by any standards.

TRAIN

Stockholm's main train station, Centralstationen (Map 4, F1; the central train station, Stockholm C), has good long-distance connections with other parts of Sweden and continental Europe. Lines to Norway and Finland are rather slow in comparison, but the slow section of the line to Oslo (west of Arvika) is to be upgraded and modern high-speed trains will be running on this route by January 2002.

Information

Centralstationen (Map 4, F1) is open 5am to 12.15am daily. The SJ domestic ticket office windows are open 7.30am to 8pm weekdays, 8.30am to 6pm Saturday and 9.30am to 7pm Sunday. International train tickets can be purchased between 10am and 6pm on weekdays only. If your train departs outside these times, you can buy a ticket from the ticket collector on the train, but you are strongly recommended to get your ticket in advance.

The Tågkompaniet ticket office, in the entrance hall, is open 7.45am to 8.15pm daily (closing noon to 3pm weekends).

Other Parts of Sweden

Sweden has an extensive railway network and trains are certainly the fastest way to get around. There are four long-distance train operators in Sweden, but the national network of Sveriges Järnväg (SJ; ☎ 020 757575, 🔲 www.sj.se) covers most of the main lines. The main exceptions are the overnight trains from Stockholm to Boden and Narvik, and the summer-only line from Boden to Haparanda (Tågkompaniet ☎ 0920-233333 or ☎ 020 444111, 🔲 www .tagplus.se). Several counties run regional länstrafik train networks.

SJ's flag carriers are the X2000 fast trains running at speeds of up to 200km/h, with services from Stockholm to Gothenburg, Malmö, Karlstad, Mora, Växjö, Jönköping, Sundsvall and other destinations.

Tickets for journeys on X2000 trains include a compulsory seat reservation; on other trains you're advised to reserve a seat (Skr30). Night train supplements are required for sleepers (from Skr165 per bed) or couchettes (from Skr90), but not for seats. First- and 2nd-class seats and sleepers are available on almost all trains (night trains don't have 1st-class seats).

Bicycles can be carried on many län-strafik trains without reservation, unlike on SJ trains, where bikes (when allowed) must go as registered baggage (Skr150).

Train Passes The Sweden Rail Pass, Eurodomino tickets and the international passes Inter-Rail, Eurail, ScanRail and Railplus cards (giving 25% discount on tickets) are accepted on SJ services and most other operators, such as regional trains (they often cooperate closely with SJ). Exceptions include the SL *pendeltåg* (local trains) around Stockholm. The X2000 trains require pass holders, except Railplus, to pay a supplement of Skr50 (which includes the obligatory seat reservation). Reservation supplements for non-X2000 trains (Skr30) aren't obligatory, and there are no supplements at all for regional trains. Rail passes are also accepted on SJ-run buses.

You're strongly advised to buy rail passes in advance; some cannot be bought in Sweden and ScanRail has restrictions in the country of purchase. Details about rail passes can be found on the Internet at **W** www.railpass.com. Discounts on Scan-Rail tickets are offered to children (under 11), youths (12 to 25) and seniors (over 60). The adult ScanRail prices are as follows:

duration	2nd class (US$)	1st class (US$)
5 days/2 months	204	276
10 days/2 months	310	420
21 days	360	486

Costs Due to restrictions, obtaining discount rail tickets in Sweden isn't entirely convenient, but they can be arranged in advance through Sweden Booking (☎ 0498-203380) for a Skr100 fee (this may rise to Skr150) and you can pay by credit card. Students (with Swedish CSN or SFS student cards only) and people aged under 26 get discounts on the standard adult fare.

Rail ticket prices quoted in this book are always the cheapest available. These are called *förköpsbillet* and must be bought at least a week in advance. Tickets for travel on Friday and Sunday are always more expensive.

Most länstrafik have one-day tourist cards (a few also have three-day passes), valid on local trains as well as buses.

Neighbouring Countries

Currently, one to three daily trains run between Stockholm and Oslo in Norway (Nkr372, six hours), but this should be upgraded to six trains per day by 2002 and journey times will be reduced. There are also twice-daily train services from Stockholm to Trondheim (Nkr317, 11 hours) and from Stockholm to Narvik (Nkr515 including couchette, from 19 hours). Seat reservation is obligatory on high-speed X2000 trains, which should be running on the Stockholm-Oslo route by 2002.

Around seven daily X2000 trains run from Copenhagen in Denmark to Stockholm (Dkr320, from 5¼ hours) via the new Öresund bridge.

Train passengers can reach Boden or Luleå in Sweden (from Stockholm) and Kemi in Finland (from Helsinki). Passenger trains run in summer (13 June to 20 August) from Boden to Haparanda on the Finnish border – contact Tågkompaniet (☎ 0920-233333 or ☎ 020 444111) for details. Bus connections between Boden/Haparanda and Kemi are free for rail pass holders.

Hamburg (Germany) is the Central European gateway for Scandinavia, with several direct trains daily to Copenhagen, where you normally have to change trains to get to Stockholm. The ferry between Germany and Denmark (Puttgarden to Rødby Havn) is included in the ticket price.

There's a direct day train and an overnight train every day from Malmö to Berlin (from 14 hours) and Dresden via the Trelleborg to Sassnitz ferry. Travelling to/from Stockholm may require changing trains in Malmö. For fares and timetables, see the Web site **W** www.berlin-night -express.com.

Travelling by train from the UK to Sweden is more expensive than flying, but you can stop en route in either direction. From London a return 2nd-class train ticket to Stockholm, valid for two months, will cost around UK£390, including couchettes in each direction and a ScanRail pass for five days out of two months. Note that the lowest equivalent air fare is UK£81.40! For tickets, contact Deutsche Bahn UK (London ☎ 0870 243 5363) or European Rail (London ☎ 020-7387 0444).

CAR & MOTORCYCLE

Basic road rules conform to EU standards, using international road signs. In Sweden, you drive on and give way to the right. Headlights should be dipped but must be on at all times when driving. Seat belt use is obligatory, and children under seven years old should be in appropriate harnesses or in child seats, if fitted.

You only need a recognised full driving licence, even for car rental. If bringing your own car, you'll need your vehicle registration documents. In case your vehicle breaks down, telephone the Larmtjänst 24-hour towing service (☎ 020 910040). Insurance Green Cards are recommended. Petrol costs around about Skr9.50/L.

The blood-alcohol limit is a stringent 0.02%. The maximum permitted speed on motorways and remote highways is 110km/h. Other speed limits are 50km/h in built-up areas, 70km/h on narrow rural roads and 90km/h on highways. The speed limit for cars towing caravans is 80km/h. Automatic speed cameras are very rare in Sweden, but police can use hand-held radar equipment and impose on-the-spot fines of up to Skr1200.

In many parts of Sweden, wild elk (moose) are a serious road hazard, particularly around dawn and dusk. If you do hit something, report the incident to the police – failure to do so is an offence.

The national motoring association affiliated to Alliance Internationale de Tourisme (AIT) is Motormännens Riksförbund (☎ 020 211111 or ☎ 08-690 3800, fax 08-690 3820), Sveavägen 159, SE-10435 Stockholm.

For details about driving in and around Stockholm, and about rental cars, see the Getting Around chapter.

Other Parts of Sweden

Sweden has good roads and the excellent E-class motorways don't usually have traffic jams. There are no public toll roads or bridges in the country.

The motorways leading out of Stockholm include the E4, which heads northwards to Uppsala, and southwards to Helsingborg where it joins the E6 for Malmö. The E18 runs westwards towards Västerås and Oslo and the E20 leads west, then south-west, for Gothenburg.

Neighbouring Countries

The main highway between Stockholm and Norway is the E18 to Oslo. Otherwise, follow the E4 northwards, then take the E14 from Sundsvall to Trondheim, the E12 from Umeå to Mo i Rana, or the E10 from just north of Luleå to Bjerkvik. Many secondary roads also cross the border.

You can now drive across the Öresund toll bridge on the E20 motorway from Malmö to Copenhagen (see Other Parts of Sweden earlier for road links between Malmö and Stockholm). The tolls cost Skr275 (Dkr230) for a car of up to 6m long and a motorcycle will cost Skr150 (Dkr125).

Between Sweden and Finland, the main road is the E4 from Stockholm to Kemi via Umeå.

BICYCLE

Sweden is a flat country and it's ideal for cycling from May to September. Cycling is an excellent way to look for points of interest en route to Stockholm, such as prehistoric sites, rune stones, parish churches and quiet spots for free camping. In most areas around Stockholm you'll find many towns and villages, with shops for supplies, within a day's ride. However, bear in mind that Stockholm is a long way from other countries and it's 516km from Oslo, the nearest foreign capital by road.

Airlines may consider your bike as luggage, but check this before booking.

International ferries to Stockholm usually charge a small fee for bicycles. Helmet use is compulsory in Sweden.

Other Parts of Sweden

You can cycle on all roads except motorways (green sign, with two lanes and a bridge) and roads for motor vehicles only (green sign with a car symbol). Other highways usually have a hard shoulder, which keeps cyclists well clear of motor vehicles. Secondary roads are better for cyclists; they're mostly quiet and reasonably safe by European standards. Remember to cycle on the right.

If you get fed up of the long distance to Stockholm, you can take your bicycle on some länstrafik trains and most regional buses (free, or up to Skr40). Long-distance buses don't accept bicycles. Bikes go as registered baggage for Skr150 on SJ trains (advance booking only), but dismantled bicycles can be taken as luggage.

There are special cycle routes in country areas and a few of them lead to or pass through Stockholm. For details, contact Svenska Cykelsällskapet (Swedish Cycling Association; ☎ 08-751 6204, fax 751 1935, ⓔ info@svenska-cykelsallskapet.se), Box 6006, SE-16406 Kista. Web site: ⓦ www.svenska-cykelsallskapet.se.

For further information about cycling, see Bicycle in the Getting Around chapter, or contact your national cycle touring club.

HITCHING

Hitching isn't entirely safe and we don't recommend it. Travellers who decide to hitch should understand that they're taking a small but potentially serious risk. People who choose to hitch will be safer if they travel in pairs and let someone know where they're planning to go.

If you try hitching around Sweden, you'll find it isn't popular and the consensus is that you'll have less luck getting lifts than in other countries. However, the main highways (E4, E6, E10 and E22) aren't too bad and very long lifts are possible. Remember, it's prohibited to hitch on motorways and you should only hitch where it's safe for drivers to stop.

BOAT

Ferry connections between Sweden and Denmark, Estonia, Finland, Germany, Lithuania, Norway, Poland and the UK provide straightforward links, especially for anyone bringing their own vehicle. Note that in most cases, the quoted fares for cars (usually up to 6m long) also include up to five passengers. Most lines offer substantial discounts for seniors, students and children, and cruises and other special deals may be available – always ask when booking.

DFDS Seaways (☎ 0990-333000) in the UK can make reservations for Silja Line's Baltic ferry services.

If you're travelling by international ferry from Estonia, Finland (via Åland), Latvia, Norway or Poland, consider buying your maximum duty-free alcohol allowance on the boat, as alcohol (particularly spirits) is expensive in Sweden. Even if you don't drink, it will make a welcome gift for Swedish friends.

Passengers leaving from Sweden by ship don't have to pay a departure tax.

Estonia Tallink (☎ 08-732 4000, fax 732 4001, ⓦ www.tallink.ee) departs once every two days (overnight) from Tallinn to its Stockholm terminal (Map 4, C9, #57), taking around 15 hours. Deck tickets start at 510/615EEK in low/high season and cars cost 800EEK year-round. Supplements for berths in cabins start at 320EEK. The breakfast buffet and the evening smörgåsbord cost 90EEK and 240EEK, respectively. Various offers are available, including return-trip fares. The company has an office at the Frihamnen terminal building.

Finland Silja Line has two luxurious liners, *Silja Symphony* and *Silja Serenade*, which sail overnight every day of the year from its Stockholm terminal (Map 4, A7, #54) to Helsinki, taking around 15 hours. Cabin berths (Fmk200 to Fmk2915 per person) are compulsory and cars up to 6m long cost Fmk160 (excluding passengers); bicycles/motorcycles cost Fmk40/90. In summer, breakfast costs Fmk40 and the famous Silja smörgåsbord costs Fmk135. The ships call briefly at Mariehamn in Åland; the islands are exempt from the abolition of duty-free within the EU. Note that there's a lower age limit of 18, unless travelling with parents. Silja Line (☎ 09-180 4510, fax 180 4452, W www.silja.com/english) is at Bulevardi 1A, POB 659, FIN-00101 Helsinki. There's also a sales outlet (Map 6, B7, #35) (☎ 08-222140, fax 611 9162) at Kungsgatan 2, Stockholm.

Two other ships in Silja Line's impressive fleet, *Silja Europa* and *Silja Festival*, sail by day and night all year between Stockholm and Turku (Åbo in Swedish), via Mariehamn. The journey takes around 11 hours. Some journeys in the low season sail to Kapellskär, about 80km north-east of Stockholm. Day/night seat tickets cost from Fmk90/110 to Fmk135/205, depending on the time of year, and cabins range from Fmk100/120 to Fmk1070/1495. Cars (passengers not included) cost Fmk115/145 by day/night, and bicycles/motorcycles cost Fmk40/90 at all times. There's a Silja Line office (☎ 02-335255, fax 335 6375) at the departure terminal in Turku.

Viking Line operates ferries overnight from Helsinki to its Stockholm terminal (Map 5, B9, #49) via Mariehamn. Tickets cost from Fmk173 to Fmk400 and cars (passengers not included) cost from Fmk75 to Fmk219. Cabin berths range from Fmk105 to Fmk2730. It takes 16 or 17 hours and sails once daily all year. Viking Line also sails from Stockholm to Turku via Mariehamn (11 hours) twice daily all year, including an overnight crossing. Passenger/car fares from Stockholm to Turku cost Fmk85/50 to Fmk195/109 (cheaper during the day). Overnight berths range from couchettes to suites and cost Fmk63 to Fmk2220. Bicycles are charged Fmk25 on all Viking Line routes and motorcycles range from Fmk35 to Fmk110.

Buffet meals are served on all Viking Line services. The company has a strict minimum age limit of 20 on Saturday, all public holidays, the 8am Stockholm to Turku departures and the 2.35pm Mariehamn to Stockholm departures. Travelling with parents or evidence in writing giving a valid reason for travelling (studies, visiting relatives, business etc) is acceptable. In Helsinki, you'll find Viking Line (☎ 09-12351, W www.vikingline.fi) at Mannerheimintie 14; in Turku (☎ 02-33311) it's at Hansa-Thalia Aurakatu 10. The company also has an office at Stockholm's Cityterminalen (Map 6, E2, #137) (the central bus station; ☎ 08-452 4000). Note that the price information is on the Swedish Web pages.

Two other companies run daily 'booze cruises' between Stockholm and Mariehamn on Åland. Birka Cruises only offers return fares from Stockholm. However, Ånedin-Linjen (Map 6, F4, #157) (☎ 08-456 2200, fax 100741), Vasagatan 6, Stockholm, runs daily passenger ferries from Stockholm to Mariehamn (six hours). One-way fares start at Fmk35 (couchette) and rise to Fmk470 for a suite. The couchettes are a very good deal. Breakfast, lunch and dinner packages start at Fmk150.

SeaWind Line (toll free ☎ 9800 6800, W www.seawind.fi), Linnankatu 84, FI-20100 Turku, sails once daily except Saturday from Turku to Stockholm Värtahamnen (Map 4, A8, #55), via Langnäs (Åland). The trip takes 11 hours, and tickets (from Fmk290/520 day/night one-way) include a car (maximum length 5m), up to four passengers, a cabin and breakfast (overnight sailings only). The ship isn't suitable for disabled travellers. In Sweden, call ☎ 020 795331.

Latvia To find out if the ferry service from Riga to Stockholm has been reinstated, contact your nearest Swedish tourist office; Latvia Tours (☎ 07-085005, fax 820020, e inese@latviatours.lt), Kalku 8, Riga; or ScanSov Offshore (☎ 08-402 5690 or ☎ 402 5600, fax 249689) in Stockholm.

Lithuania Lisco Line (☎ 06-395050, fax 395052, e passenger@krantas.lt, W www.shipping.lt), Perkelos st 10, LT-5804 Klaipeda, sails twice weekly from Klaipeda to Stockholm Frihamnen (Map 4, C9, #58) (17½ hours). Passenger fares, including meals, start at 250Lt (one way), and

View of Centralbron (bridge), the black-spired Riddarholmskyrkan and Stadshuset (city hall)

All aboard the STF boat hostel *af Chapman*

Riddarholmskyrkan, Gamla Stan

JON DAVISON

It's unlikely you'll leave Stockholm without at least one boat ride through Stockholm's waterways.

VERONICA GARBUTT

Schooner docked near Gamla Stan

CHRISTOPHER WOOD

The *Prins Carl Philip* awaits you...

VERNICA GARBUTT

Grand Hôtel Stockholm (1874) overlooking a quay popular with anglers and boat trippers.

car/motorcycle fares are 250/100Lt. You can also contact Lisco Line in Vilnius (☎ 02-313314, fax 629120, ⓔ vilnius@krantas.lt), Pylimo st 4, LT-2001 Vilnius, and in Stockholm (☎ 08-667 5235, fax 667 5235, ⓔ stockholm@krantas.lt).

Poland Polferries (☎ 058-343 1887, fax 343 6574, ⓔ pax.gdansk@polferries.pl, ⓦ www.polferries.pl), ul Przemyslowa 1, PL-80542 Gdansk, sails from Gdansk to Nynäshamn three days per week (19 hours). Passenger fares start at 185zl (plus at least 35zl for a cabin berth) and car tickets, including the driver, cost from 380zl. In Sweden, contact Polferries (☎ 08-520 18101, fax 520 18120, ⓔ info@polferries.se), Färjeterminalen, SE-14930 Nynäshamn.

The UK DFDS Seaways (UK ☎ 08705 333000, ⓔ travel.sales@dfds.co.uk; Gothenburg ☎ 031-650650, ⓔ info@dfdsseaways .se) has two crossings per week from Newcastle to Gothenburg via Kristiansand (Norway) on its vessel M/S *Princess of Scandinavia*. From Gothenburg, you'll need onward transport by air, rail, bus or car to reach Stockholm (478km). Return fares from Newcastle to Gothenburg begin at UK£84 but a car with up to five passengers starts at only UK£374.

ORGANISED TOURS

If you're short of time or you have a specialised interest, it may be worth looking into an organised tour. North American operators tend to offer general Scandinavian tours, but ask if stays in Stockholm can be extended. Operators in the UK are usually more flexible and most offer city breaks of varying length. Note that most tours aren't escorted and you'll usually pay hefty commissions and booking fees. Air fare components in organised tours are usually much higher than tickets bought by yourself. A full listing of tour operators is given in *Sweden*, the annual guide published by the Swedish Travel & Tourism Council and obtainable from Swedish tourist offices abroad.

Local travel agencies in towns and cities around the UK may offer better deals;

hotel rates through these agencies may be discounted compared to the advertised rates in Sweden.

Reputable operators offering itineraries concentrating either on Scandinavia in general or Sweden in particular are listed as follows:

USA & Canada

Bennett Tours (☎ 800 221 2420, fax 212-697 2065) 342 Madison Ave, New York, NY 10173-0999. This company specialises in coach tours, both city and countryside, and it can arrange fly/drive tours.
Web site: ⓦ www.bennett-tours.com

Brekke Tours (☎ 800 437 5302, fax 701-780 9352, ⓔ tours@brekketours.com) 802 N 43rd St, Grand Forks, ND 58203. Brekke Tours caters mainly to North Americans of Scandinavian descent. It runs a 14-day escorted coach tour through Denmark, the Norwegian fjords and various parts of Sweden, including Uppsala and Stockholm, for US$3475 per person, including air fare from Minneapolis/St Paul. It also organises independent tours, rail passes and car rental.
Web site: ⓦ www.brekketours.com

Maupintour (☎ 800 255 4266, ⓔ info@maupintour .com). Maupintour offers a 15-day Scandinavian Capitals & Fjords tour, which includes two nights in Stockholm, with visits to Drottningholm and Vasamuseet. There are six guaranteed departures yearly and it costs US$3495 (plus air fare US$1050 and single supplements US$895).
Web site: ⓦ www.maupintour.com

Scanditours
Florida: (☎ 561-585 9779, fax 561-585 9903, ⓔ florida@scanditours.com) Ye Tower Plaza, 934 South Dixie Hwy, Lantana, FL 33462
Ontario: (☎ 800 432 4176, fax 416-482 9447, ⓔ toronto@scanditours.com) 308-191 Eglinton Ave E, Toronto, Ontario M4P 1K1
Vancouver: (☎ 800 377 9829, fax 604-736 8311, ⓔ vancouver@scanditours.com) 210-1275 W 6th Ave, Vancouver, BC V6H 1A6
This company offers a variety of escorted tours throughout Scandinavia, the Baltic states and Russia, which include visits to Stockholm.
Web site: ⓦ www.scanditours.com

Scantours (☎ 800 223 7226, ⓔ info@scantours .com). Scantours offers the upmarket City Package, with three nights (including breakfast and a sightseeing tour) for US$220 (flights extra).
Web site: ⓦ www.scantours.com

GETTING THERE & AWAY

The UK

Bridge Travel Service (☎ 0870 727 5973, fax 456609, ⓔ scandinavia@bridge-travel.co.uk) Bridge House, 55-59 High Rd, Broxbourne, Hertfordshire, EN10 7DT. This company organises city breaks at Scandic hotels in Stockholm.
Web site: Ⓦ www.bridge-travel.co.uk

Cresta Holidays (☎ 0870 161 0909). Cresta Holidays has over 30 years experience with short breaks but they're expensive; prices start at UK£308 for three nights in Stockholm.
Web site: Ⓦ www.crestaholidays.co.uk

Norvista (☎ 020-7409 7334, fax 020-7409 7733, ⓔ reservations@norvista.co.uk) 227 Regent St, London, W1R 8PD. Norvista is one of the UK's longest established tour operators and it organises overnights in the finest Stockholm hotels (and flights with Finnair).
Web site: Ⓦ www.norvista.co.uk

Scantours (☎ 020-7329 2927, fax 7839 5891, ⓔ info@scantoursuk.com) 47 Whitcomb St, London, WC2H 7DH. Scantours offers a seven-day, non-escorted tour of Sweden, including three nights in Stockholm. The tours are very flexible, allowing you to vary schedules or add extra nights.
Web site: Ⓦ www.scantoursuk.com

Thomas Cook (☎ 08705 666222). This well-known name has offices around the UK. It organises tailor-made, unescorted tour packages to Stockholm but you should carefully check its commission before you accept a quote.
Web site: Ⓦ www.thomascook.co.uk

Travelscene (☎ 0870 777 4445 or ☎ 020-8424 9648, fax 020-8861 4154, ⓔ reservations@travelscene.co.uk) 11-15 St Ann's Road, Harrow, Middlesex, HA1 1LQ. Accommodation prices in city hotels are very reasonable but flights are expensive when booked with this company.

Ireland

Go Holidays (☎ 01-874 4126, fax 872 7958, ⓔ info@goholidays.ie) 28 North Great George's St, Dublin 1. Go Holidays offers three-night city breaks in Stockholm from IR£328, including flights with SAS from Dublin (tax extra).
Web site: Ⓦ www.goholidays.ie

Australia

Bentours (☎ 02-9241 1353, fax 9251 1574, ⓔ scandinavia@bentours.com.au) Level 7, 189 Kent St, Sydney 2000. Bentours is an Australian travel agency specialising exclusively in Scandinavian travel, including city stopovers, sightseeing and car rental. Staff can also organise rail passes and escorted coach tours.
Web site: Ⓦ www.bentours.com.au

Wiltrans/Maupintour (☎ 02-9255 0899) Level 10, 189 Kent St, Sydney 2000. This company offers a range of pricey, luxury tours in Scandinavia.

Getting Around

THE AIRPORT

Stockholm has three major airports, but most people arrive at Arlanda (W www .arlanda.lfv.se), which is 40km north of central Stockholm. Some domestic flights use the much smaller Bromma airport, 10km west of the city centre. Ryanair flies to/from London and tiny Nyköping Skavsta airport, 109km south-west of Stockholm, and Västerås airport, 102km west of the city.

Arlanda has four terminals (currently numbered from two to five) and a new terminal, currently under construction, will open by 2004. When alterations to comply with the Schengen agreement are completed, terminal numbers will cease to exist and the airport will be renamed Arlanda North and Arlanda South.

The centrally located Sky City complex, with shops, restaurants and hotels, is close to the SAS international terminal (No 5), but some other international flights arrive and depart from Terminal No 2, beyond the SAS domestic terminal (No 4). Terminal No 5 has separate arrival, departure and transit halls (depart from the upper level, arrive at the lower level); Terminal No 2 has an arrival/departure hall and a transit hall. A free bus runs between the terminals but there are also indoor passageways. Tax-free shopping is available in the transit halls of Terminal Nos 2 and 5. It's easy to find your way around – all the important signs are in Swedish and English.

The post office and the Handelsbanken bank are in Sky City, but there are also Bankomat ATMs in Terminal Nos 2, 4 and 5. The Forex and X-Change currency exchange offices are at Terminal Nos 2 and 5 respectively. VAT refunds are available in the transit areas of Terminal Nos 2 and 5.

Left-luggage lockers, which will accept coins, are available at all terminals and in Sky City.

There isn't a tourist information office, but you'll find airport information desks at Terminal Nos 2, 4 and 5, which sell bus and train tickets and phonecards. The information desks at Terminal No 5 are open 24 hours.

Car rental can be arranged with AVIS, Budget, Europcar and Hertz (see Car & Motorcycle later in this chapter). Parking near the terminals is very expensive and costs from Skr10 to Skr40 per hour or Skr130 to Skr230 per day. The E4 motorway, which runs north to Uppsala and south to Stockholm, is about 4km south-west of Arlanda.

TO/FROM THE AIRPORT
Bus

Between 6.40am and 10pm daily, the Flygbussarna services (☎ 600 1000, e info @flygbussarna.com, W www.flygbussarna .com/flygbussarna/en/index.html) between Arlanda airport and Cityterminalen, via Hagaterminalen and St Eriksplan, depart every 10 or 15 minutes (Skr60/30 adult/child one way, 40 minutes). Buy your ticket in advance from airport information desks. The bus stops outside Terminal Nos 2, 4 and 5. In the opposite direction, departures from Cityterminalen run from 4am to 10pm daily. See also FlygbussarnaTaxi under Taxi later in this chapter. Flygbussarna also runs buses from Arlanda to Täby Centrum (7.30am to 11.10pm, weekdays only) and Brommaplan (7.40am to 11.10pm daily).

Other companies run buses to Uppsala (see the Excursions chapter) and various local destinations around Arlanda.

Train

Trains (Arlanda Express ☎ 020 222224, W www.arlandaexpress.com/english/index .htm) run from the basement at Arlanda to Centralstationen (Map 6, F3) in the city centre (Skr120/60 one way, 20 minutes). Departures from Arlanda are between 5.05am and 12.35am daily, every 15 minutes (weekdays and 2 to 11pm on Sunday) or every 30 minutes (other times). In the opposite direction, departures are from 4.35am to 12.15am daily (with the same frequency). The frequency is reduced in summer and around public holidays.

Long-distance X2000 SJ express trains (W www.sj.se) also stop in the basement and run to Stockholm, Uppsala, Sala and other places in Sweden, but they're relatively infrequent.

Taxi

Arlanda to central Stockholm by taxi costs from Skr300 to Skr440, depending on the time of day. Agree on the fare before getting in and don't use any taxis without a contact telephone number displayed. Taxi Stockholm (☎ 150000), Stockholm Transfer (☎ 020 350000) and Taxi Kurir (☎ 300000) are reputable and use meters. FlygbussarnaTaxi is a special connecting taxi service for Flygbussarna passengers with competitive fixed fares of Skr100 in the central area or Skr170 to most suburbs. If going to Arlanda, call ☎ 686 1010 for bookings; in the other direction, arrange with the driver. FlygbussarnaTaxi connects with Flygbussarna bus at Cityterminalen (taxi journeys in central area) or Hagaterminalen (for suburban taxi journeys). These are the only places to change from taxi to bus (and vice versa).

Bromma Airport

If you're using Bromma airport for domestic flights, Flygbussarna runs frequently from Cityterminalen from 6.15am to 7.35pm on weekdays (20 or 21 trips), with a reduced service on weekends (six runs from 7.45am to 3.15pm on Saturday, 10 runs from 10.15am to 7.40pm on Sunday). The fare is Skr50/80 one-way/return. A taxi between the city centre and Bromma should cost Skr170.

Skavsta Airport

Flygbussarna runs three buses on weekdays (two on both Saturday and Sunday) from Cityterminalen (Map 6, E2, #138) Gate 24 to Nyköping Skavsta airport in connection with Ryanair flights to/from London Stansted (Skr100/150 one-way/return, 80 minutes). Buses will call at Södertälje Syd on request.

PUBLIC TRANSPORT

Storstockholms Lokaltrafik (SL; ☎ 600 1000, W www.sl.se/international) runs the comprehensive and generally efficient transport network throughout Stockholm county, including all *tunnelbana* (T) metro trains, *pendeltåg* (J) commuter trains, and buses. The Transport System map at the back of this book covers metro lines and commuter trains, which radiate outwards from the hubs Centralstationen (with T-Centralen) and Slussen. The extensive county bus network is centred around suburban and rural terminals. City centre buses run along fixed routes (both cross-city and radial) and converge around Sergels Torg, Fridhemsplan and Slussen.

The SL-Center (information and ticket office) in the Centralstationen basement (Map 4, F1) is open the longest hours (6.30am to 11.15pm Monday to Saturday, from 7am Sunday and holidays). There's also an SL office at the T-Centralen Sergels Torg entrance (Map 6, D5), which is open 7am to 6.30pm weekdays and 10am to 5pm weekends, and another at the T-Centralen Vasagatan entrance (Map 6, E3) on the eastern side, open 7am to 7pm weekdays, 10am to 5pm weekends. The staff can provide free timetables and also sell city and county transport maps (Skr35 each, not available in Centralstationen basement), SL Tourist Passes and the general Stockholm Card. You'll find SL booths at all metro stations, but services are usually basic (apart from at the SL-Centers at Slussen, Tekniska Högskolan, Fridhemsplan, Gullmarsplan and several other places). International rail passes aren't valid on either the metro or SL commuter trains.

Tickets

The Stockholm Card (see Documents in the Facts for the Visitor chapter) covers travel on all SL metro trains, commuter trains and buses in Stockholm county. The SL Tourist Passes (Skr70/135 for 24/72 hours, Skr40/80 children and seniors) also cover transport. The 72-hour pass gives free admission to Kaknästornet and Gröna Lund, and 50% discount on admission to Skansen. However, it's a much cheaper alternative if you just want transport and it's especially good value if you take a long journey (for instance, as far as some of the more distant archipelago harbours). SL Tourist Passes can be bought from SL-Centers, metro stations, commuter train stations and some Pressbyrån shops/kiosks.

If you're staying in the city for a while or you want to explore the county in more depth, ask for a monthly SL Pass (Skr450/270 adult/child and senior). It's valid for 30 days from the date of purchase, photo ID isn't required and the card is transferable (but it can't be used by more than one person at a time!). Four calendar-month season cards cost Skr1745/1050 (January to April and September to December) or Skr1295/780 (May to August). An annual season ticket (valid from the issue date) costs Skr4785/2870.

All period tickets are valid from midnight on the first day of validity until 4.30am the day after the final day of validity. Period tickets can be shown to SL staff or used to open automatic barriers in stations.

You can also buy coupons from SL-Centers, metro stations, commuter train stations and SL bus drivers. These cost Skr8 each, but better value 20-coupon strips *(rabattkuponger)* are Skr110/70. Greater Stockholm is divided into five concentric zones – to travel within any zone requires two coupons, and to travel in two/three/four or five zones requires three/four/five coupons. Coupons are valid for an hour, you can change as often as you like during this time, and return journeys within the hour are allowed. Coupons are valid on night buses and the normal tariff applies. Coupons must be stamped by SL staff at the start of the journey.

Travelling without a valid ticket is a bad idea – the fine is now Skr1000.

For more information, ask at an SL-Center for the multilingual leaflet *Price information* and the Swedish-language leaflet *SLs sortiment & priser*, which has a map showing the zones.

Bus

Although bus timetables and route maps are complicated, studying them is no waste of time. City buses can be replaced by the metro or walking, but there are useful bus connections to suburban attractions. Ask at an SL-Center for the free handy timetable booklet and route map *Stockholms innerstad busslinjerna* (inner-city bus routes). Always get on a bus at the front door and present your ticket to the driver.

Inner-city buses radiate from Sergels Torg, Odenplan, Fridhemsplan and Slussen. Bus No 47 runs from Sergels Torg to Djurgården and bus No 69 runs from Centralstationen and Sergels Torg to the Ladugårdsgärdet museums and Kaknästornet. Useful buses for hostellers include bus No 65, which goes from Centralstationen (on the eastern side of Vasagatan) to Skeppsholmen, and bus No 43, which runs from Regeringsgatan to Södermalm. Bus Nos 1, 3 and 4 are frequent and run at least every eight minutes throughout the day, decreasing to once every 15 minutes in the evening.

Inner-city night buses, detailed in the booklet *Stockholms innerstad busslinjerna*, run from around 1am to 5am every night. Most operate from Centralstationen, Sergels Torg, Slussen, Odenplan and Fridhemsplan to the suburbs.

There are several regional bus hubs for outlying areas. Unfortunately, some buses rarely run, so you should check timetables carefully. The islands of the Ekerö municipality (including Drottningholm Slott) are served by bus Nos 301 to 323 from T-Brommaplan. Bus Nos 670 and 671 run to the Vaxholm archipelago terminal from T-Tekniska Högskolan and the Rydbo commuter train station respectively. For Tyresö and Lidingö, go to Gullmarsplan and T-Ropsten respectively. The Haninge (also called Handenterminalen) and Västerhaninge commuter train stations are important southern hubs, with archipelago connections; buses from the former run to Tyresö Centrum and Dalarö, while buses from the latter run to Arsta Havsbad. Odenplan is the hub for northern suburbs, including Hagaparken (bus No 515). For more information, see the individual destinations.

Train

Local pendeltåg commuter trains are useful for connections to Nynäshamn (for ferries to/from Poland and Gotland), to Haninge (Handenterminalen) and Västerhaninge (for buses to Dalarö and Arsta Havsbad), to Märsta (for buses to Sigtuna and the short hop to Arlanda airport) and Södertälje. These trains depart from Centralstationen (Map 6, F3) up to four times per hour, from around 5am to around 1am daily.

There are also services to Nockeby (from T-Alvik), to Lidingö (from T-Ropsten), to Kårsta, Österskär and Näsbypark (from T-Tekniska Högskolan) and to Saltsjöbaden and Solsidan (from T-Slussen).

There's a lost-and-found office by the pendeltåg platform doors in the basement at Centralstationen. It's open 10am to 6pm weekdays.

Tram

The historical *Djurgårdslinjen* No 7 tram runs between Norrmalmstorg and Waldemarsudde, passing most of the attractions on Djurgården, including Skansen. Tickets cost Skr20/10 adult/child and senior; SL period card holders may have to pay. The Stockholm Card isn't valid, but the one- and three-day SL Tourist Passes are. For information, call ☎ 660 7700 or check the Internet at Ⓦ www.ss.se/english.

The new Tvärbanan tram line started running in June 2000 and crosses the south-western side of the city from Gullmarsplan to Alvik. It's of little interest to tourists.

Metro

The most useful mode of transport in Stockholm is the tunnelbana (T), which converges on T-Centralen, connected by an underground walkway to Centralstationen. There are three main through lines with branches – check beforehand that the approaching train is actually going your way. Trains run roughly from 5am to 1am on weekdays and 6am to 3am or 4am on weekends. Service can be as frequent as every five minutes during rush hours. See the Transport System map at the back of this book.

Stockholm's Metro Art

The artwork now featured in over 70 metro stations along 110km of track is considered to be the longest art exhibition in the world. Originally presented in 1955 to the City Council as a motion designed to improve the aesthetics of bleak metro stations, around 130 artists have now contributed paintings, engravings, reliefs, sculptures and mosaics to the metro art project. Restoration is continuous and the SL Art Council spends Skr2.5 million annually on improvements and additions. Displays well worth a look include the metro stations at Kungsträdgården (Map 6, E7, #189; classical pieces, ferns and dripping water), Fridhemsplan (Map 3, E3; terracotta tiles celebrating Carl von Linné) and Östermalmstorg (Map 6, B9; women's rights and peace and environmental movements). For information about metro art at all the stations, visit Ⓦ www.sl.se/international on the Internet.

Metro diagrams are available from SL and there's one near the back of the free tourist booklet *What's On – Stockholm*. The 'blue' and 'green' lines serve Kungsholmen (T-Fridhemsplan) and the western suburbs; the 'red' line goes to the north-eastern suburbs; and the 'red' and 'green' lines serve Södermalm and places further south. All metro stations feature modern art – see the boxed text 'Stockholm's Metro Art'.

CAR & MOTORCYCLE

Driving in the city isn't recommended; traffic can be fairly heavy, signs are often poorly placed and getting lost isn't unusual. There are also iniquitous levels of taxation through high petrol prices and the excessive coverage of parking meters (which you'll even see in suburban car parks and rural areas!). There are *P-hus* (parking houses) in the city centre and they're shown on city maps. The parking house Konserthusgaraget (Sveavägen 17) charges up to Skr40 per hour but, along with many other such places, there's a fixed evening rate of only Skr25 (from 6pm to midnight).

You'll still find some free street parking in parts of Södermalm and Östermalm, from 5pm to 9am daily. Beware of street cleaning night; signs are only in Swedish and you'll get a hefty fine (Skr700) if you leave your car in the street. On Skeppsholmen, hostellers can buy discounted parking tickets (Skr25 per day) from the Svenska Turistföreningen (STF). Parking at inner-city hotels costs around Skr250 per day. Street parking is free (in metered spaces) for Stockholm Card holders.

Shell (Map 6, E10, #72) on Strandvägen is a centrally located petrol station. It's open 6.30am to midnight daily (from 8am weekends).

Note that Djurgårdsvägen is closed at night, on summer weekends and some holidays. Don't attempt to drive through the narrow streets of Gamla Stan.

Car Rental

Car rental normally requires signing an 'open ended' credit card agreement, but be warned that your bill can be amended upwards by the rental company without further signature. I've had a lot of trouble with car rental in Sweden, so I suggest you consider other modes of transport first.

To rent a car you'll normally have to be at least 18 (sometimes 25) years of age and need to show a recognised licence (in some cases, an international driving permit).

The international rental chains start hiring at around Skr600 per day with unlimited kilometres and third-party insurance for smaller models (typically a Renault Clio or Ford Fiesta). Fly-drive packages can bring some savings, and weekend or summer packages may also be offered at discount rates. All the major firms have offices at or near Stockholm's Arlanda airport and Statoil has many outlets around the city and beyond. The following agencies organise car rental:

AVIS (☎ 020 788200, W www.avis-se.com) Vasagatan 10B (Map 6, F4, #157); Ringvägen 90 (Map 5, D6, #78). This company charges from Skr985 for three-day hire including unlimited kilometres and third-party insurance (fully comprehensive insurance costs Skr1250 extra). Special three-day offers start from Skr900 in the low season. Weekly hire starts at Skr1985.

Europcar (Map 6, F4, #158) (☎ 020 781180, W www.europcar.se) Tegelbacken 6. Day hire from Skr170, plus Skr1.70 per kilometre. Weekly hire costs Skr2750, with unlimited kilometres. Prices include insurance and collision damage waiver.

Hertz (☎ 020 211211, W www.hertz.nu) Vasagatan 26. Car rental starts at Skr250/1250 per day/week (plus Skr2.50 per kilometre) or Skr750/3750 including unlimited kilometres. Collision damage waiver is from Skr75 per day extra.

Statoil (Map 6, F3, #147) (☎ 020 252525) Vasagatan 16. Charges start at Skr150 per day (plus Skr1.50 per kilometre). Two-day hire with unlimited kilometres costs Skr1050.

TAXI

There's usually no problem finding a taxi in Stockholm, but they're expensive. Always arrange the fare before getting in – rip-offs aren't uncommon. Expect to pay around Skr76 per 2km. The reputable firms are Taxi Stockholm (☎ 150000), Taxi 020 (☎ 020 939393), Stockholm Transfer (☎ 020 350000), Taxi Card (☎ 970000) and Taxi Kurir (☎ 300000). Taxi Card has a maximum fare of Skr92 for inner-city journeys 'between the tulls', but not between 7am and 7pm on weekdays.

At night, women should ask about *tjej-taxa*, a discount rate offered by Taxi Card.

BOAT

Djurgårdsfärjan (☎ 679 5830) ferry services connect Gröna Lund Tivoli (Map 4, G6, #104) on Djurgården with Nybroplan and Slussen (via Skeppsholmen). Ferries run from 7.30am to midnight daily (from 9am weekends), as frequently as every 10 minutes in summer; a single trip costs Skr20/15 adult/child and senior (free with the SL Tourist Pass). Bicycles cost Skr20.

Archipelago boats, departing from Ström-kajen, Nybroplan (Nybroviken) and Strandvägen, serve various coastal towns and offshore islands. Other boats depart from coastal villages around Stockholm. For details, see the relevant sections in the Excursions chapter.

BICYCLE

Stockholm has a reasonable network of bicycle paths and in summer you'll not regret hiring a bicycle. The tourist offices have maps for sale (see Maps in the Facts for the Visitor chapter), but they're not really necessary. Some city centre roads have dedicated bicycle lanes with traffic signals featuring red/green (stop/go) bicycle symbols.

The top-five day trips are: Djurgården; a loop from Gamla Stan to Södermalm, Långholmen and Kungsholmen (on lakeside roads); Drottningholm (return by steamer); Hagaparken; and the adjoining Ulriksdal Park. Some islands in the archipelago, including Utö, are ideally suited for exploration by bicycle. You can hire bikes on a few islands, or you can hire one in Stockholm and take it with you on the ferry. Some long-distance routes are marked all the way from central Stockholm. Nynäsleden to Nynäshamn joins Sommarleden near Västerhaninge and swings west to Södertälje. Roslagsleden leads to Norrtälje (linking Blåleden and Vaxholm). Upplandsleden leads to Märsta north of Stockholm and you can ride to Uppsala via Sigtuna. Sörmlandsleden leads to Södertälje, south of Stockholm. See also Bicycle in the Getting There & Away chapter.

Bicycles are carried free on SL commuter trains, except between 6am and 9am and 3pm and 6pm weekdays. Bikes aren't allowed in Centralstationen or on the metro.

Rental & Repairs

Some hostels organise bike hire for guests. Cykel & Mopeduthyrning (Map 4, E5, #67) (☎ 660 7959), Strandvägen kajplats 24, offers rental (around Skr150 per day) and repairs. It's open 9am to 9pm daily (closed in winter).

Free bike hire is available 8am to 4.35pm weekdays (to 4pm Friday) from Stadsdelsförvaltningen Kungsholmen (☎ 508 08050). The bikes are fairly basic – they don't have gears and you use the pedals to brake.

For bike repairs, you can also try ABC Cykel & Sport (Map 4, A1, #1) (☎ 612 1739), Birger Jarlsgatan 127.

WALKING

Walking is an excellent way to appreciate the beauty of Stockholm, the varied architecture and the open spaces of water. For more details, see the Walking Tours special section.

ORGANISED TOURS

For the latest information on organised tours, contact the Excursion Shop (Map 6, D6, #180) (☎ 789 2490, fax 789 2491, e utflyktsbutiken@stoinfo.se), Sverigehuset (Sweden House), Hamngatan 27. All the following tours are available in English.

Bus

City Sightseeing (Map 6, F6, #167) (☎ 587 14030, e sightseeing@stromma.se, w www .citysightseeing.com), Gustav Adolfs Torg, runs daily bus tours of the city, departing from the booth outside Operan (the Opera House) (Map 6, F6, #168) at Gustav Adolfs Torg. Ask if free hotel pick-up is available.

The 90-minute 'Stockholm Panorama' tour runs two- to seven-times daily all year and costs Skr150. 'Royal Stockholm' and 'Historical Stockholm' are more in-depth three-hour tours, but they only run from early April and mid-October (at 10am and 2pm respectively; Skr260 each).

Open Top Tours (☎ 587 14030, e sight seeing @stromma.se, w www.citysightsee ing.com), in collaboration with City Sightseeing, runs sightseeing tours around Stockholm from April to December using distinctive yellow and purple open-top double-decker buses (roofs are added during bad weather). The routes, varying slightly by season, pass most of the main sights and you can get on and off as often as you like during the day. The first departure is from Sverigehuset (Map 6, D6, #180) at 9.20am and buses run every 20 minutes until dusk (varying depending on the season); tickets cost Skr140. Tickets allow a discount of Skr30 on any boat tour with Stockholm Sightseeing.

Boat

Stockholm Sightseeing (Map 6, F8, #195) (☎ 587 14020, ⓔ sightseeing@stromma.se, ⓦ www.stockholmsightseeing.com), Skeppsbron 22, runs interesting hourly cruises from early April to mid-December around the central bridges and canals from Strömkajen (near the Grand Hotel) or Nybroplan. The one-hour 'Royal Canal' and 'Historical Canal' tours go to Kungsholmen and the archipelago (Fjäderholmarna), respectively; both cost Skr90, and are free for Stockholm Card holders. The Historical Canal tour only runs from early June to mid-August. 'Under the Bridges of Stockholm' takes two hours and passes under 15 bridges on its way around Södermalm (Skr140, May to October only). 'Sightseeing Anno 1935' visits central areas in an open wooden boat, from 30 June to 19 August (Skr110, one hour). 'Brunnsviken Runt' is a one-hour boat tour around Brunnsviken, in the northern suburbs; departures are hourly from Haga Forum, 10am to 3pm, late June to early August (Skr40, with discounts for local attractions). You can stop at various places, including Bergianska Trädgården, Frösundavik, Fjärilshuset and Haga Slott. The 3pm departure includes tour guiding in English.

City Sightseeing runs four-hour tours with the boat *Prins Carl Philip* to Drottningholm, including visits to the palace, theatre and/or the Chinese Pavilion. Departures are daily from 9 June to 19 August and lunch is available on board (Skr260).

Svea Viking (Map 7, A5, #14) (☎ 532 57200, ⓔ viking@marite.se, ⓦ www .sveaviking.se) run 1¾-hour trips around the inner archipelago in a Viking longship (complete with Viking warriors!). Departures are five times daily, 10.45am to 7.45pm, late June to late August; Skr150/50 adult/child (Viking food and drinks included).

Strömma Kanalbolaget (☎ 587 14000), Skeppsbron 22, sails daily to the Fjäder-holmarna islands in the archipelago. Departures from Nybroplan are once or twice hourly, 10 am to 11.30 pm, 28 April to 9 September (Skr70 return). 'Salmon & Shrimp Sails' on Lake Mälaren depart every evening at 7.30pm, from 23 April to 22 September (Skr240, including buffet dinner; 3½ hours). For information on other destinations (Birka, Drottningholm, Sandhamn and Vaxholm), see the Excursions chapter.

Air

An exciting way to see Stockholm is from a hot air balloon. Trips of varying length are possible, starting at around Skr1000 for a one-hour flight with champagne 'christening' for first timers! Contact Ballongflyg Upp och Ner (☎ 695 0100, fax 695 0102, ⓔ info @uppner.se, ⓦ www.uppner.se/indeng.htm), Hammarbyvägen 37. Several other companies offer flights – contact the tourist office for details.

Helicopter flights around Stockholm and the inner archipelago, organised by Stockholm Helicopter Tours (☎ 656 9070, ⓦ www.helicoptertours.nu), cost from Skr750.

Other Tours

City Sightseeing also does an interesting walking tour, the 'Old Town Walkabout', departing Gustav Adolfs Torg at 11.30 am and 2.30 pm, running from 9 June to 19 August (Skr85, 1½ hours). It also runs 45-minute horse-and-carriage trips through Gamla Stan, departing from Mynttorget (by the Royal Palace) every half-hour between noon and 4.30pm (30 June to 19 August only). 'Stockholm in a Nutshell' features a 90-minute coach tour of the city, then a one-hour boat trip to the Fjäderholmarna islands in the archipelago; departures are three to seven times daily from April to September (Skr260).

WALKING TOURS

WALKING TOURS

Most of central Stockholm's sights can be visited on foot, following four routes (which are all shown on the maps in this special section). Each of these routes will take you a good couple of hours to complete. Better still, take a whole day to explore the medieval heart of the city – Gamla Stan – but it's best to visit when the teeming coach parties aren't there.

For details of commercial walking tours, see Organised Tours in the Getting Around chapter.

City Centre & Gamla Stan (Tour No 1)

Start your walk at **Centralstationen**, the main railway station, which dates from 1867 but has been altered many times since. Cross Vasagatan and enter the side street Vattugränd. Turn left onto Klara Västra Kyrkogatan, past the **Klara kyrka** (1), then turn right onto Klarabergsgatan. This is one of Stockholm's main modern shopping streets, with designer shops, expensive boutiques and the **Åhléns** department store (2). Looking down Klara Östra Kyrkogatan, you'll see **Läkaresällskapets hus** (3), a fine brick building dating from 1906, built in National Romantic style but with Art Nouveau windows and interior.

At **Sergels Torg**, named after the local 18th-century sculptor Johan Tobias Sergel, you'll see ghastly metallic sculpture (which doesn't look so bad at night) and fountains. There are occasional demonstrations in the open-air basement arena of **Kulturhuset** (4; the Cultural House) and there's also a Christmas market in December. Kulturhuset has a library and an Internet cafe, and it hosts regular art exhibitions (see later). Continue a short way along Hamngatan, passing the **NK** (5; Nordiska Kompaniet, opened in 1915) department store on your left. Turn right after **Sverigehuset** (6; Sweden House, the tourist office), into the pleasant **Kungsträdgården**. This park, originally Gustav Vasa's kitchen garden and later an orchard, was opened to the public in 1763 and is now popular with people relaxing in the summer sun or skating in winter. The 17th-century **St Jakobs kyrka** (7) is worth a visit.

Walk through the park to its southern end at **Karl XII's Torg**, where there's a statue of the warmongering king, Karl XII. On your right there's **Operan** (8), the royal Opera House (opened in 1896), and across the road you'll see the narrow strait **Norrström**, which is the freshwater outflow from Lake Mälaren. Continue along the waterfront, past Operan and **Gustav Adolfs Torg**, to the grandiose **Arvfurstens palats** (9; also called the Sophia Albertina palace, now housing the Foreign Ministry) and the adjacent small white house, **Sagerhus** (10), which is the prime minister's official residence. Beyond Drottninggatan is **Rosenbad** (11); originally a 17th-century steam bath was on this site,

Top left: A gilded royal crown decorates the bridge to Skeppsholmen. (Photo: Jon Davison)

but a block of commercial and residential premises was constructed here in 1904 and it now contains government offices.

Turn left over the bridge Riksbron, at the foot of Drottninggatan. The route continues across **Helgeandsholmen** (Island of the Holy Spirit), between the two parts of Sweden's parliament building, **Riksdagshuset** (12). After crossing the short bridge Stallbron, you'll arrive on **Stads-holmen** (City Island), which is the medieval core of Stockholm.

Cross Mynttorget and follow Västerlånggatan for one block, then turn left into Storkyrkobrinken to reach **Axel Oxenstiernas palats** (13), a mansion built by a famous 17th-century chancellor, and **Storkyrkan** (14), the city's cathedral and the oldest building in Gamla Stan. Facing the cathedral across the cobbled square is **Kungliga Slottet** (15), the 'new' Royal Palace. Behind the cathedral lies **Slottsbacken**, a large open area with a central **obelisk**. The southern side of Slottsbacken features **Finska kyrkan** (16; the Finnish church) and **Tessinska palatset** (17), a late 17th-century palace now used by the Stockholm county governor.

The lane Källargränd leads southwards from Slottsbacken to the square **Stortorget**, where the Stockholm Blood Bath took place in 1520. Three sides of the square are formed by quaint tenements painted in different colours and there's an interesting sensation of long history here. On the fourth side of the square there's **Börsen** (18), the Stock Exchange and Swedish Academy building, completed in 1778. The Stortorget Christmas market in December is well worth looking around.

The narrow streets of the eastern half of Gamla Stan are medieval enough, still winding along their 14th-century lines and linked by a fantasy of lanes, arches and stairways. Walk down Köpmangatan to the small square **Köpmantorget**, where there's a statue of St George and the dragon. Turn right into **Österlånggatan**, where you'll find antique shops, art galleries, handicraft outlets and **Den Gyldene Freden** (19), which has been serving food since 1722.

Follow Österlånggatan as far as **Järntorget**, where metals were bought and sold in days long past. On the south-eastern side of the square

Right: The neobaroque Operan (Opera House) is a popular venue for classical music and ballet performances.

GRAEME CORNWALLIS

stands **Gamla Riksbankhuset** (20), which was completed in 1682 and is the oldest extant national bank building in the world. From Järntorget, keep right and turn into Västerlånggatan, looking out for **Mårten Trotzigs Gränd** by No 81; this is Stockholm's narrowest lane, at less than 1m wide. If you follow Prästgatan, you'll come to the lavishly decorated German church, **Tyska kyrkan** (21).

Västerlånggatan, lined with shops and boutiques selling tourist tat, attracts dense crowds, so you're advised to follow the quieter parallel street Stora Nygatan instead. On reaching Riddarhustorget, turn left and cross the short bridge Riddarholmsbron to **Riddarholmen** (Knight Island). The large **Riddarholmskyrkan** (22), formerly a church, has an amazing modern spire. Across Birger Jarls torg, **Stenbockska palatset** (23) dates from the 1640s and is one of Nicodemus Tessin the Elder's best-preserved mansions; it now houses the supreme court. Beyond Riddarholmskyrkan, you'll come to the far side of the island; on your right is the southern tower of the **Wrangelska palatset** (24), part of the medieval city wall (1530s). Further north, **Birger Jarls torn** (25) is another of Vasa's brick watchtowers, built around 1530 from the remains of the demolished Klara monastery. There are great views across the lake to the impressive **Stadshuset** (city hall) and the eastern end of **Kungsholmen** (King's Island).

Retrace your steps to Riddarhustorget, then turn left into Vasabron and pass between **Riddarhuset** (26; the House of Nobility) and **Bondeska palatset** (27), another of Tessin the Elder's 17th-century mansions, which is now used by the appeal court. Continue across Vasabron and along Vasagatan back to Centralstationen.

Skeppsholmen, Djurgården & Östermalm (Tour No 2)

Start this walking tour at Sverigehuset (Sweden House) tourist office. Follow Hamngatan a short way eastwards, then turn right into Kungsträdgårdsgatan. This street is lined on one side by large buildings facing Kungsträdgården. The head office of Systembolaget, at No 14, contains **Bolagsmuseet** (28), which has an entertaining description of the history of alcohol in Sweden.

If you go a short way along Wahrendorffsgatan, you'll find **synagogan** (29; synagogue), with a magnificently decorated interior. At Kungsträdgårdsgatan 8, there's **Stockholms Enskilda Bank** (30), with a neoclassical facade, Carl Milles sculptures by the entrance, and a grey limestone bank hall with an extensive glass roof. **Handelsbanken** (31), Kungsträdgårdsgatan 2, is another magnificent building, open during regular banking hours.

Just north of Handelsbanken, turn into Arsenalsgatan, where there's the eastern entrance to the metro station **T-Kungsträdgården** (32). This metro is known for its fine metro art, based on casts from the ruins of the Makalös Palace, the former Royal Dramatic Theatre which was destroyed by fire in 1825 (you'll need a valid metro ticket to see the art). From Arsenalsgatan, turn right into Blasieholmstorget, a cobbled square with two bronze horses cast from the four at San Marco in Venice.

Turn right again, into Stallgatan, then left along Södra Blasieholms-hamnen. The large building on the left is the **Grand Hôtel Stockholm** (33), originally built in 1874 with an internal carriageway (now the Winter Garden, with a glass roof) and wrought-iron balconies. Residents can marvel at the hotel's **Hall of Mirrors**, with its gilded stucco, classical columns, chandeliers and mirrors, formerly used for the Nobel Prize dinners. The hotel has absorbed the next building, **Bolinderska huset** (34); its particularly fine interior was restored in the 1990s. On your right is the quay **Strömkajen**, popular with anglers and also a departure point for boats to the archipelago. The next large building on your left is the impressive **National Museum** (35), which contains fine murals by Carl Larsson. Completed in 1866 and designed to house the royal art collection, which had been available for public viewing since 1794, the museum has been enlarged, rebuilt and restored several times.

Cross the bridge to the island **Skeppsholmen**. You'll see the impressive **Gamla Amiralitetshuset** (36) straight ahead. It was the original headquarters of the Swedish Admiralty (1650), but it was rebuilt as a

Right: The Svenska Handelsbanken building on Kungsträdgårdsgatan

VERONICA GARBUTT

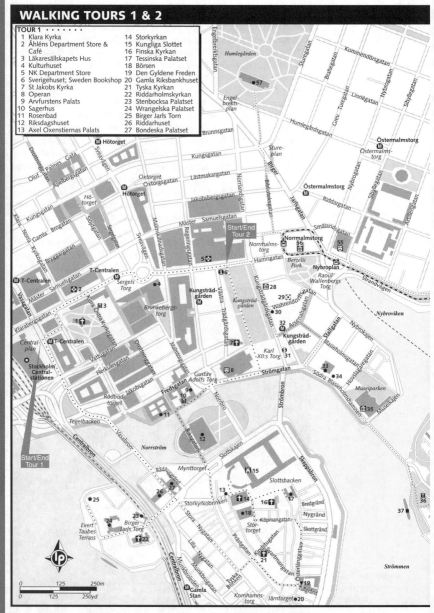

WALKING TOURS 1 & 2

TOUR 1 · · · · · · ·
1 Klara Kyrka
2 Åhléns Department Store & Café
3 Läkaresällskapets Hus
4 Kulturhuset
5 NK Department Store
6 Sverigehuset; Sweden Bookshop
7 St Jakobs Kyrka
8 Operan
9 Arvfurstens Palats
10 Sagerhus
11 Rosenbad
12 Riksdagshuset
13 Axel Oxenstiernas Palats
14 Storkyrkan
15 Kungliga Slottet
16 Finska Kyrkan
17 Tessinska Palatset
18 Börsen
19 Den Gyldene Freden
20 Gamla Riksbankhuset
21 Tyska Kyrkan
22 Riddarholmskyrkan
23 Stenbocksa Palatset
24 Wrangelska Palatset
25 Birger Jarls Torn
26 Riddarhuset
27 Bondeska Palatset

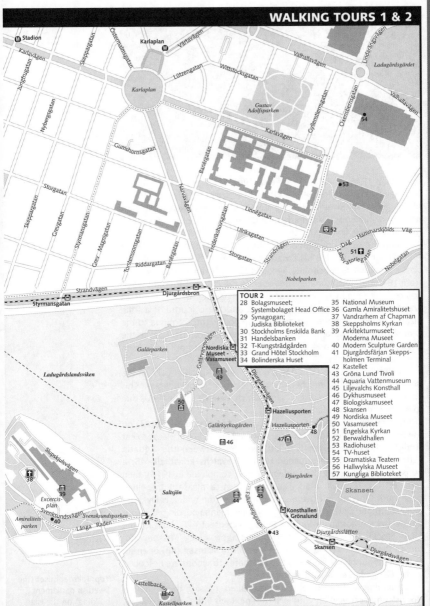

TOUR 2 --------
28 Bolagsmuseet;
   Systembolaget Head Office
29 Synagogan;
   Judiska Biblioteket
30 Stockholms Enskilda Bank
31 Handelsbanken
32 T-Kungsträdgården
33 Grand Hôtel Stockholm
34 Bolinderska Huset
35 National Museum
36 Gamla Amiralitetshuset
37 Vandrarhem af Chapman
38 Skeppsholms Kyrkan
39 Arkitekturmuseet;
   Moderna Museet
40 Modern Sculpture Garden
41 Djurgårdsfärjan Skeppsholmen Terminal
42 Kastellet
43 Gröna Lund Tivoli
44 Aquaria Vattenmuseum
45 Liljevalchs Konsthall
46 Dykhusmuseet
47 Biologiskamuseet
48 Skansen
49 Nordiska Museet
50 Vasamuseet
51 Engelska Kyrkan
52 Berwaldhallen
53 Radiohuset
54 TV-huset
55 Dramatiska Teatern
56 Hallwylska Museet
57 Kungliga Biblioteket

ANDERS BLOMQVIST

barracks in 1846, when the spectacular turrets and gables were added. The navy departed in 1969 and it's now used by Svenska Turistföreningen (STF; Swedish Touring Club). Keep right, past some cannons, and you'll reach **Vandrarhem af Chapman** (37), one of Sweden's most interesting floating hostels.

Go up the steps opposite *af Chapman* and pass the rear of Gamla Amiralitetshuset. On the hill ahead of you, there's the octagonal neoclassical church **Skeppsholms kyrkan** (38), with an original interior from 1842 but, unfortunately, not open to the public. Turn right when you reach the roadway (Svensksundsvägen), passing **Arkitekturmuseet** and **Moderna Museet** (39) on your left and the colourful, if a trifle bizarre, **modern sculpture garden** (40) on your right. Continue to the Djurgårdsfärjan boat terminal (41), where you can catch a boat to the Gröna Lund terminal on Djurgården (Skr20; the boat goes via Slussen from autumn to spring).

If you have time, you can pay a quick visit to **Kastellet** (42) on the island Kastellholmen, reached by bridge from Skeppsholmen. This strange little structure replaces a fort which blew up in the 1840s due to a botched gunpowder experiment.

On arrival in Djurgården, you'll see the **Gröna Lund Tivoli** (43) on the right (which opened in 1883) and some fairly average places to eat straight ahead. Take the first left, wander between the **Aquaria vattenmuseum** (44; an aquarium) and **Liljevalchs konsthall** (45; a purpose-built city-owned art exhibition hall, completed in 1916), then turn left on the main road, Djurgårdsvägen, a pleasant tree-lined boulevard. On your left between the road and the water, is **Dykhusmuseet** (46; the Diving Museum), in a former marina building. On your right is the extraordinary-looking **Biologiskamuseet** (47), built for the 1897 Stockholm Exhibition in 'Nordic dragon style'; just beyond, there's the Hazelius entrance to the wonderful **Skansen** (48) open-air museum, mountain railway and zoo (all these attractions are described in the Things to See & Do chapter).

Continuing northwards on Djurgårdsvägen, passing the grandiose **Nordiska museet** (49) on your left, turn next left into Galärvarvsvägen, towards **Vasamuseet** (50) and the rear of the naval officers' cemetery

Top: Riksdaghuset (the Swedish parliament building) on the islet Helgeandsholmen

Galärkyrkogården, where you'll find the controversial **Estonia monument** (see the boxed text 'The *Estonia* Ferry Disaster' in the Things to See & Do chapter). Return to Djurgårdsvägen, turn left and cross the bridge to the mainland.

Turn right into Styrmansgatan which becomes Strändvägen, passing the park **Nobelparken** on your right, and continue on Dag Hammarskjölds väg as far as **Engelska kyrkan** (51), the obviously English-looking church. Retrace your steps by 200m, then head north on Oxenstiernsgatan, passing **Berwaldhallen** (52; a concert hall) and **Radio-huset** (53; the headquarters of national Swedish radio) on your right. Turn left into Karlavägen, one of Östermalm's impressive 19th-century boulevards, before you reach **TV-huset** (54; national Swedish television).

Follow Karlavägen as far as **Karlaplan**, a large circular area with a central pond and fountain, then take a left into Styrmansgatan and continue to Strandvägen. Turn right on Strandvägen and you'll pass an interesting three-sided courtyard and impressive Art Nouveau-style hotels around No 7. At the extreme western end of Strandvägen, opposite Nybroplan, there's the ornate Art Nouveau **Dramatiska teatern** (55).

Beyond the major artery Birger Jarlsgatan, there's **Hallwylska museet** (56) and the square Norrmalmstorg. Turn right and follow the pedestrian street Biblioteksgatan through the heart of the trendy part of town, to

Right: One of the many streets in central Stockholm lined with beautiful buildings

JOHN BORTHWICK

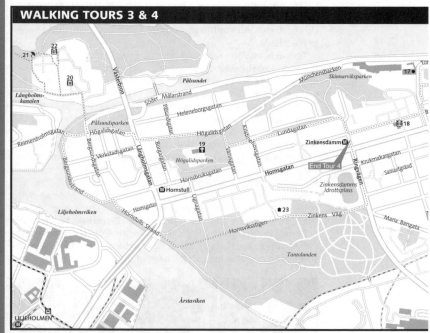

WALKING TOURS 3 & 4

Stureplan and **Kungliga Biblioteket** (57), the national and royal library, which is set in the pleasant and quiet **Humlegården** park. Return to Norrmalmstorg and turn right on Hamngatan to end your walk at Sverigehuset.

Eastern Södermalm (Tour No 3)

This walk begins at metro station T-Slussen. Leave the station using the main upper-level exit onto Södermalmstorg and turn immediately left into the lane Peter Myndes backen, between **Stadsmuseet** (1; the city museum) and **Hotell Anno 1647** (2). Take the first street on your left, **Götgatan**, which is the main shopping street in Södermalm and has some of Stockholm's most interesting stores. The second lane on your left is Klevgränd and, at No 3, one of the oldest buildings in Södermalm still displays late-medieval clamp irons on its walls. From Götgatan, take the next left after Klevgränd and ascend the stairs to Urvädergränd, which climbs steeply past **Bellmanhuset** (3), a small yellow house where Sweden's well-known bard Carl Michael Bellman lived from 1770 to 1774.

You'll get the best view of the **Slussen clover-leaf junction**, built in 1935 for right-hand drive traffic, by following the mesh-covered walkway on the left out to the upper entrance to **Katarinahissen** (4), which is a lift dating from 1936. Return to the top of Urvädergränd, where

WALKING TOURS 3 & 4

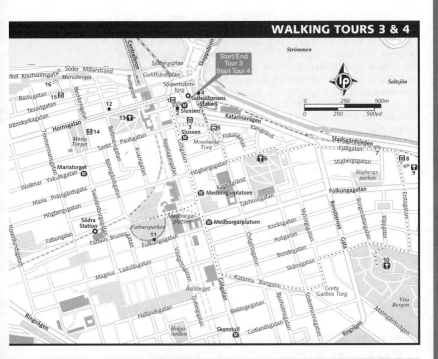

WALKING TOURS 3 & 4

TOUR 3 . . . .
1 Stockholms Stadsmuseum
2 Hotel Anno 1647
3 Bellmanhuset
4 Katarinahissen Lift
5 Södra Teatern
6 Katarina Kyrka
7 Cliiftop Viewpoint
8 Ersta Diakonimuseet
9 Kapell Ersta Diakonissanstalt

10 Sofia Kyrka
11 Bofills Båge

TOUR 4 --------------
12 Hornspuckeln Shopping
   District & Galleries
13 Maria Magdalena Kyrka
14 Leksaksmuseet
15 Ivar Lo-Museet
16 Viewpoint Mariaberget

17 Ludvigsberg
18 Måleriyrkets museum
19 Högalidskyrkan
20 Långholmens fängelsemuseum; Långholmen Hotell,
   Vandrarhem & Restaurant
21 Långholmens Strandbad
22 Bellmanmuseet
23 Zinkensdamm Hotell &
   Vandrarhem

you'll find **Södra teatern** (5), a theatre dating from the 1850s. It also faces **Mosebacketorg**, a pleasant square with the statue **Systarna**.

Follow Östgötagatan southwards from Mosebacketorg for one block, then turn left into Högbergsgatan. On your right, you'll see the church **Katarina kyrka** (6), a faithful replica of the 17th-century original, which was gutted by fire in 1990. The church is surrounded by a pleasant park. Beyond the church, continue along Mäster Mikaels Gata, which has some small, wooden 19th-century houses.

Cross Katarinavägen and follow Fjällgatan, passing more old houses, but be sure to stop at the spectacular **cliff-top viewpoint** (7) on the left. Further along the street, Fjällgatan makes a sharp right turn and becomes Erstagatan, separating the specialist hospital **Ersta sjukhus** and **Ersta diakonisällskap**, both run by a charitable religious foundation. If you turn left into the latter, you'll find the interesting **Ersta Diakoni-museet** (8), hotel and cafe, and **Kapell Ersta diakonissanstalt** (9), an octagonal chapel with a pointed roof.

Return to Erstagatan and follow it for about 400m south to Skånegatan; turn right for 150m, then cross the street and climb up to **Sofia kyrka** (10), an early 20th-century church on top of the hill Vita Bergen. You'll be able to see the **Globen** dome far to the south. Return to Skånegatan and follow it west towards Södermannagatan, then turn left for 150m to reach **Greta Garbos Torg**, which features three pink elephants, a rather strange street sculpture.

From Greta Garbos Torg, follow Katarina Bangata north-westwards; at its junction with Skånegatan, there's another odd artwork, this time featuring a woman with a pram. Continue to the main drag, Götgatan, then turn right and walk as far as Södermalm's central square **Medborgarplatsen**, which has a market hall, cinema and a library. From the square, the narrow street Bangårdsgatan leads west into **Fatbursparken**, a small park dominated by the immense and rather odd post-modern semicircular building **Bofills Båge** (11), clearly with classical influences. Retrace your steps to Götgatan and follow it northwards to T-Slussen.

Western Södermalm & Långholmen (Tour No 4)

This walk also starts from T-Slussen. Head northwards, past Stadsmuseet, then turn left into Hornsgatan. Cross Hornsgatan and follow its northern side until you reach Pustegränd, where there's an embankment with shops and galleries collectively known as **Hornspuckeln** (12). On the other side of Hornsgatan, you'll see the church **Maria Magdelana kyrka** (13). One city block to the west and lying south of Hornsgatan, the square **Mariatorget** has restaurants, bars, clubs and **Leksaksmuseet** (14), a museum dedicated to hobbies and toys.

From the northern side of Hornsgatan, turn into Blektornsgränd, then left into Bastugatan. About 200m to the west, is **Ivar Los Park**, which is named after Ivar Lo-Johansson, a well-known author whose apartment on Bastugatan is now the **Ivar Lo-museet** (15). There are fine views across Riddarfjärden from the top of the cliff **Mariaberget** (16).

Near the western end of Bastugatan, at Torkel Knutssonsgatan 2, there's the former foundry and engineering works **Ludvigsberg** (17), the best surviving example of 19th-century industrial architecture in the city; adjacent is the owner's mansion with an octagonal tower. Cross Torkel Knutssonsgatan and follow Brannkyrkagatan; on your left is the substantial building containing the **Måleriyrkets Museum** (18).

Continue walking along Brannkyrkagatan, then turn right into Lunda-gatan. Ahead of you you'll see **Högalidskyrkan** (19), completed in 1923 and the only twin-spired church in Stockholm.

Turn right at the end of Lundagatan, then left into Högalidsgatan, which terminates at the busy Långholmsgatan. Cross this street using the pedestrian crossing then walk downhill, skirting **Pålsundsparken**, turn right and cross the **Pålsundet** strait on a road bridge to reach the quiet suburban island **Långholmen**. Keep left and walk around the former **Långholmen prison** (20), which is now a hotel, hostel and restaurant; there's also an interesting **prison museum** here. **Långhol-mens strandbad** (21), on the northern shore of the island, is a pleasant beach for swimming in Mariebergsfjärden. The nearby **Bellmanmuseet**, (22) located in a 17th-century wooden customs house, features more about the life and times of the troubadour Carl Michael Bellman.

Return to Pålsundet; keep right after the bridge and cross to the residential island **Reimersholme**. In the 19th century, prisoners from Långolmen built a textile factory on Reimersholme, which was later used to make paraffin before a wealthy industrialist converted it into a distillery. There's still a variety of Swedish *snaps* called Reimersholme, but it's no longer made on the island.

Re-cross the bridge to Södermalm, then turn right along the shore and pass under the bridge Liljeholmsbron. About 1km ahead, crossing Årstaviken, you'll see **Årstabron**, a railway bridge from 1929, which looks like a Roman aqueduct. Well before reaching Årstabron, turn left onto Hornviksstigen, with **Tantolunden Park**, its allotments and huts on your right. You'll pass the quietly located **Zinkensdamm Hotell & Van-drarhem** (23) on your left as the roadway becomes Zinkens väg. Continue to the main road Ringvägen, then turn left, passing the sports field **Zinkensdamms idrottsplass** on your left. The tour ends at T-Zinkensdamm, which you'll find on the northern side of Hornsgatan.

Things to See & Do

Highlights

The following list features some of the finest attractions in Stockholm, although not necessarily the most popular and not in any particular order:

- Vasamuseet
- Kungliga Slottet
- Storkyrkan
- Skansen
- Stadshuset
- Tyska Kyrkan
- Drottningholms Slottsteater & Kina Slott
- The Gold Room, Historiska Museet
- Riddarhuset
- Polishistoriska Museet

Visitors and residents alike never tire of strolling along the wonderful streets and lanes in Gamla Stan, or visiting the multitude of excellent museums and churches the city has to offer. Some of the most interesting attractions aren't promoted by the tourist office and it remains for the reader to explore beyond the beaten track to find them. Remember that many attractions are closed on public holidays and may also be closed (or have drastically reduced opening hours) for several days before or after a holiday. The Stockholm Card is valid for free or reduced admission to most attractions.

Gamla Stan

KUNGLIGA MYNTKABINETTET

Europe's first economic museum, Kungliga Myntkabinettet **(Map 7, B5, #34)** *(the Royal Coin Cabinet; ☎ 519 55300, W www .myntkabinettet.se, Slottsbacken 6; Skr45/12 adult/child; open 10am-4pm Tues-Sun all year)*, is just across the square from the Royal Palace and the collection was initiated by Johan III in the 1570s. You'll find displays of coins (including Viking silver) and banknotes covering the history of money over the last 2600 years. There are also replicas of bank offices, medal collections and a section designed for children.

The **world's oldest coin** (a Swedish copper plate weighing 19.7kg, from 625 BC) and the **world's first banknote** (issued in Sweden in 1661) can all be found here. The finest ancient coin on display shows a lion's head on one side and was minted by King Croesus of Greece in 550 BC. A sad example of hyperinflation can be seen on the lengthy German banknote 'Tausend Mark', which is a mere DM1,000,000,000,000.

Information and floor plans are available in English and there's also a cafe and souvenir shop.

STORKYRKAN

Storkyrkan **(Map 7, B4, #31)** *(Stockholm cathedral; ☎ 723 3000, Trångsund; Skr10/ free May-Aug, otherwise free, Stockholm Card not valid; open 9am-6pm daily May-Aug, otherwise closes at 4pm)* is next to Kungliga Slottet and Sweden's monarchs used to be crowned in this impressive place. This brick-built church was consecrated in 1306, replacing a smaller church on the same site which was gutted by fire. However, the exterior is baroque.

The ceilings feature some medieval paintings, including work by Albertus Pictor in the **Chapel of the Souls** cross vault. The ancient and ornate interior contains a life-sized statue of **St George** and his horse confronting the mythical dragon, sculpted by the German sculptor Berndt Notke in 1494. You'll also see the extravagant **pulpit** from 1700 (the Hebrew word is 'Yahweh', meaning God), two large royal-box pews with crown-shaped canopies and the 350-year-old **silver altar**. Left of the altar sits a 2m-high **bell**, dating from 1493. In front of the altar, there's a 15th-century **seven-branched candlestick**, while on the wall to

Stockholm For Free

Squeezing money out of tourists is big business in Stockholm – even some churches charge admission fees! However, some of the best experiences you can have are free. The following list gives suggestions of free sights and activities:

- Self-guided walking tours of the city (especially Gamla Stan), the architecture and street sculpture
- Visits to churches, especially Storkyrkan (NB: admission fee in summer), Tyska Kyrkan and Spånga Kyrka; there are also free lunch concerts in some churches
- Free off-season admission to some museums; this is rare, and usually applies for only a few hours each week
- The art collections in Konstakademien
- Some exhibitions at Kulturhuset
- Dramatiska teatern – the entrance hall, staircase and restaurant are free to enter
- Stockholms Läns Museum
- The Riksdagshuset tour

- Östermalms saluhall
- Watching yachts on Lake Mälaren
- Visiting parks, including Ulriksdal and Haga
- Small free festivals – see Public Holidays & Special Events in the Facts for the Visitor chapter
- Metro Art in the metro stations, but you'll need a valid train ticket to see it
- Watching ice skating, bandy or other sports at the Kungsträdgården skating rink, Östermalms idrottsplass or Zinkensdamms idrottsplass (at the last two, admission fees are charged early but late arrivals may see the end for free; training and watching from outside is free)
- Watching canoeists fighting the current in Norrström, outside Operan

the left there's a 9m-high painting of the **Last Judgment** (1696). The **Parhelion Painting** (Vädersolstavlan), actually a 1630s copy of the original, depicts Stockholm during a spectacular display of atmospheric optics in 1535; it's on the southern wall, near the entrance.

A more-detailed floor plan costs Skr2 but there's also a lavish colour booklet for Skr65. Both are available in a variety of languages. The Sunday service (in Swedish) is at 11am. Classical music concerts lasting one to two hours are held every two or three weeks in the cathedral, usually on Sunday. Tickets usually cost from Skr70 to Skr130 (sometimes as high as Skr400), but multi-ticket discounts are available. Call ☎ 723 3009 for details.

TYSKA KYRKAN & FINSKA KYRKAN

Tyska Kyrkan **(Map 7, C4, #58)** *(German Church; ☎ 411 1188, Svartmangatan 16; free; open noon-4pm daily early May-late Sept, otherwise noon-4pm Sat & Sun only)* is one of Stockholm's finest churches. It dates from the 1570s, but was enlarged to

its current size from 1638 to 1642. All the church windows are stained glass and there are 119 unique **gallery paintings** (1660–65). The finest parts of the interior include the **royal gallery** (1672), the gold-painted **altar** and the astonishing ebony and alabaster **pulpit** (1660).

Finska Kyrkan *(Finnish Church; ☎ 206 140, Slottsbacken 2C; no set opening hrs)* was a former indoor tennis court given by Fredrik I to the Finnish community in the 1740s for use as a church. It currently contains an early 18th-century inventory from a church near St Petersburg.

RIDDARHOLMSKYRKAN

Riddarholmskyrkan **(Map 7, C2, #5)** *(☎ 402 6130, Birger Jarls torg; Skr20/10; open 10am-4pm daily 15 May-31 Aug, noon-3pm Sat & Sun Sept)*, on the nearby island Riddarholmen, was built by Franciscan monks in the late-13th century and was extended in the mid-15th century. The church has been the royal necropolis since the burial of Magnus Ladulås in 1290 and is home to the armorial glory of the Serafim knightly order.

STORKYRKAN

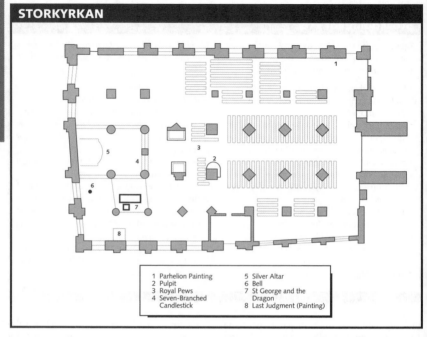

1 Parhelion Painting
2 Pulpit
3 Royal Pews
4 Seven-Branched
  Candlestick
5 Silver Altar
6 Bell
7 St George and the
  Dragon
8 Last Judgment (Painting)

The last regular church service was held in 1807 but funeral services still take place here.

To the right of the altar, there's the **Gustavian chapel**, with the marble sarcophagus of Gustav II, Sweden's mightiest monarch; directly opposite is the **Carolean chapel**, with the black marble sarcophagus of Karl XII. Look out for the massed wall-plates displaying the arms of the knights.

RIDDARHUSET

The Swedish parliament met in the 17th-century Riddarhuset **(Map 7, B2, #7)** *(the House of Nobility; ☎ 723 3990, Riddarhustorget 10; Skr40/10; open 11.30am-2.30pm daily)*, until 1865. There are 2345 coats of arms belonging to Sweden's nobility on display in the impressive **Great Hall**. Look out for the precious **Land Marshal's chair**, carved in ivory and dating from at least 1650. It is still used by the chairman during the Assembly of Nobles, which takes place every third year.

In the chancellery there's a unique collection of 525 pieces of **heraldic porcelain** displaying 170 different Swedish coats of arms. There's also a display of around 1600 **signets**, each with a family crest, and various portraits of historically important Swedes.

A colour booklet is available, in English, for Skr40.

POSTMUSEUM

The Postmuseum **(Map 7, C3, #65)** *(☎ 781 1755, Lilla Nygatan 6; Skr60/30; open 11am-4pm Tues-Sun, closing 7pm Sept-Apr)* features temporary and permanent exhibits and there are usually descriptions in English. There's a thorough description of the 360-year-long Swedish postal service history, which includes post office reconstructions and displays of Swedish stamps from 1855 to the present day. The knowledge centre, Post F@ktum, has 220,000

[Continued on page 93]

KUNGLIGA SLOTTET

The 'new' Royal Palace (Map 7, C4, #17) (☎ 402 6130, W www.royalcourt.se; Skr100/70 adult/child for general admission or Skr120/60/30 family/adult/child per unit; open 10am-4pm daily 15 May-31 Aug, otherwise noon-3pm Tues-Sun & closed Mon) is one of Stockholm's highlights and it was constructed on the site of the 'old' royal castle, Tre Kronor, which burned down in 1697. The walls of the north wing of the castle survived the fire and were incorporated in the palace, but the medieval designs are now concealed by a baroque exterior. The palace, designed by the court architect Nicodemus Tessin the Younger, wasn't completed until 57 years later and, with 608 rooms, it's the largest royal castle in the world still used for its original purpose.

The Changing of the Guard usually takes place in the outer courtyard at 12.10pm daily June to August (but at 1.10pm on Sunday and public holidays); the rest of the year it's on Wednesday, Saturday and Sunday only. It can last over 20 minutes and is quite an interesting spectacle.

By the outer courtyard, there's a shop selling souvenir books and kitschy gifts. Indoor photography in Kungliga Slottet isn't permitted.

The Royal Apartments

The royal apartments (☎ 402 6130; free guided tours in English 1.15pm daily) count as one unit and are open to the public except during state functions. Originally, there were eight suites on the 1st and 2nd floors of Kungliga Slottet, with state rooms facing outward and smaller private rooms facing the inner courtyard. Allow at least an hour for viewing the royal apartments with their rococo and baroque

Top: On guard at the Royal Palace (Photo: Veronica Garbutt)
Right: The Changing of the Guard in the palace grounds

SUNA KANGA

designs, 18th- and 19th-century furnishings, portraits, porcelain and silverware. A descriptive booklet with good colour photographs is available from the palace bookshop for Skr40.

From the main entrance, a wide staircase with an impressive painted ceiling leads to the 1st and 2nd floors. Turn left on the 1st floor for the **Bernadotte apartments**, a suite of 13 rooms featuring some uncomfortable-looking furniture and **Lovisa Ulrika's audience chamber**, including her throne and wall tapestries. There are also two small octagonal rooms, chandeliers, a gallery of royal portraits and unique mid-19th-century porcelain from Sèvres (France). Turning right leads to the Hall of State via the **apartments of the Royal Orders of Chivalry**, which feature vestments and other costumes, medals, sceptres and brightly coloured heraldic shields. The impressive 50m-long **Hall of State**, reminiscent of a Greek temple, is where the Swedish parliament was opened by the monarch every year from 1755 to 1975. It contains **Queen Kristina's silver throne**, a gift from Magnus Gabriel de la Gardie in 1650.

On the 2nd floor, turn left for the nine-room **guest apartments**, which include three small rooms facing the inner courtyard. Of particular interest is the mosaic table in the Guardroom (a gift from Pope Pius IX), plus wool tapestries, chandeliers, beds, couches and other furniture. On the right, the **State apartments** were intended as living quarters for the king and queen, but most monarchs resided elsewhere. Of the 10 rooms, the most impressive are the neoclassical **Gustav III's State bedchamber** (where that autocratic king died from gunshot wounds), the ornate **Karl XI's Gallery** banquet hall (with display cases full of unusual items in porcelain, ivory and ebony) and the large salon known as **The White Sea**, with an unusual wooden floor, display cases of royal silver and magnificent ceiling artwork.

Below: Kungliga Slottet

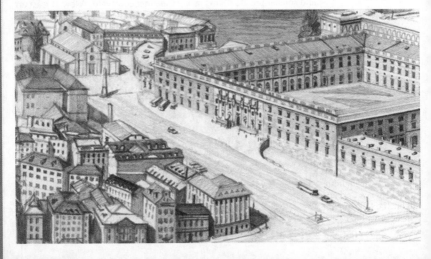

Slottskyrkan

Slottskyrkan (Map 7, C4, #16) *(the Royal Chapel; free; open for Sun services year-round & 10am-4pm daily May-Aug)*, on the 1st floor of the south wing, is reached by the staircase at the south entrance to the palace, on Slottsbacken. The three ceiling paintings depict Christ's ascension into heaven and the altarpiece features Christ in the Garden of Gethsemane. Parts of the pews were made for the Tre Kronor castle chapel and saved from the great blaze.

Skattkammaren

Skattkammaren (Map 7, C4, #16) *(the Royal Treasury; free guided tours in English 12.15pm daily)*, in the basement of the south wing (enter from Slottsbacken), has several small rooms with display cases featuring the Swedish regalia, coronation cloaks, crowns, orbs, sceptres, keys and medals. Most impressive are Oskar II's ermine and velvet coronation cloak (1872), Karl XI's extraordinary silver-coated baptismal font and Gustav Vasa's sword of state, with a magnificently etched blade depicting Old Testament scenes from the burning bush to the drowning of the Egyptians in the Red Sea.

A colour souvenir booklet is available for Skr50.

Gustav III's Antikmuseum

This museum (Map 7, B4, #13) *(Gustav III's Museum of Antiquities; open normal palace hours in summer, noon-3pm Sat & Sun 1 Sept-14 May)*, in the basement of the north wing, displays the marble Mediterranean treasures (particularly sculptures) acquired by that

KELLI HAMBLETT

eccentric monarch during his Italian tour of 1784. The smaller hall features busts of Roman emperors and generals, while the larger hall displays the muses, such as music, poetry, drama. The rumour is that some of them, probably the ones in good condition, are 18th-century fakes!

Museum Tre Kronor

This museum (Map 7, B4, #13), opened in December 1999 was originally a 16th-century wood-storage cellar. Now it features the foundations of 13th-century defensive walls, exhibits rescued from the medieval castle during the fire of 1697, and a variety of mundane objects of medieval vintage. However, it's a bit disappointing and it's certainly not the best part of the palace. The model and pictures of Tre Kronor castle are of passing interest but the displays of things such as animal bones and coins could do with improvement.

Livrustkammaren

Livrustkammaren (Map 7, C5, #15) *(Royal Armoury; ☎ 519 55544, Slottsbakken 3; Skr65/20 adult/child; open 10am-5pm daily June-Aug, otherwise 11am-5pm Tue-Sun, closing 8pm Thur; free guided tours in English 1pm Mon-Fri, 2pm Sat & Sun, 26 June-3 Sept)* is part of the palace complex but it must be visited separately. Its displays cover 500 years of royal history and there's a large collection of royal memorabilia, including armour, weapons, ceremonial costumes and five colourful carriages. There's usually a large temporary exhibition in the upstairs section.

Among the most interesting exhibits are **Gustav II Adolf's horse**, Streiff (its hide is fitted over a wooden frame), and two suits worn by the king during the 1627 Polish campaign, which have been on public display continuously since 1633. It's also worth looking out for **Karl XII's hat**, complete with the assassin's bullet hole (1718), and **Gustav III's costume**, which he was wearing at the opera when he was murdered in 1792. However, the jar with the stomach contents of Baron Bielke (one of the conspirators, who committed suicide by taking arsenic) is certainly one of the oddest things in the museum.

The downstairs section features royal coaches, saddles and sedan chairs. The most notable item is the **Austrian sleigh** (Vienna, c.1740), which was presented by the Austrian Empress to Gustav III in 1777. It's pulled by a spectacularly plumed white horse and sculpted and gilded in Viennese rococo style with a livery of blue-green velvet and gold embroidery.

[Continued from page 88]

documents, including books on stamps and postal history. There's also a miniature post office for children, a cafe/bistro and a shop. The museum is on the Internet at W www.posten.se/museum.

CORNELISMUSEET
This museum (Map 7, C4, #30) (☎ 667 7365, Trångsund 8; Skr20/free; open noon-4pm Sat & Sun, noon-4pm daily 15 June-15 Aug) displays memorabilia, including records, instruments, prizes and clothes, which relate to the hugely popular troubadour Cornelis Vreeswijk, who died in 1987.

HELGEANDSHOLMEN
This little island, in the middle of Norrström, is home to Riksdagshuset (Map 7, A3, #10) (the Swedish parliament building; ☎ 786 4000, Riksgatan 3A; open for free 1-hr guided tours in English, 12.30pm & 2pm Mon-Fri June-Aug, otherwise 1.30pm Sat & Sun only).

The older front section (facing downstream) dates from 1905 and includes an impressive central stairwell with pillars and a glass roof, a circular hall, and a glass cupola with heraldic shields. The more modern part, which incorporates a former bank building, contains the currently used debating chamber, the MP's club, a post office and restaurants. When the parliament is sitting, you can visit the public gallery and listen to a riveting debate in Swedish.

Popular with adults and kids alike, Medeltidsmuseet (Map 7, A4, #11) (Medieval Museum; ☎ 508 31790, Strömparterren; Skr40/5; open 11am-4pm Tues-Sun & closed Mon from Sept-June, closed 6pm Wed year-round & Tues-Thur July & Aug) is at the eastern end of the island. A 55m-long section of city wall dating from around AD 1530, 10 boats, 9000kg of human bones and 700 shoes were discovered here when an underground car park for Riksdagshuset was being excavated (1978–80) and you can now get a taste of medieval Stockholm by exploring faithful, on-site reconstructions of houses,

sheds and workshops. You can also see real skeletons, a secret 18th-century passage leading to Kungliga Slottet, medieval boats, weapons and a grim hanging exhibit called Gallows Hill. Free guided tours in English start at 2pm daily in July and August.

Central Stockholm

STADSHUSET
The excellent Stadshuset (Map 6, G2, #140) (city hall; ☎ 508 29058, Hantverkargatan 1, Kungsholmen; Skr50/ free; open for 45-min guided tours in English at 10am & noon daily year-round, also 11am, 2pm & 3pm from June-Aug) looks more like a large church, but its size is deceptive since it has two internal courtyards. Climb its dominant brown-brick square tower (Skr15/free; open 10am-4.30pm daily May-Sept) for a good view of Gamla Stan; it's topped with a golden spire and the symbol of Swedish power, the three royal crowns.

Inside the building, you'll find the beautiful mosaic-lined Gyllene salen (Golden Hall, made with 10kg of gold), the impressive council meeting chamber (with a roof like an overturned boat), Prins Eugen's own fresco re-creation of the lake view from the gallery, and the Blue Hall where the annual Nobel Prize banquet is held. Outside, by the lake, there's a pleasant terrace, with sculptures by Carl Eldh.

Note that the tour schedule may be interrupted from time to time by special events.

KONSTAKADEMIEN
Konstakademien (Map 6, F5, #161) (the Royal Academy of Fine Arts; ☎ 232945, Fredsgatan 12; free; open 11am-5pm Tues-Fri, noon-4pm Sat & Sun, closed Mon), in a former mansion designed by Nicodemus Tessin the Elder and originally constructed in 1672, has actually been rebuilt several times. The royal academy presents temporary exhibitions on art and architecture, which change roughly once a month.

MEDELHAVSMUSEET

The collections in Medelhavsmuseet **(Map 6, F6, #164)** *(the Museum of Mediterranean Antiquities; ☎ 519 55380, Fredsgatan 2; Skr50/free under 20; open 11am-8pm Tues, 11am-4pm Wed-Fri, noon-5pm Sat & Sun)*, in a former bank building near Gustav Adolfs Torg, include Egyptian, Greek, Cypriot and Roman artefacts. Unfortunately, the museum is often overlooked by tourists.

Some displays are rather off-beat, such as the **stone body parts** which had been donated to an Etruscan temple, the late 18th-century **model buildings** made from cork, and the **terracotta figures** excavated by Swedes from a previously undisturbed temple in northern Cyprus. The magnificent soft limestone **Assyrian palace relief** from Nimrud (now in Iraq) dates from around 870 BC; it was stolen by English adventurers who sawed it into six parts and shipped it to Britain. The relief was later sent as a present to the Swedish Queen Josephine. There are also displays of Islamic art, pottery and glassware. The basement has an etched slate showing an Egyptian hippopotamus hunt, from the early 4th millennium BC.

The secure **Gold Room**, open 12.30pm to 1pm and 2.30pm to 3pm daily, has displays of gold Greek burial wreaths and an extremely rare Hittite gold jug.

DANSMUSEET

Located in a neoclassical former bank building, Dansmuseet **(Map 6, F6, #166)** *(Dance Museum; ☎ 441 7650, Ⓦ www.dansmuseet.nu, Gustav Adolfs Torg 22-24; Skr50/free under 12, Skr30 students; open 11am-4pm Tues, Wed & Fri, 11am-7pm Thur, noon-4pm Sat & Sun)* covers all aspects of staging and costume and has a high standard of exhibits. The Tibetan, Indian and African masks and costumes are particularly fine and there are also displays of Chinese and Japanese puppets. There's a Russian ballet exhibit and an explanation of European dance history. You can also watch videos of dancers in action. The cafe serves hot meals and snacks and the friendly staff can advise on dance classes.

ST JAKOBS KYRKA

St Jakobs kyrka **(Map 6, E7, #174)** *(☎ 723 3000, Jakobs torg; free; open 11am-3pm daily, 9am-6pm daily in summer)* was completed in 1643 but features both Renaissance and Gothic architecture and has a magnificent vaulted ceiling. Of particular note are the ornate **pulpit** (1828), **high altarpiece** (1937), **heraldic shields**, stained glass windows and elaborate southern entrance. There's a colour brochure in English (Skr5) and an English service at 6pm every Sunday.

KLARA KYRKA

Construction of Klara kyrka **(Map 6, E4, #149)** *(☎ 723 3000, Klara Västra Kyrkogatan; free; open 10am-5pm daily)* was ordered by Johan III at the same location as the convent which his father demolished in 1527. It was completed in 1590 but the church was badly damaged by fire in 1751 and it has been rebuilt and renovated several times since.

The church is noted for its fine **ceiling paintings**; the central four are Old Testament scenes. There are also four **wall paintings** depicting church history and two large stained-glass windows. The famous Swedish bard Carl Michael Bellman is interred in the churchyard.

Free lunch concerts, usually organ but sometimes choir, start at noon on weekdays and last up to 45 minutes. The church cafe stays open until 3pm. The summer tourist bureau (☎ 723 3028), open 10am to 5pm (closed for lunch, noon to 12.45pm) daily, June to August, can advise on all of Stockholm's churches.

KULTURHUSET

Completed in 1974, Kulturhuset **(Map 6, D5, #154)** *(☎ 508 31508, Sergels Torg 3; free to Skr210; open 11am-7pm Tues-Fri, 11am-5pm Sat & Sun)* is a glass-fronted monstrosity. However, it presents a wide range of activities and events, including **Lava** (an independent youth culture project where you can listen to demo tapes, read fanzines and watch videos), **Rum för Barn** (activities for children under 12) and many temporary art and photography exhibitions,

Let the Traveller Beware

Some of the popular attractions are overrated, including Drottningholms Slott and its gardens and the pretentious Moderna Museet. Money-making scams, both official and unofficial, are surprisingly common for such a so-called 'developed country' and many travellers aren't impressed by the Stockholmers attitude towards making a fast buck.

Particular things to avoid or be aware of include:

- Paying admission fees to enter churches (in summer) and run-of-the-mill restaurants, ostensibly so your jacket doesn't hang on the back of your chair
- Walking down Västerlånggatan (Gamla Stan) or Drottninggatan on a busy afternoon – you'll be a fine target for pickpockets
- Speaking to staff in art museums, who are notoriously unfriendly and only seem interested in parting you from your cash
- Asking people in the street for assistance – don't be surprised if they're rude and unhelpful
- Parking – over-zealous issuing of parking tickets is endemic
- Trying to enter the Grand Hôtel in casual clothes and expecting to be served
- Queuing outside clubs and restaurants in the cold and expecting to be admitted by bouncers, depending on your 'style'

which change every four or eight weeks. Some activities and events have special opening hours; for details, check the program booklets that are issued several times yearly.

HALLWYLSKA MUSEET

The delightful Hallwylska Museet **(Map 6, D8, #80)** *(Hallwyl Museum; ☎ 519 55599,* W *www.lsh.se, Hamngatan 4; Skr60/25; 1-hr tours at 1pm Sun year-round, at 1pm daily 26 June-13 Aug)* is a private palace that was already wired for electricity when completed in 1898. From the age of 10, Wilhelmina von Hallwyl collected items as diverse as kitchen utensils, Chinese pottery, 17th-century paintings, silverware, sculpture, her children's teeth, weapons (Swedish, German and some Oriental guns, crossbows, swords and suits of armour) and

jewellery. In 1920, this lady and her husband donated their entire house (including contents) to the nation. The ornate baroquestyle **great drawing room** is particularly impressive with a gilded stucco ceiling and a rare, playable grand piano. The **ladies salon** has rococo furniture, late-16th-century tapestries and ceiling paintings.

It's also possible to join one of the more regular tours in Swedish.

BOLAGSMUSEET

One of the city's lesser-known museums, Bolagsmuseet **(Map 6, D7, #183)** *(☎ 789 3500, Kungsträdgårdsgatan 14; Skr20, Stockholm Card not valid; 1-hr tours 10am & 2pm Wed)*, located in Systembolaget's head office, traces the fascinating history of alcohol, drunkenness and state control in Sweden.

In 1467, 'burnt wine' was first imported for use in gunpowder but, in the late 16th century, vodka was brought home by Swedish troops who had fought in Russia and serious boozing became a national pastime. By the early 19th century, Swedes were consuming 46L of pure alcohol per person annually and drunkenness was rife. It's no surprise that the temperance movement gained popularity and, in 1849, King Oskar I asked parliament to consider controls on opening hours and age limits. Regulations became stricter and put most alcohol-sales premises out of business. See also the boxed text 'Systembolaget' in the Places to Eat chapter.

The excellent museum displays include details of rationing and the 1922 prohibition referendum, and lots of reconstructions, including a noisy 19th-century pub and alcohol-monopoly stores from 1907 to 1991.

Although the text on the displays is in Swedish, there's a detailed hand-out in English. Bookings of tours at other times *(9am-5pm Mon-Fri, minimum 5 people, Skr20 per person)* can be made by calling ☎ 789 3642.

NATIONAL MUSEUM

The National Museum **(Map 6, G9, #200)** *(☎ 519 54300, W www.nationalmuseum.se, Södra Blasieholmshamnen; Skr75/free, students Skr60; open 11am-5pm Tues-Sun, closed 8pm every Tues & 8pm Thur, Sept-Dec)* is Sweden's largest art museum and has the main national collection of painting, sculpture, drawings, decorative arts and graphics, ranging from the Middle Ages to the 20th century. Some of the art became state property on the death of Gustav III in 1792, making this one of the earliest public museums in the world.

The **staircase frescoes** by Carl Larsson include the notable *Gustav Vasa riding into Stockholm* and, on the opposite wall, the highly controversial *Midwinter Sacrifice.*

Currently, there are around 16,000 paintings and sculptures on display, including magnificent works by artists such as Cézanne, Goya, Rembrandt and Rubens. The collection of 18th-century art is among the finest in the world. Design 19002000 describes the history of Swedish design and exhibits feature furniture and glassware. There are around 30,000 items of decorative artwork in the museum, including porcelain, silverware and late-medieval tapestries.

The museum regularly hosts large temporary exhibitions, including topics relating to fine art and architecture. There's also an excellent museum shop and a pleasant cafe.

SKEPPSHOLMEN

Across the bridge on Skeppsholmen, up on the hill and by the church, **Östasiatiska Museet (Map 7, A7, #50)** *(Museum of Far Eastern Antiquities; ☎ 519 55750, W www .mfea.se; Skr50/free under 20; open noon-5pm Tues-Sun, closing 8pm Tues)* displays ancient and contemporary ceramics, paintings and sculpture in temporary and permanent exhibitions. The museum has one of the best collections of Chinese art, stoneware and porcelain in the world (mainly from the Song, Ming and Qing dynasties). There's also a fine exhibit of Hindu and Buddhist sculptures.

Nearby are **Moderna Museet (Map 7, B8, #51)** *(☎ 519 55200, W www.modernamuseet .se, Exercisplan 4; Skr75/free under 16, Skr50 student; open 11am-8pm Tues-Thur & 11am-6pm Fri-Sun)* and the adjoining **Arkitekturmuseet (Map 7, B8, #51)** *(Museum of Architecture; ☎ 587 27000, W www .arkitekturmuseet.se, Exercisplan 4; Skr60/ free under 16, Skr30 student; open same hours as Moderna Museet).* Moderna Museet features a basically pretentious collection of modern art, including paintings, sculpture and photographs; until there's a major improvement in standards, it isn't worth your time or money. However, Arkitekturmuseet is much more interesting. It's in an extraordinary building and has displays on Swedish and international architecture, with a permanent exhibition covering 1000 years of Swedish architecture, from cabins to castles, and an archive of 2.5 million documents, photographs, plans, drawings and models. There's also a seasonal program of temporary exhibitions and the museum arranges seminars (in Swedish; Skr50/20 adult/student) and architectural walks (Skr60).

Bird's-eye view of the picturesque Gamla Stan (Old Town), surrounded by Lake Mälaren

CHRISTOPHER WOOD

Gamla Stan's Tyska Kyrkan, dating from the 1570s

GRAEME CORNWALLIS

South tower of Wrangelska palats, Gamla Stan

Kungliga Slottet, with 608 rooms, is the world's largest royal palace still used for its original purpose.

A royal guard doing his job at Kungliga Slottet

Side view of Riksdagshuset (parliament building)

Also on Skeppsholmen is the **Svensk Form Designcenter (Map 7, C8, #45)** *(Swedish Society of Crafts & Design; ☎ 463 3136, W www.svenskform.se, Holmamiralens väg 2; Skr20/free; open noon-7pm Tues-Thur & noon-5pm Fri-Sun)* which features temporary exhibitions on Swedish and international design and has a bookshop and sales outlet.

MARIONETTMUSEET
The friendly and privately funded Marionettmuseet **(Map 6, B6, #36)** *(Puppet Theatre Museum; ☎ 103061, Brunnsgatan 6; Skr30/15; open 1pm-4pm Tues-Sun, closed Mon)* covers both Swedish and international puppet theatre. There's a lot to see, including anatomically correct Burmese puppets, horsemen and elephants from India, wild-looking red-faced puppets from Indonesia, and some magnificent Nepalese puppets. An English-language CD tour costs an extra Skr15.

Marionetteatern (Puppet Theatre), in the same building, puts on regular shows from mid-September to late April. Family shows (50 minutes) cost Skr65 per person but there is also more adult puppet entertainment (one hour; Swedish language) on some weekends for Skr130/100 adult/student. Contact the museum for details and tickets.

KONSERTHUSET
The design competition for the neoclassical and Art Deco Konserthuset **(Map 6, C4, #101)** *(☎ 786 0200, W www.konserthuset.se, Hötorget 8; Skr30; open for 1-hr tours in Swedish 11.30am Sat once per month Sept-May)* was won by Ivar Tengbom. Although it was completed in 1926, the main hall was rebuilt in the 1970s to improve the acoustics (but it lost its illusion of depth). The blue-coloured facade, with 10 enormous classical columns, belies a fairly mundane interior. However, the excellent neo-Renaissance, palatial-style smaller hall has renowned murals and ceiling paintings by the famous Swedish artist Isaac Grünewald. The statues in the entrance hall and the sculpture of Orpheus with his lyre (in Hötorget) are by Carl Milles.

STRINDBERGSMUSEET
Strindbergsmuseet **(Map 6, A2, #5)** *(☎ 411 5354, W www.strindbergsmuseet.se, Drottninggatan 85; Skr35/25/free adult/student/child under 16; open noon-4pm Tues-Sun, closed Mon, also until 7pm Tues, Sept-May)* is in the preserved apartment where August Strindberg spent his final four years. You'll see his dining room, bedroom, study and interesting library. On the table in the study, you'll see Strindberg's spectacles. All objects on display in the museum are liable to change but, at the time of research, they included Strindberg's camera, flute, guitar, some of his paintings, program sheets from his time as a director, and a copy of his **Ockulta Dagboken** diary (1896–1908). See also the boxed text 'August Strindberg'.

APOTEKSMUSEET
This low-profile museum **(Map 6, B2, #13)** *(Pharmacy Museum; ☎ 723 5000, Wallingatan 26A; Skr500 for group of 10, Stockholm Card not valid; open by arrangement)*, in the Swedish Academy of Pharmaceutical Sciences building, is well worth a visit if you can get at least 10 people together. Much of the enjoyment arises from the entertaining explanations given during the 90-minute guided tour in English. The museum describes the history of pharmacy, from primitive potions to modern medicine and includes collections of pharmacy signs and mixing jars, laboratory equipment for drug preparation, reconstructions of pharmacies and an exhibit about the famous Swedish chemist CW Scheele. There's also a display about Astra Pharmaceuticals, the Swedish company that marketed Losec, a drug that helped cure stomach ulcers around the world.

POLISHISTORISKA MUSEET
Although it's another relatively unknown museum, Polishistoriska Museet **(Map 3, F4, #50)** *(Police History Museum; ☎ 401 9053, Polhemsgatan 30, Kungsholmen; Skr500 for groups of 10, then Skr50 per extra person, Stockholm Card not valid, minimum age 16; open by appointment)* has

August Strindberg

August Strindberg was born in Stockholm in 1849, but his mother died when he was 13 and the stage was set for the chaotic life of this tortured genius who was eventually hailed as the 'writer of the people'.

Strindberg periodically studied theology and medicine at Uppsala University from 1867 to 1872, but left without a degree. He then worked as a librarian and journalist prior to becoming a productive author, writing novels, plays, poetry and over 7000 letters. He was also a talented painter of moody scenes.

His breakthrough as a writer came in 1879 with publication of the novel *The Red Room*. In 1884, Strindberg became notorious after publication of *Marriage*, a collection of short stories which led to his trial (and acquittal) for blasphemy in the City Court of Stockholm. Much of his work deals with radical approaches to social issues and it didn't go down well with the conservative Swedish establishment. In *Miss Julie* (1888), Strindberg's most frequently performed play, a count's daughter seduces her valet on Midsummer's Eve, but she's wracked with guilt and commits suicide the next day.

Strindberg married three times, but each marriage ended in divorce. His first wife was Siri von Essen (married 1877, divorced 1891) and they had four children. During his stay in Central Europe (1892–99), he led an 'artist life' with people such as Edvard Munch and Gaughin and also had a short-lived marriage to the Austrian Frida Uhl (married 1893, separated 1894, dissolved 1897), which led to the birth of a daughter. As his instability deepened, Strindberg took an interest in the occult, but the crisis was over on publication of *Inferno* (1897), an accurate description of his own emotional shambles. After returning to Stockholm in 1899, he married the Norwegian Harriet Bosse in 1901 (divorced 1904) and had yet another daughter.

His work *Dance of Death* (1900) features an old couple who live on an isolated island. They celebrate their silver jubilee but have always hated each other. In *A Dreamplay* (1901), the daughter of the god Indira visits Earth to find out how people are getting along and finds out how hard human life is.

In 1912, Strindberg was awarded an 'Anti-Nobel Prize' (funded by ordinary people from around Sweden) as compensation for not receiving the Nobel Prize for Literature. Although the conservative Swedish Academy basically ignored his work, Strindberg was appreciated by many Swedes and his death, in 1912, was seen as the loss of the country's greatest writer.

some of the finest and most unusual exhibits in the city and it's well worth getting a group together for a visit.

You'll see displays covering police history from the 1720s, including spies, forgery, fingerprinting, uniforms, illegal stills and insurance swindles. However, the most extraordinary exhibits include events connected to the **terrorist attack on the West German Embassy** in 1975 (look out for pages from the Red Army Faction terrorist handbook) and the **murder room**, which covers some particularly disturbing crimes. There's also a reconstruction of a **bank vault** as it was during a bizarre five-day robbery and siege at Norrmalmstorg in 1973. When the police used tear gas to clear out the robber, his accomplice and the four

hostages, the hostages sided with the robber in the first known case of what's now called 'The Stockholm Syndrome'.

TULLMUSEET

Tullmuseet **(Map 3, E3, #30)** *(Customs Museum;* ☎ *653 0503, Alströmergatan 39, Kungsholmen; Skr40/free, Stockholm Card not valid; open 11am-4pm Tues-Sun)* explains the history behind Stockholm's inland customs stations (Skanstull, Hornstull, Norrtull and Roslagstull), which operated from 1622 to 1810 and taxed agricultural goods. There's also a section on the coast guard service and a reconstruction of a 1920s customs warehouse and office. The main part of the exhibition deals with **smuggling** of animals, alcohol, guns, cigarettes and drugs, and how it has been controlled. Some of the dioramas are rather startling! Unfortunately, the exhibits are only described in Swedish, but there is a little leaflet with some English text.

The attached restaurant serves a weekday lunch (10.30am to 1.30pm) for Skr58.

STOCKHOLMS LÄNS MUSEUM

Many tourists turn up here expecting a major exhibition, but the museum **(Map 3, D5, #22)** *(Stockholm County Museum; ☎ 690 6960,* **W** *www.lansmuseum.a.se, Sabbatsbergsvägen 6; free; open noon-4pm Tues-Thur & Sun)* consists of only one room. It covers such subjects as archaeology, cultural heritage, history and art and there's a continually changing program of temporary exhibitions.

OBSERVATORIEMUSEET

Gamla observatoriet (the Old Observatory) contains Observatoriemuseet **(Map 4, C1, #22)** *(Observatory Museum; ☎ 315810,* **W** *www.observatoriet.kva.se, Drottninggatan 120; Skr40/20, Stockholm Card not valid; open for 1-hr guided tours in Swedish only at noon, 1pm & 2pm Sat & Sun & 6pm Tues in winter)* with temporary and permanent exhibits. Group tours can be arranged by day or night (from Skr600, plus Skr20 per person, maximum 30 people), but you'll need a fairly big party. A basic leaflet is available in English (free).

The observatory, commissioned by the Royal Swedish Academy of Sciences in 1748, promoted studies of astronomy, geography and meteorology. The museum, open since 1991, includes **Wargentins study**, continuous weather records since 1756, the **old meridian room** with a clock from 1748 and a transit instrument, the **observation room** with three 18th-century telescopes, and the **Vega Room**, with details about Nordenskiöld's journey through the Northeast Passage from 1878 to 1880 (see the boxed text 'Adolf Erik Nordenskiöld').

The Tuesday evening tour is followed by an hour at the telescope, with a chance to observe Saturn's rings, the moons of

---

Adolf Erik Nordenskiöld

The great Swedish explorer and scientist, Adolf Erik Nordenskiöld (1832–1901), is best known for the first successful sailing through the Northeast Passage.

After settling in Stockholm in 1858, Nordenskiöld became curator of mineralogy at Naturhistoriska Riksmuseet and later led a series of successful expeditions to Svalbard, the group of Arctic islands between Norway and the North Pole. In 1870, he visited Greenland, but five years later his interest switched to the east and he sailed as far as the Yenisey River, which flows into the Kara Sea. In 1878, Nordenskiöld's steamship *Vega* sailed from Tromsö in Norway and reached Cape Chelyuskin, the northernmost point of Siberia, just one month later. The ship became trapped in pack ice near the Bering Strait and the crew had to stay the winter there, from September 1878 to July 1879. After the break up of the ice, *Vega* continued to Alaska, then returned to Europe via China, Ceylon (now Sri Lanka) and the Suez Canal.

When the explorers returned to Stockholm in April 1880, they were given a rapturous welcome and Nordenskiöld was created a baron by King Oskar, in recognition of the impressive achievement.

Jupiter etc. There will also be a special opening in 2004 during the transit of Venus across the face of the sun.

JUDISKA MUSEET

The small but very interesting Judiska Museet **(Map 3, C5, #17)** *(Jewish Museum; ☎ 310143, Hälsingegatan 2; Skr40/free under 10, Skr20 students, Stockholm Card not valid; open noon-4pm Sun-Fri)* describes the lives of Swedish Jewry from 1774. Topics covered include Nazi death camps, Raoul Wallenberg, Torah silverware and accessories, ceremonial items relating to the Sabbath and Passover (including a fine collection of silver spice boxes), and a cast featuring the Menorah, a unique seven-branched candlestick which was looted from Jerusalem by the Romans in AD 70. Male visitors may want to look out for the circumcision knives!

Leaflets giving descriptions in English and coffee, tea and biscuits are available.

GUSTAF VASA KYRKA

This magnificent church **(Map 3, C5, #9)** *(☎ 736 0335, Odenplan; free; open 11am-6pm Mon-Thur & 11am-3pm Fri-Sun)* has a **baroque high altar** sculpted in plaster in 1731, a **marble pulpit** and a 60m-high **cupola** with ceiling frescoes. The creepy **columbarium** *(crypt; ☎ 324920; free; open 11am-3pm Wed, Fri-Sun, 11am-6pm Tues & Thur; closed Mon)* has places for around 35,000 burial urns and is entered from the Västmannagatan side of the church.

STOCKHOLMS MINIATYR-MUSEUM

Appealing mainly to kids and families, the Stockholms Miniatyrmuseum **(Map 4, C1, #17)** *(Stockholm Miniature Museum; ☎ 303 403, Ⓦ www.realtimemusic.se /stockholmsminiatyrmuseum, Hagagränd 2; Skr35/20, Stockholm Card not valid; open 10am-4pm Wed-Fri & noon-4pm Sat & Sun)* has numerous mechanical models with scenes from prehistoric times to the Wild West and the futuristic colonisation of a distant planet. There are also exhibits of vintage model cars (including unusual scrap yard collections), a display of 'McDonald's Collectibles', a more typical doll's house (complete with Barbie and friends), and an exhibit of dolls in national costumes from around the world.

VIN & SPRITHISTORISKA MUSEET

Vin & Sprithistoriska Museet **(Map 3, B4, #3)** *(Wine & Spirits History Museum; ☎ 744 7070, Ⓦ www.vinosprithistoriska.a.se, Dalagatan 100; Skr40/free under 12, Skr30 student; open 10am-7pm Tues, 10am-4pm Wed-Fri & noon-4pm Sat & Sun)* sounds eccentric but it helps explain the weird stories behind *brännvin* (snaps), *punsch* (like punch) and the birth of the conservative Swedish alcohol policy. It's housed in

Brännvin Distilleries

In the mid-17th century, after grain took over from wine as the raw material for *brännvin* (also called aquavit), stills were no longer only found in the homes of the rich and most of the population was distilling at home and imbibing the drink on a daily basis. The amounts of alcohol consumed were incredible and state control was only a matter of time. In 1756, there was a temporary ban on home distilling and around 180,000 household stills were confiscated. In 1775, King Gustav III introduced the first of 60 crown distilleries and again made home distilling illegal, but the people defied the law and the last crown distillery was closed in 1824.

In 1830, there were around 175,000 private distilleries in Sweden, but potato-based distillation, which required larger production units, gradually took over and the number of home-based stills dwindled. State control reasserted itself in 1855 and the number of legal distilleries fell to 591 by 1861. In 1910, the distillers amalgamated into one company, which became Vin- och Spritcentralen in 1917. By 1970, only one of the distilleries remained open – Gärdsbränneriet, in Nöbbelöv (Skåne) – the others were closed to maximise efficiency, even the distillery on Reimersholme, which pioneered new techniques back in the 1860s. Rectification (the purifying process) now takes place in Åhus (Skåne) and in Stockholm, but all Vin- och Spritcentralen spiced aquavit is produced in Skåne.

the former headquarters of Vin- och Spritcentralen (from 1920), the former state liquor import monopoly. Look out for bunches of plaster grapes hanging from the eaves.

Among the most interesting exhibits is the multimedia presentation of Swedish drinking habits (available in English); a chilling machine for spiced vodka from the 1890s; a reconstructed wine shop from the 1880s; primitive distillation processes; stills, pumps and the control room from the former Reimersholme distillery; a spice organ with

55 different spices; and a 1920s bottling plant (see the boxed text 'Brännvin Distilleries').

Guided tours are conducted in Swedish at 2pm on Wednesday and Sunday (also at 12.30pm Sunday) and there are occasional historical guided tours where you'll be shown around by staff in fancy dress. There's also an 'educational' wine bar (open regular museum hours). Cheese and wine-tasting evenings take place in summer; contact the museum for details.

The museum is in Vasastaden, north of the centre; take bus No 69 from Sergels Torg or walk from T-Odenplan metro station.

MUSIKMUSEET

Musikmuseet **(Map 6, C9, #76)** (☎ *519 55490,* W *www.musikmuseet.se, Sibylle-gatan 2; Skr40/20; open 11am-4pm Tues-Sun, closed Mon),* in **Kronobageriet** (Crown Bakery), where bread was baked for the admiralty from 1645 to 1958, is a well-presented collection. You can handle and play some of the musical instruments and see original ABBA paraphernalia. The 2nd-floor exhibit, Tutti, has an incredible range of 500 instruments from around the world, from Madagascan zithers to Sami shaman drums. Children enjoy the music workshop in the basement and there are also regular children's activities. Concerts are held in the King's Hall on the 2nd floor up to three times weekly (Skr80 to Skr250).

ARMÉMUSEUM

The newly opened Armémuseum **(Map 6, C9, #66)** (☎ *788 9560,* W *www.armemuseum .org, Riddargatan 13; Skr60/30, conces-sionary rates for Stockholm Card holders; open 11am-8pm Tues & 11am-4pm Wed-Sun)* has graphic depictions of the horrors of war and definitely isn't suitable for chil-dren or people with a nervous disposition. It's an interesting place and it certainly doesn't set out to glorify war – quite the op-posite, in fact. Information sheets in Eng-lish are available from the admission desk.

There are three floors, with medieval and Renaissance times on the top floor. Look out for the grim medieval representation of a city being invaded by an army of skeletons and the rows of human skulls on the floor. The **trophy collection** includes various items seized by Swedish troops from the Danes, Poles and Russians during the 17th- and 18th-century wars. There are fascinating **model armies** and incredibly lifelike **dioramas** of charging horsemen, starving civilians and the frozen corpses left behind by Armfeldt's retreating army at New Year 1719. On the 1st floor, highlights include films of the **Finnish winter war** (1939–40) and a reconstruction of a mid-1960s barracks. The ground floor has a shop with some rather expensive models, a cafeteria, and a display of artillery from a medieval cannon (1400) to the latest laser-guided missile technology.

KUNGLIGA HOVSTALLET

At Kungliga Hovstallet **(Map 6, D9, #69)** *(Royal Mews;* ☎ *402 6000,* W *www .royalcourt.se/hovstallet, Väpnargatan 1; Skr30/10 adult/child under 13; open for 1-hr guided tours in English at 2pm Mon-Fri 25 June-10 Aug, Sat & Sun 11 Aug-16 Dec & 13 Jan-27 May)* you'll see stables, horses, ceremonial coaches, harnesses and uniforms. The current building was com-missioned by King Oskar II in 1894, but Kungliga Hovstallet had been kept in vari-ous quarters around Stockholm since it was founded by Gustav Vasa in 1535. There are now 14 horses, 11 cars, and 40 coaches dating from the mid-19th century to the early-20th century, including the **Seven-Glass coach**, which is used during state visits.

HISTORISKA MUSEET

The main national historical collection is at Historiska Museet **(Map 4, E5, #65)** (☎ *519 55600,* W *www.historiska.se, Nar-vavägen 13; metro T-Karlaplan; Skr60/free under 13; open 10am-5pm daily 15 May-14 Sept, otherwise 11am-5pm Tues-Sun, closing 8pm Thur).* It covers nearly 14,000 years of Swedish history and culture (up to 1520), including arrowheads from around 12,000 BC, the oldest skeleton found in Sweden (8730 years old) and archaeological finds from the Viking town, Birka. There's also a of a Stone Age cult community, which lived in a swamp 3000 years ago.

Don't miss the incredible **Gold Room** in the basement, with its rare treasures in gold, silver and iron. The most astonishing artefact is the 5th-century seven-ringed gold collar with 458 carved figures, which weighs 823g. It was found in Västergötland in the 19th century and was probably used by pagan priests in ritualistic ceremonies.

Also, look out for the medieval triptychs, altar screens and textiles (including a 15th-century coffin pall and the 11th-century Kyrkås coverlet) on the 1st floor. The Iron Age exhibit has a pair of cowbone ice skates and a **picture stone** from Gotland. A new Viking Age exhibition opened in 2001, but don't look for helmets with horns – they didn't exist. The excellent Web site includes a virtual tour of the museum.

OTHER ATTRACTIONS

The **Royal Mint (Map 6, G1, #139)**, at the junction of Hantverkargatan and Samuel Owens Gatan, is housed in the former Samuel Owens foundry and engineering workshop from 1809. It isn't open to the public, but the spectacular gateway is worth a look. The Stockholm County Council meets in **Landstingshuset (Map 3, F4, #55)** *(Hantverkargatan 45; not open to the public)*, formerly the military hospital Garnisonssjukhuset (1816–34) and extended in 1970. This neoclassical building, featuring a temple-style gable, large columns and a south-facing external semicircular staircase with a double stair and cornice, is quite distinctive.

Karlbergs Slott (Map 3, D2, #29) *(☎ 562 81305, Karlbergsstrand; open to groups only, by arrangement)* was commissioned by Magnus Gabriel de la Gardie in the 1670s and swallowed up a smaller early-17th-century building. This substantial palace was extended in the 18th century and became a training school for military officers. Take bus No 42 or 72 to Karlsbergs station, then walk 500m.

In 1923, the cinema **Biografen Skandia (Map 6, B3, #19)** *(Drottninggatan 82)* was added to Warodellska House, one of the earliest apartment buildings in Stockholm (1850s). The interior is noted for its spectacular classical style, including an ornate balcony and a row of excellently preserved doors. At the time of writing, the cinema was closed. Formerly Stockholm University's Law and Humanities faculties building before the move to Frescati in the 1960s, **Juridicum (Map 4, C1, #19)** *(Norrtullsgatan 2-6; not open to the public)* is another spectacular neoclassical building with red walls and a temple-style gable.

Dramatiska teatern (Map 6, D8, #75) *(☎ 665 6100, Nybroplan; Skr40; guided tours in English 3pm Sat, July & Aug)* has impressive marble halls and stairways, gilded stucco, and wonderful painted ceilings in the theatre restaurant. Some of the interior can be seen without taking the tour and it's well worth a look.

The impressive **Östermalms saluhall (Map 6, B9, #54)** *(Nybrogatan 26-28, Östermalmstorg; free; open 9.30am-6pm Mon-Thur, 9.30am-6.30pm Fri, 9.30am-4pm Sat, 2pm Sat in summer)* is constructed of brick on a cast-iron frame, with turrets and pinnacles, vaulted windows and considerable decorative detail. It was completed in 1889 and is still used for its original purpose as a market hall. Inside, you'll find lots of shops selling meat, fish, cheese, fruit, vegetables and traditional Swedish foods. There are also several restaurants.

Djurgården

No serious traveller should miss the Royal Park and its museums. The main attractions are Skansen and the extraordinary Vasamuseet (one of the world's top tourist destinations), but there are many other interesting places to visit in the park.

Cycling is the best way to get around Djurgården, but if you're just visiting for the attractions, take bus No 47 from Centralstationen at Vasagatan, or the summer Djurgården ferry services from Nybroplan, Skeppsholmen or Slussen. You can also go by vintage tram from Norrmalmstorg.

Parking is limited during the week and prohibited on summer weekends, when Djurgårdsvägen is closed to traffic.

SKANSEN

Skansen **(Map 4, G7, #86)** (☎ *442 8000,* **e** *info@skansen.se,* **w** *www.skansen.se; Skr30/20-Skr60/30, 50% discount with 72-hr SL Tourist Pass; open 10am-10pm daily June-Aug, 10am-8pm May, 10am-5pm Sept & 10am-4pm Oct-Apr),* the world's first open-air museum, was founded in 1891 by Artur Hazelius to let visitors see how Swedes lived in previous times. Skansen organises many special events throughout the year (see the Special Events section in the Facts for the Visitor chapter for details). A map (Skr5) and an excellent 24-page booklet (Skr30) are available (in English and other languages) to guide you around.

Today, around 150 traditional houses (inhabited by staff in period costume) and other exhibits from all over Sweden occupy this attractive hill top. It's a spectacular 'Sweden in miniature' and you could spend all day here; most buildings are open 11am to 5pm (or later) daily from May to September but at other times of year, only a few buildings are open 11am to 3pm daily. There are 46 buildings from rural areas around the country, including a Sami camp (with reindeer), farmsteads representing several regions, a manor house and a school.

The **Bergbana** mountain railway **(Map 4, F6, #92)** *(Skr20/free under 6)* climbs from the Hazelius (northern) entrance to the top of the hill. Near the upper station, look out for the **Forestry Information Centre (Map 4, F7, #89)** and **Älvros Gården**, a quaint farmstead arranged around a courtyard. Nearby, there's a small pine wood and a spectacularly-painted **rune stone**. Look out for the daily activities that take place on Skansen's stages, including **folk dancing** at 7pm on weekdays and 2.30pm and 4pm on Sunday from June to August. The church **Seglora kyrka (Map 4, G7, #81)** is located almost at the geographic centre of Skansen. **Skogaholms Herrgård (Map 4, G7, #82)** is a manor house brought to Skansen from

Närke, west of Stockholm. The excellent **Town Quarters**, consisting mostly of buildings from Södermalm, include a pharmacy, bakery, bank, cafe, many types of workshops, summer houses, Charles Tottie's summer residence and Hazelius' mansion.

The eastern edge of Skansen has a rather good **zoo** with Nordic animals in a reasonably natural environment, including lynx, bears, elk, wolves and wolverines. The aquatic section has otters and seals. Feeding time is at 2pm daily. Next to the zoo, you can climb the **Bredablick Tower (Map 4, F7, #80)** for a great view and enjoy a coffee and a sandwich in the cafe.

Trace the unhealthy history of smoking on three floors at the **Tobacco & Match Museum**. This fascinating building, near the main southern entrance to Skansen, was built in 1816 and moved to its current location in 1864. It contains a working tobacco factory, an extensive matchbox collection (including the bizarre Kali Safety Match box, which shows a beheading) and a display of some of the 300,000 clay pipes found at Slussen in 1984.

The **Skansen Aquarium** *(☎ 660 1082; Skr60/30 supplementary admission fee; open 10am-4pm Mon-Fri, closing 6pm in June & Aug, closing 1 hr later Sat & Sun 7 & 8pm daily in July)* is also a must. En route to the fish (including piranhas and sharks) you'll walk among the lemurs, snakes, spiders and bats, and see pygmy marmosets, the smallest monkeys in the world. The display of rats running around a house is also quite memorable.

There are several places to eat around Skansen, from small cafes to full-blown restaurants.

NORDISKA MUSEET

Nordiska museet **(Map 4, F6, #94)** *(National Museum of Cultural History; ☎ 519 56000,* **w** *www.nordm.se, Djurgårdsvägen 6-16; Skr60/20; open 10am-8pm Tues & Thur, 10am-5pm Wed & Fri-Sun)* was also founded by Artur Hazelius. At 126.5m long and 24m high, the museum is the second largest indoor space in Sweden and it's housed in an enormous, eclectic, four-storey

Renaissance-style castle. The gigantic seated statue of Gustav Vasa, in the Great Hall, was created by Carl Milles. Guided tours in English (no extra charge) run at 1.30pm daily except Monday in summer. There are also architectural tours of the building at 11am in summer.

There are notable temporary exhibitions (changing annually) and endless Swedish collections from 1520 to the present day, with a total of 1.5 million items. Information is available in English, either in leaflet form, on the exhibit information plaques, or from free CD-players (which have several hours of English commentary).

Of greatest interest is the superb **Sami exhibition** in the basement, which includes a shaman's drum and an extraordinary 1767 drawing of a rather cool-looking reindeer being castrated by a Sami using his teeth! The **Strindberg painting exhibition** indicates the depth of this man's tortured soul and the intriguing 'small object exhibition' includes previously ordinary items that have now become rare and valuable. On the 4th-floor gallery, the **Swedish Home** exhibition allows a peek into the lives of both rich and poor in times past. Other exhibitions include fashion from the 17th to 20th centuries, the 'table settings' exhibition (running continuously since 1955), Swedish traditions and national costume, and furniture.

The museum cafe serves *dagens rätt* (daily special) for Skr70. There's also a book and souvenir shop.

VASAMUSEET

The professionally run Vasamuseet **(Map 4, F5, #96)** *(Vasa Museum;* ☎ *519 54800, Galärvarvsvägen 14,* e *vasamuseet@sshm .se,* w *www.vasamuseet.se; Skr70/40/10 adult/student/child, Skr50 adult after 5pm Wed; open 9.30am-7pm daily 10 June-20 Aug, otherwise 10am-5pm & closing 8pm Wed)*, behind Nordiska museet on the western shore of Djurgården, allows you simultaneously to look into the lives of 17th-century sailors and to appreciate a brilliant achievement in marine archaeology. You'll need around 1½ hours to appreciate this amazing place. Guided tours in English run

hourly from 10.30am in summer and at least twice daily at other times (25 minutes).

On 10 August 1628, the 69m-long top-heavy flagship *Vasa* overturned and went straight to the bottom of the Saltsjön within minutes of being launched. Tour guides will explain the extraordinary and controversial 300-year story of its death and resurrection. After being raised in 1961, the incredible wooden sculptures on the ship were pieced together like a giant 14,000-piece jigsaw and almost all of what you see today is original.

On the entrance level, there's a model of the ship at scale 1:10 and a cinema that shows a 25-minute film, covering topics not included in the exhibitions (it's screened in English at 11.30am and 1.30pm daily, 1 June to 31 August). There are three other levels of exhibits, including temporary exhibitions (two or three yearly), life on board (displays of artefacts salvaged from the *Vasa*), naval warfare, the sculptures, and 17th-century sailing and navigation.

Light levels are kept low and there are strict controls on temperature and humidity to protect the ship. On-going research is looking into the original colours – the *Vasa* was probably brightly painted.

The bookshop is worth a visit and there's also a restaurant, noted for its 17th-century-style foods, including *mejramkorv* (herb-flavoured sausage). An excellent *kanonkula* (heavy chocolate cannonball) and coffee costs Skr40.

Just outside the museum, there's a walkway to two more modern ships, **Museifartygen** *(Museum Ships; separate admission fee Skr30/10; open noon-5pm daily 9 June-31 Aug, closing 7pm 30 June-19 Aug)*. The vessels are Sweden's first sea-going icebreaker *Sankt Erik* (launched in 1915) and the characteristic red-and-white lightship *Finngrundet* (1903), which had a crew of eight until decommissioning in 1969.

JUNIBACKEN

Junibacken **(Map 4, F5, #95)** *(*☎ *587 23000, Galärparken; Skr85/60 adult/child aged 3-15; open 9am-6pm daily June-Aug, otherwise 10am-5pm Tues-Sun)* recreates the fantasy scenes of Astrid Lindgren's children's books, which will stir the imaginations of children and the memories of adults familiar with her characters. You'll go on a 10-minute train journey past miniature landscapes, you'll fly over Stockholm, observe Swedish historical scenes and traditions, and pass through houses. It's a very professional and rather unusual form of entertainment. In Villekulla cottage, kids can shout and squeal and dress up like Pippi (complete with wigs!). The average age of visiting children is around five years.

The Stockholm Card allows Skr20 discount from 9am to 11am June to August and 10am to noon September to May. There's also a cafe and a well-stocked children's bookshop.

GRÖNA LUND

The crowded Gröna Lund Tivoli (Map 4, G6, #104) (☎ 587 50100, W www.gronalund .com; Skr45/free under 7, free with 72-hr SL Tourist Pass; open varying hours: noon, 3pm or 5pm-8pm, 11pm or midnight most days from 28 Apr-2 Sept) fun park has 28 rides, ranging from the easy circus carousel to the terrifying 'Free Fall', where you drop from a height of 80m in two seconds, and 'Extreme', where you get whirled around and subjected to high G-forces. The new ride for 2001 is 'Drop 'n Shot', where you're shot 60m upwards at 3.5G, then downwards at -1G! There are lots of places to eat and drink in the park, but whether you could keep anything down is another matter.

All rides except the Haunted House (Skr25) are covered by Gröna Lund's ride coupon scheme (Skr10 per coupon); individual rides range from one to four coupons each. The Grönakortet season pass gives free admission to the park (Skr100). There are lots of easy rides for small children but some of the other rides have minimum height restrictions.

PRINS EUGENS WALDEMAR-SUDDE

Prins Eugens Waldemarsudde (Map 2, D7, #25) (☎ 545 83700, W www.waldemar sudde.com, Prins Eugens väg 6; Skr45/ free; open 11am-5pm Tues-Sun but closing at 8pm Thur May-Aug, otherwise 11am-4pm Tues-Sun but closing 8pm Thur & 5pm Sat & Sun), at the southern tip of Djurgården, was the private palace of the painter-prince who preferred art to royal pleasures.

The palace now holds his large collection of Nordic art, including fine works by Zorn and Larsson and some rather good oil paintings of landscapes in Sweden and Italy by the prince himself. The downstairs furnishings are quite impressive and the buildings, including an old windmill, are surrounded by picturesque gardens. However, some security guards look fierce and they follow you around; it's most disconcerting. After extensive renovations, the palace will reopen in October 2001.

ROSENDALS SLOTT

On the northern side of Djurgården, the prefabricated wooden palace Rosendals Slott (Map 4, F9, #78) (☎ 402 6130, W www .royalcourt.se, Rosendalsvägen; Skr50/25; guided tours in English hourly, noon-3pm Tues-Sun 15 May-31 Aug, Sat & Sun Sept) was built as a retreat for Karl XIV Johan and his family in the 1820s. It features sumptuous, typically royal furnishings and is the finest example in the city of the so-called Empire style. The furnishings from Karl XIV Johan's bed chamber at Kungliga Slott were moved to Rosendals Slott in the 20th century to make this palace museum more complete. Take bus No 47 from Centralstationen to the Djurgården terminus, then walk 700m.

THIELSKA GALLERIET

At the eastern end of Djurgården you'll find Thielska Galleriet (Map 2, D8, #24) (☎ 662 5884, Sjötullsbacken 6; Skr50/free, Skr30 student, Stockholm Card not valid; open noon-4pm Mon-Sat, 1pm-4pm Sun). It was purpose-built for the tycoon Ernest Thiel, who patronised the arts, and was completed in 1907. It now contains Thiel's notable collection of late-19th- and early-20th-century Nordic art on three floors, including Anders Zorn's portraits and nudes, Carl Larsson's portraits, Bruno Liljefors' excellent wildlife paintings and August

Strindberg's wild landscapes. Unfortunately, some staff members need retraining in dealing with the public and the cafe looks like a public toilet.

From the grounds, you can watch huge ferries sailing by. About 400m east of the gallery, at Blockhusudden, there's **Stora Sjötullen**, a former customs station from 1727, which kept an eye on ships sailing into the harbour. To reach the gallery, take bus No 69 from Centralstationen.

LILJEVALCHS KONSTHALL

Liljevalchs konsthall **(Map 4, G6, #101)** *(Liljevalchs Art Gallery; ☎ 508 31330, Djurgårdsvägen 60; Skr50/free; open 11am-5pm Wed & Fri-Sun, 11am-8pm Tues & Thur, closed Mon)* is a marvellous building which is the result of a competition in 1913. It's partly neoclassical, with cast-iron pillars on the south-facing facade. The statues by the entrance (an archer and wolves) are by Carl Milles. The main hall has interesting windows placed high up, allowing natural light to illuminate the contents to best advantage.

The gallery covers 20th-century international art in temporary exhibitions of video, photography, painting, sculpture, drawings and etchings. There are four to six major exhibitions per year. Every year in February and March there's an art show where everything is for sale. Guided tours (in Swedish) start at 2pm, daily except Monday.

AQUARIA VATTENMUSEUM

The excellent Aquaria Vattenmuseum **(Map 4, G6, #100)** *(Aquaria Water Museum; ☎ 660 4940, Falkenbergsgatan 2; Skr55/25; open 10am-6pm daily 15 June-15 Aug, otherwise 10am-4.30pm Tues-Sun, closed Mon)* has a waterfall on either side of its entrance. The museum features a hot and steamy tropical forest complete with thunderstorm, rain torrents and a bridge over a pool of piranhas. You'll also see huge red-tail catfish, mudskippers (which come out of the water) and a colourful coral reef. There's a sewer you can explore, a mountain pool with trout and arctic char, and a salmon ladder where wild Baltic salmon

come-and-go between the museum and the sea. The cafe offers fine views and serves meals and snacks.

BIOLOGISKAMUSEET

The design of **Biologiskamuseet (Map 4, F6, #93)** *(Museum of Biology; ☎ 442 8215, Hazeliusporten; Skr20/10; open 10am-4pm daily Apr-Sept, otherwise 10am-3pm Tues-Sun)* is based on Norwegian stave churches, but the double spiral staircase is curiously reminiscent of DNA. Admission is included in the price of Skansen admission, but you must visit Biologiskamuseet first. There are two dioramas of stuffed creatures – High Arctic wildlife and Swedish wildlife. The latter is illuminated by natural light. Look out for the amusing **skvader**, a stuffed combination of a capercaillie hen and a mountain hare.

Ladugårdsgärdet

North of Djurgården is a huge open paddock for the royal sheep, but the museums are considerably more interesting. Ladugårdsgärdet is part of Ekoparken (W www.ekoparken.com), the first National City Park in the world. Ekoparken is 14km long and stretches from the Fjäderholmarna islands all the way to Ulriksdal, in the northern suburbs of Stockholm (see Northern Suburbs later in this chapter).

Take bus No 69 from Centralstationen or Sergels Torg for the attractions covered in this section.

SJÖHISTORISKA MUSEET

Sjöhistoriska Museet **(Map 4, E8, #74)** *(National Maritime Museum; ☎ 519 55000, W www.sjohistoriska.nu, Djurgårdsbrunnsvägen 24; Skr50/20, free under 7; open 10am-5pm daily, closing 8.30pm Tues Feb-Apr & Sept-Nov)* has extensive exhibits of maritime memorabilia. It's in a beautiful curved neoclassical building with a round central tower and a copper roof, purpose-built and opened in 1935. Information in English is available on plastic-coated cards.

There are over 1500 model ships, including Swedish boats from AD 300, ferries, freighters, liners, sailing ships, naval vessels, tankers and tugs. The oldest model ship dates from the mid-17th century (the votive ship *Solen* was built in Lübeck in 1669) but the most extraordinary model is the fantasy galleon which bristles with cannons. There's also a model oil rig, a lighthouse and full-size reconstructions of living quarters on board a freighter and a barquentine, the *Hoppet*.

Other displays in the museum cover Swedish shipbuilding, the Swedish navy, the Karlskrona naval base, sailors and pleasure cruising. There are many full-size boats in the museum, from canoes to motor boats and yachts, and unusual collections of anchors, figureheads and outboard motors. Look out for the excellent model of Södra Varvet in Södermalm, showing shipbuilding in progress in 1781.

As well as the permanent exhibit, there's usually a temporary exhibition. There's also a kids' playroom, a shop and a cafe on site. Drivers should note that the car park costs Skr7/15 for one/three hours.

TEKNISKA MUSEET, TEKNORAMA SCIENCE CENTRE & TELEMUSEUM

The vast Tekniska Museet & Teknorama Science Centre **(Map 4, E9, #75)** *(Museum of Science & Technology;* ☎ *450 5600,* W *www.tekmu.se, Museivägen 7; Skr50/20; open 10am-5pm Mon-Fri, until 9pm Wed, 11am-5pm Sat & Sun)* is just around the corner from Sjöhistoriska Museet and you'll need at least two hours to appreciate it. There are exhaustive exhibits on technology, machinery and transport, including Swedish inventions and their applications. Information sheets are available in English. Telemuseum, part of the same complex, keeps the same hours and admission is included with the Tekniska Museet ticket. There's a cafe and a museum shop in the complex.

Tekniska Museet

The **machinery hall** is packed with cars, bicycles, motorcycles and aircraft, including the first motor car in Sweden from 1897.

There's also a fascinating **steam-powered fire engine** from 1878. Downstairs in the artificial mine **Ferrum** you'll see mining dioramas, read about the miners' strike in 1969, and find out about mining in Sweden today. The smelting and uses of steel exhibit could be better.

The older upstairs exhibits (on Levels 3 and 4) include engineering, a **Foucalt pendulum**, Swedish domestic technology, the uses of timber and the development of chemistry. Also on Level 4, there's a handmade Swedish **model railway**, which runs at 1pm daily and at noon and 3pm on weekends and features typical trains from the 1950s.

At the far end of the southern corridor, you'll find the interesting **history of electric power** exhibition. It covers magnetism, transformers, generators, motors, trains, lifts and trams. There's a section on the developer of the **voltaic pile**, Alessandro Volta. There are displays about the development of power stations and excellent reconstructions of rooms with early electric light apparatus.

The **Wallenberg Hall**, in the centre of the museum complex, has large temporary exhibitions which are usually on show for about a year.

Teknorama Science Centre

The Teknorama Science Centre (at the rear of the complex) has 'hands-on' displays and activities for everyone, especially children. The Discover-Investigate-Experience section presents the basic principles of physics to the kids in an entertaining fashion using a huge seesaw, a chute and a hot air balloon. Adults will enjoy using TV cameras to record their own show or winding-up an old-fashioned telephone.

Telemuseum

The two-storey Telemuseum **(Map 4, E9, #75)** *(Telecommunications Museum;* ☎ *670 8100)* is within the complex and covers radio, television, the telegraph and telephone. In the centre of the museum, there's a two-floor reconstruction of a lavishly decorated part of the **LM Ericsson & Co** telephone factory (for more about the company,

LM Ericsson & Co

Lars Magnus Ericsson was born in a rural area of western Sweden in 1847. After working as an unskilled labourer, he was taken on by a telegraph workshop at the age of 20. The director recognised Ericsson's potential and sent him to Germany and Switzerland for 2½ years training.

After returning to Sweden, Ericsson founded the LM Ericsson & Co electrical engineering workshop in 1876. Soon afterwards, he started designing and manufacturing telephones and the first models were sold in November 1878. Although the American Bell Company set up the first Swedish phone network only two years later, Ericsson set up a rival network and, in 1883, he cooperated with the newly founded Stockholm Telephone Company by providing them with their first cord-operated telephone exchange. Ericsson became the main supplier to the Stockholm Telephone Company and his business expanded rapidly once the high quality and superior design of his products became widely known.

From 1884, the Ericsson factory was located in Tulegatan in Stockholm; the LM Ericsson memorial room in the Telemuseum was originally an exhibition room at this factory. By the 1890s, Ericsson had 500 staff and the company had many foreign customers and even a few foreign subsidiaries. The company expanded steadily throughout the 20th century and moved into the mobile phone market in the 1980s. Now renamed Ericsson, it's a world leader in telecommunications and mobile Internet technology, with over 23,000 research and development engineers and technicians worldwide and markets in over 140 countries.

see the boxed text). There's also a reconstruction of a radio studio from the 1930s. The LM Ericsson & Co stand from the 1897 Stockholm Exhibition, the display of telephone receivers from 1880 to the present and the telegraph station from 1853 are particularly worth seeing.

The small coffee shop has several Apple Mac computers offering 20 minutes of free Internet access.

FOLKENS MUSEUM ETNOGRAFISKA

The excellent Folkens Museum Etnografiska (Map 4, E9, #76) (National Museum of Ethnography; ☎ 519 55000, Djurgårdsbrunnsvägen 34; Skr50/10; open 11am-5pm Tues & Thur-Sun, 11am-8pm Wed, closed Mon) covers non-European races and cultures and has interesting temporary exhibitions.

There's a large exhibition about native North Americans, which includes fine examples of Pueblo ceramics, baskets, Navajo carpets, and extraordinary **dance masks**. Among the Asian collections from the explorer Sven Hedin there's a **Mongolian tent** with an exquisite interior. You'll see some interesting masks from Africa (look out for the crocodile mask from Mali) and displays about the Inuit people in Greenland, including a polar bear suit. On the ground floor, there's a section about the religious cities of the world.

In the grounds of the museum there's a **Japanese tea house**, open at 5.30pm on Wednesday and Sunday afternoons. There's also an **ethnographic workshop** (contact the museum for details), a museum shop (with lots of Swedish and ethnic music), and a restaurant which serves food from around the world. Guided tours are available (in Swedish) at 2pm on Sunday.

KAKNÄSTORNET

About 500m from the museums is the 155m-high Kaknästornet (Map 4, D10, #77) (Kaknäs Tower; ☎ 789 2435, Mörka kroken; Skr25/15 lift fee, free with 72-hr SL Tourist Pass; open 9am-10pm daily May-Aug, otherwise 10am-9pm), opened in 1967 and still the tallest building in the city. It's the automatic operations centre for radio and TV broadcasting in Sweden. The upper floors have two square plans aligned at 45 degrees to each other, creating a startling star shape at the top of the tower. This is where you'll find an observation deck and a restaurant, but the tourist office on the ground floor has been closed. The restaurant windows are made from gold-coated glass, which reflects 75% of the sun's heat.

Södermalm & Långholmen

Mostly residential, Södermalm also has more character than other parts of Stockholm. However, things are beginning to change here, with the arrival of trendy overspill from Östermalm. For evening walks, head to the northern cliffs for the old houses and good views; see also the Walking Tours special section.

KATARINAHISSEN
You'll also get great views from Katarinahissen **(Map 7, F5, #80)** *(☎ 743 1395, Slussen; Skr5/free; open 7.30am-10pm Mon-Sat, 10am-10pm Sun)*, a lift dating from 1936 and replacing a previous lift from 1881, which takes you up 38m to the magnificently located Gondolen restaurant and the heights of Slussen. The lift inside the adjacent Cooperative Association office building is free and takes you to the other end of the elevated 'bridge'.

STOCKHOLMS STADSMUSEUM
Stockholms Stadsmuseum **(Map 7, F4, #84)** *(Stockholm City Museum; ☎ 508 31600, W www.stadsmuseum.stockholm.se, Slussen; Skr50/10; open 11am-5pm Tues-Sun, closing 9pm Thur Sept-May, otherwise closing 7pm Thur)* is housed in the late-17th-century building Ryssgården, designed by Nicodemus Tessin the Elder and subsequently put to a variety of uses. Exhibits cover the history of the city and its people and it's worth a visit once you develop a romantic attachment to Stockholm.

On the 1st floor, the 'Proud City' exhibition, named after one of Carl Michael Bellman's songs, features Bellman-era memorabilia and includes his **cittern** (a type

of musical instrument). The magnificent **Lohé Hoard** consists of silver found in Gamla Stan in 1937. Look out for the reconstruction of **Stadshuskällaren**, a popular cellar inn (in the basement of the current museum building) during the mid-18th century, which was frequented by Bellman.

The 2nd floor has some interesting local archaeological finds, a reasonable exhibit on the metro and a good reconstruction of a cottage from the 1940s. The 3rd floor has more reconstructions – a registry office, a primary school from around 1900 and factory workers' home life in 1897.

Temporary exhibitions change several times yearly. There's also a museum shop and the cafe serves light lunches.

BELLMANHUSET
During one of the most productive periods of his life (1770 to 1774), the Swedish poet and songwriter Carl Michael Bellman lived in this house, which is now a museum **(Map 7, F5, #105)** *(☎ 640 2229, e stockholm@ par-bricole.a.se, Urvädergränd 3; variable fees, Stockholm Card not valid; guided tours at 1pm, first Sun of the month)*. Guided tours, with music or singing, are also given during *Bellmansveckan*, which is usually the last week in July (except Monday). For an events program, contact the museum directly.

Carl Michael Bellman (1740–95), one of Sweden's most-loved troubadours

THINGS TO SEE & DO

ALMGRENS SIDENVÄVERI MUSEUM

This unique place **(Map 7, G4, #111)** *(Almgren's Silk Weaving Mill & Museum;* ☎ *642 5616, Repslagargatan 15; Skr55/ free under 12; open 9am-5pm Mon-Fri, 11am-3pm Sat & Sun, but telephone in advance)* opened in 1991 as a working museum and the only full-time silk mill in Scandinavia. The two full-time staff still use the ancient equipment to hand-weave traditional patterns.

Originally the factory opened in 1833 using the latest Jacquard punch-card technology (amazingly, machinery parts were smuggled from France to Sweden hidden in barrels of cognac and crates of prunes!), which was a forerunner to modern computers. The factory moved to the current location in 1846 and produced up to 90,000 silk scarves per year, but was closed from 1974 to 1991. You can see a warping machine, watch the workers using the Jacquard looms (weekdays only), see displays of silk (including patterns ordered by royalty) and watch an excellent slide show and video (each six minutes and in English).

The museum shop sells soap, cream, shuttles, silk ties and silk scarves. It's the best place in Stockholm for hand-woven quality products.

MARIA MAGDALENA KYRKA

This cruciform-plan church **(Map 7, F3, #101)** *(Church of St Mary Magdalene;* ☎ *640 5334, Hornsgatan 21; free; open 11am-5pm Thur-Mon, 11am-8pm Wed)* was consecrated in 1634 and was later restored by both Nicodemus Tessin the Elder and the Younger. In 1759, most of the church was destroyed by fire but it was rebuilt by 1763 and has remained basically the same since. Of greatest interest are the *Adoration of the Shepherds* **altarpiece painting** (dating from around 1800) and the rococo-style **pulpit**, placed in the church in 1763 and featuring a medallion of Mary Magdalene. A free leaflet describing the church inventory is available in English. Free lunch concerts are held from 12.15pm to 12.35pm on Thursday.

LEKSAKSMUSEET

Leksaksmuseet **(Map 7, G2, #98)** *(Hobby & Toy Museum;* ☎ *641 6100, Mariatorget 1C; Skr40/25; open 10am-4pm Tues-Fri & noon-4pm Sat & Sun, also 10am-4pm Mon late June-mid-Aug)* is an oversized fantasy nursery full of everything you probably ever wanted as a child (and may still hanker after as an adult!).

There are four floors with model railways (ancient and modern), planes, cars, boats, fire engines, clockwork animals, a toy zoo, dolls, excellent miniature room scenes and old board games. There's also an accordion display, polyphones, musical clocks, early phonographs (from 1890) and a bizarre birdcage with three singing toy birds. In the attic, don't miss the **superb dioramas** of historical and fictional events, including Greek mythology, Roman and ancient Egyptian scenes.

Children will enjoy themselves with Lego in the playroom and at the daily children's theatre (Skr50, including museum admission).

IVAR LO-MUSEET

This museum **(Map 7, F1, #93)** *(*☎ *658 2584, Bastugatan 21; Skr50/free, Stockholm Card not valid; open by appointment)*, in the former apartment of the proletarian writer Karl Ivar Lo-Johansson (see Literature in the Facts about Stockholm chapter), remains as it was when he died in 1990. It features his clothing and furniture, including a writing table. Unfortunately, members of staff don't speak English so, if you're determined to visit, make arrangements through your hotel, hostel, or the tourist office.

MÅLERIYRKETS MUSEUM

This museum **(Map 5, B4, #17)** *(Building Painters' Museum;* ☎ *668 6619, Brännkyrkagatan 71; free; open 3pm-6pm Thur Sept-Apr)* isn't terribly interesting itself, but it's in a building with impressive oak panelling, stone floors and furniture, including a magnificent marble desk. The exhibits feature the building painters' equipment, such as brushes and tubs of different colours of paint.

The *Estonia* Ferry Disaster

On 28 September 1994, the passenger and car ferry M/S *Estonia* capsized and sank off the Finnish coast, with a loss of 852 lives. Most of the victims were Swedish or Estonian and there were only 137 survivors, making this Europe's worst ferry disaster since WWII.

At 1am, the ship was 35km south-east of Utö, an island in the outer reaches of the Turku archipelago. Despite the stormy weather and waves up to 5m, the ship was sailing at full speed, directly from Tallinn towards Stockholm. It has since been found that the bow visor was torn off by the waves, then the hydraulic latches on the forward ramp opened, allowing water onto the car deck leading to rapid loss of stability and a severe list. To make matters worse, the ship's officers reacted badly – the *Estonia* didn't initially slow down and the alarm wasn't raised for five minutes, by which time the list was so severe, it would've been virtually impossible to get out anyway. There was also difficulty using lifesaving equipment and no information was forwarded to the terrified passengers.

After the disaster, a joint Estonian, Swedish and Finnish commission produced a report, which was widely criticised as incompetent. The manufacturer reported that the bow door hinge latches had been rewelded in a substandard fashion and it was also suggested that the boat was unseaworthy when it left Tallinn. Rumours of cover-ups and conspiracies have been fuelled by the bizarre plan to seal the entire vessel in concrete, despite the fact that 700 bodies are still inside the wreck, but this was abandoned when furious relatives intervened.

The monument at Galärkyrkogården in Stockholm has been vandalised with text saying that the sinking wasn't an accident and the Swedish government is lying. There's also a memorial cross at Ersta Diakoni, the hospital where some survivors went for counselling.

Official reports of the disaster can be found on the Internet at W www.estoniaferrydisaster.net and W www.multi.fi/estonia, but there's also an interesting conspiracy view espoused at W www.sociamedia.nl/~wise/452/4471.html.

ERSTA DIAKONIMUSEET & KAPELL ERSTA DIAKONISSANSTALT

Run by the Ersta Society for Parish Welfare, a Christian charity which provides medical and geriatric care, support for the poor and homeless, and further education, **Ersta Diakonimuseet (Map 7, G10, #116)** *(Ersta Parish Welfare Museum; ☎ 714 6348, Erstagatan 1M; Skr10/free, Stockholm Card not valid; open 9am-4pm Mon-Fri & 1 Sun per month June-Aug)* provides an interesting insight into the development of Swedish nursing. Across the road, Ersta Hospital now specialises in gastroenterology.

The museum building has, in the past, been a soup kitchen for the homeless and there was once an orphanage for 20 children upstairs. You'll see an oblatmaskin, which makes communion bread, and an unusual collection of bedpans on the staircase. Upstairs, you'll find out about the orphanage

and see original children's beds. There's also a nurse display, blood transfusion equipment and surgical equipment from the 19th century (look out for the amputation saw) to the present day.

Kapell Ersta Diakonissanstalt (Map 7, G10, #118) *(Ersta Chapel; free; open 8am-6pm daily)* is a wonderful octagonal church. The text surrounding the congregation (on the balcony) is 1 Timothy 2:4–6. Prayers are held at 8.15am and noon daily, with services at 6pm on Wednesday and 11am on Sunday. Nearby, there's a **monument** to the victims of the *Estonia* disaster (see the boxed text).

SPÅRVÄGSMUSEET

Spårvägsmuseet **(Map 5, C10, #50)** *(Stockholm Transport Museum; ☎ 559 03180, Tegelviksgatan 22; bus Nos 46 & 55; Skr20/10; open 10am-5pm Mon-Fri, 11am-4pm Sat & Sun)* is in the Söderhallen bus depot and near the Viking Line terminal.

THINGS TO SEE & DO

Public transport in the city from rowing boats circa 1700 to the latest innovations in buses, trains and on the metro is covered. There are nearly 60 vehicles, including horse-drawn carriages, Stockholm metro trains, vintage trams and buses. There's a **horse-drawn tram** from 1877 (used for the museum logo), a two-compartment **motor bus** from 1928 (in working order) and a red-painted **city bus** from 1938, which you can go aboard (it has very comfortable seats!). Look out for the restored kiosk from Ängbyplan, which dates from the 1930s, the centrally placed exhibit on metro art, the 'tunnel trams' and the videos showing the development of the metro (in Swedish). You can also create your own computer-generated public transport network.

In spring and autumn, the museum organises one-hour tours in a double decker bus twice per day on weekends. Contact the museum for information and ticket prices. The museum has a children's train, bookshop and cafe (coffee Skr9, including refill).

OTHER ATTRACTIONS IN SÖDERMALM

Lilla Blecktornet (Map 5, D8, #70) *(Lilla Blecktornsparken; not open to the public)*, a distinctly odd little neoclassical-style mansion from 1781, has octagonal towers at either end. The park is always open and the building is definitely worth a look.

The 27-storey landmark **Folksamhuset (Map 5, D7, #81)** *(☎ 772 6000,* **W** *www .folksam.se, Bohusgatan 14; not open to the public)*, another strange-looking structure (with narrow rectangular windows), was built in 1959. It's the headquarters of Folksam, one of Sweden's largest insurance companies. Inside, there are notable artworks by well-known artists, including Carl Malmsten, Isaac Grünewald and Lennart Lindqvist.

The beautiful **Katarina Kyrka (Map 7, G6, #114)** *(Katarina Church; ☎ 743 6800, Högbergsgatan; free; open 9am-5pm Mon-Fri & 10am-5pm Sat & Sun Apr-Sept, otherwise closing 4pm)* is on the site of a former late-14th-century chapel. The church was badly damaged by fire in 1723 and was rebuilt in the form of a Greek cross

with a central altar. A more serious fire in 1990 caused the cupola to collapse and the interior was completely gutted. The church was rebuilt authentically along 17th-century lines for Skr270 million, despite the lack of original plans, and it was reconsecrated in 1995.

LÅNGHOLMEN

This island in Lake Mälaren once housed the notorious Kronohäktet prison. The worthwhile **Långholmens fängelsemuseum** *(Prison Museum; ☎ 668 0500,* **W** *www.langholmen.com; Skr25/10, Stockholm Card not valid; open 11am-4pm daily)* is in one of the former prison's wings – the rest of the building has been converted into a quirky hotel, restaurant and STF hostel. Displays cover 250 years of prison history and the curious story of how, in the 19th century, the formerly barren island was transformed into a park after the prisoners had covered it in mud from the lake. You'll also see a reconstructed guard's office and find out about escapees, the prison hospital, executions and chains weighing 40kg.

Just north of the prison museum, tiny **Bellmanmuseet (Map 5, A1, #1)** *(☎ 669 6969, Stora Henriksvik; Skr30/free, Stockholm Card not valid; open noon-6pm daily June-Aug, noon-4pm Sat & Sun May & Sept)* commemorates Carl Michael Bellman, the 18th-century composer of daring drinking songs. It's mostly of local interest, but guided tours for groups are available all year on request.

To get to Långholmen, take the metro to Hornstull, then walk north along Långholmsgatan and turn left onto Högalidsgatan.

Southern Suburbs

SKOGSKYRKOGÅRDEN

The Unesco World Heritage-listed graveyard **Skogskyrkogården (Map 2, G8)** *(☎ 508 30193, Sockenvägen 492, Enskede, metro T-Skogskyrkogården; free; open all times)* has a pine woodland setting and features several functionalist and neoclassical

A gilded royal crown decorates the bridge to Skeppsholmen, home to several good museums

The mosaic-lined Gyllene salen (Golden hall) of Stadshuset was made using 10kg of gold.

The silhouette at sunset of Stadshuset (city hall) on the islet of Kungsholmen

GRAEME CORNWALLIS

JOHN BORTHWICK

Elaborate street lamp

Gothic light bearers

JOHN BORTHWICK

GRAEME CORNWALLIS

Storkyrkan, Gamla Stan

Non Violence on Sergelgatan – one of the city's striking sculptures

JON DAVISON

The Renaissance-inspired Drottningholms Slott was designed by Nicodemius Tessin the Elder.

buildings, including a crematorium and several chapels. Skogskyrkogården is dominated by a massive granite cross and is known as the final resting place of Hollywood actress Greta Garbo (1905–90), who hailed from Stockholm. Her ashes were interred in Skogskyrkogården in 1999. Guided tours (in English) of the cemetery run at 5pm on Monday, from 1 May to 18 September (Skr50).

Northern Suburbs

The areas just north of the city centre are noted for their green and open spaces, stretches of water and woodland trails. Several large parks, spanning from Djurgården in the south, form Ekoparken (the National City Park), the first such protected city area in the world. Hagaparken is particularly pleasant for walks and bicycle tours. It's possible to walk all the way around Brunnsviken bay in 2½ hours.

CARL ELDHS ATELJÉMUSEUM

This sculpture museum (Map 2, C6, #21) (☎ 612 6560, Lögebodavägen 10; Skr40/15; guided tours in English 1pm Tues-Sun June-Aug, 1pm Sat & Sun May & Sept, 1pm Apr & Oct) is the former home and studio of Carl Eldh (1873–1954) and features over 400 of his works, moulds and belongings. You'll see many bronze statues by Eldh around the city.

The studio is a curious building, with rustic tarred vertical weatherboards and an attached circular house complete with cupola. It was specially designed to allow the best possible natural light conditions inside and was used by Eldh from 1919 to 1954.

Guided tours in Swedish are considerably more frequent; contact the museum or the tourist office for details. To get to the museum, take bus No 46 to Sveaplan, then it's a short walk through Bellevueparken. Motorists can park at the distinctive Wenner-Gren Center, on the north side of Sveaplan.

Current plans to build a highway through Bellevueparken, which would dramatically affect the museum, are being resisted locally.

MEDICINHISTORISKA MUSEET

The excellent Medicinhistoriska museet (Map 3, A4, #2) (Medical History Museum; ☎ 545 45150, W www.medhm.se, Karolinska Sjukhuset Eugenia T-3; Skr40/10, Skr30 students, Stockholm Card not valid; open 11am-4pm Tues, Thur & Fri, 11am-7pm Wed, noon-4pm Sun, closed Sat), in a former school and living quarters for disabled children, features medical and dental equipment, documents, art, and temporary exhibitions which change every few months. The enthusiastic and pleasant staff here make a pleasant change from the attitudes at the well-known touristy museums elsewhere in the city. A descriptive colour booklet is available in English for Skr10.

Near the entrance hall, notice the cases of wax casts from syphilis victims and various unpleasant skin conditions. If that hasn't put you off, proceed upstairs to see excellent displays including reconstructions of a 19th-century dental practice, operating theatres and hospital ward. Some of the old traction equipment in the orthopaedics room and the horrors in the psychiatry room are reminiscent of medieval torture chambers. Look out for the x-ray of the footballer Thomas Brolin's broken fibula (Sweden-Hungary match, 1994). There's also an interesting treatment of folk medicine and the history of medical practices.

Take frequent bus No 3 from T-St Eriksplan to Karolinska Sjukhuset, then walk through the hospital grounds (follow signs).

MILLESGÅRDEN

The superb sculpture garden and museum Millesgården (Map 2, B7, #22) (☎ 446 7590, W www.millesgarden.se, Carl Milles väg 2; Skr80/20; open 10am-5pm daily May-Sept, otherwise noon-4pm Tues-Fri & 11am-5pm Sat & Sun) is on Lidingö island and has great views across to the mainland. There's only very basic free information in English and the staff are keen for you to buy the detailed 32-page catalogue and map (in English; Skr15).

The house was sculptor Carl Milles' home and studio and the gardens feature

Raoul Wallenberg

Of all the 'righteous gentiles' honoured by Jews around the world, one of the most famous is Swedish diplomat Raoul Wallenberg, known for his part in the rescue of as many as 35,000 Hungarian Jews during WWII.

Wallenberg's father died before he was born into one of Sweden's most prominent families on Lidingö in 1912, and he was subsequently raised by his mother. After leaving school, he studied in the US in 1931, then gained employment in Cape Town. From there, he moved to work for a Dutch bank in Haifa and came into contact with Jews who had escaped from Nazi Germany.

In 1944, Wallenberg was appointed first secretary at the Swedish legation in Budapest, which was then part of the Nazi empire. The American War Refugee Board financed a project to rescue the Hungarian Jews, which Wallenberg was to implement – with the full knowledge of the Swedish government. Wallenberg's office issued 'Protection Passes' to tens of thousands of Jews, who were moved to safe houses displaying the Swedish coat of arms before being taken to Sweden. Amazingly, the protection passes were actually completely worthless, but the Nazi authorities were easily influenced by such symbolism and failed to deal with what was happening. Even more incredible, Wallenberg threatened the German military commander, General Schmidthuber, with death by execution after the war if he massacred the remaining 97,000 Jews in Budapest – and the massacre plan was cancelled at the last minute.

However, after the Russians entered Budapest in 1945, Wallenberg was summoned by the Russian authorities and he disappeared without trace. The Russians claim he died in detention in Moscow in 1947, but rumours about Wallenberg being alive in the 1970s have surfaced, even quite recently. Claims that senior figures in the Swedish government washed their hands of Wallenberg and left him to his fate appear to be well supported.

Whatever happened to Wallenberg may always be a mystery, but he has become a worldwide symbol to victims of persecution. For more information, see the booklet *Swedish Portraits – Raoul Wallenberg*, available from the Swedish Institute.

lots of his outdoor sculptures (some with fountains), including a replica of his *Poseidon* statue in Gothenburg (1930). The **Little Studio** has a rather good art collection, including pieces by Milles' wife and elder sister. In the **music room**, you'll see an organ reputedly played by Mozart's father, a tapestry and medieval church sculptures. Milles' fine indoor collection of ancient Egyptian, Greek, Etruscan and Roman items, including sculpture, coins and rings, is excellent. Look out for the 7th-century BC **Egyptian cat** statuette, complete with gold earrings. There are also temporary exhibitions, a museum shop and a cafe.

Take the metro to T-Ropsten, then bus Nos 205 or 225 to Torsvik (running every 15 to 30 minutes). A 10-minute walk along Herserudsvägen leads to Millesgården (follow the signs).

RAOUL WALLENBERG STATUE

This intriguing 4m-high bronze statue was erected in 1999 and shows Wallenberg holding out protection passes towards Jews trying to escape Nazi tyranny. It's located in Stadshusparken on Lidingö. Take bus No 205 or 225 from T-Ropsten to Lidingö Stadshus, on Lejonvägen. See also the boxed text on Wallenberg.

NATURHISTORISKA RIKSMUSEET & COSMONOVA

The extensive three-floor **Naturhistoriska Riksmuseet (Map 2, B6, #19)** *(National Museum of Natural History;* ☎ *519 54000,* Ⓦ *www.nrm.se, Frescativägen 40; Skr60/35, student Skr40; open 10am-7pm Tues-Sun, closing 8pm Thur)* was founded by Carl von Linné in 1739. It's now Sweden's largest museum and includes the usual stuff like dinosaurs, sea life and the fauna of the polar regions. Many displays are dioramas; one of the best shows baby dinosaurs breaking out of eggs. The volcano video is quite impressive. On the 1st floor, 'Life in Water' is supported by models, charts and videos. The tour around the human body has hands-on exhibits and computerised features with English text. There are also fairly large temporary exhibitions and a restaurant. The metro station T-Universitetet is a five-minute walk down the road (or take bus No 40).

In the same complex there's **Cosmonova** *(☎ 519 55130, W www.nrm.se; Skr70/45)*, a combined planetarium and Omnimax theatre, which shows films in the world's largest format using seven projectors and a 760-sq-m hemispherical screen. Films are entertaining, informative and impressive and English sound is available on request. The diverse topics covered include the Arctic, dolphins and UFOs. Cosmonova screens films on the hour, 10am to 7pm inclusive, daily except Monday (also open Monday during weeks eight, nine, 15-33 and 44); tickets cost Skr65/40 (the Stockholm Card gives a Skr10/5 discount), and advance reservations are recommended. Combined entry with Naturhistoriska Riksmuseet costs Skr105/70 (Skr90 student).

BERGIANSKA TRÄDGÅRDEN

Just across the road from Naturhistoriska Riksmuseet and by the shore of Brunnsviken, the pleasant Bergianska Trädgården **(Map 2, B6, #18)** *(Bergius Botanic Garden; ☎ 156545; free; open all times)* was donated to the Swedish Academy of Sciences in 1791. It's now Stockholm University's botanic garden and has over 9000 plant species. The park contains trees and shrubs from around Europe, America and Asia. There are also beds of Nordic and Mediterranean flowers, and a Japanese garden with a pond. A special **environment trail** describes environmental problems and research.

Don't miss the spectacular **Victoriahuset** *(Victoria House; ☎ 162853; Skr10/free; open 11am-5pm daily May-Sept)*, a tropical greenhouse with giant water lilies *(Victoria*

cruziana) and tropical crops (banana plants, rice, yams etc). The other must-see is **Edvard Andersons Växthus (Map 2, B6, #18)** *(Edvard Andersons Conservatory; ☎ 156 545; Skr40/free; open 11am-5pm daily)*, which opened in 1995. This attractive building contains a winter garden of Mediterranean flora, but there are also many other flowering plants from areas around the world with a Mediterranean climate. Look out for the flesh-eating plants in the tropical rooms.

Regular tours of the park (Skr30) and the conservatory (included in the admission fee) are conducted in Swedish.

Take the metro to T-Universitetet, walk northwards past Naturhistoriska Riksmuseet on Frescativägen, then turn left (under the main road) on Bergiusvägen. Alternatively, take bus No 40 from metro stations T-Odenplan or T-Universitetet directly to Bergiusvägen. See also the Organised Tours section in the Getting Around chapter for details of the 'Brunnsviken Runt' boat tour.

HAGAPARKEN

King Gustav III, who was interested in country pursuits as well as French and Italian culture, organised the development of Haga as an English-style park but with a palace simi-lar to Versailles. Although work on the palace started in 1786, it was halted when the king was assassinated in 1792. Near the incomplete structure (called Slottsruinen, but not a ruin at all) lies another royal palace, **Haga Slott**, which was built from 1802–04. It's an official Swedish government residence and isn't open to the public.

A few minutes' walk from the Haga Norra bus stop brings you to the amazing brightly-painted **Koppartälten (Map 2, B5, #15)** *(Copper Tent; open 10am-5pm daily June-Aug, otherwise 11am-4pm)*, built in 1787 as a stable and barracks for Gustav III's personal guard. It now contains a cafe, an inn and **Haga Parkmuseum (Map 2, B5, #17)** *(☎ 402 6130; free; open noon-4pm Tues-Sun May-Aug)*, with displays about the park, its pavilions and Haga Slott.

About 200m away, in a former royal kitchen garden dating from 1785, is the friendly **Fjärils & Fågelhuset (Map 2, B5, #16)** *(Butterfly House;* ☎ *730 3981,* W *www .fjarilshuset.se; Skr60/25; open 10am-4pm Tues-Fri & 11am-5.30pm Sat & Sun Apr-Sept, otherwise 10am-3pm Tues-Fri & 11am-4pm Sat & Sun)*, with free-flying birds and butterflies. Some birds, such as parrots, are in cages. There are around 35 species with a total of 400 mainly tropical butterflies; to see them at their best, visit on a sunny day (or a sunny day with snow in winter). There are also Japanese fish and birds, cactuses, spectacular **long-tailed finches** and comical diminutive **Chinese quail**. The cafe serves good sandwiches and drinks.

From the butterfly house, follow the **touristpromenad** (tourist trail) east, then south to Haga Slott and Slottsruinen (see earlier). On your left, you'll see the odd **Ekotemplet** *(Echo Temple; free; always open)*, designed as a summer dining room for Gustav III and with excellent, recently restored ceiling paintings. **Gustav IIIs Paviljong (Map 2, B6, #17)** *(*☎ *402 6130,* W *www.royalcourt.se; Skr50/25; open for hourly guided tours in Swedish noon-3pm inclusive Tues-Sun 15 May-31 Aug, Sat & Sun in Sept)* is a superb example of neo-classical style and is one of the finest such buildings in Europe. The mainly original furnishings and decor reflect Gustav III's interest of things Roman after his Italian tour in 1782.

Beyond Gustav IIIs Paviljong, another trail leads south alongside Brunnsviken; it splits then reconverges at Haga Södra (the southern entrance to the park). Between the eastern trail and Brunnsviken, you'll see the ornate **Kinesiska paviljongen** (Chinese pavilion; 1787). The western route passes near **Turkiska paviljongen**, another of Gustav III's architectural wonders.

To reach the park, take bus No 515 from Odenplan to Haga Södra or Haga Norra.

ULRIKSDALS SLOTT

Further north is the yellow-painted royal Ulriksdals Slott **(Map 2, A5, #4)** *(Ulriksdal Palace;* ☎ *402 6130,* W *www.royalcourt .se; Skr50/25, free under 7; open 10am-4pm Tues-Sun 15 May-31 Aug, Sat & Sun in Sept)*, in Ulriksdals Park and on the waterfront at Edsviken.

This large, early-17th-century building was home to King Gustav VI Adolf and his family until 1973. You can visit several attractive apartments on two floors. The **living room** is one of the finest 20th-century interiors in Sweden and Gustaf VI Adolf's **drawing room**, which dates from 1923 and contains part of his art collection, contains furniture designed by Carl Malmsten. In the northern wing, you'll see rooms from the time of Karl XV; the southern wing contains the offices of the World Wide Fund for Nature.

The nearby **Orangery** *(*☎ *402 6130; Skr50/25; same hours as Ulriksdals Slott)* contains Swedish sculpture and Mediterranean plants. You can also see **Queen Kristina's coronation carriage** *(*☎ *402 6130; Skr20/10; guided tours in English 1.40pm & 3.40pm Tues-Sun May-Aug)*.

A ticket for combined admission costs Skr80/40 (free for kids under 7). To reach the palace, take the metro to T-Bergshamra, then bus No 540.

SPÅNGA KYRKA

The stone-built Spånga kyrka **(Map 2, A2, #2)** *(*☎ *362650, Spånga Kyrkaväg; free; open by arrangement)* is one of Stockholm's oldest churches – and one of its best. The nave dates from the end of the 12th century and has impressive 15th-century **wall and ceiling frescoes** featuring biblical scenes. Some earlier works have been dated to the mid-14th century. Look out for St George and the dragon, God holding Christ on his cross and a lion painting, all from the 1460s. The **porch** also has impressive artwork. Among the inventory, there's a **pulpit** from 1759 and a **communion plate** from around 1500.

In the grounds, there are three spectacular **rune stones** from the 11th century. A segment of another rune stone is located in the southern wall. A colour booklet (in Swedish only) is available for Skr10.

Take the metro to T-Tensta, then it's a 15-minute walk.

OTHER ATTRACTIONS

Polistekniskamuseet (Map 2, A4, #3) *(Police Technique Museum; ☎ 401 9053 9am-11am Tues-Fri, Polishögskolan, Sörentorp; Skr500 for groups of 10 people, then Skr50 per extra person, minimum age 16, Stockholm Card not valid; open by appointment)* is in the grounds of the police academy. It displays vehicles from 1903 (including a fine collection of BMW motorcycles, all in working order) and other things such as radio equipment. Public transport, apart from taxis, isn't feasible.

The original residence of artist Olle Olsson Hagalund, who painted with knives, **Olle Olsson-huset (Map 2, B5, #14)** *(☎ 839744, Hagalundsgatan 50; Skr30/free, Stockholm Card not valid; open noon-4pm Sun-Thur)* is now a gallery of modern art. It's a traditional house with temporary exhibitions changing monthly. Take bus No 515 from T-Odenplan to Kolonnvägen or take the metro to T-Solna Centrum.

One of the oddest museums in Stockholm is **Frisörmuseet (Map 2, C2, #9)** *(Museum of Hairdressing; ☎ 870430, Per Ekströms väg 3, Bromma; T-Islandstorget; admission fee on request, Stockholm Card not valid; open by arrangement)*. It describes the work of hairdressers from 1896 to the present day.

Activities

Stockholm offers a great variety of activities for everyone and the tourist office can provide details on organised activities and suggestions for things you can do yourself. The tourist office Web site, [w] www .stockholmtown.com, has a good listing of outlets offering organised activities.

Friluftsfrämjandet (Map 2, E4, #26) *(☎ 556 30740, [e] info@frilufts.se, Instrumentvägen 14, SE-12653 Hägersten)*, is an outdoor activity organisation which organises courses and events in climbing, skiing, hiking, canoeing/kayaking, sailing and cycling. Members get discounts at events and membership costs Skr200/100/50 adult/youth (13 to 25)/under 13.

HIKING

Hiking trips around the city are fairly limited, but there are some good walks in the parks – the most popular area for short walks is Djurgården, but Hagaparken is better for longer hikes. The city's parks, gardens and shorelines are also favourite outdoor venues for picnics.

The 2½-hour walk around Brunnsviken passes through Hagaparken, but it requires some road walking. Another fine place for strolling around is the small island Tranholmen. Although it's quite heavily built up, there's a network of narrow streets and some interesting old houses. No cars are allowed, making it a great place to explore on foot. A ferry runs from near the metro station T-Ropsten three times daily, June to August (Skr50 return).

For more on walks around Stockholm, see the Walking Tours special section.

CLIMBING

Climbers have better options, with around 150 cliffs within 40 minutes' drive of the city. There's a cliff in Nacka but the closest to the city centre is the vertical face just west of the Viking Line terminal and near Ersta sjukhus (Ersta hospital).

The 12m-high unconventional climbing wall, **Klättercenteret Original (Map 5, E8, #82)** *(☎ 644 9091, Hammarby Kajvägen 24B; Skr70 per day)* is an enjoyable place to climb but bring your own karabiner and friction device.

Further from the city centre, the 14m-high **Klätterverket** *(☎ 641 1048, [e] info@ klatterverket.se, Järnvägsgatan 7, Nacka; J-Sickla; Skr70 per day; open noon-10pm Mon-Fri, 10am-8pm Sat & Sun)* offers around 1000-sq-m of artificial climbing. Climbing courses are also organised here (for around Skr250).

CYCLING

Cycling is best in Ekoparken (the national city park) and away from the busy central streets and arterial roads, but some streets have special cycle lanes (often shared with pedestrians) and cyclist's traffic signals. The tourist office sells maps of cycle routes.

For more details, see Bicycle in the Getting Around section.

ICE SKATING

Whenever it's cold enough (usually November to March), outdoor ice skating takes place in Kungsträdgården at **Kungsans isbana (Map 6, D7, #177)** *(free; open 9am-5pm Mon, Tues & Thur, 9am-9pm Wed & Fri, 11am-5pm Sat & Sun)*. The ice rink is floodlit at night. Skate hire is available for Skr30/10 adult/child. Skating on frozen lakes or the sea isn't recommended for beginners, but trips with experienced skaters are arranged by Friluftsfrämjandet (see earlier in this section).

TENNIS

Although Sweden has produced some of the world's finest tennis players, tennis isn't as popular as you might think. **Tennisstadion (Map 4, A4, #52)** *(☎ 215454, Fiskartorpsvägen 20; open 7am-11pm Mon-Fri, 8am-9pm Sat & 8am-10pm Sun)* charges around Skr165 per hour; hire of rackets and a ball costs extra. **Kungliga Tennishallen (Map 4, A6, #53)** *(☎ 459 1500, Lidingövägen 75)* is more expensive.

FITNESS CENTRES

You'll find many fitness centres (with gyms and aerobics classes) in the city. Some are associated with luxurious 'health' clubs (such as Sturebadet) which charge astronomical membership fees. However, the more reasonable **Friskis & Svettis (Map 3, E3, #35)** *(☎ 429 7000, Jympalatset, St Eriksgatan 54; open variable hours daily)* offers weight training, exercise bikes etc and charges from Skr70 per 55-minute session. For other Friskis & Svettis centres, look up the Pink Pages phone book. See also Centralbadet under Swimming in this section. Look out for **free outdoor aerobics** in summer at Hagaparken, Rålambshovsparken (Kungsholmen) and Tantolunden.

GOLF

Golf is popular in Sweden and there are lots of clubs in the Stockholm area. For a complete listing, contact Stockholmsgolfför-

bund *(☎ 731 5370, fax 731 5377, ⓔ info@ stockholmsgf.golf.se; Box 1035, SE-18121 Lidingö)*. The Web site at Ⓦ www.golf.se has a directory *(golfguiden)* of clubs and their facilities, but it's only in Swedish.

Mini golf is also available; try **Bredäng Minigolf (Map 2, E2, #28)** *(☎ 972068, Stora Sällskapets väg 51)* or check the Web site at Ⓦ www.stockholmtown.com for a complete listing.

GO-KARTING

Mainly aimed at children and youths, this activity is rapidly gaining in popularity. **Svenska Go-karthallen (Map 5, E9, #83)** *(☎ 462 9755, Hammarbyvägen 37; Skr60/90 for 5/8mins; 'drop-in' available noon-5pm Sun)* has a 340m-long indoor track.

SWIMMING & SAUNA

This is a national pastime in summer and there are several places in the city with free lake swimming, including **Långholmens strandbad**, with a good beach, and **Smedsuddsbadet** on Kungsholmen, with a short sandy beach, a small hut with changing facilities, and a toilet.

Eriksdalsbadet (Map 5, E6, #79) *(☎ 508 40250, Hammarby slussväg 8)* has indoor pools (Skr45/30 adult/child), one with chutes, and an open-air (Skr30/20) pool; opening hours vary, but it's generally open 8am to 8pm or 9pm.

The open-air adventure pool **Vanadisbadet (Map 4, B1, #2)** *(☎ 301211, Sveavägen 142; Skr50; open 10am-6pm daily 20 May-23 Aug)* is in a pleasant park north of the city centre.

First Hotel Reisen (Map 7, B5, #40) *(☎ 223260, Skeppsbron 12; Skr125 for 90 min; open noon-9pm for nonresidents)* has a superb cold (16°C) pool and sauna in a medieval brick-arched cellar, with separate men's and women's sections.

If you want a relaxing swim in an extraordinary Art Nouveau bathing salon, try **Sturebadet (Map 6, B8, #57)** *(☎ 501500, Sturegallerian 36)*, but note that six-month membership costs Skr3950. Much cheaper is **Centralbadet (Map 6, B3, #20)** *(☎ 242 402, Drottninggatan 88; from Skr110; open*

7am-10pm Mon-Fri & 10am-10pm Sat June-Aug, otherwise 6am-10pm Mon-Fri & 8am-10pm Sat & Sun), which doesn't require membership, but is still a pleasant spa. Admission includes access to the gym, sauna, jacuzzi and sunbathing terrace. Swimsuit hire is available and there's also a pool bar and restaurant.

BOATING

With all its water and islands, Stockholm is ideal for boating activities. For kayaking trips, contact Friluftsfrämjandet (see earlier in this section). One-day or multi-day sailing trips in the archipelago with an experienced captain can be organised with the tourist office between 1 June and 24 September (from Skr790/1350 day/weekend; weekend prices also include meals and accommodation).

If you prefer to hire your own boat, contact **Tvillingarnas (Map 6, E10, #73)** *(☎ 663 3739, Strandvägskajen 27)*. The boat hire is run by a floating restaurant, open 8am to 1am daily, April to September. Pedalboats for splashing around Ladugårdslandsviken cost Skr100 per hour. A one-person mini yacht costs Skr250 for the first hour, then Skr200 for each following hour. Two- to four-person yachts are Skr800/1200 for four hours/one day. There are also many types of motorboats, from Skr3500/9900 per day/week, and powerful RIB Zodiac 310s cost Skr2000 per day.

Courses

Stockholm University (Map 2, B6, #20) *(☎ 162000, fax 161757, [W] www.su.se, SE-10691 Stockholm)* and **Kungliga Tekniska Högskolan** *(Royal Institute of Technology; ☎ 790 6000, fax 790 6500, [W] www.kth.se, SE-10044 Stockholm)* both offer masters degree programs taught in English. See also the University section in the Facts for the Visitor chapter.

LANGUAGE COURSES

Full details of all courses in Swedish offered for foreigners staying in Sweden can be found in the booklet *Swedish in Sweden*, which is published annually by the Swedish Institute.

Studiefrämjandet i Stockholm *(☎ 441 5200, fax 441 5210, [e] 0101@sfr.se, Box 6361, SE-10235 Stockholm)* offers 48-hour eight-week spring and autumn courses for beginners and intermediate learners (Skr2245). Intensive 60-hour five-week courses cost Skr2975.

Studieförbundet Vuxenskolan (Map 3, F5, #56) *(☎ 693 0390, fax 693 0397, Hantverkargatan 26, SE-11221 Stockholm)* organises twice-weekly 24- and 30-hour beginners, conversation and continuation classes in February, each costing from Skr800 to Skr975.

Skeppsholmens Folkhögskola (Map 7, B8, #52) *(☎ 679 2804, [e] hellerud@post .utfors.se; SE-11149 Stockholm)* offers an 11-day course in August for Skr1500 (basic knowledge of Swedish required). A huge range of 26-day intensive language courses is run year-round by **Folkuniversitetet i Stockholm** *(☎ 789 4190, fax 679 9541, [e] info.sprak@folkuniversitetet.se, [W] www .folkuniversitetet.se, Box 26210 SE-10041 Stockholm)*; each costs Skr4000 and starting levels range from beginners to advanced. Extra-intensive, 50-hour 12-day courses in July and August cost Skr3500.

OTHER COURSES

Some museums (including Folkens Museum Etnografiska) offer short courses, but they're all presented in Swedish. Contact the tourist office for details.

Free Swedish folk dance classes are organised by Skeppsholmens Folkhögskola (see the previous section) every Sunday from 6pm, including a two-hour session for beginners. **Södra Teatern (Map 7, G5, #108)** *(☎ 556 97200, Mosebacketorg 1-3)* offers free dance classes (waltz, foxtrot, tango, ballroom etc) in July and August.

Places to Stay

PLACES TO STAY – BUDGET
Camping

Some camping grounds are open all year, but the best time for tent camping is from May to August. Prices vary according to facilities and season; kitchen and toilet facilities are usually included and reasonable rates are offered to hikers and cyclists. Ask the tourist office for the free annual booklet *Camping – Stockholm*, which has details of camping grounds in and around the city. The nearest free camping is in Tyresta National Park – see the Excursions chapter for details.

Primus and Sievert supply gas for camping stoves and containers are available at petrol stations. *T-sprit Röd* (methylated spirit/denatured alcohol) for Trangia stoves can be bought at petrol stations. *Fotogen* (paraffin/kerosene) is sold at paint shops such as Fargtema and Spektrum.

Bredäng Camping (Map 2, E2, #28) (☎ 977 071, fax 708 7262, ⓔ *bredang camping@swipnet.se, Stora Sällskapets väg 51)* Metro: T-Bredäng, then 700m walk. Camping fees Skr90 (walker or cyclist) or Skr155-185 (with car, caravan or camper van), including shower. Four-bed room Skr450. Chalets Skr620-820. Open 9 April-28 October, full service 29 May-28 October. Bredäng Camping is 10km south of Stockholm and well signposted from the E4/E20 motorway (junction Bredängsmötet). It has a pleasant grassy location, with patches of trees, near Lake Mälaren. Facilities include self-service laundry, grocery store, licensed cafeteria, sauna, children's play area and a public phone. Bike hire, golf and fishing are available.

Ängby Camping (Map 2, D2, #11) (☎ 370420, fax 378226, ⓔ *reservation@ angbycamping.se*, ⓦ *www.angbycamping.se, Blackebergsvägen 24)* Metro: T-Ängbyplan, then 600m walk. Camping fees Skr80 (walker or cyclist) or Skr115-165 (with vehicle). Cabins (1-5 people) and rooms Skr400-675, caravans (1-4 people) Skr300. Open year-round, full service 8am-10pm

daily, 1 May-15 September. This forested camping ground, 10km west of Stockholm, is by an inlet of Lake Mälaren. Facilities include self-service laundry, grocery store, cafeteria, sauna, children's play area, tennis, golf, fishing and a public phone.

Klubbensborgs Camping (Map 2, E3, #27) (☎ 646 1255, fax 646 4545, ⓦ *www .welcome.to/klubbensborg, Klubbensborgs-vägen 27)* Metro: T-Mälarhöjden, then 900m walk. Camping fees Skr60 (walker or cyclist) or Skr140 (with vehicle), 6-bed cabin Skr4500 per week. Reception open 8am-8pm daily June-Aug. This excellent camping ground by Lake Mälaren has mixed grassland and woods adjacent to some quaint old houses and a former inn. You'll find a laundry, shop, swimming, canoe rental and a cafeteria/bakery. There is also hostel accommodation (see Hostels later in this section).

Östermalms Citycamping (Map 4, B5, #51) (☎ 102903, fax 214412, *Östermalms Idrottsplass, Fiskartorpsvägen 2)* Metro: T-Stadion, then 600m walk. Open 25 June-12 Aug. This new city-centre camping ground, by the Östermalm sports ground, offers spaces for tents, caravans and camper vans, but prices weren't available at the time of writing.

Hostels

Stockholm has more than a dozen hostels within easy reach of the city centre, both Hostelling International-affiliated hostels and independent hostels. The choice includes four boat hostels and one in an old prison. Most hostels fill up during the late afternoon in summer so arrive early or book in advance; bookings through tourist offices cost Skr20. The free annual tourist office booklet *Hotels & Youth Hostels in Stockholm* lists all hostels in Stockholm county.

Svenska Turistföreningen (STF; ☎ *463 2100, fax 678 1958,* ⓔ *info@stfturist.se,* ⓦ *www.meravsverige.nu, Box 25, SE-10120*

The History of *af Chapman*

This wonderful fully rigged sailing ship, launched in 1888 at Whitehaven (England) with the name *Dunboyne*, was the last of this type of three-masted vessel to be built. Initially, it worked as a cargo ship for British then Norwegian owners, but it ended up in Gothenburg in 1915 and was renamed *GD Kennedy*. After a few years as a training ship, the Swedish Navy purchased the boat in 1923 and changed the name again to *af Chapman*, in honour of the renowned 18th-century Swedish naval architect Fredrik Henrik af Chapman. The navy used *af Chapman* for training ship's boys until 1934, then it was retired to the Karlskrona naval base. In 1947, Stockholm city council bought *af Chapman* and asked Svenska Turistföreningen to run it as a hostel. It opened two years later, with 136 beds for guests.

Stockholm), is part of Hostelling International (HI) and an HI membership card yields a Skr45 discount. Children under 16 pay about half price but only adult HI members' rates are quoted in this book. Nonmembers can buy an HI Guest Card for Skr175, then pay members' rates. Facilities are excellent and all STF hostels have kitchens. Breakfast may be available for Skr40 to Skr55 extra (if you reserve it the previous day). Sleeping bags are allowed if you have a sheet and pillowcase to cover the mattress and pillow; otherwise you can hire sheets for Skr50 per stay (it's recommended that you take your own). Clean up after yourself, or face 'cleaning fees' of up to Skr100.

The 'rival' *Sveriges Vandrarhem i Förening* (SVIF; W *www.svif.se*) has several hostels in and around the city and membership isn't required. Few SVIF hostels in Stockholm have kitchens and you may need your own utensils. Breakfast is available at some hostels. Pick up the free booklet at tourist offices or SVIF hostels, or check the Web site.

Some hostels aren't members of either organisation.

Although most inner-city hostels now have 24-hour reception, some hostels in Stockholm have restricted access. Phone and make a reservation during reception hours (generally between 5pm and 7pm); you'll be given instructions on how to get in. You'll be charged for one night's stay if you cancel after 6pm the day before arrival. Even in winter, reservations are advised – hostels are often full.

Lockers are usually available at hostels. Some require coins, others just need a padlock (bring your own).

Skeppsholmen Most travellers head first to Skeppsholmen, just east of the city centre; take bus No 65 from the eastern side of Vasagatan, across the street from Centralstationen, or just walk (20 minutes).

Vandrarhem af Chapman & Skeppsholmen (Map 7, C7, #43) (☎ 463 2266, fax 611 7155, e *info@chapman.stfturist.se*, *Flaggmansvägen 8*) Dorm beds Skr115-145, doubles Skr350. Open 12 Jan-16 Dec; 24-hour reception. The large and popular, recently restored STF boat hostel *af Chapman* has done plenty of travelling of its own, but is now well anchored in a superb, quiet location, swaying gently in sight of the city centre (see the boxed text). Bunks in dorms below decks have nautical ambience and staff members are friendly and helpful. Apart from showers and toilets, all facilities are on dry land in the adjacent Skeppsholmen hostel, where you'll find a good kitchen with a laid-back common room and a separate TV lounge. Laundry facilities (Skr35 for wash and dry) and 24-hour Internet access are available. The excellent KRAV-marked ecological buffet breakfast costs Skr55. Car parking (for guests only) is Skr25 per day and bike hire is available for Skr50/90 half/full day. Stays on the boat are normally limited to five nights from May to September.

City Centre & Vasastaden *City Backpackers* (Map 6, B2, #16) (☎ *206920, fax 100464,* e *citybackpackers@swipnet.se, Upplandsgatan 2A)* Beds in 8-/4-bed dorms Skr160/190. Doubles Skr470. 2- to 6-bed apartments Skr1500 per day. Open year-round; reception 8.30am-noon & 2pm-7pm. Closest to Centralstationen is the recently renovated City Backpackers (SVIF), one of the cleanest and best-equipped hostels in Stockholm. It's a friendly, bright and airy 19th-century building, located off a quiet street. The hostel has a kitchen, satellite TV, sauna (Skr10) and laundry (Skr50). Internet access costs Skr30 (allowing one hour, with free return later). Sheets are available for Skr20 per week. Ask for Gunnars' Bistro breakfast buffet tickets which are available at reception (Skr37).

Hostel Mitt i City (Map 6, B1, #9) (☎ *217630, fax 217690,* e *reservation@ stockholm.mail.telia.com,* w *www.stores .se/hostal.htm, Västmannagatan 13)* Dorm/4-bed room Skr175/225, including breakfast. Doubles Skr570. Open year-round; 24-hour reception. This SVIF hostel occupies the entire 5th floor in an old-style building on a quiet street and is reached by either stairs or an antique lift. It's a trifle claustrophobic (some rooms have very small windows), but it's reasonably clean and friendly. However, there are no kitchen or laundry facilities.

Vandrarhemmet Brygghuset (Map 3, C5, #6) (☎ *312424, fax 310206,* e *youth .hostel.brygghuset@snfr.se, Norrtullsgatan 12N)* Metro: T-Odenplan. Dorm beds Skr140.

Doubles Skr340. Open 27 May-9 Sept. Further north in the Vasastaden district, this SVIF hostel is an ex-brewery building next to Hamburger Bryggeriet, the original brewery (now closed). There isn't a cafe or any kitchen facilities, but you can do your laundry.

Hostel Bed & Breakfast (Map 4, C1, #11) (☎/fax *152838,* e *hostelbedandbreakfast@ chello.se,* w *www.hostelbedandbreakfast .com, Rehnsgatan 21)* Metro: T-Rådmansgatan. Dorm beds Skr90-175. Singles/doubles Skr275/380. Open year-round; telephone reception 8am-midnight. This is a bright, pleasant informal and well-equipped basement hostel with a kitchen and laundry (Skr35). The large summer dorm across the street is open June to August. The buffet breakfast is Skr25, sheet hire is Skr45 and Internet access is Skr25/45 per 30/60 minutes.

Östermalm *Backpackers Inn* (Map 4, D6, #62) (☎ *660 7515, fax 665 4039, Banérgatan 56)* Metro: T-Karlaplan. Dorm beds Skr105. Open 25 June-11 Aug; reception 7am-11am & 4pm-2am. The STF Backpackers Inn, located in a fairly modern school building (during the summer holidays only), has 260 beds in seven-bunk classrooms and 40 beds in four-bed family rooms. There is no kitchen but the cafeteria serves alfresco breakfasts (Skr45). Showers are in the adjacent sports hall. Street parking is free at night.

Östra Reals Vandrarhem (Map 4, D5, #49) (☎/fax *664 1114, Karlavägen 79)* Metro: T-Karlaplan. Dorm beds from Skr125 (10% student discount with ISIC card). Open 16 June-12 Aug; telephone reception available year-round. Östra Reals Vandrarhem (SVIF) is also in a school, which looks old-fashioned and austere. There are no kitchen facilities but there is a cafeteria.

Södermalm & Långholmen There are plenty of hostels in and around Södermalm, many within walking distance of both the Viking Line terminal and Centralstationen. Views from the boat hostels are wonderful from on deck and from cabins facing the water.

Gustaf af Klint (Map 7, F6, #77) (☎ 640 4077, fax 640 6416, Stadsgårdskajen 153) Metro: T-Slussen. Dorm beds from Skr120. Hostel doubles Skr340. Basic hotel rooms Skr395/650. Open all year; reception 7am-11pm. This clean and friendly boat hostel, a former naval cartography vessel from 1942, is now a little dilapidated but it has atmosphere. There's no guest kitchen, but the licensed restaurant on board serves reasonably priced meals. Sheets cost Skr50 and breakfast is Skr45.

Mälaren Den Röda Båten (Map 7, E2, #91) (☎ 644 4385, fax 641 3733, e info@ rodabaten.nu, w www.rodabaten.nu, Söder Malärstrand, Kajplats 6) Metro: T-Slussen. Dorm beds Skr185-215. Singles/doubles Skr400/450. Prices include sheets. Open all year; reception 8am-11pm. Docked west of the Slussen railway lines, this red boat carried timber around Mälaren from 1914 but became a Göta Canal steamer in the 1920s. It's easily the cosiest of Stockholm's floating hostels thanks to lots of dark wood, nautical memorabilia and friendly staff. There are also excellent hotel-standard rooms (see the Mid-Range section later in this chapter). Breakfast (Skr45) and dinner are served on the floating restaurant *Ludvigshafen* from June to August; at other times, breakfast and snacks are available on the main boat.

M/S Rygerfjord (Map 7, E1, #92) (☎ 840830, fax 840730, e hotell@rygerfjord .se, w www.rygerfjord.se, Söder Malärstrand, Kajplats 12) Metro: T-Slussen. Beds in 12-bed dorms Skr165. Doubles Skr370. Hotel rooms Skr625-850. Open all year. This SVIF hostel, launched in Bergen in 1950 as a *hurtigruten* (the coastal steamer) vessel for the Norwegian coast, is a bit further west. The hostel section is rather ordinary but the public areas, including the restaurant, are very pleasant. Most on-board berths are fairly ordinary hotel rooms. The buffet breakfast is Skr45 and sheets are Skr55. Reasonably priced lunches (including refill) and dinners are also served in the restaurant.

Zinkensdamm Hotell & Vandrarhem (Map 5, B3, #13) (☎ 616 8100, fax 616 8120, e zinkensdamm@telia.com, Zinkens

väg 20) Metro: T-Hornstull. Beds in 4-bed dorm Skr145/185. Doubles Skr435/540, without/with private bathroom. Hotel B&B singles/doubles Skr995/1295 (discounted weekends & summer Skr695/995). Open year-round; 24-hour reception. In the western end of Södermalm, this STF hostel is a large, 466-bed complex in a quiet location by Tantolunden Park. It's well equipped with kitchen facilities, but the hostel is often crowded and noisy. The loud TV in the kitchen suppresses most attempts at conversation. The hostel breakfast buffet isn't too great (Skr50), but the hotel breakfast is much better (hostellers can buy this separately for Skr65). Laundry costs Skr45 and bike hire is Skr60/80 per half/full day. The comfy Zinkadus bar serves snacks and drinks all day.

Långholmen Hotell & Vandrarhem (Map 5, A1, #2) (☎ 668 0510, fax 720 8575, e vandrarhem@langholmen.com, w www .langholmen.com, Kronohäktet) Metro: T-Hornstull, then 750m walk. Cells without/ with private bathroom Skr165/195. Hotel B&B Skr995/1295 (discounted to Skr695/ 995). Open year-round; 24-hour reception. In a former prison on the small island of Långholmen, off the north-western corner of Södermalm, this hotel and STF hostel is a most unusual place to stay. It's highly recommended and most staff members are friendly and efficient. There are good kitchen and laundry facilities, and the pleasant restaurant Långholmens Wärdshus serves breakfast (Skr60) and other meals; there's also a pub and a summer terrace.

Other Areas If you're having trouble finding a bed and things get desperate, there are more than 20 other hostels in Stockholm's *län* (county), which can be reached by SL buses or trains or archipelago boats within an hour or so. Some options are mentioned in the Excursions chapter and others are mentioned here.

Solna Vandrarhem & Motelcamp (Map 2, A4, #6) (☎ 514 81550, fax 514 81551, e info@solna-vandrarhem.se, w www.solna -vandrarhem.se, Enköpingsvägen 16) Commuter train: J-Ulriksdals station, then walk

500m (follow signs). Dorm beds Skr150. Singles/doubles Skr225/380. Open year-round. This 374-bed former barracks in the northwestern suburbs is worth trying when the city hostels are full. Accommodation is in prefabricated huts, which are kept well heated in winter. The hostel has a small guest kitchen but a buffet breakfast is available for Skr40. The attached restaurant and bar is open daily except Sunday.

STF Vandrarhem Jakobsberg (☎ 445 7270, fax 445 7273, e vandrarhemmet .majorskan@swipnet.se, Kaptensvägen 7, SE-17738 Järfälla) Commuter train: J-Jakobsberg, then bus No 567 to IKEA & walk 5 min. Dorm beds Skr165. Singles/doubles Skr255/330. Open 2 Jan-21 Dec; reception hours 8am-7pm Mon-Fri (closed noon-1pm), 4pm-7pm Sat & Sun. This comfortable hostel, in former offices for a military airport, offers kitchen facilities, bike hire and a sauna. It's located just off the E18, near IKEA in Jakobsberg, about 18km north-west of the city centre.

Bredängs Vandrarhem (Map 2, E2, #28) (☎ 976200, fax 976030, e bredang -camping@swipnet.se, Stora Sällskapets väg 51) Metro: T-Bredäng, then 600m walk. Dorm beds Skr135-190. Open 8 Jan-21 Dec. Just along the street from Bredäng Camping, in a pleasant suburb near Lake Mälaren, this is a clean and pleasant hostel with a well-equipped kitchen. When the camping ground is open (9 April to 28 October), laundry facilities, a cafeteria and shop are available there (see Camping earlier in this chapter).

Klubbensborg Hostel (Map 2, E3, #27) (☎ 646 1255, fax 646 4545, w www .welcome.to/klubbensborg, Klubbensborgs-vägen 27) Metro: T-Mälarhöjden, then 900m walk. Dorm beds from Skr130. Open year-round; reception hours 8am-8pm daily June-Aug, otherwise 10am-4pm Mon-Fri, 10am-5pm Sat & Sun. This wonderful lakeside SVIF hostel has a rural atmosphere and several buildings dating back to the 17th century. The hostel has a kitchen, laundry and camping ground. Breakfast is available in the attached cafe and there's also an excellent bakery.

STF Vandrarhem Hökarangen (Map 2, G6 #31) (☎/fax 941765, Munstycksvägen 18, SE-12357 Farsta) Metro: T-Hökarangen, then walk 800m (follow the signs). Dorm beds Skr130. Doubles Skr260. Open 25 June to 9 August. This summer STF hostel is located in a colourful Waldorf school and in a quiet suburb. Car parking is free of charge. Breakfast is available for Skr45.

Motels

Hotel Formule 1 (Map 2, E4, #30) (☎ 744 2044, fax 744 2047, Mikrofonvägen 30) Metro: T-Telefonplan. Rooms with shared bathroom Skr219. Open year-round. This motel, by the Västberga exit on the E4 motorway, about 4km due south-west of the city centre, is a modern place with basic rooms. Breakfast costs Skr30 extra. Book well in advance.

PLACES TO STAY – MID-RANGE

The accommodation listed here costs between Skr200 to Skr800 for a single room.

Private Rooms

Hotellcentralen (Map 6, F3, #146) (☎ 789 2490, fax 791 8666, e hotels@stoinfo.se) at Centralstationen can organise B&B in private rooms (Skr50 fee). The following agencies can also arrange either B&B in private homes or apartment accommodation from around Skr200 to Skr500 per person per night.

Bed & Breakfast Agency (☎ 643 8028, fax 603 8078, e info@bba.nu, w www.bba.nu)
Bed & Breakfast Center (☎ 730 0003, fax 730 5214, e stockholm@bbc.nu, w www.bed-and-breakfast.se)
Bed & Breakfast Service (☎ 660 5565, fax 663 3822, e info@bedbreakfast.a.se, w www.bedbreakfast.a.se)
Gästrummet (☎/fax 650 1006, e gastrummet@ telia.com, w www.gastrummet.com)
Rent a Room (☎/fax 712 3300, e rent.a.room@tyreso.mail.telia.com, w welcome.to/rentaroom)
Stockholm Guesthouse (☎ 396900, fax 648 1648, e info@stockholmguesthouse.com, w www.stockholmguesthouse.com)

Guesthouses & Hotels

Many options in this section only have rooms with shared bathroom. They're all clean and tidy but the decor may be rather old-fashioned and slightly shabby.

Rates are usually the same all year but, in some cases, there are small discounts, either summer (late June to early August) or weekend (Friday and Saturday night). Breakfast is normally included in quoted prices. *Hotellcentralen* (Map 6, F3, #146) (☎ 789 2490), at Centralstationen, can usually find you suitable accommodation for a Skr50 fee.

Some hostels offer better quality single/double rooms at lower prices (see the earlier Hostels section).

City Centre & Vasastaden *Good Night Hotell Danielsson* (Map 6, B1, #10) (☎ 411 1065, fax 317020, Västmannagatan 5) Metro: T-Centralen. Singles/doubles with shared bathroom Skr450/550, with private bathroom Skr550/750. This friendly Finnish-Polish, family-run hotel is well placed for the city centre. All of the 20 rooms are decorated in different styles but none have phones. Family rooms are available. The common room has a TV and free coffee, tea and juice.

Hotell Bema (Map 6, A1, #7) (☎ 232675, fax 205338, ℮ hotell.bema@stockholm.mail.telia.com, Upplandsgatan 13) Metro: T-Centralen. Singles/doubles Skr780/850 (discounted Skr550/650). Just north of the centre and opposite the quiet Tegnér-lunden Park you'll find this friendly hotel, with 12 very nice twin and double rooms, all with shower and TV, and excellent value.

Queen's Hotel (Map 6, B3, #18) (☎ 249460, fax 217620, ℮ queenshotel@queenshotel.se, Drottninggatan 71A) Metro: T-Hötorget. Singles/doubles with shared bathroom Skr625/680; with private bathroom Skr995/1100. In an early 20th-century building on the pedestrian mall, this friendly old-fashioned hotel has marble staircases and an antique lift.

Wasa Park Hotel (Map 3, D4, #24) (☎ 545 45300, fax 545 45301, St Eriksplan 1) Metro: T-St Eriksplan. Singles/doubles Skr495/595 to Skr535/695 (discounted Skr475/575 to Skr495/595). Reception is on the 1st floor of an ordinary six-storey, yellow painted city block, with an entrance located in the tunnel leading from St Eriksplan to Völundsgatan. There are 15 functional rooms, most with shared bathroom and toilet.

Rosinge Gästvåning (Map 3, C4, #18) (☎ 336770, fax 508 60815, Sigtunagatan 6-8) Metro: T-St Eriksplan. Singles/doubles Skr550/750-850 (discounted Skr500/650-750). This five-room guesthouse, in a former bank building, has a basement swimming pool and sauna. The breakfast buffet is particularly good. Don't just turn up here – there's usually no one around.

Hotell Haga (Map 3, B5, #4) (☎ 545 47300, fax 545 47333, ℮ info@hagahotel.se, Hagagatan 29) Metro: T-Odenplan. Singles/doubles from Skr740/985 (discounted Skr540/725). Although it's a characterless, modern place above a car showroom, this hotel is in a quiet area of town.

Pensionat Oden (Map 4, C1, #6) (☎ 612 4349, fax 612 4501, ℮ info@pensionat.nu, ⓦ www.pensionat.nu, Odengatan 38) Metro: T-Rådmansgatan. Singles/doubles with shared bathroom Skr670/69, with private bathroom Skr795/895 (discounted Skr570/650). This small six-room guesthouse is on the 2nd floor of an ordinary city block. The pleasant rooms feature wooden floors and decor of the early 1900s.

Östermalm *Stureparkens Gästvåning* (Map 4, C4, #43) (☎ 662 7230, fax 661 5713, Sturegatan 58) Metro: T-Stadion. Singles/doubles Skr480/795-1500. This older-style guesthouse is on the 4th floor of a featureless six-storey building opposite the small Stureparken Park. The superior double room has a private bathroom. There's a common room with TV and breakfast is served there. The owner's dog is called Chivas!

Hotell Östermalm (Map 4, D4, #47) (☎ 660 6996, fax 661 0471, Karlavägen 57) Metro: T-Stadion. Singles/doubles Skr790/990 (discounted Skr690/790). The Hotell

Östermalm is another old-fashioned place, on the 2nd floor of a nondescript city block. This Yugoslav-run establishment has 18 basic rooms (some with shared bathroom) and narrow corridors. The staff members don't speak English.

A&Be Hotell (Map 4, D4, #46) (☎ 660 2100, fax 660 5987, Grev Turegatan 50) Metro: T-Ostermalmstorg. Singles/doubles with shared bathroom Skr490/690; Skr790/ 890 with private bathroom. Breakfast is not included. Situated on the eastern side of the city centre, this small, old-fashioned 12-room hotel on the 1st floor of a city block is good value. The hallway is adorned with tapestries, and English isn't spoken.

Hotell Örnsköld (Map 6, C9, #64) (☎ 667 0285, fax 667 6991, Nybrogatan 6) Metro: T-Östermalmstorg. Singles/doubles from Skr675/1275 (discounted Skr475/ 975). This pleasant, laid-back 19th-century style hotel has old but well-looked-after facilities still in very good order. Some rooms facing Nybrogatan have wrought-iron balconies.

Södermalm *Mälaren Den Röda Båten* (Map 7, E2, #91) (☎ 644 4385, fax 641 3733, ⓔ info@rodabaten.nu, ⓦ www.roabaten .nu, Söder Malärstrand, Kajplats 6) Metro: T-Slussen. Singles/doubles with private bathroom Skr665/915 to Skr775/1150. The rooms, on board the sister vessel *Ran*, are great value. The finest is the captain's cabin (behind the bridge), with dark wood, nautical paintings, en suite, TV, phone and great views across the lake to the Stadshus (city hall). For information on the other vessel, see Hostels earlier in this chapter.

Pensionat Oden Söder (Map 7, G1, #94) (☎ 612 4349, fax 612 4501, ⓔ info@ pensionat.nu, ⓦ www.pensionat.nu, Hornsgatan 66B) Metro: T-Mariatorget. Singles/ doubles with shared bathroom Skr595/785; with bathroom Skr920/1015 (discounted Skr550/685 without bathroom, Skr820/925 with bathroom on weekends). This is a pleasant, early 20th-century-style guesthouse, which was last renovated in 1999, and has wooden floors and 17 rooms, all with cable TV.

Hôtel Tre Små Rum (Map 5, B5, #25) (☎ 641 2371, fax 642 8808, ⓔ info@ tresmarum.se, ⓦ www.tresmarum.se, Högbergsgatan 81) Metro: T-Mariatorget. Singles/doubles both Skr595. In a quiet district of Södermalm and now with six rooms, this quaint 18th-century basement hotel has Italian-style interior decor, high ceilings and wooden floors. It's one of the nicest hotels in Stockholm and it's hard to beat on value. Bike rental costs Skr85 per day.

Alexandra Hotel (Map 5, C6, #29) (☎ 455 1300, fax 455 1350, ⓔ info@ alexandrahotel.se, Magnus Ladulåsgatan 42) Metro: T-Medborgarplatsen. Singles/ doubles from Skr695/1095 (discounted Skr585/775). This modern hotel has rooms with or without private bathroom. There's also a pleasant breakfast room.

Columbus Hotell & Vandrarhem (Map 5, B7, #44) (☎ 644 1717, fax 702 0764, ⓔ columbus@columbus.se, Tjärhovsgatan 11) Metro: T-Medborgarplatsen. Singles/ doubles from Skr695/795 (discounted Skr595/695). Hostel-standard doubles with shared bathroom Skr500. Columbus Hotell, in a quiet part of Södermalm, has a pleasant cobbled courtyard, stone staircases and wooden floors. It was originally a brewery and dates from 1780. There are many types of rooms, with or without private bathroom; for the hostel-standard accommodation only, breakfast costs Skr55 and sheets are Skr50.

Ersta Konferens & Hotell (Map 7, G10 #117) (☎ 714 6341, fax 714 6351, ⓔ konferens@ersta.se, Erstagatan 1K) Metro: T-Medborgarplatsen. Singles/doubles with shared bathroom Skr450/650; with private bathroom Skr850/1050. Reception open 8am-6pm Mon-Fri & 8am-3pm Sat & Sun. This hotel has pleasant, rather old-fashioned rooms, each with phone, desk and TV. Although breakfast is included, there's also a kitchen for self-caterers. The hotel, near the Viking Line terminal, is run by the parish welfare society. There's also a cafe and restaurant nearby.

Other Areas If city centre hotels are full, or if you want free parking, you can try a suburban hotel – the following have good public transport connections and are great value.

Ibis Stockholm-Syd (Map 2, F3, #29) (☎ 566 32330, fax 976427, e booking@ goodmorninghotels.se, W www.ibishotel .com, Västertorpsvägen 131, SE-12944 Hägersten), Metro: T-Västertorp, then 500m walk. Rooms Skr650 (1-3 people), discounted to Skr530. Breakfast Skr45. This modern hotel is in the southern suburbs, 8km south-west of the city centre and just off the E4/E20 motorway (junction Bredängsmotet). All rooms have cable TV, phone, private bathroom. You'll also find a bar/restaurant, as well as a sauna and a fully equipped gym.

Ibis Stockholm-Väst (☎ 362540, fax 760 9293, e booking@goodmorninghotels.se, W www.ibishotel.com, Finspångsgatan 54, SE-16353 Spånga) Commuter train: J-Spånga station, then 1km walk. Rooms Skr680 (1-3 people), discounted to Skr520. Breakfast Skr45. This hotel is located near the E18 highway in the north-western suburbs about 15km from the city. The rooms each have cable TV and private bathrooms, and the hotel has a bar/restaurant and a sauna.

PLACES TO STAY – TOP END

Most top-end hotels in this section offer en suite rooms with a buffet breakfast, satellite TV, mini bar, room service, a bar/restaurant or cafe, laundry service and sauna (exceptions are noted in the reviews). The standard rate for a single room is over Skr800. An extra bed may normally be included for around Skr150 to Skr250. Garage parking costs around Skr250 for 24 hours. Staff members are well trained, efficient and friendly.

Almost all top-end hotels offer great-value weekend (Friday and Saturday) and summer (late June to early or mid-August) rates, often below Skr700 for a double – about 30% to 40% lower than the rest of the year.

Many hotels are members of chains, such as Radisson SAS (W www.radissonsas .com), Scandic Hotels (W www.scandic -hotels.com), Sweden Hotels (W www

.swedenhotels.se) and First Hotels (W www .firsthotels.com). Online bookings are possible but ask about discount schemes such as coupons, hotel passes or cheques.

Good-value, cut-price packages include a hotel room, free entry to most city attractions, free parking and free local transport; for details, see 'Stockholm Package' under Documents in the Facts for the Visitor chapter.

Hotellcentralen (Map 6, F3, #146) (☎ 789 2490, fax 791 8666, e hotels@ stoinfo.se), at Centralstationen, can usually find you suitable accommodation for a Skr50 fee. It's open 7am to 9pm daily May to September (9am to 6pm daily October to April). Booking is available on the Internet at W www.stockholmtown.se. The handy booklet Hotels & Youth Hostels in Stockholm, available free from tourist offices, lists most hotels and their room rates.

Gamla Stan First Hotel Reisen (Map 7, B5, #40) (☎ 223260, fax 201559, e info@ firsthotels.se, Skeppsbron 12) Metro: T-Gamla Stan. Singles/doubles from Skr1749/1349 to Skr2899/2899 (discounted Skr1249/ 1349). Suites Skr3800/4800. Located in an eight-storey waterfront building with a distinct 'sea-faring' atmosphere, the recently redecorated rooms in this luxurious hotel feature dark wood panelling, wooden floors and sumptuous furnishings. The Chapman suite is one of the finest hotel rooms in the city. There's also a popular piano bar, and an extraordinary swimming pool and sauna in the brick-vaulted cellar.

Victory Hotel (Map 7, C3, #64) (☎ 506 40000, fax 506 40010, e info@victory -hotel.se, Lilla Nygatan 5) Metro: T-Gamla Stan. Singles/doubles from Skr2090/2390 (discounted Skr1150/1750). This early 17th-century building is now literally full of nautical antiques, grandfather clocks, model ships and art. Most rooms are fairly small but the museum-like suites are larger. The hotel's restaurant is Leijontornet (see Places to Eat).

Lord Nelson Hotel (Map 7, C3, #21) (☎ 506 40120, fax 506 40130, e info@ lord-nelson.se, Västerlånggatan 22). Metro:

T-Gamla Stan. Singles/doubles from Skr1320/ 1570 (discounted Skr720/1250). This odd pink-painted building, only 6m wide, features maritime antiques and small rooms with nice woodwork and brass, each with a model ship. You'll find a 'deck' on the roof. The restaurant only serves breakfast and the buffet has a limited selection.

Lady Hamilton Hotel (Map 7, B4, #20) (☎ 506 40100, fax 506 40110, e info@ lady-hamilton.se, Storkyrkobrinken 5) Metro: T-Gamla Stan. Singles/doubles from Skr1950/2250 (discounted Skr990/ 1590). Dating from the 1470s, this quiet and unique place to stay lies in the heart of Gamla Stan, next to Storkyrkan and the Royal Palace. It's packed out with antiques, pictures of Lady Hamilton, rocking horses and art. However, the bathroom facilities are definitely up-to-date. There's a breakfast room, but no other meals are served.

Mälardrottningen (Map 7, C2, #3) (☎ 545 18780, fax 243676, e receptionen@ malardrottningen.se) Metro: T-Gamla Stan. Singles/doubles from Skr950/1075 (discounted Skr790/890) to Skr2050/2050. This cosy vessel, launched in 1924 and now anchored off Riddarholmen, was once the world's largest motor yacht. All cabins have private bathroom and are very well appointed. The deep blue carpets, the wooden floors, ceilings and chairs, and the wonderful restaurant (with a bar in the bridge, above) create a great maritime atmosphere.

City Centre & Vasastaden *Comfort Hotel Prize* (Map 6, D2, #119) (☎ 566 22200, fax 566 22444, e comfort.prize -stockholm@choicehotels.se, Kungsbron 1) Metro: T-Centralen. Singles/doubles from Skr1205/1365 (discounted Skr725/895). This modern business-class hotel in the World Trade Center includes 'Japanese-style' rooms (without windows) and larger multi-bed rooms. There's also a New York-style bar/restaurant.

Radisson SAS Royal Viking Hotel (Map 6, D2, #131) (☎ 506 54000, fax 506 54001, e guest@stozs.rdsas.com, Vasagatan 1)

Metro: T-Centralen. Singles/doubles from Skr2829/3079 (discounted Skr1599/1849). Located in a modern tower block, with all the usual luxury mod-cons, this impressive hotel has up-to-date rooms in fine Swedish style. For seriously expensive meals, visit the attached fish restaurant. The Sky Bar on the 9th floor offers great views.

Central Hotel (Map 6, D3, #125) (☎ 566 20800, fax 247573, e bokningen@ centralhotel.se, Vasagatan 38) Metro: T-Centralen. Singles/doubles from Skr1475/ 1675 (discounted Skr795/1095). This comfortable and appropriately named hotel features subdued contemporary design, particularly friendly staff and a fine buffet breakfast (but no cafe or restaurant).

Adlon Hotel (Map 6, D3, #124) (☎ 402 6500, fax 208610, e hotel@adlon.se, Vasagatan 42) Metro: T-Centralen. Singles/ doubles from Skr1295/1950 (discounted Skr895/1550). Located in a fine building dating from 1884 (complete with circular tower and cupola), Adlon Hotel offers modern rooms with Internet facilities through its LAN.

Freys Hotel (Map 6, D3, #126) (☎ 506 21300, fax 506 21313, e freys@freyshotels .com, Bryggargatan 12) Metro: T-Centralen. Singles/doubles from Skr995/1690 (discounted Skr745/990). Freys Hotel opened in 1989 and features rooms with heavy 1980s and 1990s styles. The reception resembles an art gallery.

Nordic Hotel (☎ 505 63000, fax 505 63420, e info@nordichotels.se, Vasaplan) Metro: T-Centralen. Singles/doubles from Skr1500/2400 (discounted Skr750/1450). Excelling in modern design, the two parts of this new hotel, Nordic Hotel Light **(Map 6, D3, #127)** and Nordic Hotel Sea **(Map 6, E3, #132)**, feature black-and-white and nautical blue-and-white styles, respectively. Nordic Hotel Sea, which is in a former police station, has an impressive 9000L aquarium in the reception area and many rooms face a quiet internal courtyard.

Sheraton Stockholm (Map 6, F4, #158) (☎ 412 3400, fax 412 3409, e sheraton _stockholm@sheraton.com, Tegelbacken 6)

Metro: T-Centralen. Singles/doubles from Skr2700/2900 (discounted Skr1280/1380) to Skr7900/7900. The ugly breeze-block facade conceals a wonderful, modern interior complete with strikingly stylish rooms, a remarkably inexpensive cafe, and a top-quality a la carte restaurant.

Rica City Hotel (Map 6, C4, #112) *(☎ 723 7220, fax 723 7299, Kungsgatan 47)* Metro: T-Hötorget. Singles/doubles Skr1440/1640 (discounted Skr825/1125). Located in the upper five floors of the PUB department store building (where Greta Garbo started her working career), this hotel has very comfortable rooms furnished in modern Scandinavian style.

Hotell August Strindberg (Map 6, A1, #1) *(☎ 325006, fax 209085, ⓔ info@ hotellstrindberg.se, Tegnérgatan 38)* Metro: T-Rådmansgatan. Rooms Skr1150-1400 (discounted Skr850-1000). This quiet family-run hotel, pleasantly situated in a courtyard, has 21 traditional-style rooms and a spiral staircase. There's no sauna or restaurant, and some rooms have shared bathroom.

Hotel Tegnérlunden (Map 6, A2, #3) *(☎ 545 45550, fax 545 45551, ⓔ info .tegner@swedenhotels.se, Tegnérlunden 8)* Metro: T-Rådmansgatan. Singles/doubles from Skr1200/1460 (discounted Skr800/ 990). Near the Strindberg statue in Tegnérlunden Park, this is another modern hotel furnished in tasteful styles. There is a cafe, but no restaurant.

Hotell Lilla Rådmannen (Map 6, A2, #2) *(☎ 506 21500, fax 506 21515, ⓔ radmannen@ freyshotels.com, Rådmansgatan 67)* Metro: T-Rådmansgatan. Singles/doubles from Skr995/1390 (discounted Skr695/990). This recently renovated 36-room hotel has small-ish but tastefully decorated rooms. Staff members are particularly welcoming and the breakfast buffet is excellent. There is no sauna or restaurant.

Kom Hotel (Map 4, D2, #37) *(☎ 412 2300, fax 412 2310, ⓔ bokningen@ komhotell.se, Döbelnsgatan 17)* Metro: T-Rådmansgatan. Singles/doubles from Skr990/ 1450 (discounted Skr800/965). Kom Hotel, in a quiet location opposite Johannes kyrka and just north of the city centre, has interesting contemporary architecture and notably friendly staff. There is no bar/ restaurant, cafe or room service.

Hotell Gustav Vasa (Map 3, C5, #11) *(☎ 343801, fax 307372, ⓔ gustav.vasa@ wineasy.se, Västmannagatan 61)* Metro: T-Odenplan. Singles/doubles from Skr800/ 1100 (discounted Skr575/775). Refurbished in 2001 and located in a 19th-century listed building with wrought-iron balconies, this family-owned place has no frills, modern-style rooms but no restaurant. The discounted rates are good value.

Hotel Oden (Map 3, C5, #10) *(☎ 457 9700, fax 457 9710, ⓔ hotel@hoteloden.se, Karlsbergsvägen 24)* Metro: T-Odenplan. Singles/doubles Skr985/1230 (discounted Skr685/850). Hotel Oden occupies the upper six floors above a supermarket in a busy part of town. The characterless brick facade doesn't inspire confidence but the rooms, in traditional and modern styles, are very pleasant. There's a coffee bar, but no restaurant.

Crystal Plaza Hotel (Map 6, A6, #38) *(☎ 406 8800, fax 241511, ⓔ bokning@ crystalplazahotel.se, Birger Jarlsgatan 35)* Metro: T-Östermalmstorg. Rooms from Skr995-3900 (discounted Skr595/895 singles/doubles). With an impressive eight-storey tower, neoclassical columns and classical-style artwork, this wonderful hotel offers both old-fashioned and modern rooms with excellent facilities. The circular-plan tower rooms are especially nice.

Berns' Hotel (Map 6, D7, #185) *(☎ 566 32200, fax 566 32201, ⓔ info@berns.se, Näckströmsgatan 8)* Metro: T-Kungsträdgården. Singles/doubles from Skr1945/ 2295 (discounted Skr995/1290). Rooms in this modern hotel, all equipped with CD players, range from 19th-century classical to the latest styles featuring marble and lots of dark wood. The attached restaurant (see Places to Eat), dating from 1863, is one of the grandest in the city.

Radisson SAS Strand Hotel (Map 6, E9, #192) *(☎ 506 64000, fax 506 64001, ⓔ sales@stozh.rdsas.com, Nybrokajen 9)*

Metro: T-Kungsträdgården. Singles/doubles from Skr3049/3299 (discounted Skr1699/1949). Not only does this hotel dominate Nybroviken with its tower, ivy-covered facade and copper roof, it also has a wonderful glass-roofed courtyard and luxurious rooms with wooden floors, individualistic styles and great views.

Grand Hôtel Stockholm (Map 6, F8, #197) (☎ 679 3500, fax 611 8686, [e] hotel .grand@grandhotel.se, Södra Blasieholms-hamnen 8) Metro: T-Kungsträdgården. Singles/doubles from Skr2595/3195 (discounted Skr1110/1690). The Grand Hôtel is one of the city's most sumptuous lodgings. Some rooms are in royal Gustavian style but others are intriguing traditional/modern mixes. All rooms have Internet access. Room No 701 has a unique tower with a 360-degree view and No 702 is the astounding Nobel Room, where the literature prizewinners stay overnight. It's an impressive stone building with a copper roof and great views of the Kungliga Slottet (new Royal Palace); many public rooms are quite astonishing, but styles are often heavy.

Scandic Hotel Sergel Plaza (Map 6, E5, #155) (☎ 517 26300, fax 517 26311, [e] sergel.plaza@scandic-hotels.com, Brunk-ebergstorg 9) Metro: T-Centralen. Singles/doubles from Skr1780/2560 (discounted Skr1250/1350). Situated just off Sergels Torg, this fine establishment has ornate 1980s-style decor. The superb roofed and carpeted internal courtyard features live piano music. Room rates include three different types of buffet breakfast – the Japanese breakfast is very popular.

Östermalm *Scandic Hotel Park* (Map 4, C3, #44) (☎ 517 34800, fax 517 34711, [e] park@scandic-hotels.com, Karlavägen 43) Metro: T-Stadion. Singles/doubles from Skr1587/2005 (discounted Skr1150). Opposite Humlegården Park, this fine hotel has a wonderful bistro and rooms with wooden floors and renowned Hästens beds.

Lydmar Hotel (Map 6, B7, #48) (☎ 556 11300, fax 566 11301, [e] info@lydmar.se, Sturegatan 10) Metro: T-Östermalms-torg. Singles/doubles from Skr1850/2200

(discounted Skr1225/1465). The Lydmar Hotel, a functionalist glass and concrete building from 1930, has rooms from antique to modern minimalist, with heavy emphasis on black. The bizarre lift has push buttons giving 10 choices of music! The trendy ground floor bar/restaurant features an hour of live music on most nights (see the Entertainment chapter).

Castle Hotel (Map 6, C8, #63) (☎ 679 5700, fax 611 2022, [e] receptionen@castle -hotel.se, Riddargatan 14) Metro: T-Öster-malmstorg. Singles/doubles Skr1650/1900 (discounted Skr825/950). The family-run Castle Hotel features rooms and public areas in pleasant, subdued Art Deco styles.

Hotel Esplanade (Map 6, D10, #70) (☎ 663 0740, fax 662 5992, [e] hotel@ esplanadesto.se, Strandvägen 7A) Metro: T-Östermalmstorg. Singles/doubles Skr1495/2095 (discounted Skr995/1495). Built in 1910 and facing a quiet courtyard, this excellent and welcoming hotel has individually decorated rooms and a superb breakfast room in Art Nouveau style. There's no restaurant.

Hotell Diplomat (Map 6, D10, #71) (☎ 459 6800, fax 459 6820, [e] info@dipl omat-hotel.se, Strandvägen 7C) Metro: T-Östermalmstorg. Singles/doubles from Skr1795/ 2295 (discounted Skr1095/1595). This Art Nouveau hotel, dating from 1911, has many different styles of rooms, all luxurious and some with excellent harbour views.In the finest rooms you'll find a jacuzzi and a sauna. Staff members are attentive and efficient.

Pärlan Hotell (Map 6, C10, #68) (☎ 663 5070, fax 667 7145, Skeppargatan 27) Singles/doubles Skr975/1175 (discounted Skr700/950). Metro: T-Östermalmstorg. This very popular and homely nine-room hotel has quaint public areas and tastefully decorated rooms with private bathroom. There's also a balcony with views of the internal courtyard. There's no restaurant or sauna.

Mornington Hotel (Map 6, A9, #52) (☎ 507 33000, fax 507 33039, [e] stockholm @ mornington.se, Nybrogatan 53) Metro: T-Stadion. Singles/doubles Skr1895/2020 (discounted Skr1370/1570). This seven-floor, recently renovated (2001), English-style hotel has a unique library of around 5000 books at reception. Rooms are typical of most modern hotels.

Södermalm *Hotel Anno 1647* **(Map 7, F4, #103)** *(☎ 442 1680, fax 442 1647,* e *hotell@ anno1647.se, Mariagränd 3)* Metro: T-Slussen. Singles/doubles from Skr795/995 (discounted Skr595/795). This historical building has labyrinthine hallways and a range of rooms, most with private modern bathrooms and wooden floors. Some rooms have tiled Swedish stoves, toilets with chains, chandeliers or rococo wallpaper. Only a few rooms have good views. There's no restaurant but there's a cafe and bakery on the premises.

Scandic Hotel Sjöfartshotellet **(Map 7, F5, #106)** *(☎ 517 34900, fax 517 34911,* e *sjofart@scandic-hotels.com, Katarinavägen 26)* Metro: T-Slussen. Singles/doubles from Skr1022/1334 to Skr1787/2099. One of the city's best Scandic hotels, just a few minutes' walk from Gamla Stan, Hotel Sjöfartshotellet has a distinctive nautical atmosphere with brass, cherry, oak and extensive use of blue shades. Views, however, are restricted.

Scandic Hotel Slussen **(Map 7, E4, #87)** *(☎ 517 35300, fax 517 35311, Guldgränd 8)* Metro: T-Slussen. Singles/doubles from Skr1618/2036 (discounted rooms from Skr1000-1750). Perched between the chaotic Slussen interchange and Södermalm's underground highway, Scandic Hotel Slussen features grand marble staircases and bathrooms. Rooms are strongly influenced by contemporary design and those facing north have a great view of Gamla Stan.

Scandic Hotel Malmen **(Map 5, B7, #38)** *(☎ 517 34700, fax 517 34711,* e *malmen@ scandic-hotels.com, Götgatan 49-51)* Metro: T-Medborgarplatsen. Singles/doubles from Skr1413/1831 (discounted rooms from Skr950-1650). This functionalist building dating from 1951 has the only piano bar in Södermalm, and the pleasant rooms feature up-to-date design.

Other Areas *Scandic Hotel Täby (☎ 517 35400, fax 517 35411,* e *taby@scandic -hotels.com, Näsbyvägen 4, SE-18330 Täby)* Singles/doubles Skr1090/1402 (discounted by Skr710 per room). If city hotels are full, try the modern Scandic Hotel Täby, located just off the E18 motorway in the northern suburbs. The nearest metro station is T-Mörby Centrum, then take bus No 614. The evening and night bus No 691 from Odenplan or T-Mörby Centrum also passes the hotel.

LONG-TERM RENTALS
Finding a flat in central Stockholm is very difficult due to a serious accommodation shortage, astronomical prices and very high demand. Locals reputedly use methods that are technically illegal and you're advised to steer well clear of this. *Hotellcentralen* **(Map 6, F3, #146)** *(☎ 789 2490)* should be able to advise you on rental.

Solna Vandrarhem & Motelcamp offers long-term rental to students from October to April, and some other hostels may also provide rooms for extended periods. For information, see the earlier Hostels section.

PLACES TO STAY

Places to Eat

FOOD

Stockholm has thousands of restaurants, ranging from inexpensive lunch cafeterias to gourmet establishments with outrageously fine decor. The city may not be one of the world's cheapest places to eat, but the quality is generally high. Many people will have heard of the Swedish chef on *The Muppet Show*, but cooking in Sweden is no laughing matter and *haute cuisine* is all the rage.

Restaurant reservations are recommended, particularly on Friday and Saturday evenings. Due to licensing restrictions, pubs must offer a full menu, sometimes with high prices to discourage potential customers (drinks sales make higher profits). Some pubs accept reservations for meals, but it's not really necessary; see Bars & Pubs in the Entertainment chapter. Almost all restaurants have nonsmoking sections and some don't allow smoking at all.

Many restaurants in Stockholm, particularly pretentious touristy places, levy an entry charge of Skr10 or Skr15. It's disguised as a 'cloakroom fee' and applied across the board by average premises and classy establishments alike. Many people, including locals, find this practice unacceptable and wish to avoid these places on principle. For this reason, admission fees (if any) are mentioned in this chapter.

Breakfast

The day begins with *frukost* (breakfast) – the initial fruit juice (apple or orange) is usually followed by cereal such as muesli, taken with *filmjölk* (cultured milk) or fruit-flavoured yoghurt. Winter alternatives are hot oat or rice porridge, bacon, sausages, meatballs and scrambled eggs. There's usually a buffet of several types of bread, pastries, ryebread, crispbread and/or rolls, with *pålägg* (toppings) including butter, margarine, sliced cheese, sliced meat, spicy sausage or salami, liver pate, pickled herring, sliced cucumber and pepper, jam and marmalade. Coffee is the main breakfast drink.

Breakfast at restaurants is normally only available to residents of the attached hotel or hostel, but a few American-style cafeterias have now opened for business.

Lunch

In restaurants, look for *dagens rätt* (daily special), usually only available 11.30am to 2pm on weekdays. It offers great value and normally includes a main course (meat or fish), salad, drink (lingonberry juice or light beer), bread and butter and coffee. Prices are low, with most restaurants charging between Skr50 and Skr65, but many places also offer more expensive a la carte menus (see also the Dinner section). A few restaurants are only open for lunch.

Alternatively, try takeaways (burgers, pizzas or kebabs – see the Dinner section) or bakeries, cafes and coffee shops (for open sandwiches, filled baguettes, pastries, pies, salads etc, from around Skr15 to Skr45). In cafes, a coffee of any size for less than Skr15 is rare, but ask for *påtår* (free refill). Museum cafes generally offer the cheapest coffee in town.

Dinner

Stockholm is well known for its seafood, which features strongly on many menus, but surprisingly there are few specialist seafood restaurants. Finding traditional Swedish cuisine isn't particularly easy either, since most restaurants now have international or crossover styles. The city also offers a wide range of foreign cuisine.

Most dinner restaurants have menus in English but, if not, the staff will normally be happy to translate for you. Service is generally not up to standard and can be very slow in Asian restaurants. Notable exceptions include the finer restaurants, where the staff have been properly trained to serve their guests.

Ask the tourist office for a free copy of the 136-page *Stockholm Restaurangguide*, which includes 12 pages of maps and lists many of Stockholm's restaurants. It's issued twice yearly and has some text in English.

Swedish Cuisine You will spend at least Skr100 on a main course from a *middag* (dinner) menu in a good restaurant and gourmet restaurants charge from around Skr200 to Skr400. Starters typically cost between Skr60 and Skr120 and desserts range from Skr40 to Skr90.

Starters may include Baltic herring with crispbread or cheese, *gravad lax* (marinated salmon), duck or goose liver pate and prawns. Main courses are dominated by fish, beef and game but lamb and chicken dishes are becoming more common. Look out for *rödingfilé* (grilled fillet of char), *gösfilé* (grilled pike), *marulk* (baked monkfish/anglerfish), *rökt hjortytterfilé* (smoked venison) and *entrecôte* (grilled sirloin steak). These dishes are traditionally served with sauce and vegetables, mainly potatoes. However, adventurous chefs are now serving meals in a more modern international (usually Mediterranean) style. Dessert menus may have a more limited choice, but favourites are *crème brûlée* and warm *hjortron* (cloudberries) with cream or ice cream. See also Traditional Foods in this chapter.

Drinks in these restaurants are expensive: typically, a coke is at least Skr20, a light beer is around Skr24, a full strength beer is Skr40 to Skr50 and a glass of wine costs from Skr35 to Skr70 (some fine wines in the best restaurants will cost over Skr100 per glass). Many restaurants have extensive wine lists, with imports from around the world. *Fullständiga rättigheter* means fully licensed.

Look out for small, low-profile restaurants associated with gourmet kitchens and normally with a separate entrance. These are known as *bakfickan* (literally, 'back pocket') and they offer excellent food (often traditional) at reasonable prices, usually with main courses under Skr100.

Foreign Cuisine Italian restaurants offer a wide range of pasta dishes and pizzas, but meat and fish courses are usually much more expensive. A few places serve Spanish and French food but they're mostly overpriced for what you get, with exceptions including the French dining room in the Grand Hôtel, which is one of the best restaurants in Sweden. Greek restaurants are popular and there's a cluster of them in Södermalm. Solid Polish and Czech meals are also available in town, with main courses under Skr150.

Asian restaurants generally have lower prices. Indian restaurants serve authentic Indian food and are particularly good value. There are many Chinese restaurants in Stockholm, but flavours are notably directed towards Western palates and only a few places are reasonably authentic. Thai restaurants are often better and there are several great places in town. Japanese sushi bars can be found around town, and there's only one Vietnamese restaurant but it's very expensive. You'll also see several Mongolian barbecue restaurants around Stockholm; although some are reasonable, several are not too good. Eat-all-you-like buffets aren't common, but note that food quality may be substandard in these places.

There are a few American-style fried chicken places that also serve things such as fried beans and Texas wraps. There's now a Cuban restaurant, and a Caribbean, Creole and South American restaurant has recently opened, indicating further expansion of interest in exotic foreign tastes.

Vegetarian Cuisine Soup and vegetarian courses (apart from salads) are relatively uncommon on menus, or there may be a limited choice. However, there are several places in Stockholm that specialise in vegetarian cuisine and some places (particularly Asian restaurants) will rustle up vegetarian meals on request. The Hare Krishna-run Govindas restaurant offers excellent vegetarian food at budget prices.

Budget Eating Budget-conscious travellers may want to avoid the expensive dinner menus in restaurants and opt for self-catering, takeaways, or *husmanskost* (traditional Swedish home cooking). The cheapest places to eat dinner are hamburger bars (Sibylla and Scan are reputable chains), McDonald's (a Big Mac, medium chips and medium drink costs Skr39) and the hugely popular pizza, kebab, salad and felafel outlets.

There are hundreds of budget pizza outlets in the suburbs plus a few near the city centre. Many of these places are run by immigrants who don't speak English. Most pizzas are large with thin crust and the least expensive range from Skr29 to Skr45. *Avhämtning* (takeaways) are always cheaper than eating in. Beware of the very spicy cabbage *pizza sallad*. Real salads and vegetarian pizzas also appear on menus and usually cost upwards of Skr40.

The Kungshallen, Hötorgshallen and Centralstationen food courts all contain moderately priced eating places.

Husmanskost, *smårätt* or *Lätt och Gott* (light meals), feature on menus in some pub/restaurants and in bakfickan (see Swedish Cuisine earlier in this chapter). You'll find meals such as *köttbullar och potatis* (meatballs and potatoes), *lövbiff & strips* (thinly sliced fried meat and chips), *pytt i panna* (Swedish hash) and *Falukorv & potatis* (sliced Swedish sausage, potatoes and a fried egg), ranging from Skr45 to Skr100. They're generally filling and good value.

Traditional Foods

In Sweden, some traditional foods are associated with certain times of year. At Skansen, you'll see preparation of traditional foods at the appropriate times. There's also the five-day food festival, Restaurangernas Dag, which takes place from late May to early June. See Special Events in the Facts for the Visitor Chapter.

Smörgåsbord The best-known Swedish food tradition is the *smörgåsbord* buffet, which generally includes a large range of hot and cold dishes, followed by a choice of dessert and coffee.

Potatoes are a strong feature of the smörgåsbord and are eaten along with meat stews or sliced meat freshly cut from steaming joints; grilled or baked trout, char or salmon; or herring, either pickled or in mustard or lemon sauce. The potatoes may be boiled, baked, or sliced with onion and anchovies, then oven-baked with lots of cream. Another great smörgåsbord favourite is gravad lax and potatoes stewed with dill. A full range of other vegetables is normally available, often boiled, but sometimes prepared in more interesting ways.

There's usually a selection of types of bread (eaten with butter), including sweet dark rye bread, tasty *tunnbröd* (thin barley crispbread) and *knäckebröd*, a hard bread made from wheat or rye. The best desserts are *crème brûlée*, strawberries or blueberries and cream, *spettekaka* (Skåne meringue), and warm cloudberry jam with ice cream.

The *julbord* (Christmas smörgåsbord), includes *lutfisk* – this is dried ling or saithe which has been soaked for several days in lye to make it gelatinous. It's then stewed in white sauce and served with boiled potatoes, ground pepper and mustard. Sweet rice pudding with cinnamon is often served for dessert.

Other Dishes Sausages are popular in Sweden and you'll see many types in supermarkets. *Falukorv* is a fairly bland, pale-coloured pork sausage which is best fried but can be boiled; *rotmos och fläskkorv* is mashed turnip and boiled pork sausage; and *isterband* is a sausage with a mixture of pork, beef and barley.

Meat, game and poultry dishes are the mainstay of Swedish menus. Fillets of beef, pork and elk are usually served with a sauce and vegetables. Cheaper restaurants may serve steaks with too much Béarnaise sauce. There's usually at least one lamb and one chicken dish (in white sauce) on a restaurant menu, but more adventurous menus have things such as guinea fowl and reindeer.

Pytt i panna is a mix of diced sausage, beef or pork fried up with onion and potato and served with sliced beetroot and a fried egg. Meatballs and potatoes are commonly served in Swedish households.

Traditional Swedish Foods

Gravad Lax

Marinated salmon can be served smörgåsbord-style or it can be enjoyed along with dill stewed potatoes.

Ingredients
1kg fresh or well-thawed salmon in two equal size fillets
4 tbsp sugar
4 tbsp salt
2 tsp coarse pepper
1 posy of dill, finely chopped
1 lemon

Method
Clean and dry the salmon, leaving the skin intact. Mix the sugar, salt and pepper, then rub the mixture into both salmon fillets. Place the fillets together, nose-to-tail, with the skin facing outward. Pop the fillets in a sealed plastic bag and place in a fridge for around 36 hours, turning the bag over after 18 hours. Remove the seasoning and thinly slice the salmon. Serve with sliced lemon and chopped dill garnish.

Swedish Meatballs

Meatballs are best eaten along with boiled or steamed vegetables such as potatoes, carrots and peas.

Ingredients
3½ tbsp breadcrumbs
300g beef mince
1 tbsp grated onion
1 egg
butter or margarine suitable for frying
100mL water
pinch salt
pinch pepper

Method
Place the breadcrumbs in a bowl and add the water. Leave standing until the water is absorbed. Add the mince, onion, egg, salt and pepper, and work until you have a rubbery-feeling paste. Roll sections of paste into balls around 2cm in diameter. Fry the meatballs over a moderate heat until they're suitably brown.

Fish can be prepared in a variety of ways, but frying and grilling are popular, for example, fried fillet of whitefish, fried char, and grilled salmon and trout. Gravad lax, smoked eel and herring, pickled and fermented herring, caviar, crayfish and shrimps are all considered delicacies, but *surströmming* (fermented herring) is definitely an acquired taste. A variety of pickled herring is available on some restaurant menus and lots of jars may be seen in Swedish supermarkets. Fish dishes are also often used as appetisers (starters) in Swedish restaurant meals.

On Luciadagen (the Lucia festival; 13 December), *lussekatter* (saffron-flavoured wheaten buns), *pepparkakor* (ginger biscuits) and *glögg* (spicy mulled wine) are served.

There is a huge range of hard regional cheeses available in Stockholm, but most are fairly bland. However, *Västerbottens ost* is an excellent, strongly flavoured cheese, which is often eaten along with herring as an appetiser.

DRINKS
Nonalcoholic Drinks

Coffee is Sweden's unofficial national drink, but tea is also widely available. Coffee costs between Skr15 and Skr20 per cup in most cafes. Fizzy drinks, including international brands, are popular but expensive; they're cheapest when bought in 1.5L plastic bottles from supermarkets (around Skr20). The bottles and aluminium cans can be recycled, with supermarket disposal machines giving Skr4 per bottle and Skr0.50 per can. *Saft* (concentrated fruit juice) is commonly made from lingonberries and blueberries and *Festis* is a pleasant, noncarbonated fruit drink.

Tap water is safe to drink in Stockholm so you may want to carry a water bottle.

Mineral water is available in supermarkets for around Skr5 per 330ml bottle, but the price rises steeply to as much as Skr40 in expensive restaurants.

Alcoholic Drinks

Beers are ranked by alcohol content. Good-value light beers (*lättöl;* less than 2.25%) and folk beers (*folköl;* 2.25% to 3.5%) account for about two-thirds of all beer sold in Sweden and can be bought in supermarkets. Medium-strength beer (*mellanöl;* 3.5% to 4.5%) and strong beer (*starköl;* over 4.5%) can only be bought at outlets of the state-owned alcohol store, Systembolaget, or ordered through its agents in remote places. Swedes generally drink strong beer on special occasions.

Sweden's largest breweries, including Spendrups, Pripps, Kopparbergs, Falcon and Åbro, produce a wide range of drinks from cider to light and dark lagers, porter and stout. Pear cider is usually less than 2.25% and may even be alcohol-free. The most popular strong Swedish beers are Norrlands Guld Export, Mariestads Export and Pripps Extra Strong. For a good genuine Stockholm beer, try the excellent fresh lager (which is 5% alcohol by volume) from the little brewery Gamla Stans Bryggeri.

Wines and spirits can only be purchased at Systembolaget, where prices are kept high as a matter of policy (for details see the boxed text 'Systembolaget'). Pick up a copy of the free price list (with an extensive range of mainly imported products), which is updated every two months. Vin & Sprit (V&S) produce some fruit wines and glögg.

Sweden produces its own spirit, *brännvin*, *snaps* or *aquavit* (vodka), which is a fiery and strongly flavoured drink, usually distilled from potatoes. Renat Brännvin (the classic purified Swedish vodka, 39% alcohol by volume; Skr202 per 700ml) tops the liquor league with home sales of 2.1 million litres in 1999.

The legal drinking age in Sweden is 18 years, but many bars and restaurants impose significantly higher age limits – these

Systembolaget

The goal of Swedish alcohol policy, as stipulated by the Swedish parliament, is to reduce alcohol consumption and therefore alcohol-related illness. This seems to work, since Sweden has one of the lowest death rates from liver cirrhosis in Europe.

Limiting private profit from alcohol sales is an integral part of the Swedish alcohol policy since private profit and competition increase both sales and the negative effects of too much alcohol consumption. Sweden, along with a majority of Nordic countries, most Canadian provinces and some US states, operates a government monopoly on the sale of alcohol.

The Swedish Alcohol Retailing Monopoly (*Systembolaget*), a wholly state-owned company, is responsible for selling strong beer, wine and spirits to the general public. The monopoly, which has 411 stores and 580 local agents throughout Sweden, employs 3246 people and sales in 1999 amounted to Skr16.6 billion. Due to EU trading regulations, changes are likely and the future of Systembolaget will be decided by parliament by 2003. It seems likely that the monopoly will be split up and sold off – much to the benefit of big business.

Systembolaget doesn't favour any particular brand nor does it promote Swedish products over imported brands; as a result, the choice available from the company's catalogue is impressive. Supermarket-style outlets are rapidly replacing the former queue-by-number liquor stores and extended hours (both evenings and Saturday opening) are under trial.

usually differ for men and women (which, incidentally, flout the EU sex discrimination laws).

Systembolaget In central Stockholm, you'll find 22 outlets of the state-owned alcohol monopoly, Systembolaget; a complete listing is given at the back of the

Systembolaget price list or on the Internet at Ⓦ www.systembolaget.se. Details of four are given here.

(Map 6, C6, #95) (☎ 796 9810) Regeringsgatan 44. Open 10am to 7pm weekdays, 10am to 2pm Saturday

(Map 6, B8, #60) (☎ 611 2270) Grev Turegatan 3. Open 10am to 6pm weekdays (closing 7pm Thursday, 6.30pm Friday), 10am to 2pm Saturday

(Map 3, E3, #32) (☎ 653 1058) Fleminggatan 56. Open 10am to 6pm weekdays (closing 7pm Thursday and Friday), 10am to 2pm Saturday

(Map 5, B2, #7) (☎ 669 7105) Långholmsgatan 21. Open 10am to 6pm weekdays (closing 7pm Thursday and Friday), 10am to 2pm Saturday

PLACES TO EAT – BUDGET

Budget eating in Stockholm doesn't just mean burgers, kebabs and pizzas. Some cafes and budget restaurants offer reasonable quality meals and more upmarket establishments also offer excellent lunch deals (see the Mid-Range and Top-End sections later in this chapter).

Gamla Stan

Hermitage **(Map 7, C3, #27)** *(☎ 411 9500, Stora Nygatan 11)* Daily special Skr60-70, salads Skr55. Open daily. Hermitage, a modern cafe in a 17th-century building, rustles up fine vegetarian fare from around the world.

Coffee Cup **(Map 7, C4, #67)** *(☎ 244200, Västerlånggatan 57)* Coffee & snacks Skr28-50. Cakes & giant biscuits from Skr15. Open 7am-7.30pm Mon-Fri, 9am-6pm Sat & 10am-6pm Sun. This very cheerful American-style coffee bar in Gamla Stan serves acceptable snacks and is one of the rare places for breakfast.

Sundbergs Konditori **(Map 7, D5, #73)** *(☎ 106735, Järntorget 83)* Daily specials Skr59. Open daily. Sundbergs is the oldest bakery in Stockholm, dating from 1785, and has a fine early 20th-century-style interior. The cafe serves delicious hot sandwiches, pies, omelettes, lasagne and an assortment of other snacks.

City Centre & Vasastaden

Eken **(Map 6, G2, #142)** *(☎ 785 9934, Stadshuset, Hantverkargatan 1)* Lunch Skr65. Open 11am-2pm Mon-Fri. In this bright, modern lunch restaurant you'll serve yourself from a buffet in a wooden rowing boat. Soup, main course, salad, bread, butter and coffee are all included.

Vetekatten **(Map 6, C3, #123)** *(☎ 218 454, Kungsgatan 55)* Tea, coffee & snacks from Skr19. Open 7.30am-8pm Mon-Fri, 9am-5pm Sat & noon-5pm Sun. Popular with shoppers and families, Vetekatten is one of the city's most traditional cafes, with lots of small rooms and a great atmosphere. You can also buy baked goods, large sandwiches and cakes.

Café Vivels **(Map 6, B6, #88)** *(☎ 200157, Kungsgatan 7)* Husmanskost Skr65-75. Open 8am-10pm Mon-Thur, 8am-1am Fri, 11am-1am Sat & 1pm-10pm Sun. Vivels is a fairly large and bright cafe, which serves breakfast, salads, wok dishes, club sandwiches and desserts.

Piccolino **(Map 6, E7, #176)** *(Kungsträdgården)* Sandwiches Skr30-60. Closed winter. A reasonably good spot for coffee and substantial sandwiches but the prices seem a bit high.

Åhléns Café **(Map 6, D4, #134)** *(☎ 676 6000, Klarabergsgatan 50)* Husmanskost Skr59, wok & pasta dishes Skr49/59 small/large (weekdays). Open 10am-6.30pm Mon-Fri, 10am-5.30pm Sat & noon-3.30pm Sun. This shopper's cafe, in the Åhléns department store, also has a large weekday vegetarian buffet and offers 25% discount on takeaways.

Collage **(Map 6, C8, #77)** *(☎ 611 7551, Smålandsgatan 2)* Weekday lunch Skr68, Sun brunch buffet Skr79, evening buffets Skr48 6pm-9.30pm daily. At Collage the buffets change style every fortnight and the food's reasonably good. It's got a kitschy interior but it's popular with a wide range of people and tends to have a party atmosphere late in the evening. There are also Mediterranean and Asian dishes and other main courses on the menu.

Sturekatten **(Map 6, C8, #62)** *(☎ 611 1612, Riddargatan 4)* Snacks, cakes & pies

PLACES TO EAT

Skr15-70. Open 8am-8pm Mon-Fri, 10am-6pm Sat & 11am-6pm Sun. The Sturekatten cafe has good food and a quaint late-19th-century ambience, with antique chairs, paintings and lamps. Cheese and ham pie costs Skr70 and filled baguettes are Skr55.

11350 Café & Deli (Map 4, C1, #12) (☎ 157445, Sveavägen 98) Sandwiches/salads from Skr26/48. Various pies Skr52, including bread, butter & salad. Open 9am-9pm Mon-Fri, 11am-5pm Sat & noon-6pm Sun. This trendy place appeals to the 18-30 set, with its loud music and excellent pasta salads.

Café Sirap (Map 4, B1, #4) (☎ 642 9419, Surbrunnsgatan 31A) Weekday breakfast Skr50 9am-11am, weekday lunch Skr52-54 11am-3pm, sandwiches Skr20-54, American pancakes Skr45-52. Open until 7pm daily. This is a small, popular, no-frills place with a huge menu and pleasant ambience.

Razmahal Indian Restaurant (Map 3, D4, #23) (☎ 311333, Torsgatan 27) Most mains under Skr65. Open daily except lunchtime Sat & Sun. Razmahal is a good budget restaurant with vegetarian dishes and a kid's menu. Beer is only Skr28 at the bar.

Lundberg (Map 3, D4, #27) (☎ 305747, Rörstrandgatan 14) Mains Skr59-89. Open 11am-11pm Mon-Sat. At Lundberg you'll find brick walls, modern design and an international menu with fairly good food. Service is also good and there's a 10% discount on takeaway.

Kungsholmen

Indian Curry House (Map 3, F5, #58) (☎ 650 2024, Scheelegatan 6) Lunch from Skr45, specials Skr50-60, most mains Skr55-75. Open daily. The food in this small, basic restaurant is delicious and includes samosas, curries, thali and murgh dishes. Takeaways are possible.

Café Julia (Map 3, F3, #46) (☎ 651 4515, St Eriksgatan 15) Dagens rätt Skr59, soup special Skr49. Open 10.30am-9pm Mon-Thur & 10.30am-7pm Fri-Sun. The attractive art and minimalist style in this airy cafe complement the food perfectly. Try the rather good home-made cheese here.

Govindas (Map 3, E3, #40) (☎ 654 9004, Fridhemsgatan 22) Lunch/dinner Skr49/69. Open 11am-7pm Mon-Fri (from noon Sat). The authentically decorated Hare Krishna-run Govindas restaurant is cafeteria style and offers an imaginative vegetarian buffet, which changes daily.

Södermalm

Restaurang Connection (Map 5, B2, #6) (☎ 669 8942, Långholmsgatan 32) Daily husmanskost specials Skr45; pizzas, kebabs & wok dishes Skr55-65. A comfortable cafe/restaurant with warm, eclectic decor, friendly staff and great-value food.

Van Der Nootska Palace (Map 7, G3, #100) (☎ 644 2370, St Paulsgatan 21) Lunch mains Skr60-71. Open 11.30am-2pm Mon-Fri. This private palace, built for a Dutch mercenary in the 1670s, now offers lunch in a magnificent setting.

Crêperie Fyra Knop (Map 7, G5, #113) (☎ 640 7727, Svartensgatan 4) Crepes from Skr28, desserts Skr35-48, mains Skr54-74. Open 5pm-11pm Mon-Fri, noon-11pm Sat & Sun. A cosy and intimate little place, with lots of small rooms, serves excellent crepes. It is unique in Stockholm.

AH's Glassbar (Map 5, C8, #55) (Skånegatan 85) Sandwiches from Skr30, weekday lunch Skr50. You'll get the best ice cream in town at this little ice-cream parlour; two scoops in a cone costs Skr15.

Primo Delikatessbutik (Map 5, C8, #57) (Bondegatan 44) Pizzas from Skr42. A warm Italian food store and cafe serving brick-oven fired pizzas and lasagne.

Café String (Map 5, C8, #58) (☎ 714 8514, Nytorgsgatan 38) Buffet breakfast & other meals Skr55. Open daily. Café String, a hugely popular and atmospheric place, looks like a second-hand shop and almost everything is for sale – you can buy your cup or even your chair. The food's good and includes pies and baked potatoes for Skr55.

Zucchero (Map 5, B8, #47) (☎ 644 2287, Borgmästargatan 7) Sandwiches Skr30, pasta dishes Skr65, mains Skr85. Open daily. Zucchero has a 1950s Italian-style, slightly kitschy atmosphere and it can get a bit smoky. The food's fairly good.

Fast Food

The cheapest snacks are to be found in the numerous *gatukök* (takeaway) outlets that serve chips, burgers and sausages. The main gatukök and hamburger restaurant chains found around town include Sibylla, Burger King and McDonald's. Sausages start at around Skr10 and meal deals (burger, chips and a drink) are around Skr45 to Skr55.

There's a *Burger King* in Centralstationen **(Map 6, F3)** and another at Sergelgården **(Map 6, D5, #153)** (the arcade beneath the fountain at Sergels Torg). You'll find an unusual *McDonald's* **(Map 6, C9, #65)** on Nybrogatan (complete with statues, greenery and a library) and another on Vasagatan (outside Centralstationen) **(Map 6, E3, #135)**, which is open 24 hours. On the Drottninggatan mall, *Sibylla Klaragrillen* **(Map 6, F5, #163)** is generally better than the others and also serves meatballs and chips.

Food Courts

Kungshallen **(Map 6, C4, #103)** (☎ 218005, Kungsgatan 44) Open 9am-11pm Mon-Fri, 11am-11pm Sat & noon-11pm Sun. This is a genuine food centre where you can eat anything from Tex-Mex to Indian at budget prices, but things change fast in here and the quality is sometimes dubious. The American-style coffee shop *Robert's Coffee* serves ice cream, milk shakes and a good range of speciality coffees (Skr17 to Skr32). The upstairs sushi bar *Ikki* is excellent; the weekday lunch special is Skr60 and eight/11-bit sushi is Skr72/98. A range of fast food bars in the basement churn out kebabs, pasta, wok dishes, curries and excellent fish and chips.

Centralstationen Food Court **(Map 6, F3)** (Centralstationen) The array of budget eating places here changes quickly, but there's usually somewhere serving pasta, baked potatoes, salads, pizza or wok dishes. Prices tend to be high but the quality isn't unreasonable.

Pizzas & Kebabs

Hundreds of budget pizza and kebab places offering takeaway and eat-in can be found on the outskirts of the city centre.

Gamla Stans Kebab **(Map 7, B3, #23)** (☎ 215133, Storkyrkobrinken 11) Kebabs & pizzas, mostly Skr40-55. Open 10am-8pm daily. Interestingly ornate and old-fashioned, this place seems an unlikely Arabian-style kebab outlet.

Stora Nygatans Grill **(Map 7, B3, #24)** (Stora Nygatan 1) Burger & kebab meals Skr40-60. Open daytime, and summer evenings. This fast food joint also serves traditional Swedish dishes such as tunnbröd wrap with mashed potato and sausage.

Carinas Pizzeria **(Map 6, B1, #8)** (☎ 218687, Upplandsgatan 9B) Daily special pizza Skr29, pan pizzas Skr45/80 small/medium. Open 10.30am-10pm Mon-Fri, noon-10pm Sat & Sun. For great food and soft drinks at very reasonable prices, try this little pizzeria. Salads and lasagne cost Skr45.

Pavonas Grill Pizza Kebab **(Map 3, E3, #33)** (Fleminggatan 95) Kebabs/pizzas from Skr30/40. A small and rather basic place with a few tables, but most business is takeaway.

Pizzeria Vicky **(Map 5, B2, #3)** (☎ 669 9859, Högalidsgatan 48) Weekday lunch Skr45. Pizzas from Skr40, salads from Skr45. A friendly place serving tasty pizzas, but no English is spoken.

Angelos **(Map 5, B4, #21)** (☎ 669 9027, Rosenlundsgatan 18) Pizzas Skr40-65. Open 10am-10pm Mon-Fri, noon-10pm Sat & Sun. Acceptable pizzas are served and imported Italian groceries are sold here.

Jerusalem Royal Kebab (Götgatan 61) Kebabs & felafel from Skr15 (Skr45 with rice). Open 24 hours. This rather unprepossessing place is actually quite popular and the food is OK.

Other Outlets

Rooster **(Map 6, C6, #91)** (☎ 225902, Regeringsgatan 48) Snacks & fried chicken from Skr35. Open 11am-7pm Mon-Fri & noon-5pm Sat. At Rooster, you'll get noodles, fried beans, fried chicken and burgers. The BBQ chicken meal is Skr55.

Gelateria Italiana **(Map 3, F3, #41)** (☎ 653 0140, Drottningholmsvägen 22) Sandwiches from Skr35. A small coffee shop serving excellent toasted sandwiches and home-made ice cream, also known as a haunt of SL bus drivers.

Yogurt Shoppen **(Map 6, E5, #156)** *(Gallerian)* Soft frozen yoghurt Skr15-25, toppings Skr23-35. Enjoy an unusual and tasty dessert while sitting around a rectangular bar in the middle of the Gallerian shopping centre.

Nystekt Strömming (Södermalmstorg) For some of the best fried herring in Stockholm, visit this little trailer outside the metro station T-Slussen.

SELF-CATERING

Making your own meals is easy enough if you're hostelling or camping. In supermarkets, both the item price and comparative price per kilogram have to be shown by law. Plastic carrier bags usually cost Skr1 or Skr2 at the checkout.

Supermarkets aren't easy to find in Stockholm and you'll need to know where to look. The main chains Vivo and Konsum have outlets at major metro stations. Shop at Rimi for much lower prices.

Supermarkets

ICA Baronen (Map 4, C1, #7) (Odengatan 40) Open 8am to 10pm daily
Klippet (Map 3, E3, #36) (T-Fridhemsplan, northern entrance) Open 8am to 10pm daily
Konsum (Map 5, B2, #7) (Birkagatan 30) Open 9am to 10pm daily
Rimi (Map 5, B3, #12) (Hornsgatan 138) Open 9am to 9pm Monday to Saturday, 11am to 9pm Sunday
Vivo T-Jarlen (Map 6, C8, #61) (T-Östermalmstorg, Grev Turegatan entrance) Open 7am to 9pm weekdays, 10am to 7pm Saturday, noon to 6pm Sunday

Bakeries

Stockholm's traditional bakeries are fairly similar and offer fantastic confections at outrageous prices. Most have attached cafes.

Gunnarssons Specialkonditori (Map 5, C7, #75) (Götgatan 92) Closed Sunday
Konditori Ritorno (Map 5, C5, #16) (Odengatan 80)

Källströms Konditori (Map 3, E3, #37) (Fleminggatan 83)
Munken Konditori (Map 5, B8, #45) (Renstiernas Gata 19) Closed Sunday
Tjärhovsbagarn (Map 5, B7, #40) (Tjärhovsgatan 1) Opens 3am

Market Halls

The colourful market halls are excellent places to sample local and exotic tastes.

Hötorgshallen **(Map 6, C4, #104)** *(Hötorget)* Open 10am-6pm Mon-Thur, 10am-6.30pm Fri & 10am-4pm Sat. Located in the basement below the Filmstaden cinema, Hötorgshallen has several Asian fast-food outlets, a good fish restaurant and many fine specialist food shops selling meat, fish, cheese, groceries, coffee and tea. There's a daily street market (flowers, fruit and vegetables) in Hötorget.

Östermalms Saluhall **(Map 6, B9, #54)** *(Östermalmstorg)* Open 10am-6pm Mon, 9am-6pm Tue-Fri & 9am-3pm Sat. Excellent for fresh fish and meat, but there are also places selling bread, cheese, fruit and vegetables. There are some fast-food outlets and restaurants, including *Depå Sushi* and the more expensive bistro *Tysta Mari*.

Söderhallarna **(Map 5, B6, #33)** *(☎ 714 0984, Medborgarplatsen)* This more modern market hall includes a vegetarian restaurant, delis, a cheese shop, an Asian supermarket and a pub.

PLACES TO EAT – MID-RANGE

A typical place to eat and drink in the evenings is the *kvarterskrog* (neighbourhood pub), which generally combines excellent cuisine with a fully licensed bar. Most of these places are in Vasa Staden and Södermalm. Krogs are generally open 5pm to 1am or so, although about 10 places in the city stay open until 5am at least once a week. See also Pubs in the Entertainment chapter.

Gamla Stan

Michelangelo **(Map 7, D4, #69)** *(☎ 209 391, Västerlånggatan 62)* Pizzas Skr78-102, mains Skr87-199. Open daily. This is an Italian restaurant, with great classical-style atmosphere, paraffin lamps, painted ceilings and Roman statues, and the food's not bad either.

Café Art (Map 7, D4, #68) (☎ *411 7661, Västerlånggatan 60)* Snacks & light meals from Skr40. Open 11am-11pm daily. A trendy barrel-vaulted and brick-lined cellar – just the place for a coffee and cake, a waffle, quiche or lasagne.

Kristina (Map 7, D4, #70) (☎ *208086, Västerlånggatan 68)* 2-/3-course meals Skr209/235, pasta dishes Skr101-110, salads Skr35-79, mains Skr101-225. Open daily. This rather old-fashioned place had lost popularity, but the daily live jazz (free) is now drawing people back. Most main courses seem rather overpriced.

Siam Thai Restaurant (Map 7, C4, #62) (☎ *200233, Stora Nygatan 25)* Weekday lunch Skr65, mains Skr95-165. Closed Sun. A friendly and flexible restaurant in a brick cellar offering a range of authentic mild to spicy Thai dishes. The food is excellent, portions are large and the service is great.

Maharajah (Map 7, C3, #63) (☎ *210404, Stora Nygatan 20)* Most mains Skr69-89, clay oven tandoori dishes Skr75-119. Open daily. This cosy Indian restaurant, with appropriate music and an open fire in winter, serves excellent food at keen prices. The Swedish songwriter Carl Michael Bellman lived here from 1787 to 1789.

Cattelin (Map 7, B3, #22) (☎ *201818, Storkyrkobrinken 9)* Buffet weekday lunch Skr65, mains Skr90-160. Open daily in summer, Mon-Fri only in winter. Cattelin, with old-fashioned decor (and garden seating in summer) serves reasonably priced Swedish dishes and specialises in fish.

Zum Franziskaner (Map 7, D5, #75) (☎ *411 8330, Skeppsbron 44)* Weekday lunch Skr65, Franziskaner Classics Skr92-149, other mains Skr114-209. Cloakroom fee Skr10. Closed Sun & 4-22 Jan. Founded in 1421 by German monks and claiming to be the oldest restaurant in the city, Zum Franziskaner still serves German and Austrian beers, sausages and meals. Although the current building dates from 1906, it looks like a museum inside, with well-preserved wooden stalls, ornate cabinets and ceiling artwork.

Gamla Stans Bryggeri (Map 7, C6, #42) (☎ *202065, Tullhus 2, Skeppsbrokajen)* Mains Skr145-195. Bar menu: salads Skr50-130, mains Skr135-145. Open daily 4pm-11pm (bar closes 1am, 3am Sat & Sun). Minimum age 20/23 women/men. This huge restaurant has its own brewery and you'll see two huge copper brewing vats surrounded by the bar. In summer, you can eat on the veranda, with nice views across the water. The food here is quite good and the international-style menu has Spanish influences.

City Centre

Bakfickan (Map 6, F7, #173) (☎ *676 5809, Karl XII:s torg)* Mains Skr65-192. Open 11.30am-midnight Mon-Sat. With superb service, Art Nouveau decor, stools around the bar and opera-related photos, this little restaurant serves gourmet-quality Swedish husmanskost at moderate prices. Try the assorted herring, boiled potatoes and crispbread (Skr85).

Normans Mat & Form (Map 7, B7, #46) (☎ *611 9989, Skeppsholmen)* Lunch around Skr80. Open 11.30am-2.30pm Mon-Fri. A bright and airy lunch restaurant with small, temporary exhibits of modern design. The food is good, especially the bread, and servings are generous.

Allemans Bar & Matsal (Map 6, D5, #97) (☎ *212885, Malmskillnadsgatan 40)* Daily specials Skr79 including beer or wine. Pasta dishes Skr79-89, mains Skr129-159. Open daily for lunch & dinner. This is a relaxed pub, which serves notably good-value food, including light meals, grilled steak, lamb or fish, and vegetarian dishes.

Djingis Khan (Map 6, B4, #25) (☎ *216385, Sveavägen 36)* Mongolian buffet Skr138. Buffet available every evening, and afternoons Sat & Sun. Djingis Khan is an outrageously ornate restaurant serving Chinese a la carte but better known for its vast buffet which includes soup, bread, seven main courses, a salad bar and dessert.

Bistro Boheme (Map 6, B3, #18) (☎ *411 9041, Drottninggatan 71A)* Mains Skr62-162. Open daily. This odd place has weird designer furniture, a tiled contemporary bar with loud music, and a beer garden in summer. The menu includes Czech goulash soup and vegetarian lasagne. You can also try Swedish *punsch* here.

Leonardo (Map 4, D1, #24) (☎ *304021, Sveavägen 55)* Pasta dishes Skr86-124, stone oven-baked pizza Skr73-95, mains Skr155-188. Open daily. There's a huge menu at this excellent, cosy Italian restaurant and pizzas are also available for takeaway.

Café Piastowska (Map 4, C2, #28) (☎ *212508, Tegnérgatan 5)* 2-course dinner Skr160, including beer or wine. Mains Skr135-155. Open 6pm-11pm Mon-Sat. An extraordinarily quaint place with unusual decor, a vaulted cellar and genuine Polish cooking. A different soup is offered every day.

Restaurang Spice House (Map 6, B2, #12) (☎ *141032, Upplandsgatan 6)* Lunch Skr55 inclusive, mains around Skr80. Open daily. Fairly minimalist decor features in this authentic Indian restaurant. Portions are large and the vegetable dishes are recommended.

Sabai Sabai (Map 6, A2, #6) (☎ *790 0913, Kammakargatan 44)* Mains Skr85-179. Open daily (dinner only). Friendly and laid-back Sabai Sabai, an award winning Thai restaurant, serves great Thai food and has a rather ornate tropical-style interior. The extensive menu includes wok, noodle, curry, fish and seafood dishes.

Tures (Map 6, B8, #56) (☎ *611 0210, Sturegallerian 10)* Mains Skr88-165. Highly recommended, this pleasant eating place sits in the middle of a trendy shopping mall. Try the excellent fried herring and Västerbottens ost.

Sturehof (Map 6, B7, #58) (☎ *440 5730, Stureplan 2)* Shellfish platter Skr330, mains Skr95-330. Open to 2am daily (kitchen closes 1am). Known as one of Sweden's busiest restaurants, bright and modern Sturehof has a menu vast enough to satisfy every taste. Fish dishes are recommended.

Vasastaden & Djurgården

Svea Bar & Matsal (Map 4, D1, #25) (☎ *315950, Sveavägen 53)* Pizzas Skr58-75, pasta dishes Skr67-77 & other mains Skr95-145. Open daily. There's a wide range of international dishes at this modern split-level place. Look out for the blackboard specials. A disco booms nightly from Wednesday to Saturday.

La Habana (Map 4, C1, #13) (☎ *166465, Sveavägen 108)* Mains Skr100-150. La Habana is a recommended Cuban restaurant with friendly staff, good service and great food. Beer and rum are served. There's a casual atmosphere here plus there's salsa music, with dancing in the basement.

Storstad (Map 4, C1, #8) (☎ *673 3800, Odengatan 41)* Mains Skr150-200. You'll get a good meal and excellent service in this modern design-style (but unpretentious) restaurant. The international-style menu includes a reasonable range of meat and fish dishes.

Sibiriens Soppkök (Map 4, B1, #3) (☎ *150014, Roslagsgatan 25)* Daily soup specials Skr55 inclusive, a la carte soups Skr67-121. Open 9am-9pm Mon-Fri & noon-6pm Sat. Sibiriens Soppkök is a small, traditional-style soup kitchen, but the soups are from around the world. Main courses and baguettes are also available.

Haga Restaurang & Delikatesser (Map 4, B1, #16) (☎ *319695, Hagagatan 18)* Pizzas Skr79-89, pasta Skr94-129, other mains Skr139-179. Open daily (kitchen closes 10.30pm). This cosy and friendly Italian-style family restaurant includes an old-fashioned tiled deli section and Italian wines are served. Antipasti and desserts also feature on the menu; the pizzas are particularly good.

Narknoi Bar & Restaurang (Map 3, D4, #19) (☎ *307070, Odengatan 94)* Mains Skr121-184. Open daily (lunch Sat & Sun only). Excellent Thai food is available at this award-winning, friendly and unpretentious restaurant. It's fairly small, with minimalist styles. The mild to hot dishes on the menu include many types of meat and fish and a less expensive vegetarian selection. Book well in advance.

Rabarber (Map 3, C4, #20) (☎ *311775, Karlbergsvägen 52)* Mains under Skr100. Meals served 4pm-1am daily. The bar in this friendly neighbourhood restaurant is

PLACES TO EAT

popular with an after-work crowd and serves tasty traditional Swedish meals. It doubles up as an art gallery, with some fairly wild stuff.

Broncos Bar (Map 4, D2, #32) (☎ 160215, Tegnérgatan 16) Mains Skr59-119. Open daily. Bright and airy Broncos Bar, renowned for its fast service and good, filling husmanskost, has its own beer and is run by a former weightlifter. The extensive menu includes meatballs, falukorv and pytt i panna (all Skr79).

Restaurang Patpong (Map 4, D2, #31) (☎ 458 9567, Luntmakargatan 63) 4-course lunch buffet Skr60-70, 3-course dinner Skr185, soups Skr35-55, mains Skr85-135. Open daily. This fine Thai restaurant has minimalist decor but a luxurious atmosphere. Try the Thai fondue with marinated meat and seafood (Skr185).

Restaurang Malaysia (Map 4, C1, #9) (☎ 633 5669, Luntmakargatan 98) Mains Skr115-170. Open daily. The excellent food in this tropical-style restaurant has been recommended by Asian visitors to Stockholm and it includes noodle and rice dishes, beef, lamb, duck, fish and cuttlefish.

Blå Porten Cafe (Map 4, G6, #102) (☎ 663 8759, Djurgårdsvägen 64) Mains Skr65-105. Open 11am-7pm daily (9pm Tue & Thur); longer hours in summer. The Swedish and international meals in this popular cafe, which is next to Liljevalchs Konsthall in Djurgården, are particularly recommended.

Kungsholmen

Mamas & Tapas (Map 3, F5, #57) (☎ 653 5390, Scheelegatan 3) Small Spanish dishes Skr30, mains Skr68-148. Open 4pm-1am Mon-Fri & noon-1am Sat & Sun. Mamas & Tapas serves reasonable food and it tends to be busy. Its modern styles include a tiled bar and Spanish art.

Salzer Restaurant & Bar (Map 3, G4, #54) (☎ 650 3028, John Ericssongatan 6) Mains Skr120-170, from Skr80 in 'Propeller bakfickan' (so called because John Ericsson, after whom the street is named, invented the propeller). Modern design and excellent service feature strongly here.

Menus have Swedish and continental choices, including vegetarian. You can also try the local Kungsholmen brew, 'Lundbergs lager'.

Hot Wok Café (Map 3, F3, #48) (☎ 654 4202, Hantverkargatan 78) Lunch Skr59-95, mains Skr119-179. Open 11am-midnight Mon-Fri, 1pm-midnight Sat & Sun. Contemporary art and trendy music feature strongly in this busy place. Staff are friendly and meal portions are large, but prices seem high.

Ristorante la Rustica (Map 3, F3, #47) (☎ 651 4051, Hantverkargatan 73) Specials Skr70-179, pasta Skr85-105, mains Skr159-185. Open daily. This large, pleasant restaurant has a vaulted interior and Italian scenes on the side of the bar. The food's not bad but it's a bit on the pricey side.

Pic-Nic (Map 3, E3, #31) (☎ 652 3819, Fleminggatan 70) Lunch & evening specials from Skr79. Open daily. In this very nice place, you can enjoy your candle-lit meal at a wooden table while viewing the art exhibits. The menu includes beef, pork, fish and pasta.

Södermalm

Restaurang Ho's (Map 5, C2, #5) (☎ 844 420, Hornsgatan 151) Mains around Skr150. Closed Mon & lunchtime Sat & Sun. One of the most authentic Chinese restaurants in Stockholm, Hos has none of the kitsch but all of the quality. Well worth a visit.

Restaurang Ming Palace (Map 7, G1, #96) (☎ 640 8686, Mariatorget 2) Weekday lunch from Skr58, mains Skr90-125. Open daily. Ming Palace is another authentic Chinese restaurant, with elegant black-and-white decor, a goldfish pond and a waterfall. The four small courses and the ice cream with preserved ginger are particularly recommended.

Fenix (Map 5, B6, #36) (☎ 640 4506, Götgatan 40) Mains Skr64-192. Open daily. This colourful and modern international-style restaurant, with art and designer furniture, is a busy place serving things such as nachos, wok dishes, Cajun tortillas and sushi.

Hermans Trädgårdscafé (Map 7, G8, #115) (☎ 643 9480, *Fjällgatan 23A*) Lunch/dinner Skr65/95. Open daily to 9pm (11pm in summer). Here you'll get excellent budget vegetarian buffets and tables in two barrel-vaulted basement rooms or summer veranda seating with a five-star view. Home-made snacks are also available.

La Scudetto (Map 5, B8, #46) (☎ 640 4215, *Åsögatan 163*) Pasta dishes Skr88-99, other mains Skr172-198. Closed Sun. La Scudetto is a pleasant, minimalist-style restaurant serving some of the best Italian food in town, a notable wine rack and good friendly service.

Dionysos (Map 5, C8, #52) (☎ 641 9113, *Bondegatan 56*) Weekday lunch Skr58-60. 2-course meals Skr160-170, mains Skr95-178. Open daily. Dionysos is a charming and friendly place which opened in 1974 – the first Greek restaurant in Stockholm. The menu includes tzatziki, moussaka and a vegetarian dish. Greek wines are available.

Sonjas Grek (Map 5, C8, #53) (☎ 702 2229, *Bondegatan 54*) Lunch from Skr82, mains Skr75-178. Open daily. Close to Dionysos, this restaurant offers stylish dining, the usual Greek dishes, and an ouzo bar.

Matcultur (Map 5, B9, #48) (☎ 642 0353, *Erstagatan 21*) Mains Skr73-193. This is a bright, arty restaurant offering rather good international-style Swedish and exotic food, from clam chowder to Vietnamese chicken. World music is played by the DJ at the bar.

Mest (Map 5, B7, #35) (☎ 641 3653, *Götgatan 46*) Mains Skr85-110. Cloakroom fee Skr8. Open afternoon until late. You'll get good food and good service in this large, modern-style bar. Check the daily specials menu.

Little Persia (Map 5, C7, #61) (☎ 644 8569, *Östgötagatan 32*) Salads Skr65-75, mains Skr110-175. Open daily to 11pm (1am Sat & Sun). Expect the best in Persian home cooking here, but you'll need to relax among the huge cushions and the pleasant atmosphere, since your dinner will take most of the evening to be served. The menu includes vegetarian and kebab dishes.

Koh Phangan (Map 5, C7, #67) (☎ 642 6865, *Skånegatan 57*) Lunch Skr65, mains Skr90-220. Open daily until late (from 2pm Sat & Sun). This outrageously kitsch Thai restaurant has to be seen to be believed. It's best at night, when you can enjoy your meal in a real tuk-tuk to the accompanying racket of crickets and a tropical thunderstorm. The food is fairly good, but service is moderate. There's a DJ after 10pm, Tuesday to Sunday.

Indira Indisk Restaurang & Bar (Map 5, C7, #62) (☎ 641 4046, *Bondegatan 3B*) Vegetarian Skr70-80, mains Skr75-120. Open 5pm-11pm Mon, 3pm-11pm Tue-Fri, 1pm-11pm Sat & Sun. You'll find Indian-style decor, an aquarium and a huge menu of good authentic food in this popular restaurant.

Faros (Map 5, C8, #69) (☎ 442 1414, *Sofiagatan 1*) Mains Skr98-175. Open daily. With a rather dark interior, some condescending staff and mixed reports from diners, this might not be your first choice of Greek restaurant.

Pelikan (Map 5, C7, #74) (☎ 556 09090, *Blekingegatan 40*) Mains Skr74-182. Open for dinner daily & for lunch Sat & Sun. Minimum age 23. The well-established place has a unique atmosphere with rooms in three different styles, including a German-style beer hall with monkeys painted on the pillars and ceiling. The food is good – husmanskost is on the menu and there's usually a vegetarian special on the blackboard.

PLACES TO EAT – TOP END

Reservations are essential at top-end restaurants, especially on Friday and Saturday evenings. Few places accept orders after 10pm, although they may stay open until midnight or 1am. Many restaurants are closed on Sunday – always phone to check.

Gamla Stan

Pontus in the Greenhouse (Map 7, C5, #38) (☎ 238500, *Österlånggatan 17*) Starters Skr215-400, mains Skr295-365. Open 11.30am-3pm & 6pm-11pm Mon-Fri, noon-4pm & 5.30pm-11pm Sat. Just across from the St George monument, this stylish

Many *konditori* (bakeries) have attached cafes.

10.20am in Stortorget – a great place to brunch

Street corner in late June, Gamla Stan

Historic, multicoloured buildings, west of Stadshuset, as seen from across Lake Mälaren

You can buy bananas, beetroots and bouquets at the daily street market in Hötorget.

Cafe-dwellers in historic Stortorget square

The fine art of cone-making...

You'll drool over the glassware in Stockholm.

modern restaurant with greenish decor was declared the best in Sweden in 2000 and it deserves the fine reputation. You can eat while seated at a central bar or at regular tables. Courses, including Beluga caviar and Greenhouse canapes, are exceedingly well presented.

Primo Restaurant (Map 7, C5, #40) (☎ 362500, Skeppsbron 12) Dagens rätt Skr75, mains Skr169-235. Open 11.30am-2.30pm Mon-Fri & 5pm-midnight daily. You'll find this atmospheric, contemporary restaurant, with fine food, a wooden floor, wooden tables, model ships and other nautical items, in First Hotel Reisen. There's an emphasis on seafood and it's excellent value for lunch.

Leijontornet (Map 7, C5, #64) (☎ 142 355, Lilla Nygatan 5) Starters Skr155-195, mains Skr270-320. 3-/5-course fixed-price meals Skr420/675, excluding wine. Open 6pm-10.30pm Mon-Sat, closed Sun. One of the finest city restaurants, Leijontornet's basement dining room includes the foundations of a 14th-century tower. The brick-vaulted ceilings and candlelight add to the atmosphere, but furnishings feature modern design. The superb menu features fish, duck, game and vegetarian dishes. There's also a cheaper mid-range Italian-style bakfickan menu.

Källare Restaurang Movitz (Map 7, D4, #66) (☎ 209979, Tyskabrinken 34) 2-/3-course meals Skr210/255 to Skr280/320, pub meals under Skr100. Cloakroom fee Skr10. Open 11am-11pm Mon-Thur, 11am-midnight Fri-Sun. This pleasant, 17th-century, white-painted and brick-arched cellar is a busy place, which serves traditional Swedish fare with an Italian twist. The menus include fish, lobster, beef with gorgonzola, veal and pork. Upstairs in the pub there's often live music and meals are also served.

Fem Små Hus (Map 7, C5, #39) (☎ 100482, Nygränd 10) Fixed-price menus Skr365-460, mains Skr205-265. Cloakroom fee Skr10. Open 5pm-midnight Tues-Sat, 5pm-11pm Sun & Mon. Located in several brick-vault cellars, cosy Fem Små Hus specialises in reindeer, salmon, beef and veal, but locals reckon it's overpriced.

Den Gyldene Freden (Map 7, D5, #56) (☎ 109046, Österlånggatan 51) 2-/3-course set menu Skr418/468, husmanskost Skr96-185, mains Skr248-378. Cloakroom fee Skr10. Open 5pm-midnight Mon-Fri, 1pm-midnight Sat. This incredible place, which includes three barrel-vaulted cellar dining rooms (two with plasterwork paintings), has been open continuously since 1722 and it oozes history. High standards are maintained here and the husmanskost deals are excellent.

City Centre

Restaurant Anna Rella (Map 6, E5, #155) (☎ 517 26300, Scandic Hotel Sergel Plaza, Brunkebergstorg 9) 2-/3-course pre-theatre menu Skr260/311, mains Skr95-220, lunch husmanskost Skr120. Open 11.30am-2pm Mon-Fri & from 6pm-late daily. This fine restaurant's discreet alcoves are popular with Swedish politicians for lunchtime conversations, so book well in advance. The restaurant has a heavy 1980s style with an emphasis on blue. With competitive prices, the international-style menu covers most tastes and it includes salads, fish, meat and vegetarian options.

Franska Matsalen (Map 6, F8, #197) (☎ 679 3584, Grand Hôtel Stockholm, Södra Blasieholmshamnen 8) Starters Skr185-1900, mains Skr195-450, desserts Skr95-135. 6-course set menu (including vegetarian) Skr695-1200. Open 6pm-11pm Mon-Fri only. The ornate French restaurant at the Grand Hôtel has chandeliers, lots of dark wood and deep red carpets. It has received the accolade of best restaurant in Sweden, so the food is guaranteed to be spectacular. There's also an extensive French wine list. A smörgåsbord lunch is available 11.30am to 3pm on weekdays in the Grand Veranda, also in the Grand Hôtel.

Operakällaren (Map 6, F7, #171) (☎ 676 5800, Karl XII:s torg) 7-course *Menu Dégustation* Skr1450, 3-course *Menu Végétarien* Skr500, mains Skr370-400. Open 5pm-10pm daily. The finest place within the Opera House is the century-old Operakällaren, with fantastic decor (which has to be seen to be believed), deep red carpets,

PLACES TO EAT

Alfred Nobel & the Nobel Banquet

Alfred Nobel (1833–96), Swedish chemist, engineer and industrialist, patented a detonator for highly unstable nitroglycerine in 1862. Four years later he made the remarkable discovery that kieselguhr could absorb nitroglycerine safely, but remain an explosive substance. This became known as dynamite and Nobel's factories expanded enormously to cope with demand, increasing their output 6000-fold over the next 30 years.

As a very wealthy industrialist, Nobel's will created the annual Nobel Prizes (from 1901) in physics, chemistry, medicine/physiology, literature and peace, to be awarded to those who had benefited mankind the most in the preceding year. A sixth prize, for economics, was added in 1969.

On 10 December every year, after the prize ceremony at Konserthuset, the Nobel Banquet is held in the Blue Hall at Stadshuset. There are 1353 guests, including prize winners and their families, international guests representing science and literature, members of the royal family, representatives from the government and MPs. The banquet, covered by Swedish and international media, is a vast affair. Laying the tables takes 30 people six hours and there's 240 serving staff. The 25 chefs produce three different menus; 340 bottles of champagne are consumed during the first course and 340 bottles of wine wash down the main course. The after dinner drink is a mere 330L of coffee!

Visitors to Stockholm can enjoy the latest Nobel Menu in Stadshuskällaren – see the restaurant review for details.

---

paintings and extravagant furnishings. The gourmet menu, printed in French, includes caviar, fish, hare and pigeon. Try the chocolate souffle with liquorice ice-cream dessert. Men must wear a lounge suit and a tie before being admitted. To dine here on weekends, you'll need to book a fortnight in advance.

Fredsgatan 12 (Map 6, F5, #160) (☎ 248052, Fredsgatan 12) Starters Skr135-250, mains Skr245-345. Open 11.30am-2pm Mon-Fri & 5pm-1am Mon-Sat. With minimalist modern decor and classical touches, this fine restaurant has one of Sweden's best chefs and is highly recommended. Courses include seafood, lamb, veal and duck.

Stadshuskällaren (Map 6, G2, #143) (☎ 650 5454, Stadshuset, Hantverkargatan 1) Mains Skr185-265, Nobel Menu Skr1075 including wine. Open 11.30am-11pm Mon-Fri & 2pm-11pm Sat. This very chic restaurant has two main rooms with impressive paintings on the walls and vaulted ceilings. The seasonal a la carte menu always has a variety of well-presented meat and fish dishes.

Orientexpressen Restaurang & Bar (Map 6, F3, #145) (☎ 202049, Centralstationen) Starters Skr69-125, mains Skr89-218, desserts Skr42-59, 2-course lunch/dinner Skr169/275. Open daily until late. This place is an old Stockholm favourite, with serving in authentic re-creations of railway carriages and KRAV-marked ecological standards. The food is great value in here; try the braised char in butter sauce (Skr172) or the fried root vegetables and Västerbotten cheese in a creamy basil sauce (Skr124).

Berns (Map 6, D8, #186) (☎ 566 32222, Berzelii Park) Restaurant menu mains Skr130-325, 2-/3-course set menu Skr265/325, bistro menu mains Skr95-215 & weekend brunch buffet Skr175. Open 11.30am-1am Sun-Wed & 11.30am-2pm Thur-Sat (last orders 12.30am). Looking like an ornate theatre, with gilded stucco, immense chandeliers and paintings of composers, this magnificent place was thoroughly renovated by Sir Terence Conran in 1999. August Strindberg named his novel Röda-rummet after what's now a function room. The international menus have good choices of meat and fish, but few vegetarian dishes. There's live jazz in the main hall from 9pm to 11pm Wednesday to Saturday. Evening reservations need to be made at least a week in advance.

Restaurant Riche **(Map 6, D8, #78)** *(☎ 679 6840, Birger Jarlsgatan 4)* 3-course lunch Skr295, mains Skr110-265. Open 11.30am-3am Mon-Fri & 1am-3am Sat. Restaurant Riche is a stylish establishment with a glass-fronted veranda, and classically stylish decor (including paintings and chandeliers); one room deep in the interior displays statues and wigs. The fine menu has a French touch and includes steak, fish, veal and duck. Champagne costs up to Skr3300 per bottle.

Restaurant KB **(Map 6, D8, #81)** *(☎ 679 6032, Smålandsgatan 7)* Mains Skr255-315, husmanskost Skr117, bar menu Skr75-125. Cloakroom fee Skr10. Open 11.30am-midnight Mon-Fri & 5pm-midnight Sat. Restaurant KB is a traditional, cosy restaurant with Swedish cuisine that has catered for numerous local artists and hosts occasional art exhibitions. The attached bar has wall paintings from 1931.

Grodan Grev Ture **(Map 6, B8, #55)** *(☎ 679 6100, Grev Turegatan 16)* Lunch Skr95, mains Skr97-202, dinner mains Skr127-219. Voluntary cloakroom fee Skr10. Open 11.30am-1am Mon-Thur, 11.30am-2am Fri & noon-2am Sat. This huge sophisticated place includes modern dining areas with blackboards and an 18th-century-style room with ornate plasterwork and superb paintings. The French-style meals, including venison, pike and vegetarian lasagne, are popular with young professional types.

Sture Compagniet **(Map 6, B7, #46)** *(☎ 611 7800, Sturegatan 4)* Mains Skr149-225. Open 5pm-midnight Mon-Wed & 5pm-3am Thur-Sat. Although more known for its nightlife, Sture Compagniet also has good eating prospects. The restaurant is modern and you can eat outside in summer. The menus are rather adventurous, offering things such as mint and chilli-fried shrimps (Skr79) and herb-baked halibut with zucchini-mushroom canneloni (Skr195).

Kharma Restaurant & Nightclub **(Map 6, A8, #49)** *(☎ 662 0456, Sturegatan 10)* Mains Skr148-239. Cloakroom fee Skr10. Open 5pm-11pm Mon-Sat, closed Sun. This classy and ultra-hip dinner restaurant has an attractive modern Indian-style ambience and a bar and nightclub (see the Entertainment chapter).

Rolfs Kök **(Map 6, A2, #4)** *(☎ 101696, Tegnérgatan 41)* Mains Skr156-225. Open 11am-1am Mon-Fri, 5pm-1am Sat & Sun. At this friendly modern restaurant, you can either get table service or sit on stools and eat at the central bar. The unusual decor includes chairs hanging from the walls. Fish, duck and lamb are on the menu, but the unusual wine list describes which wines are suitable for each type of course.

Vasastaden

Le Bistrot de Wasahof **(Map 3, C5, #14)** *(☎ 323440, Dalagatan 46)* Mains Skr172-206, seafood platters Skr289-1400. Open 5pm-1am Mon-Sat. Here you'll find a genuine bistro milieu, including wooden tables and lamps, a huge range of seafood (from winkles and whelks to oysters and lobsters) and an extensive wine list. Meals are beautifully presented and the service is exemplary, but you'll need to reserve a table up to three days in advance. There's also a less expensive *smårätt* (light meals) menu.

Tennstopet **(Map 3, C5, #15)** *(☎ 322518, Dalagatan 50)* Mains Skr114-267. Open 4pm-1am Mon-Fri, 1pm-1am Sat & Sun. Tennstopet, a traditional and laid-back bar/restaurant and the oldest pub in Stockholm, has a very pleasant and comfortable atmosphere with paintings, mirrors and padded chairs. There's a wide seasonal range of husmanskost and specials start at Skr90.

Café Tranan **(Map 3, C5, #7)** *(☎ 300 765, Karlbergsvägen 14)* Starters Skr55-125, mains Skr95-265. Open 11.30am-1am Mon-Fri, 5pm-1am Sat & Sun (kitchen closes 11.45pm). This stylish, modern and busy place on Odenplan is one of the best neighbourhood restaurants in Stockholm and is popular with locals. It has an excellent and comprehensive international menu, including a traditional Swedish herring platter.

MoonCake **(Map 4, C1, #10)** *(☎ 169928, Luntmakargatan 95)* Mains Skr178-265. Open 5pm-midnight Mon-Sat & 5pm-10pm

Sun. At MoonCake you'll experience modern Chinese and Vietnamese fine dining. The menu features all sorts of meat and fish, including delicious monkfish, and you can also order Cha Gio (Vietnamese spring rolls; Skr115).

Djurgården

You'll not go hungry on this touristy island – there's no shortage of restaurants.

Restaurang Hasselbacken (Map 4, G6, #88) (☎ 517 34307, Hazeliusbacken 20) 2-/3-course weekday lunch Skr155/195, lunch specials Skr89-95, 2-/3-course dinner Skr255/295, dinner mains Skr168-205. Open 1pm-10pm Mon-Sat late June to mid-Aug (restricted menu); otherwise 10am-2pm & 5pm-10pm Mon-Fri, 1pm-10pm Sat & 1pm-9pm Sun. This restaurant, in Scandic Hotel Hasselbacken, serves fine classical Swedish meals with foreign influences in a wonderful dining room dating from 1923. There is a superb ceiling and a raised dining area with alcoves and sofas.

Ulla Winbladh (Map 4, F6, #91) (☎ 663 0571, Rosendalsvägen 8) 2-course weekday lunch Skr195, mains Skr190-275 & daily herring buffet Skr125. Cloakroom fee Skr10. Named after one of Bellman's lovers, this villa was built as a steam bakery for the Stockholm World Fair (1897) and now serves fine food in an early 20th-century-style restaurant with a garden setting. The menu features international dishes and traditional Swedish meals, including meatballs and crayfish tails.

Wärdhuset Godthem (Map 4, F7, #90) (☎ 661 0722, Rosendalsvägen 9) Mains Skr175-250, 3-course theatre menu Skr375. Cloakroom fee Skr10. Open 11.30am-midnight Mon-Fri, noon-midnight Sat & Sun. Just across the road from Ulla Winbladh, this strange-looking grey building with an octagonal tower and spire is another early 20th-century-style restaurant. The rows of lightbulbs don't inspire confidence, but the food is OK. Main courses include smoked salmon, smoked reindeer and braised monkfish (anglerfish).

Södermalm

Eriks Gondolen (Map 7, F5, #81) (☎ 641 7090, Stadsgården 6) 2-/3-course lunch or dinner Skr320/395, weekday lunch husmanskost Skr85, mains Skr235-295. Cloakroom fee Skr8. Open 11.30am-1am Mon-Fri & 1pm-1am Sat. With perhaps the most unusual location in Stockholm and feeling like an airborne boat, Eriks Gondolen offers diners fantastic views, armchairs, wooden decor and fine food. Gondolen's marinated herrings (Skr105) and warm cloudberries with ice cream (Skr50) are particularly recommended. There's also a bakfickan with a lower-price bistro menu.

Entertainment

Stockholm is the entertainment capital of northern Europe, with everything from bars, pubs and nightclubs to theatres, cinemas, concert halls and a range of indoor and outdoor spectator sports. Unfortunately, most places are heavily commercial and making lots of money is the number one priority. Check the Swedish-language entertainment listing *På Stan*, which comes with the *Dagens Nyheter* newspaper every Thursday. The free tourist booklet *What's On – Stockholm* has reasonable events listings.

BARS & PUBS
Stockholm's lively bar and pub scene has boomed in recent years, thanks mainly to an easing of the formerly draconian licensing restrictions. However, all bars and pubs in Sweden must still be attached to a restaurant and a real 'pub' atmosphere is relatively rare. Some kitsch 'theme pubs' really overdo it – the so-called Scottish pubs are the worst, but they're worth a visit for a laugh if little else.

There's live music in some places and entry may be free or a 'cloakroom fee' of around Skr15 will be charged. Bars and pubs don't have a strict dress code. Although the minimum legal age for buying alcohol in Sweden is 18, most bars and pubs have significantly higher age limits and they may operate a sexist admissions policy depending on age.

Stockholm nightlife centres around neighbourhoods that offer many *krogs* (bars) conveniently within walking distance. The best bars and pubs are in Södermalm, especially in the Götgatan, Östgötagatan and Skånegatan areas. In Kungsholmen, go to Scheelegatan and Fridhemsplan, and in the northern centre (Vasastaden) try the Tegnérgatan and the Rörstrandsgatan areas.

The standard 400ml *storstark* (strong beer) costs from Skr22 to Skr53, but is typically around Skr40. A glass of wine is unlikely to be below Skr35. Most bars open by 5pm (perhaps earlier on Saturday) and many places also serve weekday bar lunches.

Gamla Stan
Wirströms Irish Pub (Map 7, C3, #28) (☎ 212874, *Stora Nygatan 13*) Open until midnight Mon-Fri, 1am Sat & Sun. Arrive early to get a seat in this excellent brick-built vaulted cellar. Bar meals (including vegetarian) cost Skr69 to Skr89 and a pint of Caffreys is Skr48. There's also live music Wednesday to Saturday evenings.

City Centre & Vasastaden
Naglo Vodka Bar (Map 6, F6, #169) (☎ 207630, *Regeringsgatan 6*) Open 5pm-midnight Tues-Thur, 5pm-3am Fri, 7pm-3am Sat & 10pm-3am Sun. This pleasant modern-design bar has around 30 vodkas and some other drinks on offer.

The Dubliner (Map 6, C8, #82) (☎ 679 7707, *Smålandsgatan 8*) Open to 1am Mon & Sun, 3am Tues-Sat. Admission Skr50 Fri & Sat; cloakroom fee Skr10/5 jacket/bag. The Dubliner is an Irish-style restaurant/pub that offers bar meals including fish and chips for Skr49 to Skr79, but the restaurant isn't particularly Irish. It's a friendly and hugely popular place which gets quite wild late at night on weekends, with dancing on the benches not unknown.

The Loft (Map 6, B6, #31) (☎ 411 1991, *Regeringsgatan 66*) Open daily until late. The Loft is a great Irish pub with wooden beams, Irish beers and whiskeys, and restaurant-quality food, including Asian wok dishes (from Skr89 to Skr112) and fish and chips (Skr86). The minimum age limit is 23.

Biblos (Map 6, C7, #85) (☎ 611 8030, *Biblioteksgatan 9*) Open 11.30am-1am Mon & Tue, 11.30am-3am Wed-Fri, 1pm-3am Sat, closed Sun. Cloakroom fee Skr14/10 jacket/bag. If you're looking for a trendy bar with loud music, this is your place. The ground floor bar/restaurant serves beer and Swedish, international and crossover dishes (Skr96 to Skr225), with reasonable portions. The two bars downstairs include the five-brands only Absolut Vodka Bar (Skr60 for 4cL). Tables spill out onto the street in summer.

Norrlands Bar & Grill (Map 6, B7, #87) (☎ 611 8810, Norrlandsgatan 24) Open 11.30am-2.30pm Mon, 11.30am-1am Tues-Thur, 11.30am-2am Fri & 6pm-2am Sat. This is a popular and atmospheric modern-design pub, with outdoor seating in summer and an evening DJ.

Bull & Bear Inn (Map 6, C7, #59) (☎ 611 1000, Birger Jarlsgatan 16) Open 4pm-1am Mon-Thur, 4pm-2am Fri, 1pm-2am Sat & 3pm-midnight Sun. In this fairly authentic English pub you'll get good draught beers, but there are also around 100 whiskies available. Pub grub here costs from Skr89 to Skr148. The minimum age limit is 23.

Kjellsons (Map 4, D3, #39) (☎ 611 0045, Birger Jarlsgatan 36) Open until 3am Sat & Sun. Kjellsons is a bright modern place with pricey meals and a DJ playing varied music on Friday and Saturday nights. It's frequently crowded and the minimum age is 20.

Tudor Arms (Map 4, E5, #66) (☎ 660 2712, Grevgatan 31) Open until 11pm Mon-Sat, 6pm Sun. The recently renovated Tudor Arms was the first English pub to open in Stockholm and it features typical Tudor styles. Beers on tap include Tennents, Guinness and McEwans. Staff members are mostly British and the pub grub menu looks like it has been plucked straight out of the shires; most mains, including fish and chips, are Skr75.

St Andrews Inn (Map 6, A9, #51) (☎ 661 1202, Nybrogatan 46) Open until midnight Mon-Thur, 1am Fri & Sat, 11pm Sun. You'll find golf kitsch on the walls and staff members in kilts in this 'Scottish' pub. The bar menu is fairly average but prices are high. The minimum age is 23.

Limerick Irish Pub (Map 4, D2, #30) (☎ 673 4398, Tegnérgatan 10) Open to 1am Mon-Thur, 2am Fri & Sat, 10pm Sun. North of the city centre, this lively Irish-style pub is reasonably authentic and has typical pub snacks (under Skr30), with the inevitable Guinness on tap (Skr51 per pint). You can catch live folk or rock music here from 9.30pm to 1am on Friday and Saturday.

Cliff Barnes (Map 3, B5, #5) (☎ 318 070, Norrtullsgatan 45) Open until 1am Mon-Sat. People come here to sing along to popular tunes, dance on the tables and get inebriated. It's a hugely popular beer hall-type place and there's also an outdoor bar in summer.

Strindbergs (Map 6, A2, #5) (☎ 201650, Drottninggatan 85) Open until 1am daily. Located in an atmospheric old shop, this small, expensive and trendy wine bar serves wine from Skr58 per glass. Modern Swedish-style main courses are between Skr115 and Skr198.

Phukets Oslag Bar (Map 6, B2, #11) (☎ 411 3311, Upplandsgatan 7) Open daily, until 1am Sat & Sun. The upstairs beach-style bar, with oriental art, serves sushi from 11am to 4pm on weekdays (Skr55/85 for eight/11 bit). The downstairs bar is open at night and is quite popular.

Bagpiper's Inn (Map 3, D3, #28) (☎ 311855, Rörstandsgatan 21) Open until 1am daily. West of St Eriksplan, this pub claims to be Scottish with an enthusiastic display of tartan and British(!) warm hospitality. Storstark starts at Skr40 and bar meals cost Skr67 to Skr155. You'll need to be over 23 to get in.

Boomerang BBQ & Steakhouse (Map 3, D3, #28) (☎ 330411, Rörstandsgatan 23) Open 5pm-midnight Mon-Thur, 5pm-1am Fri & Sat, closed Sun. Just next door to the Bagpiper's Inn, you can get an Oz beer and pub grub (including an 'Aussie Barbie') but it's an expensive place, with mains from Skr69 to Skr259.

Kungsholmen

Agra Tandoori (Map 3, F3, #45) (☎ 650 6121, Hantverkargatan 84) Open until 10pm Sun-Thur, 11pm Fri & Sat. Although looking a bit shabby, the inexpensive Indian fare in this friendly bar/restaurant is reasonably good and, all evening, storstark is only Skr23.

Södermalm

Carmen (Map 5, B7, #41) (☎ 641 2470, Tjärhovsgatan 14) Open until 1am Mon-Sat, until 11pm Sun. Carmen is a busy and rather large 1970s-style pub, which is trying to head upmarket; it now offers food for under Skr100 and storstark for Skr25/29 before/after 8pm.

Indian Star Restaurang (Map 5, B7, #41) (☎ 556 95557, Tjärhovsgatan 12) Open until midnight daily. Indian Star Restaurang is a budget Indian restaurant which doubles up as a basic pub offering storstark for Skr29. There's also a huge range of meals, mostly between Skr60 and Skr70. The ultra-strong vindaloo curry (Skr70) should soak up a few beers.

Östgötakällaren (Map 5, C7, #60) (☎ 643 2240, Östgötagatan 41) Open until 1am daily. With brick-lined and wood-panelled walls and an old-fashioned atmosphere, this is one of the best pubs in Stockholm. During happy hour (before 5pm and after 10pm), storstark is Skr26 (otherwise Skr34). There's occasional live jazz (free admission). The food here is excellent, with weekday lunches from Skr52 to Skr62 and mains and specials from Skr70 to Skr165. From 5pm to 6pm on weekdays there's 25% off food and drinks.

Kvarnen (Map 5, B7, #39) (☎ 643 0380, Tjärhovsgatan 4) Open until 3am daily. A strange mixture of Hammarby football fans and Left Party former communists frequently gather in this traditional beer hall dating from 1907. Occasionally, there's live music and queues out the door. Draught Staropramen Czech beer is Skr42 and main courses are in the Skr82 to Skr142 range.

Bonden Mat & Bar (Map 5, C7, #64) (☎ 641 8679, Bondegatan 1C) Open 5pm-1am daily. In this small bar, located by a cow sign outside the door, you'll find a strangely curved ceiling with 19th-century-style light bulbs. Storstark costs Skr39 and main courses are from Skr98 to Skr169. See also Bonden Club under Nightclubs.

Zombie Bar (Map 5, D8, #71) (Ringvägen 151) Open until 1am daily. At this wild bar, you'll get storstark for Skr25 while 1970s to 1980s punk rock and modern alternative rock booms from the loudspeakers. The minimum age is only 18, but people up to 30 come here.

Black Horse Inn (Map 5, C8, #56) (☎ 643 1616, Bondegatan 50) Open until midnight Mon-Fri, to 1am Sat & Sun. The Black Horse Inn is a pleasant English-style pub offering lots of draught ales, lagers and ciders. The bar meals on the blackboard are only Skr45 to Skr98, including 'vegetarian wok' at Skr73.

Folkhemmet (Map 5, C8, #54) (☎ 640 5595, Renstiernas Gata 30) Open 5pm-1am daily. The menu in this trendy minimalist-style bar/restaurant features Swedish traditional cooking with international influences, while the two bars have DJs playing alternative rock, hip hop and reggae. This friendly, popular place, run by socialists, doesn't have a doorman or an admission charge. Make reservations well in advance.

August Bar Bistro (Map 5, B7, #42) (☎ 644 8700, Folkungagatan 59) Open until 1am daily. Comfortable, classy and laid-back August Bar Bistro serves beer and wine along with bar food, with daily specials from Skr82 to Skr105.

Soldaten Svejk (Map 5, B7, #43) (☎ 641 3366, Östgötagatan 35) In this crowded but basic pub, with wooden floors and heraldic shields, you can get great Czech beer, including 0.5L Staropramen on tap for Skr43. There are also simple and solid Czech meals (Skr75 to Skr115); try some of the excellent smoked cheese along with your beer. Be sure to arrive early – there are often long queues for tables.

NIGHTCLUBS

Discos and nightclubs usually admit no one aged under 20, although the minimum age limit for men may be 23 or higher. Dress codes are variable but, generally, turning up in sandals, trainers or jeans is not a great idea, particularly on weekends.

Dancing (sometimes to live music) takes place on most nights of the week but busy nights are Friday and Saturday. Amazingly, there are still discos and nightclubs in Stockholm that close in July. Drinking in these places is an expensive option and there are also cloakroom fees averaging Skr20 and cover charges up to Skr150.

Hard-looking bouncers are ubiquitous and queues in the street outside busy nightclubs are common, particularly late at night. You may be selected for admission (or not, as the case may be) dependent on your sex or how much money it looks like you'll spend. Discrimination on the basis of race or language is strongly suspected at several places; well-dressed Caucasian-race English-speaking tourists seem to do fairly well at getting into Stockholm's more exclusive nightclubs. Identification will be demanded at the door, especially for proof of age – bring your passport.

Gamla Stan

Nattklubben Kolingen (Map 7, D4, #71) *(☎ 201092, Kornhamnstorg 59B)* Admission Skr60; cloakroom Skr10. Open 9pm-3am Mon-Sat. At this crowded disco there's 1970s and 1980s music during the week and 1990s/current hits on weekends. The minimum age is 23.

City Centre & Vasastaden

Café Opera (Map 6, F7, #172) *(☎ 676 5807, Operahuset, Karl XII:s Torg)* Admission Skr80 after 10pm; cloakroom fee Skr15. Open 10pm-3am daily. Café Opera is a trendy restaurant during the day, which metamorphoses into a classy nightclub after midnight. It's a wonderful place, in classical style with ceiling paintings and ornate plasterwork. The restaurant offers mains from Skr185 to Skr280. Music is fairly mixed but consists mostly of 1990s disco sounds and the nightclub appeals to wealthy young people aged 23 to 40. There's no strict dress code, but you must look smart and be aged over 23.

Heaven (Map 6, D2, #130) *(☎ 545 16000, Kungsgatan 65)* Admission from Skr25/60 to Skr40/80 member/nonmember. Open 9pm-3am Fri & 9pm-4am Sat. Heaven is Scandinavia's largest disco and it holds up to 1800 people. The Friday nightclub appeals to ages 20 to 25 (minimum ages 18/20 women/men), while the Saturday nightclub is aimed at those aged 25 to 35 (minimum ages 23/25). To get in, it's

best to accompany a member or turn up early. There are three dance floors and a wide range of contemporary music, from the 1960s to the latest chart sounds.

Sargasso (Map 6, D2, #130) *(☎ 545 18500, Kungsgatan 65)* Admission Skr80/40 men/women; cloakroom fee Skr20. Open 8pm-3am Thur & 7pm-4am Fri-Sat. Although in the same building as Heaven, Sargasso has its own entrance. It's known as a pick-up joint and has an unusual bar with water flowing along it, under the glass surface. The music in here is 1970s to 1990s pop, including ABBA. A dress code is enforced (no jeans or trainers) and the minimum age limit is 30.

Torsgatan 1 (Map 6, C1, #118) *(☎ 225 170, Torsgatan 1)* Admission free/Skr60 before/after 11pm. Open 10pm-3am Fri & Sat. Here, the DJs play soul, funk and 1980s rap on Friday and 1970s disco music on Saturday. The program and opening nights change fairly regularly. You'll need to be over 20 to get in.

Holger Bar & Mat (Map 6, C1, #117) *(☎ 411 5647, Norra Bantorget)* Admission Skr20 Wed, free Thur, Skr50 Fri & Sat; cloakroom fee Skr10. Open 9pm-3am Tues-Sat. Indie, Manchester and 1960s to 1980s alternative rock are played by DJs in this curious round building. Minimum age is 20.

Karlsson & Co (Map 6, C3, #115) *(☎ 545 12140, Kungsgatan 56)* Admission Skr40 after 9pm Wed & Thur; Skr80 after 9pm Fri & Sat; cloakroom fee Skr15. Open until 3am Mon-Sat. Karlsson & Co is a kitschy dance restaurant and nightclub with an extensive crossover menu and a disco renowned as a pick-up joint. There's a dress code (no jeans or trainers on weekends) and a minimum age of 27.

Tiger Rum & Bar (Map 6, B6, #31) *(☎ 244700, Kungsgatan 18)* Admission around Skr100. Open until 3am Wed & Thur, 4am Fri & Sat. Easily located by its completely black exterior, Tiger Rum & Bar is a classy place which plays typical club music to over 30s. There are several bars and a large dance floor.

Daily News Café (Map 6, D6, #179) *(☎ 215655, Kungsträdgården)* Admission

Skr80. Open 10pm-4am Wed, 10pm-3am Thur, 10pm-5am Fri & 9pm-5am Sat. There are two dance floors at this popular place, one playing chart hits while the other features exceptionally loud techno club music.

Level (Map 6, D8, #79) *(Hamngatan 2)* Admission Skr60. Open 10pm-3am Fri & Sat. Here you'll find a soul, hip hop and reggae club.

Sophies Bar (Map 6, C7, #84) *(☎ 611 8408, Biblioteksgatan 5)* Admission free; cloakroom fee Skr20. Open until 3am (closed Sunday). Sophies Bar is a trendy, overpriced cafe, but there's also a downstairs nightclub with black decor and an Asian touch, which the royal princesses have been known to frequent. The bouncers are particularly tough here and you have to be over 25 to get in (with the exception of Princess Madeleine). White trainers and jeans are prohibited.

East (Map 6, B7, #86) *(☎ 611 4959, Stureplan 13)* Admission free. Open until 3am daily. The restaurant at East serves Korean, Japanese, Thai and Vietnamese food but, after midnight, there's a DJ and dancing in the bar. Arrive by 11pm to ensure you get in. Music played here includes soul and rhythm and blues, and the minimum age for admission is 23.

Sturecompagniet (Map 6, B7, #46) *(☎ 611 7800, Sturegatan 4)* Admission Skr100 after 10pm. Open 10pm-5am Thur-Sat. As one of Stockholm's premier modern-style nightclubs, Sturecompagniet has several rooms with different styles, mostly playing CDs but live reggae bands play on the last Tuesday every month. The DJs play jazz, 1960s to 1980s soul and motown, and techno. In the tiled basement bar, there's thunderous hard rock.

Spy Bar (Map 6, B7, #44) *(☎ 545 03701, Birger Jarlsgatan 20)* Admission up to Skr120; cloakroom fee Skr20. Open 10pm-5am Wed-Sat. Possibly the trendiest nightclub in town, this is where celebrities and the royal princesses hang out. You'll find several bars here, along with crystal chandeliers and leather furniture. A beer in here will set you back around Skr50 for 40cL. Normally, you'll need a membership card or be on the guest list to get past the bouncers, but go before 11pm and you might get in if you're English-speaking, cool, clean and classy.

Chiaro (Map 6, B7, #43) *(☎ 678 0009, Birger Jarlsgatan 24)* Admission free; Skr100 after 11pm/10pm Fri/Sat. Open until 3am Wed & Thur, 5am Fri & Sat. This popular restaurant serves traditional Swedish lunches and Swedish, French and Asian crossovers. There's also a downstairs nightclub, which appeals to the 25 to 45 age group; DJs play a wide range of nonmainstream contemporary music including house, soul and funk (but not techno). Minimum age is 25.

Kharma Restaurant & Nightclub (Map 6, A8, #49) *(☎ 662 0456, Sturegatan 10)* Admission Skr100; cloakroom fee Skr20. Open 11pm-3am Thur-Sat. The nightclub associated with this groovy restaurant plays club house music to patrons over 23 years.

Crazy Horse Saloon (Map 6, A8, #50) *(☎ 665 9496, Sturegatan 12)* Admission free; cloakroom fee Skr15. Open 5pm-1am Tues-Thur, 5pm-3am Fri & Sat. The Crazy Horse Saloon is an American-style bar with a restaurant section, where you can get burgers and Tex-Mex mains for Skr85-138. From 9pm on Wednesday to Saturday nights, DJs play a wide range of contemporary music; there's dancing too. Minimum ages 20/22 women/men.

Santana (Map 4, D2, #34) *(☎ 248400, Kammakargatan 22)* Admission Skr50. Open 9.30pm-3am Fri. Santana is a new Caribbean and South American restaurant, which has a salsa music club on Friday night only.

Musslan (Map 3, C5, #14) *(☎ 346410, Dalagatan 46)* Open until 1am Mon-Sat. The DJs here play varied contemporary music, but you'll need to be over 20 to get in the door.

Café Tranan (Map 3, C5, #7) *(☎ 300 765, Karlbergsvägen 14)* Open 11.30am-1am Mon-Fri, 5pm-1am Sat & Sun. The cellar bar in this popular restaurant (see the Places to Eat chapter) attracts a mixed clientele. The DJs play rhythm and blues and rock on weekends.

ENTERTAINMENT

From Warship to Nightclub

The interesting ship *Patricia* was launched in 1938 at Smith's shipyard in Middlesbrough, England, with the intention of serving as a lightship off the British coast. However, when WWII broke out in September 1939, it was hastily rebuilt as a warship and pressed into service with the Royal Navy. *Patricia* was attacked by the Luftwaffe during the evacuation of Allied troops at Dunkirk in 1940, but it didn't suffer serious damage. The ship was also involved in naval operations relating to the D-day landings in Normandy during June 1944.

After the end of WWII, Patricia was rebuilt once more, this time as a luxury royal yacht and it sailed to Helsinki with Princess Elizabeth (now Queen Elizabeth II) on board in 1952. The ship ultimately came to Stockholm in 1986 and was berthed near Slussen, where it has been used as a novel restaurant and nightclub known as Lady Patricia ever since.

***Hard Rock Café* (Map 4, C1, #15)** (☎ 545 49400, *Sveavägen 75*) Admission Skr50 after 11pm. Nightclub open until 3am Fri & Sat. Perhaps better known for its restaurant (weekday lunch Skr69; burgers, salads and sandwiches from Skr75) and T-shirt sales (from Skr140), the Hard Rock Café includes the excellent downstairs hard rock bar 'Metallbaren', open after 9pm on Friday and Saturday. The main restaurant is partly cleared of tables at 11pm and DJs play things such as the Beatles, Madonna and ABBA (but no techno) to a lively mixed crowd. Sometimes there's live music from 9pm to 11pm. Upstairs, there's an ABBA room with gold records, hit lists and awards.

Södermalm

***Lady Patricia* (Map 7, E5, #78)** (☎ 743 0570, *Stadsgårdskajen 152*) Admission Skr80 after 10pm; cloakroom fee Skr15. Restaurant open 5pm Wed & Thur, 6pm Sat & Sun; nightclub open 11pm-5am Fri-Sun.

Stockholm's only nightclub aboard a ship is a unique and busy place with an extraordinary history (see the boxed text 'From Warship to Nightclub'). It's also known for its restaurant, which serves lobster, Tex-Mex fajitas and Cajun blackened steak. The nightclub has four bars, three with DJs (including a small rock bar) and the other with live contemporary music, usually featuring new bands playing unreleased material. Minimum age limits are 23/25 for women/men on Friday and Saturday, and 20 for both on Sunday. Blue jeans are prohibited on Friday and Saturday nights. Sunday is gays-only night (see Gay & Lesbian Venues later in this chapter).

***Sjögras* (Map 5, B5, #23)** (☎ 841200, *Timmermansgatan 24)* Admission is free. Nightclub open 9pm-1am Wed-Sat. In the popular basement bar at this Asian-style restaurant you'll find DJs playing reggae, soul, hip hop and rock.

***Star Bar* (Map 7, F2, #97)** (☎ 644 5418, *Hornsgatan 31)* Admission Skr40. Open 10pm-3am Thur-Sat. At this nightclub, you'll get reggae on Thursday and heavy metal on weekends.

***H62* (Map 7, F1, #95)** (☎ 615 2570, *Hornsgatan 62)* Admission free; cloakroom fee Skr10. Open until 1am most days. H62 is a party place that plays just about anything, but it may be closed for private parties on occasion. Minimum age is 18.

***Bonden Club* (Map 5, C7, #64)** (☎ 642 9913, *Bondegatan 1C)* Admission free; cloakroom fee Skr10. Open 7pm-1am Wed-Sun. The unusual music in this nightclub includes disco, hip hop, pop and house. There's also a reasonable international menu (mains Skr98 to Skr169), and storstark costs only Skr35. The minimum age limit is 22 on Friday and Saturday, otherwise it's 20.

***La Cucaracha* (Map 5, C7, #65)** (☎ 644 3944, *Bondegatan 2)* Admission free; cloakroom fee Skr15. Dancing from 10.30pm Wed-Sat. The Latin American restaurant La Cucaracha has a brick-vaulted cellar from the former Beijer Palats, and offers excellent salsa music and dancing. It's very popular, so turn up early.

MUSIC

For more details about the background to the Stockholm music scene, see Music in the Facts about Stockholm chapter. It's always best to book tickets as far in advance as possible. Tickets should be booked directly with the outfits concerned, unless otherwise noted.

Classical

Some classical concerts are held at venues better known for pop and rock events; see the sections on these events later in this chapter.

Konserthuset (Map 6, C4, #101) (☎ 102110, e biljettkontoret@konserthuset .se, W www.konserthuset.se, Hötorget) Tickets Skr50-350; lunch concerts Skr50. Konserthuset is Stockholm's main concert hall and it features classical concerts and other musical events, including the Royal Philharmonic Orchestra, which plays several times each month. Lunch concerts are held once or twice each month, usually in the smaller Grünewald hall (which is within the Konserthuset building). The ticket office, entered from Sveavägen, stocks an excellent free Swedish-language booklet which lists the concerts.

Berwaldhallen (Map 4, E6, #68) (☎ 784 1800, e biljettkontoret@bwh.sr.se, W www .sr.se/berwaldhallen, Dag Hammarskjölds väg 3) Tickets Skr50-355. Classical music featuring the Swedish Radio Symphony Orchestra, the 33-member Swedish Radio Choir and occasional visiting musicians can be enjoyed at Berwaldhallen. The Swedish radio channel P2 makes recordings here and, every year, the Radio Symphony Orchestra hosts several premieres of new works by leading Swedish or international composers. The box office is open noon to 6pm weekdays and unsold tickets go on sale at the door two hours before the concert starts. The free events calendar is in Swedish and English.

Nybrokajen 11 (Map 6, E8, #191) (☎ 407 1700, W www.nybrokajen11.srk.se, Nybrokajen 11) Tickets Skr55-140. Built as the first concert hall in Sweden in the 1870s, Nybrokajen 11 still hosts classical orchestra and choir performances several times weekly. There is also occasional jazz and foreign folk music and dance.

Café Opera (Map 6, F7, #172) (☎ 248 240, Karl XIIs torg) Tickets Skr120. Lunch concerts 12.30pm Wed & Fri. These classical lunch concerts (typically featuring violin, piano, oboe and singing) include salad, light beer, bread and butter.

Piano Bars

There are piano bars in several top-end Stockholm hotels and three are worth a visit. Strict dress codes are enforced and you'll need to be smartly turned out to get past the staff at the door.

First Hotel Reisen (Map 7, B5, #40) (☎ 223260, Skeppsbron 12) Admission free; cloakroom fee Skr15. Piano entertainment 9pm-2am/3am Mon-Sat. Arrive before 10pm on weekends to avoid the crowds.

Scandic Hotel Sergel Plaza (Map 6, E5, #155) (☎ 517 26300, Brunkebergstorg 9) Admission free. Piano entertainment 5.30pm-7pm & 9.30pm-1am Mon-Fri, 6pm-7.30pm & 10pm-2am Sat. The lobby bar in this hotel has a very pleasant atmosphere and it's a great place to relax while listening to the baby grand.

Malmens Pianobar (☎ 517 34700, Götgatan 49-51) Admission free. Piano entertainment 9pm-3am Tues-Sat. Located in the functionalist Scandic Hotel Malmen (Map 5, B7, #38), this is Södermalm's only piano bar and it's particularly popular with locals.

Jazz & Blues

Stampen (Map 7, C3, #25) (☎ 205793, W www.stampen.se, Stora Nygatan 5) Admission Skr120; cloakroom fee Skr10. Open 8pm-1am Mon-Wed & 8pm-2am Thur-Sat. In Gamla Stan, friendly Stampen has live jazz, rhythm and blues, soul and piano boogie in a street-level pub and a basement bar with a dance floor. The pub opens at 8pm daily and serves some food, such as *pytt i panna* (Swedish hash dish) for Skr80. It's a great place, with knick-knacks hanging from the ceiling and lots of 70-year-old stuffed animals in the corridor, including a bear with a trombone! You'll need to be over 18 to get in, but most of the clientele are over 35.

***Jazzclub Fasching* (Map 6, D2, #129)** *(☎ 216267, Kungsgatan 63)* Tickets Skr90-350 but normally Skr160; cloakroom fee Skr15. Open 7pm/8pm-late Mon-Sat (until 3am Sat & Sun). Jazzclub Fasching is one of Stockholm's main live jazz venues and it attracts musicians from around the world. The restaurant has lots of art and photos about jazz musicians.

***Kristina* (Map 7, D4, #70)** *(☎ 208086, Västerlånggatan 68)* Admission free. Music 7pm-10pm Sun-Thur & 8pm-11pm Fri-Sat. Kristina is a fairly average old-fashioned restaurant (see the Places to Eat chapter), but it's noted for the daily live jazz, which is pulling the customers in.

***Glenn Miller Café* (Map 6, B5, #28)** *(☎ 100322, Brunnsgatan 21A)* Admission free. Open 5pm-midnight Mon-Thur & 5pm-1am Fri-Sat. Here you'll find one of the best music pubs in Stockholm, with live jazz on Monday, Tuesday and Saturday. It's an atmospheric little place, with walls lined with photos of jazz personalities and offering a small menu of snacks and mains under Skr132.

Traditional Swedish & World Music

***Stallet* (Map 6, E8, #193)** *(☎ 407 1700, Stallgatan)* Admission Skr80-120. This converted stables offers excellent music and dance events (ranging from Celtic folk to tango) performed by groups from around Sweden, typically four days per week. Shows usually commence at 8pm.

Pop & Rock

Most Swedish pop and rock bands have lyrics in English, although whether or not they're intelligible is another matter. Concerts featuring international artistes are excruciatingly expensive. For a listing of gigs throughout Sweden, see the Internet at W www.algonet.se/~widenby/blugigs.html.

Tickets for some events can be booked on the Internet through Ticnet at W www.ticnet.se or BiljettDirekt at W www.biljett.se or on ☎ 077 170 7070 in Sweden only.

***Globen* (Map 5, G8, #85)** *(Stockholm Globe Arena; ☎ 600 3400, e info@globen.se, W www.globen.se, Arenavägen, Johanneshov)* Metro: T-Globen. Tickets Skr290-620. Concerts featuring international rock stars are held at least monthly in this huge golf-ball-like structure just south of Södermalm. It also stages classical concerts and sporting events, particularly ice hockey and football. You'll find the events program on the Web site.

***Cirkus* (Map 4, G6, #87)** *(☎ 660 1020, Djurgårdsslätten 43, e info@cirkus.se, Djurgården)* Tickets Skr150-500. Pop and rock concerts, classical concerts, theatre, musicals and things such as magic shows and variety performances take place on several days every week at Cirkus. It's an interesting building, originally from the 1890s and first used by travelling circuses in winter. Nowadays, TV programs requiring an audience are recorded here. The renovated cafe, open when there are performances, is still in 1890s style. The booking office is open 10am to 6pm and during performances.

***Södra teatern* (Map 7, G5, #108)** *(☎ 644 9900, Mosebacketorg 1-3)* Tickets Skr150-350. Beautiful Södra teatern, one of Stockholm's premier music venues, hosts all kinds of concerts, from pop and rock to Hungarian trumpets. Events take place once or twice weekly; the Re:Orient Club at 9pm on Saturday is an interesting mix of oriental music and modern hits.

***Nalen* (Map 6, B6, #37)** *(☎ 453 3400, Regeringsgatan 74)* Admission Skr40-90. Open 8pm-midnight/1am 3-4 days per week. The main room at Nalen, with mirrors and chandeliers, has a good restaurant. Live music at Club Alcazar ranges from blues and soul to hip hop and death metal. Well worth a visit.

***Tantogården* (Map 5, C4, #26)** *(☎ 668 6371, Ringvägen 24)* Tickets variable, up to Skr150. At Tantogården you'll get country music and rock and roll roughly once per week. The venue is a summerhouse in Tantogården Park but, in summer, events are held in the park itself. Tickets are available from Pet Sounds (☎ 702 9798), Skånegatan 53, or at the door.

Engelen Steakhouse & Pub (Map 7, D4, #72) (☎ 201092, *Kornhamnstorg 59B*) Admission Skr60 after 9pm. Open until 3am daily. This moderately priced restaurant (with most mains under Skr150) features loud live bands from 9pm to midnight Monday to Saturday. There's occasional music on Sunday, but the regular Sunday event is a troubadour.

Hard Rock

Anchor Pub & Restaurang (Map 4, C1, #26) (☎ 152000, *Sveavägen 90*) Admission Skr30-100. Live music 11pm-3am 3-5 days per week. You'll get a good blast of live 1980s-style hard rock here.

Other Contemporary Music

Lava (Map 6, D5, #154) (☎ 508 31400, W *www.kulturhuset.stockholm.se, Kulturhuset, Sergels Torg*) Concerts free-Skr100. Closed Mon. The popular Lava youth project at Kulturhuset, which is aimed mainly at the under-25s, hosts weekly concerts from unsigned bands, ranging from folk to rock.

Lydmar Hotel (Map 6, B7, #48) (☎ 566 11300, *Sturegatan 10*) Admission free. Live music 9.30pm-10.30pm most days. The lobby bar of this stylishly modern and laid-back hotel has live bands encompassing rhythm and blues, soul, Latin, house, funk and jazz. It's a very popular venue and attracts people in their 20s and 30s (minimum age is 23).

Golden Hits (Map 6, B5, #99) (☎ 232 015, *Kungsgatan 29*) Entertainment only Skr90-130. Shows 8pm-11pm Tues-Sat. Golden Hits, with modern eclectic decor, offers three-course meals (from Skr278 to Skr359), which are served by staff dressed as ABBA, Elvis, Gary Glitter etc. After your meal, they take to the stage and you can dance to the music. This odd cabaret-style entertainment is extremely popular so you should apply a month ahead for a weekend reservation.

Wallmans Salonger (Map 6, E9 #198) (☎ 611 6622, *Teatergatan 3*) Entertainment only Skr90-130. Shows 8pm-11pm Tues-Sat. The dressed-up waiting staff serve meals then sing and dance on stage, which is then followed by a 1970s-style disco.

Snaps (Map 5, B6, #34) (☎ 640 2868, W *www.snaps.org*, W *www.rangustangus .com, Götgatan 48*) Admission free. This two-floor establishment has a small stage in the basement bar (called Rangus Tangus), with jazz, soul, Latin music, and live reggae bands most weekends.

Mosebacke Etablissement (Map 7, G5, #107) (☎ 556 09890, W *www.mosebacke .se, Mosebacketorg 3*) Admission around Skr60. Open 5pm-1am Mon-Wed, 5pm-2am Thur-Fri, noon-2am Sat & noon-1am Sun. Everything from jazz and salsa to modern hits is played at this excellent nightclub and concert venue. For the Moserobie Jazz Club, turn up on Friday night. There are also DJs, stage shows and a restaurant.

GAY & LESBIAN VENUES

The Stockholm gay scene includes bars, discos, restaurants, cafes, nightclubs and fetish clubs. Some places are frequented only by gays and/or lesbians, while other places are mixed gay and straight. For an up-to-date listing of venues, check the Web site at W www.qx.se.

The nightclubs *Lady Patricia* (Map 7, E5, #78) and *Sturecompagniet* (Map 6, B7, #46) have gay-only nights on Sunday (until 3am) and Friday and Saturday (until 5am), respectively. For details, see Nightclubs earlier in this chapter.

Chokladkoppen (Map 7, C4, #61) (*Stortorget 18*) Open 9am-11pm daily. You'll get excellent chocolate drinks and cakes in this pleasant cafe in Gamla Stan, which has outdoor seating in summer. There's also lots of info about gay events around town.

Stargayte (Map 7, C2, #4) (*Södra Riddarholmshamnen 19*) Open 9pm-3am Sat only. The Stargayte nightclub at Restaurang Scorpios on Riddarholmen is mainly frequented by gay men. There are two dance floors, with Schlager and house music, respectively.

Tip Top (Map 4, C1, #23) (☎ 329800, *Sveavägen 57*) Bar open until 1am Mon-Tues;

bar & nightclub open until 3am Wed-Sat. Tip Top, in the same building as the RFSL office and bookstore, is Stockholm's premier gay and lesbian venue and it's very popular. It includes a gay bar, nightclub (with disco music) and Thai restaurant. Minimum age is 20.

Häcktet (Map 5, B4, #16) (☎ 845910, Hornsgatan 82) Admission free. Open 7pm-1am Wed & Fri. Häcktet, a mixed gay disco/bar at Restaurant Bysis, is a fairly cosy place but it gets crowded late.

Hjärter Dam (Map 3, F4, #49) (☎ 737 0483, W www.ix.nu/hjarter-dam, Polhemsgatan 23) Members only (see the Web site for membership details). Hjärter Dam is a mixed gay/straight fetish club that appeals to transsexuals, transvestites and people into rubber, bondage and piercing. Wild parties are held several times a year but drunkenness, drug taking and sexual activity are not permitted on the premises.

Bitch Girl Club (Map 7, E4, #83) (☎ 643 3946, W www.qx.se/bitch, Södermalmstorg 2) Admission Skr60. Open 9pm-3am every second Fri. The Bitch Girl Club is northern Europe's largest lesbian club; to find it, go downstairs from Gulagången. It has a good reputation and there are two dance floors where you can move to 1980s and 1990s music. Membership (Skr120) is required and you'll need to be over 18. Some straight women also go here.

Corkybar (Map 5, B3, #10) (W www .corky.nu, Varvsgatan 14) Admission Skr50. Open irregularly, at least twice a month. Corkybar is a popular, well-respected lesbian hang-out.

CINEMAS

Foreign films are almost always screened in the original language (usually English), with Swedish subtitles. Most of the big cinemas show mainstream Hollywood fare, but there are some smaller alternative cinemas (where 25% to 35% of movies are in English). Daily papers have comprehensive cinema listings. Tickets usually cost between Skr75 and Skr85 (possibly lower early in the week); ask about child/student/senior discounts. The following places may be worth checking:

Biografen Sture (Map 6, A7, #42) (☎ 678 8548, W www.biosture.se, Birger Jarlsgatan 28) – shows alternative films; there's children's cinema on Saturday and film festivals in May and September/October

Biopalatset (Map 5, B7, #32) (☎ 644 3100, Folkungatrappan 2, Medborgarplatsen) – screens mainstream movies

Filmstaden Sergel (Map 6, C4, #104) (☎ 789 6001, Hötorget) – offers mainstream films

Grand (Map 4, D2, #33) (☎ 411 2400, Sveavägen 45) – screens mostly mainstream but some alternative movies

Kvartersbion (Map 5, B2, #4) (☎ 669 1995, Horntullsstrand 3) – shows movies after they've finished their runs elsewhere; admission discounted to around Skr60

Royal (Map 6, B5, #100) (☎ 101020, Kungsgatan 37) – shows mainstream films

Röda Kvarn (Map 6, C7, #84) (☎ 789 6037, Biblioteksgatan 5) – fine comfortable milieu, with gilded stucco and marble floors; shows mainstream movies

Saga (Map 6, B5, #30) (☎ 789 6037, Kungsgatan 24) – superb functionalist building with a mirrored ceiling; shows mainstream films.

Zita (Map 6, A6, #39) (☎ 232020, W www.folketsbio.se/zita, Birger Jarlsgatan 37) – screens alternative movies

THEATRE

Stockholm is a theatre city, with outstanding dance, opera and musical performances – pick up the free *Teater Guide* from the tourist office for an overview. For tickets, contact the tourist office (which charges a fee), theatre box offices or BiljettDirekt (☎ 077 170 7070 in Sweden only, W www .biljett.se). Prices depend on your seat position, the length of performance, and various other factors. Saturday shows are often sold out. Shows are nearly always in Swedish and many theatres are closed in July and August. Operas are performed in their origi-nal language (usually Italian or German), or in Swedish.

English Theatre Company (Map 6, B9, #53) (☎ 662 4133, @ etc.ltd@telia.com, Nybrogatan 35) This company consists entirely of native English-speakers. Performances are held at Vasa Teatern, Södra teatern and other places.

Stockholms Stadsteatern (Map 6, E5, #152) (☎ *506 20100,* W *www.stadsteatern .stockholm.se, Kulturhuset, Sergels Torg)* Tickets around Skr200, lunch theatre Skr120 Tues-Sat. Closed Mon. At Stockholms Stadsteatern, there are regular performances of Swedish plays and Swedish versions of international plays on six stages. There are also guest appearances by foreign theatre companies. The hour-long Swedish-language lunchtime performance (reservation compulsory) includes soup, bread and butter.

Operan (Map 6, F6, #168) *(Royal Opera;* ☎ *248240,* W *www.operan.se, Gustav Adolfs Torg)* Tickets Skr130-380, but some tickets Skr35; cloakroom fee Skr12. Closed Sun. This is the place to go for opera and classical ballet, but there's also some modern ballet. The main theatre has three tiers of impressively ornate balconies reached via marble staircases. Classical concerts are held in the smaller halls.

Dramatiska teatern (Map 6, D8, #75) (☎ *667 0680,* W *www.dramaten.se, Nybroplan)* Tickets Skr120-260. Open daily. Easily the most impressive theatre in Stockholm, Dramatiska teatern presents a range of plays (from Shakespeare to Strindberg) in a fantastic Art Nouveau environment. Unsold tickets are offered an hour before shows at a 35% discount.

Oscars Teatern (Map 6, D2, #128) (☎ *205000, Kungsgatan 64)* Tickets Skr150-400. Open Tues-Sat. The classic 960-seat Oscars Teatern runs 'Broadway' musicals and occasional comedies, all in Swedish.

Vasa Teatern (Map 6, C2, #120) *(Vasan;* ☎ *248240,* W *www.operan.se, Vasagatan 19)* Tickets Skr55-260. Closed Sun & Mon. Some plays in English are staged here, as well as operas, some ballet, and musicals.

Folkoperan (Map 5, B5, #19) (☎ *616 0750, Hornsgatan 72)* Skr270-350. Open early Sept-early May. Known internationally for its unconventional productions, Folkoperan brings opera to ordinary people five or six days weekly. You can also catch some modern ballet and concerts here.

Dansens Hus (Map 6, B2, #15) (☎ *796 4910,* W *www.dansenshus.se, Barnhusgatan 12-14)* Tickets typically Skr90/150 student/adult. Modern dance and ballet performances from troupes around the world can be seen at this venue.

Regina (Map 6, B3, #18) (☎ *411 6320, Drottninggatan 71A)* Tickets Skr445, including 3-course dinner. Commences 7pm daily (5pm Sun). Italian-style opera singing is performed (in Italian) by your waiting staff after your food has been brought to your table.

Hamburger Börs (Map 6, E6, #175) (☎ *787 8500, Jakobsgatan 6)* Tickets from Skr175. Open from 9.30pm daily, meals start 7.30pm. Hamburger Börs has a cabaret restaurant with a stage that hosts stand-up comedy, song and dance. Occasionally, international artistes appear here.

Drottningholms Slottsteater (Map 2, D2, #10) (☎ *660 8225,* W *www.drottningholmsteatern.dtm.se, Drottningholm)* Tickets Skr150-545. Open irregularly 1 Jun-8 Sept. This small but beautiful 18th-century theatre still holds opera and ballet performances; for bookings contact BiljettDirekt. See also Drottningholm in the Excursions chapter.

SPECTATOR SPORTS

For information on participation sports, see Activities in the Things to See & Do chapter. The Excursion Shop at Sverigehuset (Sweden House) (Map 6, D6, #180) sells tickets to major sporting events (for a fee); otherwise, contact the organisers directly.

Globen (Map 5, G8, #85) (☎ *600 3400,* e *info@globen.se,* W *www.globen.se, Arenavägen, Johanneshov)* Metro: T-Globen. Tickets Skr150-200. Ice hockey matches take place at Globen two or three times weekly from October to April. Football fixtures take place once weekly from April to October at the adjacent Söder Stadion (home to Hammarby FC), with the same contact details and prices as Globen.

Stadion (Map 4, C4, #42) (☎ *508 28362, Lidingövägen 1)* Metro: T-Stadion. Tickets Skr150-200. Premier division (Allsvenskan) football matches take place here once weekly from April to October. There are

Ice Hockey

In Sweden, ice hockey is the second biggest sport after football. The sport originated in North America and European settlers added rules to the original native American game in 1875. Ice hockey then spread rapidly throughout Canada, the USA and Scandinavia and became an official sport at the Winter Olympics in 1920.

There are only five active players plus a goalkeeper per side. Ice hockey is extremely fast and aggressive and it's the only major sport where unlimited substitution is possible during play – active players are drawn and returned from the full team of 20 to 25 every few minutes.

Most Swedish communities have amateur teams and an *ishall*, where ice hockey matches are played during winter. There are 15 professional teams in the Premier League and important games are shown on television. Strong rivalry exists between the national teams of Sweden and Finland; some Swedish players play abroad, notably in the Canadian league.

For further details on the sport in Sweden, contact Svenska Ishockeyförbundet (☎ 08-449 0400, fax 910035), Bolidenvägen 22, Box 5204, SE-12116 Johanneshov.

also occasional track and field events in summer, and the sports festival DN Galan in mid-July (W www.dngalan.com).

Zinkensdamms Idrottsplass (Map 5, B3, #13) *(Ringvägen)* Metro: T-Zinkensdamm. Tickets around Skr100. Bandy, which is similar to ice hockey, takes place at this venue roughly twice monthly and it's a great social event. Local football teams play more regularly.

Råsunda Stadion (Map 2, B4, #13) *(☎ 735 0935, Solnavägen 51)* Metro: T-Solna Centrum. Tickets around Skr200. Råsunda is Sweden's national football stadium

and you can see the national team or AIK (Allmänna Idrottsklubben) play here.

Solvalla Travbana (Map 2, B3, #7) *(☎ 635 9000, Travbaneplan, Sundbyberg)* Metro: T-Rissne. Tickets usually Skr20. At Solvalla Travbana you'll see trotting, a sport in which horses pull little carriages, each with a driver. It's a popular spectator sport and it's closely connected to gambling. Races take place several times weekly.

Eriksdalsbadet (Map 5, E6, #79) *(☎ 508 40250, Hammarby slussväg 8)* Metro: T-Skanstull. Look out for year-round swimming competitions in the indoor arena.

Shopping

If you intend to do a lot of shopping and you're a non-EU citizen, check when making a single purchase over Skr200 if the outlet is part of the 'Tax Free Shopping' network. For more information, see Taxes & Refunds in the Facts for the Visitor chapter.

If you want to ship a large package home, some shops may be able to arrange this for you, but you'll pay dearly. You're advised to go to the post office yourself and ask for the 'box and postage' *('Kartonger och Porto')* deal, which allows you to ship up to 10kg for Skr115 to Skr270 within the European Union (EU) or Skr92 to Skr350 outside the EU (depending on the size of box and the destination).

Ask the tourist office for a free copy of the *Tax Free Shopping Guide to Sweden*, which is updated annually. It has a fairly reasonable Stockholm shopping guide, but most shops mentioned are on a fairly well-trodden tourist circuit. The monthly tourist office booklet *What's On – Stockholm* also has information for shoppers.

WHAT TO BUY

Stockholm's shops generally don't sell items you can't get outside Sweden, but there are some notable exceptions.

Quality Swedish products in glass, wood, amber, pewter or silver are relatively expensive when bought from retail outlets in Stockholm. Among the best souvenirs are glassware (such as bowls, jugs, vases and quirky glass fruit) from the Glasriket factories, typically Swedish painted wooden horses from Dalarna, wooden toys, miniature Swedish-style huts and other buildings, and beautiful amber and silver jewellery. Some foods, such as cloudberry jam and pickled herring, are also well worth taking home.

Handicrafts carrying the round token *Svensk slöjd,* or the hammer and shuttle emblem, are endorsed by Svenska hemslöjds-föreningarnas riksförbund, the national handicrafts organisation whose symbol is found on affiliated handicraft shops. Look out for signs reading *Hemslöjd*, indicating handicraft sales outlets.

If you're interested in Sami handicrafts, which are usually astronomically expensive, look for the *Duodji* label (a round coloured token of authenticity). Be careful, since some shops have been known to have fakes on the shelves. Typical Sami handicrafts include ornately carved sheath knives, drums, cups, bowls, textiles and jewellery. Reindeer bone, wood (birch), reindeer hide and tin are commonly used materials.

English-language books, apart from paperbacks, are normally very expensive, but antiquarian bookshops often have some second-hand books in English. Second-hand music stores are the best places to buy music, since new CDs are likely to be dearer than they are back home. There are lots of antique shops in the city and, although most of the stuff on offer usually has enormous price tags, there are bargains to be found. Items for sale in art galleries are priced as if the artists are all likely to become Van Goghs – but people from outside Sweden will most likely never have heard of them.

WHERE TO SHOP

Gamla Stan has a lot of touristy souvenir shops, but there are some shops on side streets that are well worth a visit. Most of the Norrmalm shopping streets are similar to what you'd find in other European cities. Vasastaden and Södermalm are the best places for antiquarian bookshops, antique and curio shops, and unusual clothes or music stores. Many of these places rarely see tourists. Hornspuckeln in Södermalm has the best concentration of art galleries.

Antique Shops

There's a large concentration of antique shops at the northern end of Upplandsgatan (metro: T-Odenplan) and each has a different speciality. Several of these shops are quite extraordinary and you could spend hours browsing the window displays alone. Other areas worth checking are Odengatan, Sibyllegatan and Hornspuckeln. Look under *antikviteter* in the Yellow Pages.

The following places can all be located on Map 3 (C5).

Antikt & Modernt (☎ 303144, Upplandsgatan 44) – glassware, ceramics, wooden figures, silver and some nice pieces of china; open noon to 6pm weekdays and noon to 3pm Saturday

Antikt Evensen Nött & Nytt (☎ 346166, Upplandsgatan 48) – chairs, lamps, glassware and porcelain; a real Aladdin's cave; open noon to 6pm Monday and Thursday, noon to 3pm Saturday

Antiques (☎ 210239, Köpmangatan 3, Gamla Stan) – porcelain, art (paintings), maps, glassware, silverware and cutlery; this shop is in a fascinating old building; open noon to 6pm weekdays and 11am to 4pm Saturday

Bacchus Antik (☎ 305480, Upplandsgatan 46) – lamps, glassware, old signs, ceramics, china, bronze candlesticks and pots; open noon to 6pm weekdays and 11am to 3pm Saturday

Carléns Antik (☎ 313401, Upplandsgatan 40) – paintings, porcelain, glassware, furniture, candelabras and chandeliers; open 11am to 5pm weekdays and 11am to 3pm Saturday

Lady Lisabeth Dream (☎ 324145, Upplandsgatan 45) – antique clothes, medals, toys, pipes, dolls, purses, cutlery and jewellery; open 10am to 6pm weekdays and 11am to 2pm Saturday

Odens Antik (☎ 346522, Upplandsgatan 41) – lamps, furniture, clocks, carpets, globes and chandeliers; open 12.30pm to 6pm weekdays and 11am to 2pm Saturday

St Eriks Antik (☎ 348900, Upplandsgatan 51) – light fittings, glasses and porcelain; open 11am to 6pm weekdays and 11am to 3pm Saturday

Trädkronan Antik (☎ 317210, Upplandsgatan 43) – paintings, glassware, furniture, chandeliers, silver cutlery and bronze candlesticks; open noon to 6pm Tuesday to Thursday, noon to 5pm Friday and 11am to 2pm Saturday

Qriosa Antik (☎ 309230, Odengatan 87) – furniture, chandeliers, silver, art, glassware, porcelain and candelabras; open noon to 6pm weekdays and 10am to 3pm Saturday

Art Galleries

You'll find most art galleries in Stockholm in Hornspuckeln on Hornsgatan, Söder-malm. Some galleries are members of Galleriföreningen Puckeln, an association that produces a quarterly exhibitions listing. Exhibitions change every three or four weeks.

Most individual galleries show similar types of art throughout the year, but there may be variations. All items on display are usually for sale and prices range from Skr4000 to Skr20,000.

The following places can be located on Map 7 (F3) unless otherwise indicated.

Ateljen Hornsgatan 34 (☎ 641 3381, Hornsgatan 34) – glassware and ceramics

blås & knåda (☎ 642 7767, W www.blas -knada.com, Hornsgatan 26) – very fine glassware and ceramics; open 11am to 6pm weekdays, 11am to 4pm Saturday and noon to 4pm Sunday

Galleri Bellman (☎ 702 0784, Hornsgatan 38) – various displays, differing styles; open noon to 5pm Tuesday to Thursday and noon to 4pm Friday to Sunday

Galleri Embla (☎ 640 7588, Hornsgatan 42) – modern paintings; open noon to 7pm Tuesday, noon to 5pm Wednesday and Thursday, noon to 4pm Friday and Saturday, 1pm to 4pm Sunday

Galleri Hera (☎ 642 1113, Hornsgatan 36) – modern paintings and sculpture; open noon to 7pm Tuesday, noon to 6pm Wednesday and Thursday, noon to 4pm Friday to Sunday

Galleri Knall (☎ 641 2580, Hornsgatan 26) – modern paintings and prints; open 11am to 6pm Tuesday to Friday and noon to 4pm Saturday to Sunday

Galleri Lucidor (☎ 640 6786, Hornsgatan 36) – modern art, glass, sculpture and textiles; open noon to 7pm Tuesday, noon to 5pm Wednesday and Thursday and noon to 4pm Friday to Sunday

Galleri Micro (☎ 640 0307, Hornsgatan 40) – traditional paintings, including Stockholm scenes; open noon to 5pm Tuesday to Thursday and noon to 4pm Friday to Sunday

Galleri Puckeln (☎ 641 2323, Hornsgatan 26) – paintings; open 11am to 4pm Tuesday and Wednesday, 11am to 5pm Thursday and noon to 4pm Friday to Sunday

Helle Knudsen (☎ 644 4072, Södermalmstorg 4) – modern art, graphic design and sculpture; open 11.30am to 5.30pm Tuesday to Thursday,

11.30am to 4pm Friday, noon to 4pm Saturday and 1pm to 4pm Sunday

Kaolin (Map 7, F2, #90) (☎ 644 4600, Hornsgatan 50B) – excellent porcelain is for sale in this gallery/shop owned by 20 artists; open 11am to 6pm weekdays, 11am to 4pm Saturday and noon to 4pm Sunday

Metallum (☎ 640 1323, W www.metallum.com, Hornsgatan 30) – excellent metallic modern art, including gold and silver jewellery; open 11am to 6pm Tuesday to Friday, 11am to 4pm Saturday and noon to 4pm Sunday

Södra Galleriet (☎ 702 0305, Hornsgatan 34) – modern paintings; open 11am to 6pm Tuesday to Thursday, 11am to 5pm Friday and noon to 4pm Saturday and Sunday

Bookshops – New Books

Books are generally expensive in Sweden and most places sell few (if any) books in English. Apart from the list below, try the excellent book store in NK (see the upcoming Department Stores section).

Akademibokhandeln (Map 6, C6, #96) (☎ 613 6100, Mäster Samuelsgatan 32) – the widest range of new books in Stockholm, mostly in Swedish; open 10am to 7pm weekdays and 10am to 4pm Saturday

Junibacken (Map 4, F5, #95) (☎ 587 23000, Galärparken) – a good selection of children's books, mostly in Swedish; open 9am to 6pm daily June to August, otherwise 10am to 5pm Tuesday to Sunday; take bus No 47

Kartbutiken (Map 6, D2, #119) (☎ 202303, Kungsgatan 74) – an excellent selection of travel books, including many Lonely Planet titles; Kartbutiken has the lowest prices for travel books in Stockholm; open 9am to 6pm weekdays and 10am to 2pm Saturday

Press Stop (Map 5, B7, #37) (☎ 644 3510, Götgatan 31) Metro: T-Slussen – a selection of English-language paperbacks and magazines; open 10am to 7pm weekdays, noon to 5pm Saturday and noon to 4pm Sunday

Press Stop (Map 6, E4, #151) (☎ 411 1193, Drottninggatan 35) – see previous entry; other stores are located at Gallerian **(Map 6, E6, #156)** and Sky City (Arlanda airport); open 10am to 6.30pm weekdays, 10am to 5pm Saturday and 11am to 5pm Sunday

Sweden Bookshop (Map 6, D6, #180) (☎ 789 2131, E bookshop@si.se, 1st floor, Sverigehuset, Hamngatan 27) – lots of touristy books in English at premium prices; mail order service is available; open 10am to 6pm weekdays, 11am to 3pm Saturday and 10am to 3pm Sunday in July and August

Bookshops – Second-Hand Books & Maps

The following is a selection of second-hand bookshops in Stockholm:

Antikvariat MIMER (Map 4, C2, #29) (☎ 612 0500, Tegnérgatan 4) Metro: T-Rådmansgatan – mainly books on philosophy and history

Bokmagasinet (Map 5, B4, #16) (☎ 668 0580, Hornsgatan 80) Metro: T-Mariatorget – new and antiquarian books, with some titles in English; open 10am to 6pm weekdays and 10am to 3pm Saturday

Centralantikvariatet (Map 6, B3, #14) (☎ 411 9136, Drottninggatan 73B) – a wide range of books, covering music, travel, history etc and including lots of books in English; open noon to 6pm Tuesday to Friday and 11am to 3pm Saturday

Flodins (Map 7, C4, #29) (☎ 204881, W www.flodins.aos.se, Västerlånggatan 37) Metro: T-Gamla Stan – antique maps and prints, Skr250 to Skr6000; open 10am to 6pm weekdays and 11am to 3pm Saturday

Halléns Antikvariat (Map 4, D2, #35) (☎ 200270, Tegnérgatan 17) Metro: T-Rådmansgatan – huge range covering history, food and fiction, with books in English (from Skr20); open 11am to 6pm weekdays and 11am to 3pm Saturday

Jones Antikvariat (Map 4, C1, #20) (☎ 307697, Norrtullsgatan 3) Metro: T-Odenplan – includes books on art, medicine and science; there are also biographies, children's books and some books in English; open 11am to 6pm weekdays and 11am to 3pm Saturday

Ryös Antikvariat (Map 3, F5, #61) (☎ 654 8086, W www.ryo.se, Hantverkargatan 21) Metro: T-Rådhuset – a wide range of books, including some rare titles; various books in English; open 10am to 6pm weekdays and 10am to 2pm Saturday (closed Saturday June to August)

Rönnells Antikvariat (Map 6, A6, #40) (☎ 679 7550, W www.ronnells.se, Birger Jarlsgatan 32) Metro: T-Hötorget – this is a huge place, with around 100,000 books and there are many modern books in English, from art and literature to travel; open 10am to 6pm weekdays and 11am to 3pm Saturday

Department Stores – Souvenirs, Speciality Foods

There are three department stores in Stockholm.

NK (Map 6, D6, #94) (☎ 762 8000, Hamngatan 18-20) – an enormous store with over 110 departments, selling cosmetics, expensive fashion clothing, Swedish handicrafts and own-brand chocolates. The basement supermarket sells some traditional foods and there's also a health food store and a book department with a particularly good English-language section. Open 10am to 7pm weekdays, 10am to 5pm Saturday, noon to 5pm Sunday (noon to 4pm Sunday, June and July); basement closes an hour later

PUB (Map 6, C4, #111) (☎ 402 1611, Hötorget) – with 59 departments, covering music, video, DIY, books, toys and cosmetics; there are several brand-name boutiques within the store; open 10am to 7pm weekdays, 10am to 5pm Saturday and noon to 5pm Sunday

Åhléns (Map 6, D4, #134) (☎ 676 6000, Klarabergsgatan 50) – with more moderate prices, Åhléns offers clothes (own-brand and designer label), glassware, books, cosmetics, sportswear, photography, computers and music. The Hemköp supermarket in the basement sells vegetarian foods; there's also a good cafe. Open 10am to 7pm Monday to Saturday and 11am to 6pm Sunday

Music

One of the best places for new CDs is the music department on the 1st floor of Åhléns (see the previous Department Stores section). Some smaller stores specialise and there are also several good second-hand record shops.

Andreas skivor (Map 5, C8, #68) (☎ 640 8839, Skånegatan 90) Metro: T-Medborgarplatsen – the knowledgeable staff here can advise on the latest club music on new CDs; fliers can be picked up here; open 11am to 6.30pm weekdays and 11am to 4pm Saturday

multikulti (Map 7, G4, #109) (☎ 643 6129, St Paulsgatan 3) Metro: T-Slussen – come to multikulti for alternative music, jazz, oriental, Middle-Eastern, African and world music; open 11am to 6.30pm Monday and Tuesday, 11am to 7pm Wednesday to Friday and 11am to 4pm Saturday

Pet Sounds (Map 5, C7, #66) (☎ 702 9798, Skånegatan 53) Metro: T-Medborgarplatsen – indie, pop, rock and dance music is available; fliers and knowledgeable staff

Record Palace (Map 3, E3, #34) (☎ 650 1990, St Eriksgatan 56) Metro: T-Fridhemsplan – the largest second-hand music store in town, with everything from classical and jazz to pop and rock; open 11am to 6pm weekdays and 11am to 3pm Saturday

Rotspel (Map 4, C2, #5) (☎ 160404, [W] www.rotspel.a.se, Tulegatan 37) Metro: T-Rådmansgatan – Scandinavian folk, Sami and world music; open 11am to 6.30pm weekdays and 11am to 4pm Saturday

Skivbörsen (Map 3, D4, #25) (☎ 320317, St Eriksgatan 71) Metro: T-St Eriksplan – lots of nonmainstream, second-hand music on LPs and CDs; open 11am to 6pm Friday and 11am to 3pm Saturday

Svala & Söderlund (Map 6, C4, #102) (☎ 109838, Kungsgatan 43) – new classical CDs

Outdoor & Sports Equipment

The following is a selection of stores which sell outdoor and sports equipment:

Friluftsbolaget (Map 6, B5, #29) (☎ 241996, Kungsgatan 26) – stockists of boots, jackets, fleeces, sleeping bags, tents, stoves and backpacks; open 10am to 6pm weekdays, 10am to 4pm Saturday and noon to 4pm Sunday

Naturkompaniet (Map 6, B7, #34) (☎ 723 1581, Kungsgatan 4A) – similar to Friluftsbolaget; open 10am to 6.30pm weekdays and 10am to 4pm Saturday

Naturkompaniet (Map 3, F4, #53) (☎ 651 3500, Hantverkargatan 38-40) Metro: T-Rådhuset – a larger and better store, also with climbing equipment, cross-country skiing and travel gear; open 10am to 6pm weekdays and 10am to 3pm Saturday

Stadium (Map 6, B6, #32) (☎ 723 0875, Kungsgatan 8) – general sports goods, including ice skating equipment; open 10am to 7pm weekdays, 10am to 5pm Saturday and noon to 4pm Sunday

Photography

The following is a selection of photography stores in Stockholm:

Expert (Map 6, D4, #109) (☎ 249320, Drottninggatan 53) – sells a range of still and video film

Kodak Image Center (Map 6, C4, #105)
(☎ 219167, Sergelgatan 29) – sells Kodak products only
OdenLab (Map 5, B5, #24) (☎ 545 41741, Timmermansgatan 32) Metro: T-Mariatorget – OdenLab develops film and provides high quality prints
Sergel Foto (Map 6, D4, #108) (☎ 205959, Slöjdgatan 1-5) – the recommended sales outlet for Fuji films; also develops slides and prints; open 9am to 6pm weekdays and 10am to 3pm Saturday

Second-Hand Shops
Not everyone in Stockholm can afford the latest designer outfits so there's a booming trade in second-hand clothing and other items; look out for nice pieces of glassware that would cost much more when new. Look up *Second Handaffärer* in the Yellow Pages.

Emmaus Praktisk Solidaritet (Map 7, F4, #85) (☎ 644 8586, Götgatan 14) Metro: T-Slussen – this charity shop deals in second-hand clothing, books and designer wares; open 10.30am to 6.30pm weekdays and 11am to 4pm Saturday
Judits Second Hand (Map 5, B4, #15) (☎ 844510, Hornsgatan 75) Metro: T-Zinkensdamm – quality second-hand goods
Myrorna (Map 5, B4, #14) (☎ 556 05982, Hornsgatan 96) Metro: T-Zinkensdamm – second-hand clothes for men and women, plus some other second-hand goods
UFF (Map 6, C3, #114) (Kungsgatan 54) – this controversial charity-shop chain has traditional and trendy clothes and shoes for both sexes; open 10am to 6pm weekdays and 10am to 4pm Saturday

Speciality Shops & Boutiques
Most of the best speciality shops and boutiques are well off the tourist trail.

Brunzell Vanja AB (Map 7, C5, #37) (☎ 212763, Köpmangatan 4) Metro: T-Gamla Stan – unique women's clothes (including dresses, coats and scarves), but very expensive; open 11am to 6pm weekdays and 11am to 4pm Saturday
Götgatsbackens Hälsokost (Map 7, G4, #112) (☎ 640 9040, Götgatan 21) Metro: T-Slussen – this health food store has organic fruit and vegetables, dietary supplements and vegetarian and vegan foods; open 9am to 6pm weekdays and 10am to 2pm Saturday

Govindas Butik (Map 3, E3, #40) (☎ 654 9002, Fridhemsgatan 22) Metro: T-Fridhemsplan – here you'll get vegetarian foods, spices, teas and Indian and Nepali clothes; open 11am to 7pm weekdays and noon to 7pm Saturday
Klädd i Konst (Map 5, B5, #20) (Hornsgatan 43) Metro: T-Mariatorget – unusual women's clothes; some silver jewellery; open 11am to 6pm weekdays and 11am to 3pm Saturday
Konsthantverkarna (Map 6, C7, #83) (☎ 611 0370, Mäster Samuelsgatan 2) – a recommended glassware and ceramics outlet, but there are also textiles, silver and wood; open 10am to 6pm weekdays and 10am to 4pm Saturday
Kus & Kompaniet (Map 7, G4, #109) (St Paulsgatan 1) Metro: T-Slussen – Swedish-made women's clothing; open 11am to 7pm weekdays and 11am to 4pm Saturday
Lush (Map 7, G4, #110) (☎ 642 0089, Götgatan 26A) Metro: T-Slussen – handmade cosmetics, natural soaps, lotions and oils; open 10am to 6.30pm weekdays, 10am to 4pm Saturday and noon to 4pm Sunday
Nanso (Map 6, B7, #86) (☎ 679 7085, Stureplan 13) – comfortable clothes for women, made in Finland

Swedish Modern Design
Sweden is rightly famous for its high standards of modern design. For a detailed listing of design shops, see W www.svenskform.se on the Internet (currently in Swedish only).

Agata (Map 5, C8, #59) (☎ 643 0980, Nytorgsgatan 36) Metro: T-Medborgarplatsen – unique modern styles in ceramics, glass and textiles; open 11am to 6pm Tuesday to Friday and 11am to 4pm Saturday
Design Torget (Map 5, B7, #37) (☎ 462 3520, Götgatan 31) Metro: T-Slussen – contemporary Swedish design, from toys and textiles to furniture; there's another outlet in Kulturhuset, at Sergels Torg; open 10am to 7pm weekdays, 10am to 4pm Saturday and noon to 4pm Sunday
DIS Inredning (Map 6, B8, #47) (☎ 611 2907, Humlegårdsgatan 19) – Swedish interior design, porcelain, glassware, furniture, baskets etc; open 10.30am to 6pm weekdays and 10.30am to 3pm Saturday
Jackson's (Map 7, C4, #59) (☎ 411 8587, Tyskabrinken 20) Metro: T-Gamla Stan – modern design, including Swedish glassware and ceramics; superb museum quality art

glass; prices up to Skr20,000; open noon to 6pm weekdays and 11am to 3pm Saturday

Kalikå (Map 7, C5, #57) (☎ 205219, Österlånggatan 18) Metro: T-Gamla Stan – old-fashioned textile and wooden toys with unique designs; open 10am to 6pm weekdays, 10am to 4pm Saturday and noon to 4pm Sunday

Nutida Svenskt Silver (Map 6, E8, #190) (☎ 611 6718, Arsenalsgatan 3) – exhibitions and sales by 50 modern Swedish silversmiths and goldsmiths, including jewellery and silverware; open 11am to 6pm weekdays and noon to 4pm Saturday (closed July)

plan ett: 1 (Map 4, D2, #36) (☎ 555 29707, Tegnérgatan 13) Metro: T-Rådmansgatan – varied Swedish design from glass to furniture; open 11am to 6pm weekdays and 11am to 3pm Saturday

Platina (Map 3, C5, #12) (☎ 300280, Odengatan 68) Metro: T-Odenplan – metal and jewellery design by Swedish and international designers; open 11am to 6pm weekdays and 11am to 3pm Saturday

Handicrafts & Traditional Souvenirs

There's no shortage of handicraft and souvenir outlets in Stockholm. You can buy all sorts of things such as soft toy elks, dolls in Swedish national dress, toy Viking boats, toy Viking warriors, trolls, excellent Dalarna horses, silverware and glassware. Some of the more interesting or unusual places are:

Carl Wennberg (Map 7, C4, #60) (☎ 201721, Svartmangatan 11) Metro: T-Gamla Stan – superb Sami art and handicrafts, including knives, silver and tin jewellery, drums, clothes and ceramics; almost everything sold here is made by Sami people; open 10am to 6pm weekdays and 11am to 3pm Saturday

Duka (Map 6, C4, #102) (☎ 206041, Konserthuset, Kungsgatan) – glassware from Småland (Orrefors, Kosta Boda, Målerås etc); also kitchenware and crockery; open 10am to 7pm weekdays, 10am to 4pm Saturday and noon to 4pm Sunday

Nordiska Kristall (Map 6, B6, #89) (☎ 104372, Kungsgatan 9) – Orrefors, Kosta Boda and Målerås glassware; open 10am to 6.30pm weekdays and 10am to 4pm Saturday

Skansen Shop (Map 4, G7, #86) (☎ 442 8268, Djurgårsslätten 49-51) – a wide range of quality traditional and modern handicrafts, artwork, souvenirs and food from around Sweden; open daily (variable hours); take bus No 47

Svensk Hemslöjd (Map 6, A4, #22) (☎ 232115, Sveavägen 44) – traditional handicrafts in wood, textiles, wool and glass, including large Dalarna horses and wicker baskets; open 10am to 6pm weekdays and 10am to 3pm Saturday

Svenskt Hantverk (Map 6, C3, #122) (☎ 214726, Kungsgatan 55) – Swedish craft and design; Dalarna horses, kitchen and eating utensils, candelabras, jugs, bowls, linen etc; open 10am to 6pm weekdays and 10am to 3pm Saturday (10am to 2pm Saturday in summer)

Svenskt Tenn (Map 6, D9, #74) (☎ 670 1600, Strandvägen 5) – interior design and gifts; furniture, china, glassware, textiles, pewter, lamps and porcelain; open 10am to 6pm weekdays and 10am and 3pm Saturday

Excursions

The delightful islands of the Stockholm archipelago are within easy reach of the city and there are regular ferry services to the populated islands for most of the year, directly from the city centre or from nearby coastal towns. Ferries aren't expensive and there's a travel pass available if you want to tour around the islands for a while. On warm and sunny summer days, you could easily believe you're in the south of France rather than in the far northern reaches of Europe.

In the other direction, the Lake Mälaren archipelago is also a delightful destination and you can take tour boats to various places around the lake, including the Viking site Birka. Also around Mälaren is Sweden's oldest town, Sigtuna, the Renaissance royal palace Gripsholms Slott, and the more modern cities of Uppsala and Västerås.

Getting Around

You can explore Stockholms Län (the county of Greater Stockholm) with the Storstockholms Lokaltrafik (SL) Tourist Pass or the 30-day pass – both allow unlimited travel on all buses and local trains. Free timetables are available from the SL-Center in Centralstationen or the (SL) terminals at Slussen or Östrastationen. For details of transport in Stockholms Län, see the Getting Around chapter. SL tickets cannot be used on archipelago boats. For details of ferry companies, schedules and fares, see Stockholm Archipelago later in this chapter.

Destinations just outside Stockholms Län are generally reached by express train or bus. Daily trains to Uppsala, Västerås and Sala are operated by Svenges Järnväg (SJ; ☎ 020 757575, ☒ www.sj.se). Express buses to these destinations are run by Swebus Express (☎ 0200 218218). Car rental is also feasible – once you're outside the city, driving is straightforward (see Car & Motorcycle in the Getting Around chapter. Details of transport options to other nearby places in Sweden can be found in Lonely Planet's *Sweden* guidebook.

VAXHOLM
☎ 08 • pop 8721

Vaxholm is the gateway to the central and northern reaches of Stockholm's archipelago and it swarms with tourists in summer. Despite that, it's a pleasant place with several attractions and is well worth a visit.

The town was founded in 1647 and has many quaint summerhouses, which were fashionable in the 19th century. The oldest buildings are in the Norrhamn area, a few minutes' walk north of the town hall, but there's also interesting architecture along Hamngatan (the main street).

The tourist office (☎ 541 31480), by the harbour at Söderhamnsplan, is open 10am to 4pm daily (also open 10am to 4pm weekends in summer). Ask for the handy leaflet *A stroll through Vaxholm*. You'll find a bank and post office on Hamngatan.

The traditional island market day is held on the third Saturday in August. You'll find the town on the Internet at ☒ www.vaxholm.se.

Things to See

The construction of **Vaxholms Fästning** *(☎ 541 72157; Skr40/10 including ferry; open 11.45am-3.45pm daily 1-22 June & 14 Aug-3 Sept, 11.45am-5.45pm daily 24 June-13 Aug)*, located on an unnamed islet just east of Vaxholm, was originally ordered by Gustav Vasa in 1544. The castle was attacked by Danes in 1612 and the Russian navy in 1719; most of the current structure dates from 1863. Nowadays, it's home to the National Museum of Coastal Defence and is due to reopen in 2002, after renovations. The ferry across to the island departs from next to the tourist office and departs every 30 minutes while the castle is open.

At the **Hembygdsgård** *(☎ 541 31720, Trädgårdsgatan 19; free; open 11am-4pm Sat & Sun mid-May-mid-Aug)*, you'll find the finest old houses in Vaxholm, including the **fiskarebostad**, an excellent example of a late 19th-century fisherman's house, with a typical Swedish fireplace.

Around the corner from the tourist office, the **Customs House** is one of the few stone buildings in town and dates from 1736. The other stone building is the **church** (Kungsgatan), which is late 18th century. Just off Hamngatan, you'll see the **town hall**, rebuilt in 1925 with an onion dome on its roof; if it's open, take a look inside.

Places to Stay
Vaxholms Camping (☎ 541 30101) Hiker/car with tent Skr80/110. Open 26 Apr-30 Sept. Vaxholms Camping is 3km west of the harbour, at the other end of the island.

Rådhusgatan 18 (☎ 541 31555, Rådhusgatan 18) Singles/doubles Skr200/300-Skr250/400. This place offers centrally placed and good-value self-catering accommodation in summer only.

Berggrens Hus (☎ 541 30279, Soldatgatan 14) Singles/doubles Skr325/450. About 1km from the harbour, Berggrens Hus offers hotel-standard rooms, but breakfast costs Skr50 extra. Self-catering facilities are available.

Waxholms Hotell (☎ 541 30150, ⓔ info@ waxholmshotell.se, Ⓦ www.waxholmshotell .se, Hamngatan 2) Singles/doubles from Skr1100/1350 (discounted Skr770/945). Waxholms Hotell has a pleasant mixture of Art Nouveau and modern styles and is just opposite the tourist office.

Places to Eat
Waxholms Hotell (☎ 541 30150, Hamngatan 2) Mains Skr98-275. The first-floor hotel restaurant offers a summer herring buffet (Skr160). The outdoor restaurant *Kabyssen*, at Waxholms Hotell, is only a little dearer.

Moby Dick Restaurang & Pizzeria (☎ 541 33883, Söderhamnsplan 1) Mains Skr65-159, takeaway pizzas from Skr55. Across the street from the tourist office, this restaurant also offers enchiladas and meat and fish dishes.

Gröna Langan (Hamngatan 16) Breakfast buffet Skr40, weekday lunch Skr45. Open 6am-4pm Mon-Fri, 8am-4pm Sat & Sun. You'll find this cosy cafe in a traditional building on the main street.

AROUND STOCKHOLM

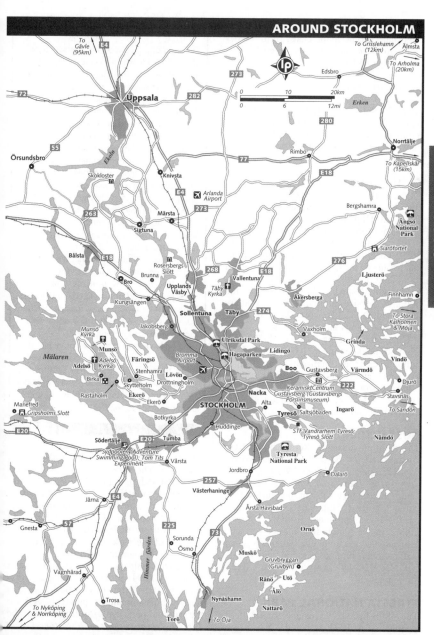

AROUND STOCKHOLM

EXCURSIONS

EXCURSIONS

There's also a popular *cafe* at the Hembygdsgård (home-made cakes from Skr14) and a ***Konsum*** supermarket (open 9am to 8pm daily) on Hamngatan.

Entertainment
Waxholms Hotell (☎ *541 30150, Hamngatan 2)* Nightclub admission Skr60. Live bands play outdoors from Wednesday to Saturday on summer afternoons, but they play inside the hotel nightclub on Friday and Saturday nights.

Getting There & Away
Vaxholm is 35km north-east of Stockholm. Bus No 670 from the metro station T-Tekniska Högskolan in Stockholm runs regularly to the town (Skr32, 45 minutes).

In summer, Waxholmsbolaget (☎ 679 5830) boats depart frequently from Strömkajen (outside the Grand Hôtel) from 8.30am to 6.30pm on weekdays, 8am to 6.30pm on Saturday, and 8am to 9.30pm on Sunday and holidays. Services at other times of year are less frequent. Tickets cost Skr50/30 adult/ child and sailings take 1¼ hours.

Cinderella Båtarna (☎ 587 14050) sails from Strandvägen (near Nybroplan) to Vaxholm three or four times daily from 20 April to 24 September and once daily Friday to Sunday from late September to early November (Skr50/25, 45 minutes). Meals are available on board.

GUSTAVSBERG
The ceramic museum, **KeramisktCentrum Gustavsberg** (☎ *08-570 35658, Odelbergs väg 5B; open 10am-5pm Mon-Fri, 10am-3pm Sat & 11am-3pm Sun),* at the tourist centre and factory shop in the Gustavsberg china factory (25km east of Stockholm) has displays of porcelain from the 19th and 20th centuries, including dinner services. You can also see an active workshop where staff members produce ceramic figures. Take bus Nos 424-440 from T-Slussen (Skr32, 40 minutes).

TYRESTA NATIONAL PARK
The 4900-hectare Tyresta National Park, established in 1993, is noted for its virgin

The Right of Public Access

The right of public access to the countryside, *allemansrätten*, which includes national parks and nature reserves, dates back to common practices in medieval times, but isn't enshrined in law. Full details can be found on the Internet at Ⓦ www.environ.se.

You're allowed to walk, ski, boat or swim anywhere outside private property but stay at least 70m from houses and keep out of gardens, fenced areas and cultivated land. You can camp for more than one night in the same place and you may pick berries and mushrooms, provided they're not protected.

Don't leave any rubbish or take live wood, bark, leaves, bushes or nuts. Fires with fallen wood are allowed where safe, but not on bare rocks. Use a bucket of water to douse a campfire even if you think that it's out. Cars and motorcycles may not be driven across open land or on private roads; look out for the sign *Ej Motorfordon* (No Motor Vehicles). Dogs must be kept on leads from 1 March to 20 August. Close all gates and don't disturb farm animals and nesting birds.

If you have a car, bicycle or you're hitching, look for free camping sites around unsealed forest tracks leading from secondary country roads. Make sure your spot is at least 50m from the track and not visible from any house, building or sealed road.

forest, which includes huge 300-year-old pine trees. The park lies only 20km southeast of Stockholm and the city is the only European capital with virgin forest so close. Tyresta is a beautiful area, with interesting rocky outcrops, small lakes, marshes, and a wide variety of birdlife. Unfortunately, sections of the park were damaged by fire during the hot summer of 1999.

The Nationalparkernashus (visitor centre; ☎ 08-745 3394) in Tyresta village, at the south-western edge of the park, charges Skr20 admission and is open daily. Ask for the national park leaflet in English and the *Tyresta Nationalpark och Naturreservat* leaflet in Swedish, which includes an excellent topographical map at 1:25,000 scale.

From Nationalparkernashus there are various trails into the park. The *Sörmlandsleden* track cuts across 6km of the park on its way to central Stockholm. There are also several 'loop' trails, from 3km to 6km long, and you can hike right across the park to Åva. Wild camping is allowed at certain places, but you must strictly obey the regulations on access (see the boxed text 'The Right of Public Access').

Access to the park is easy. Take the *pendeltåg* (commuter train) to Haninge Centrum (also called Handen station) on the Nynäshamn line, then change to bus No 834 (45 minutes from central Stockholm). Some buses run all the way to the park, others stop at Svartbäcken (2km west of Tyresta village).

GAMLA TYRESÖ
☎ 08

Gamla Tyresö, about 20km south-east of Stockholm and just north of Tyresta National Park, has a pleasant English-style park with some significant attractions.

The **church** *(free; open irregularly)* on the hill has an impressive square tower and dates from 1641. The **altarpiece** was looted from Poland and it shows a remarkable scene of the murder of Bishop Stanislaus of Kraków in 1079. There's also an interesting **votive ship** from 1620, one of the oldest in Sweden.

Work started on **Tyresö Slott** *(☎ 770 0178; Skr50/20 adult/child; guided tours on the hour noon-4pm daily mid-June-mid-Aug, noon-2pm Sun May-Oct & by appointment at other times)* in the 1620s and it was completed by 1635. The castle was rebuilt in rococo style in the second half of the 18th century and restored in 17th-century style after purchase by Claes Lagergren in 1892. On Lagergren's death in 1932, the castle and estate were bequeathed to Nordiska Museet and the interiors have been kept in excellent condition.

STF Vandrarhem Lilla Tyresö (☎ 770 0304, fax 770 0355, Kyrkvägen 3) Dorm beds Skr145-165. Open year-round. Prince Eugene, the royal artist, stayed here for 18 summers and now this small group of buildings, across the stream from the church, has been excellently restored as a hostel. Advance booking is obligatory from October to May.

You'll find a *cafe* and *restaurant* at the castle.

Take the regular bus No 805 from T-Gullmarsplan to the stop Tyresö Slott (Skr24, 30 minutes).

DALARÖ
☎ 08

Dalarö is a quaint little town which serves as a gateway to the southern archipelago and it's a great place for walks, ice skating (in winter), fishing (bring your own equipment), swimming and island visits. Dalarö is about 40km south-east of Stockholm by road. The town was a popular 19th-century resort and it still sees plenty tourists today.

The tourist office (☎ 501 50800, ⓔ turistbyran@dalaro.org, Hotellbryggan), by the ferry quay, is open 9am to 5pm Tuesday to Friday and 9am to 2pm weekends from June to August (shorter hours and also closed on Sunday at other times of year). Dalarö has a post office and an ATM, both on Odinsvägen (the main street).

A small fort was built near Dalarö in 1623 but, in 1719, the Russians sacked the town. Fortunately, the impressive church Dalarö Kyrka and its magnificent collection of artefacts was spared. The brick-built **customs house** dates from 1788 and was used by Gustav III during his royal visits. At **Anders Franzéns Sjöbod** *(Tullbacken; free; open 8am-7pm Mon-Fri, 9am-4pm Sat & Sun May-Sept)* you'll see the office and study of one of the prime movers in the raising of the *Vasa* in 1979.

Dalarö Kyrka

While appearing ordinary from the outside, this magnificent church *(Odinsvägen 4; free; open most days noon-3pm June & July)* was consecrated in 1652 and looks like an upturned boat from the inside. It contains a beautiful inlaid wood **pulpit** from 1630, a **votive ship** from 1652, and a stone grave slab from 1686. The **altar painting** shows Christ on the cross and dates from 1710. There is also a series of six paintings describing the history of Dalarö and a 17th-century Dutch tapestry behind glass.

Contact the tourist office regarding access at other times.

Dalarö Skans

Construction of this small fort, on a tiny offshore island, was ordered by Gustav II Adolf in 1623, with the intention of controlling the waterway. It is very impressive, with a circular tower and angular bastions. There's now a fine restaurant here. Boats run two or three times daily, 23 June to 17 August, from Hotellbryggan (Skr50 return).

Places to Stay & Eat

STF Vandrarhem Dalarö (*☎/fax 501 51636, Tullbacken 4*) Dorm beds Skr100 (Skr150 May to mid-Sept). Open year-round, advance bookings only mid-Sept-Apr. Sweden's smallest hostel is a former pilot station, rebuilt on the edge of the water in 1933 after a fire in 1890. You'll need to book up to four months in advance in summer.

Rosenon Spa & Friskvård (*☎ 501 53700, fax 501 53801, ℮ rosenon@rosenon .se, Rosenon*) B&B Skr370 per person. Open 26 June-24 July. Rosenon is a wonderful country house hotel, pub and restaurant on a small island 5km north-east of Dalarö. Rosenon is connected to Dalarö by road.

Skårgårdsrestaurangen Mysingen (*☎ 501 51525, Odinsvägen 10*) Mains Skr87-158. Good Swedish food is served in this rustic and friendly pub/restaurant.

Pizzeria Ankaret (*☎ 501 51690, Odinsvägen 19*) Pizzas from around Skr50, mains Skr80-120. The attached restaurant has a Swedish *husmanskost* (traditional Swedish home-cooking) menu.

For fast food, visit *Dalarö Kiosk & Grill*, by the ferry quay. There's also *Dalarö Bagariet* on Odinsvägen (with good bread and cakes) and the supermarket *Norbergs ICA (Odinsvägen 22)*, which is closed on Sunday.

Getting There & Away

Most people get to Dalarö by taking the pendeltåg to Haninge Centrum, then bus No 839 (Skr40 from central Stockholm, one hour, roughly hourly). Many buses continue to Smådalarö, near Rosenon Spa & Friskvård.

Waxholmsbolaget boats run to Stockholm (Skr95, weekends in summer only), Fjärdlång (Skr30, daily) and Utö (Skr60, weekends in summer only).

SÖDERTÄLJE
☎ 08 • pop 78,836

Södertälje, a large satellite town 38km south-west of Stockholm, offers a couple of attractions of interest to children and families.

The adventure swimming pool, **Sydpoolen** (*☎ 554 42800, [W] www.sydpoolen .se, Grödingevägen 2; 1hr Skr60/45 adult/ child under 7, 3hrs Skr75/55; open 9am-9pm daily, closing 6pm Sun*) has waves, currents, slides, diving, a lagoon for babies and a climbing wall. There's also a fitness centre and a gym.

Discover science and technology for yourself at **Tom Tits Experiment** (*☎ 522 52500, Storgatan 33; Skr85/65; open 10am-4pm Mon-Fri & 11am-5pm Sat & Sun, 10am-5pm daily late June-late Aug*), with lots of hands-on exhibits.

To get to Sydpoolen, take the commuter train from Centralstationen in Stockholm to J-Södertälje Central (Skr40, 43 minutes, four per hour), then cross the canal. Tom Tits Experiment is about a 10-minute walk north of J-Södertälje Central.

NYNÄSHAMN
☎ 08 • pop 23,341

From humble beginnings as a small fishing village, by the early 20th century Nynäshamn had developed into a thriving spa town and the most important ferry terminal for Gotland. The important modern port also handles sailings to and from Poland.

The tourist office (*☎ 520 14590, ℮ turist@ nynasnet.se*), Järnvägsgatan 2, is close to the train and ferry terminals. It's open 9am to 4pm on weekdays (9am to 6pm week-days and 9am to 3pm weekends, in June and July). The town centre is nearby and you'll find the post office at Lövlundsvägen 3, a bank (FöreningsSparbanken) at Centralgatan 6B, and Systembolaget at Mörbyvägen 3. To call a doctor, contact ☎ 520 72010.

Things to See

Find out about the cultural history of the area in the **Nynäshamn Hembygdsgård** *(Nynäshamn Folklore Museum;* ☎ *520 10050, Strandvägen; free; open noon-4pm Sun mid-June to mid-Sept, or by appointment)*, which is south of the town centre and near Nynäs Havsbad train station.

Located about 1km north of the town centre, **Järnvägsmuseum** *(*☎ *520 13955, Nickstabadsvägen 13; open 1pm-4pm Sun 15 June-15 Aug & 1pm-4pm last Sun of every month)* has exhibits covering the history of the railway.

In Sorunda, situated 19km north-east of Nynäshamn, there are fine paintings in the 12th-century **church**, and one of the largest collections of **rune stones** in Sweden. Körunda, 14km north of Nynäshamn, has **Viking Toste** *(*☎ *520 39030)*, a reconstruction of a Viking homestead where you'll find out about horn jewellery, Viking brewing techniques and Norse myths.

Places to Stay

Nickstabadets Camping (☎ *520 12780, Nickstabadsvägen)* Hiker/car with tent Skr60/110, rooms from Skr200, cabins & chalets Skr225-575. Open 15 May-15 Sept. Nickstabadets Camping lies about 1km west of the ferry terminal.

STF Vandrarhem Nickstagården (☎ *520 12780, fax 520 15317, Nickstabadsvägen 15)* Dorm beds Skr120. Open year-round. Nickstagården is a rather basic STF hostel, but there are plans for improvement. From September to May you must book in advance.

B&B accommodation can be booked through the tourist office for between Skr150 and Skr300 per person.

Skärgårdshotellet (☎ *520 11120, fax 520 10572,* e *info@skargardshotellet.com, Kaptensgatan 2)* From Skr440 per room. Skärgårdshotellet, just across from the ferry terminal, offers comfortable hotel rooms.

Places to Eat

M/S Freja (☎ *520 16230, harbour)* This restaurant/pub is very popular with young people.

Restaurang Kroken (☎ *520 10025, harbour)* Most mains Skr100-180. This is a good fish restaurant in a traditional boat house, which doubles-up as an art gallery.

Statt (☎ *520 15078, Fredsgatan 2)* The Statt restaurant has a popular nightclub and disco.

Lydias Krog (☎ *520 14001, Centralgatan 3)* This is a cosy restaurant/pub with a good menu.

Smått & Gott (☎ *520 14902, Gallerian Havet)* Here you'll get reasonable sandwiches and salads from around Skr30 to Skr60.

Moulin Rouge (☎ *520 20210, Centralgatan 2)* This is one of several pizza places in town.

Self-caterers should visit *Rökeriet*, the fresh fish shop at the harbour. The *Konsum* and *ICA* supermarkets are across from each other on Centralgatan.

Getting There & Away

Nynäshamn is 58km south of Stockholm. The ferry terminal is the main gateway to Gotland. For details of the ferry to Poland, see the Getting There & Away chapter. There are also boats to Ålö on the island of Utö and from Torö to Öja (see Stockholm Archipelago later in this chapter).

A regular local train runs from Stockholm to Nynäshamn once or twice hourly (Skr40, one hour). It takes bicycles and SL tickets, but not international rail passes.

Buses arrive and depart from outside the train station. Bus No 783 runs once an hour (every two hours on weekends) between Nynäshamn and Södertälje via Sorunda (Skr16). There are also three to seven daily buses (No 852) from Nynäshamn to Torö (Skr16).

EXCURSIONS

Getting Around

Ask the tourist office about bike hire. The local taxi firm is Taxi Nynäs (☎ 520 11111).

STOCKHOLM ARCHIPELAGO
☎ 08

Depending on which source you read, the archipelago around Stockholm has anything between 14,000 and 100,000 islands, and regular boats offer great possibilities for outings. Having a summer cottage on a rocky islet is popular among wealthy Stockholmers.

While many islands can be visited on a day trip, you'll get a better experience if you stay overnight. Most main islands have STF hostels, but they tend to only open in summer and they're often booked out months in advance. For information on cabin and chalet rental, contact Destination Stockholms Skärgård (☎ 542 48100, fax 542 41400, e dess.skarg@ dess.se, W www.dess.se), Lillström, SE-18497 Ljusterö.

Getting There & Away

Waxholmsbolaget (☎ 679 5830, W www .waxholmsbolaget.se) is the biggest ferry operator; timetables and information are available on its Web site, from its offices outside the Grand Hôtel Stockholm and at the quay in Vaxholm. Ask for the free *Stockholm Archipelago Guide*.

The ferries wind through the archipelago to Arholma, Finnhamn, Stora Kalholmen, Gällnö, Sandön, Nämdö, Ornö, Fjärdlång, Utö, Öja and many more destinations. Waxholmsbolaget's *Båtluffarkortet* (Skr300), sold at Sverigehuset (Sweden House; the main tourist office in Stockholm) and Waxholmsbolaget offices, is valid for 16 days and gives unlimited rides plus a handy island map. It costs an additional Skr25 per trip to take a bicycle on the ferries (if space is available), but bicycles can be hired on many islands. Waxholmsbolaget's vintage steamers S/S *Storskär*, S/S *Norrskär* and S/S *Saltsjön* sail daily from Strömkajen and/or Vaxholm to the islands and restaurant service is available on board.

It's worth checking what Cinderella Båtarna (☎ 587 14050, W www.cinderella -batarna.com) at Skeppsbron 22, Stockholm, has to offer. Its boats *Cinderella I & II* also go to many of the most interesting islands.

Boat frequencies described in this section are for the summer period, mid-June to mid-August. Services are reduced at other times of year and are generally very poor in January and February. Quoted ferry fares are all one-way; return tickets are normally just double the one-way fare.

Organised Tours

The highly recommended and great value 11-hour Thousand Islands Tour, which is operated by Strömma Kanalbolaget (☎ 587 14000, e strommakanalbolaget@stromma .se, W www.strommakanalbolaget.com) departs from Nybroplan at 9.30am daily from 30 June to 12 August (Skr625, including lunch, dinner, entrance fees and guided tours ashore). The vessel, M/S *Waxholm III*, calls at Strindberg's island (Kymmendö), Bullerö in the outer archipelago, Sandhamn and Vaxholm. You get around an hour ashore at each place (except Vaxholm).

Arholma

Arholma is one of the most interesting islands in the far north of the archipelago. Everything was burnt down during a Russian invasion in 1719. The **lighthouse** was rebuilt in the 19th century and it's a well-known landmark. The island became a popular resort in the early 20th century and it's noted for its traditional village and chapel.

STF Vandrarhem Arholma (☎ 0176-56018) Dorm beds Skr110. Open year-round. The hostel offers dorm beds in a renovated cow barn. Advance booking is essential.

Arholma has a summer *cafe* and a *grocery shop* by the harbour.

You can take bus No 640 from Stockholm Tekniska Högskolan to Norrtälje, then No 636 (or No 637 to Älmsta, then change to No 636) to Simpnäs (Skr40, 2¼ hours, three to five daily) followed by a 20-minute ferry crossing to the island (Skr30). Once daily from mid-June to mid-August, Blidösundsbolaget (☎ 08-411 7113) sails

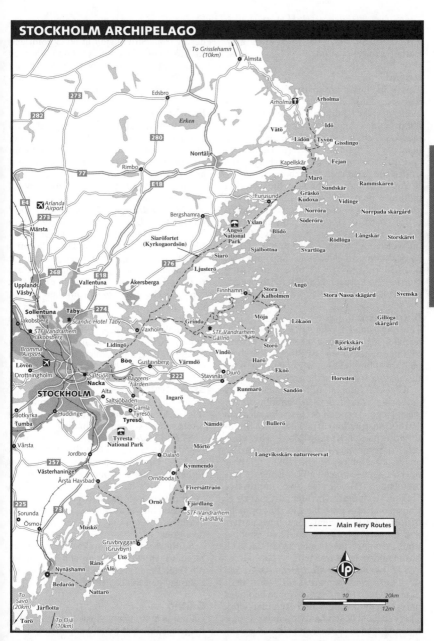

STOCKHOLM ARCHIPELAGO

To Grisslehamn (10km)

Älmsta

Arholma

Arholma

Edsbro

Idö

Vätö

Gisslingo

Lidön Tyvön

Erken

Kapellskär

Fejan

Norrtälje

Rimbo

Marö

Sundskär

Rammskären

Furusund

Gräskö

Kudoxa

Vidinge

Arlanda Airport

Bergshamra

Norröra

Norrpada skärgård

Yxlan

Ängsö National Park

Söderöra

Märsta

Blidö

Siaröfortet (Kyrkogaordsön)

Rödlöga

Långskär

Storskäret

Själbottna

Svartlöga

Siarö

Ljusterö

Vallentuna

Åkersberga

Upplands Väsby

Finnhamn

Stora Kalholmen

Angö

Stora Nassa skägård

Svenska

Sollentuna

Täby

Scandic Hotel Täby

STF Vandrarhem Jakobsberg

Jakobsberg

Vaxholm

Grinda

Möja

Lökaön

Gillöga skägård

STF Vandrarhem Gällnö

Bromma Airport

Lidingö

Vindö

Storö

Björkskärs skärgård

Lövön

Gustavsberg

Värmdö

Harö

Eknö

Horssten

Drottningholm

Boo

Stavsnäs

Djurö

STOCKHOLM

Saltsjön

Nacka

Alta

Bäggens-fjärden

Runmarö

Sandön

Saltsjöbaden

Ingarö

Botkyrka

Huddinge

Gamla Tyresö

Tyresö

Bullerö

Tumba

Nämdö

Vårsta

Tyresta National Park

Mörtö

Jordbro

Dalarö

Langviksskärs naturreservat

Västerhaninge

Kymmendö

Årsta Havsbad

Ornöboda

Fiversättraön

Sorunda

Ornö

Fjärdlang

STF Vandrarhem Fjärdlång

Muskö

Gruvbryggan (Gruvbyn)

Utö

Nynäshamn

Rånö

Ålö

Bedarön

Nattarö

To Savö (20km)

Järflotta

Torö

To Ojä (10km)

----- Main Ferry Routes

0   10   20km
0   6   12mi

LP

directly from Strömkajen in Stockholm to Arholma (Skr100, 3½ to five hours). Båtluffarkortet is valid.

Ängsö

This island lies 15km south of Norrtälje and it was declared a national park as early as 1909, despite being only 1.5km long and 600m wide. Ängsö is characterised by meadows, virgin woodland and magnificent displays of wild flowers (especially in spring). You may also see ospreys, sea eagles and great crested grebes.

You can't stay overnight in the park, but there are boat trips (from Furusund) and guided walks – contact Norrtälje tourist office (☎ 0176-71990) for current details. Bus No 621 runs every hour or two (fewer on weekends) from J-Åkersberga station (Stockholm) to Norrtälje and bus No 632/634 runs six to 12 times daily from Norrtälje to Furusund (Skr40 for the whole journey).

Siaröfortet

The tiny island Kyrkogårdsön, in the important sea lane just north of Ljusterö (40km due north-east of Stockholm), may be only 400m long but it's one of the most fascinating islands in the archipelago.

After the outbreak of WWI, the military authorities decided that Vaxholm castle wasn't a good enough defensive position. In 1916, construction of a new fort, Siaröfortet, began on Kyrkogårdsön. This powerful defence facility was never used in anger; after renovation in 1996, it's now open as a museum and a visit is highly recommended. You'll see two impressive 15.2cm cannons (incidentally, they're trained on passing Viking Line ferries!), the officers mess, kitchen, sleeping quarters and tunnels. There are no fixed opening times; contact the managers at the STF hostel to arrange a free tour.

STF Vandrarhem Siaröfortet (☎/fax 542 42149, W *siarofortet.just.nu)* Dorm beds Skr140. Open May-Sept (advance bookings only, May-mid-June & mid-Aug-end Sept). This excellent hostel has two saunas. Canoe hire and breakfast are available.

Waxholmsbolaget ferries to Siaröfortet depart from Strömkajen in Stockholm and sail to Siaröfortet via Vaxholm once or twice daily. The journey takes 1½ hours from Stockholm, or 50 minutes from Vaxholm (Skr85/75 respectively).

Finnhamn

This 900m-long island has rocky cliffs and a small beach with good family swimming opportunities. Fairly trendy, Finnhamn attracts wealthy visitors from Stockholm and beyond. You can go free camping in the woods, but you'll need to carry all your own water.

STF Vandrarhem Finnhamn (☎ 542 46212, fax 542 46133, e *info@finnhamn .nu,* W *www.finnhamn.nu)* Dorm beds Skr160. Open year-round. The Finnhamn hostel is in a large converted warehouse and advance booking is essential. There are rowing boats and boats with outboards for hire. The *Finnhamn Café* here serves good meals.

You can sail with Waxholmsbolaget from Stockholm (Strömkajen) to Finnhamn via hours). Cinderella Båtarna sails from Strandvägen to Finnhamn two or three times daily; the trip (Skr95) takes two hours.

Stora Kalholmen

Measuring only 700m long by 300m wide, this rocky islet just south of Finnhamn offers some excellent swimming.

STF Vandrarhem Stora Kalholmen (☎ 542 46023, fax 571 60125) Dorm beds Skr125. Open 10 June-20 Aug. Stora Kalholmen is a very nicely located hostel, but it doesn't have electricity or a flush toilet. There is a gas cooker and a sauna, and canoe hire is available. Meals are only available for large groups, so bring your own grub.

Sailings with Cinderella Båtarna from Strandvägen (via Vaxholm and Finnhamn) run three times each weekday and once on Saturday and Sunday (Skr95, 2¼ hours).

Gällnö

Gällnö is a strangely shaped island with a long coastline and a small population. It's a

Uppsala's cathedral took 175 years to build.

Floating wooden restaurant, Sigtuna

Try canoeing on a day trip from Stockholm!

An 11th-century rune stone, near Västerås

Silver birch woodland, near Stockholm

CHRISTOPHER WOOD

Stone parish church of Gamla Uppsala

GRAEME CORNWALLIS

GRAEME CORNWALLIS

Anundshög tumulus, just outside Västerås

13th-century Badelunda kyrka, north of Västerås

VERONICA GARBUTT

A street scene in Sweden's oldest town, Sigtuna, which was founded in AD 980

Aurora Borealis

There are few sights as mesmerising as an undulating aurora. Although these appear in many forms – pillars, streaks, wisps and haloes of vibrating light – they're most memorable when they take the form of pale curtains, apparently wafting on a gentle breeze. Most often, the aurora appears as faint green, light yellow or rose, but in periods of extreme activity it can change to bright yellow or crimson.

The visible aurora borealis, or northern lights, are caused by streams of charged particles from the sun (called the solar wind), which are diverted by the Earth's magnetic field towards the polar regions. Because the field curves downward in a halo surrounding the magnetic poles, the charged particles are drawn earthward here. Their interaction with atoms in the upper atmosphere (about 160km above the surface) releases the energy creating the visible aurora. (In the southern hemisphere, the corresponding phenomenon is called the aurora australis.) During periods of high activity, a single auroral storm can produce a trillion watts of electricity with a current of one million amps.

Although science dismisses it as imagination, most people report that the aurora is often accompanied by a crackling or whirring sound. Don't feel unbalanced if you hear it – that's the sort of sound you'd expect to hear from such a dramatic display, and if it's an illusion, it's a very convincing one.

The best time of year to catch the northern lights in central Sweden is from October to March.

great place for swimming and fishing. Camping is allowed in the woods, but bring your own water.

STF Vandrarhem Gällnö (☎ *571 66117, fax 571 66288*) Dorm beds Skr140. Open May-Sept. The Gällnö hostel is in a former schoolhouse built in the early 20th century, but some rooms are in adjacent cabins; there's also a sauna.

Near the Gällnö hostel is a small *store* which serves coffee and cakes.

Waxholmsbolaget sails from Strömkajen to Gällnö (Skr70, 1½ to 2¼ hours, two to five daily).

Sandön
pop 100

Sandön is 2.5km long and has superb sandy beaches that are reminiscent of the Mediterranean on a sunny day. Sandhamn is the northern settlement but the best beaches are at Trovill, near the southern tip of the island. The wooden houses and narrow alleys of Sandhamn are worth exploring too. However, the island is a popular destination for party goers and wealthy sailors – many regattas start or finish here. Overall, the place is rather expensive and it's best visited as a day trip. Camping is prohibited.

Sandhamns Värdshus (☎ *571 53051, fax 571 53240,* **e** *lars.mac.gregor.e@sandhamns-vardshus.se*) Singles/doubles Skr520/840. Open year-round. Sandhamns Värdshus first opened in 1672 and still serves good food, with a three-course meal for Skr263 and main courses for Skr139 to Skr191.

Dykarbaren (☎ *571 53554*) Mains around Skr130, lunch special Skr70. Just 50m from the quay, Dykarbaren is a popular and trendy restaurant/bar.

Waxholmsbolaget sails from Strömkajen to Sandhamn via Vaxholm with the vintage steamer S/S *Norrskär* once on Saturday and Sunday (Skr95, 3½ hours). It's also possible to take bus No 433 or 434 from Slussen to Stavsnäs (Skr40, 50 minutes) then sail from there (Skr60, 35 minutes to one hour, six to nine times daily).

Cinderella Båtarna (☎ *587 14050*) runs boats from Strandvägen to Sandhamn twice daily between mid-June and mid-August (Skr95, 2¼ hours), departing at 9.30am and returning at 2.30pm (6pm on weekends), allowing nearly three hours in Sandhamn (nearly 6½ hours on weekends).

Fjärdlång

Fjärdlång is a 4km-long island without roads and with very few residents. It's an ideal and very scenic place to relax and enjoy the archipelago life. Swimming, fishing and boat hire are all available. Fjärdlång is also a great place for wild berry picking (July to early August) and mushroom picking (late August).

STF Vandrarhem Fjärdlång (☎ *501 56092, fax 501 56634)* Dorm beds Skr110. Open 5 June-30 Sept. Perched on the rocks, the wonderful Fjärdlång hostel consists of a house and several chalets. There's no shop or meals service, so you must bring your own food.

The Waxholmsbolaget ferry sails from Dalarö to Fjärdlång three or four times daily (Skr60, one hour). For details of transport from Stockholm to Dalarö, see the Dalarö section earlier in this chapter. Direct boats from Stockholm to Utö stop at Fjärdlång once or twice daily (Skr90, three hours).

Utö

Utö is a fairly large, delightful island in the southern section of the archipelago – it's 13km long and up to 4km wide. There's a reasonable road and track network, so it's popular with cyclists.

You can purchase a reasonable sketch map of the island from the tourist office (☎ 501 57410), which is in a small cabin by the guest harbour at Gruvbryggan, also known as Gruvbyn, (the northernmost village). It's open 10am to 4pm on weekdays, April to September. At other times, ask at Utö Värdshus, which is just up the hill. There's also a post office in the village centre.

Things to See & Do Most of the sights are at the northern end of the island, near Gruvbryggan. The most unusual thing to see is **Sweden's oldest iron mine**, which opened in 1150 but closed in 1879. The three pits are now flooded – the deepest is Nyköpingsgruvan (215m). The **mining museum** (opposite the Värdshus) keeps variable hours, so check locally. The well-preserved 18th-century **miners' houses** on Lurgatan are worth a look. The **windmill** is open 11am to 3pm, daily. The best **sandy beach** is on the north coast, about 10

minutes' walk from the Värdshus, in the direction of Kroka. To see the **glaciated rock slabs** on the eastern coast, walk for about 20 minutes through the pine forest towards Rävstavik.

Places to Stay & Eat *STF Vandrarhem Utö* (☎ *504 20315, fax 504 20301, Gruvbryggan)* Dorm beds Skr190. Open year-round. The Utö hostel, associated with the nearby Värdshus, is in a former summer house. Reception and meals are at the Värdshus.

Utö Värdshus (☎ *504 20300, fax 504 20301,* e *receptionen@uto-vardshus.se)* B&B from Skr695-1790 per room. This overpriced establishment is the only hotel on the island and it overcharges accordingly. However, facilities aren't at all bad and the restaurant serves fine (albeit overpriced) meals.

You may prefer to try the more reasonable cafe *Dannekrogen* (☎ *501 57079).* It's located near the Gruvbryggan harbour, next to the *bakery* and opposite the *ICA supermarket.* The nearest pizzeria is *Pizza Stugan* (☎ *57350),* in Edesnäs (3km west); pizzas will cost you around Skr60 to Skr75.

Getting There & Around The easiest way to reach Utö is to take the pendeltåg from Stockholm Centralstationen to Västerhaninge, then bus No 846 to Årsta Havsbad (Skr40, one hour). From there, Waxholmsbolaget and Utö Rederi ferries connect eight to 10 times daily with Utö (Skr50, 40 minutes), but make sure you know whether your boat stops at Spränga or Gruvbryggan first. You can also sail directly from Strömkajen to Utö (via Saltsjöbaden), once or twice daily (Skr95, 3½ hours); Gruvbryggan is always the first stop. See the boxed text 'The Vintage Steamer S/S *Saltsjön*'.

If you take a ferry from Nynäshamn to Ålö, you'll have to hike most of the length of the island to reach Gruvbryggan (Skr55, one hour, two to four daily).

Ask at the guest harbour (☎ 501 57410) about bike hire.

The Vintage Steamer S/S *Saltsjön*

The wonderful old steamship S/S *Saltsjön*, launched in 1925, was specifically designed to navigate the narrow sounds between Saltsjön and Baggensfjärden, which lie between Stockholm and Utö in the southern archipelago. The ship was built with a 55HP compound steam engine and could hold 454 passengers. After WWII, S/S *Saltsjön* was moved to the northern archipelago and was eventually taken out of regular service in 1968.

Just two years later, it was renamed S/S *Björkfjärden* and started taking passengers to Birka on Lake Mälaren, but a boiler fault in 1975 put it out of business.

After being renovated by a group of enthusiasts, the boat started sailing again under its original name. The S/S *Saltsjön* can now take up to 300 passengers and has a top speed of 11 knots. There's a restaurant on board.

S/S *Saltsjön* now sails from Stockholm's Strömkajen to Gruvbryggan (Utö) via the original route on weekends from mid-June to mid-August. Departure from the city is at 9.30am and the return trip is at 8.15pm, allowing three hours on the island. The round trip costs Skr190 and *Båtluffarkortet* is valid.

Öja

pop 25

In the far south of the archipelago, Öja is 4km long but only 500m wide. Until the 1990s, the island was in a military zone and was strictly off-limits for tourists. The village at the southern tip, **Landsort**, has been a pilot station since 1535. The **labyrinth** near the village has superstitious origins and was believed to bring fishermen good luck.

Landsorts fyr (open Tues & Thur) Built in 1672, this is the oldest preserved lighthouse in Sweden. The light is still operational and can be seen 18 nautical miles away.

Lotsutkiken (☎ 520 34111, fax 520 34121) Singles/doubles Skr325/600. Open year-round. The former pilot's house now offers B&B and there's a cafe/restaurant nearby.

The ferry to Öja departs from Torö, Ankarudden (see the Nynäshamn section; 1½ hours from Stockholm), and sails to Landsort two to five times daily (Skr50, 30 minutes).

Sävö

About a one-hour drive and a short ferry trip south of Stockholm, tiny Sävö is only 1.3km long and it's a great place to escape from the summer crowds. There's a nature reserve on the island.

STF Vandrarhem Sävö (☎/fax 0156-40346) Dorm beds Skr120. Open year-round. In another former pilot's station, this old wooden building has great sea views. Breakfast and boat hire are both available. Advance bookings are compulsory from September to May.

Access is by private car only – there's no public transport. Drive south on the E4 motorway and turn off at Vagnhärad. Follow road No 219 south, then turn off for Tofsö, Källvik and Sävö. By prior arrangement, the STF hostel manager will come to the mainland by boat and pick up overnight guests (Skr50 return, five minutes).

EKERÖ

☎ 08 • pop 21,367

Just west of Stockholm and surprisingly rural, Ekerö district consists of several large islands on Mälaren, three Unesco World Heritage-listed sites and a dozen medieval churches.

Tourist information can be found on the Internet at W www.ekeroturism.se

Drottningholm

The royal residence and parks of Drottningholm on Lovön should be among the best tourist attractions in Stockholm, but the palace and gardens are disappointing considering all the hype. The Unesco listing is mainly due to the amazing Drottningholms Slottsteater and Kina Slott.

EXCURSIONS

If you're not short of time (and the weather permits it) you can cycle out to the palace. Otherwise, take the metro to T-Brommaplan and change to bus Nos 301 to 323 (eight minutes). If you're driving, there are few road signs for Drottningholm and it's difficult to find the car park! The car park is second on the left after you've crossed Drottningholmsbron.

The most pleasant way from Stockholm to the palace is with Strömma Kanalbolaget (☎ 587 14000, e strommakanalbolaget@ stromma.se); some trips are in the steamboat S/S *Drottningholm*. Departures from Stadshusbron are daily, once or twice an hour from 9.30am to 6pm in summer (reduced service from 28 April to 8 June and 20 August to 9 September); the trip costs Skr90 return.

Drottningholms Slott The Renaissance-inspired palace *(☎ 402 6280; Skr50/25, but chapel is free; open 10am-4.30pm daily May-Aug, noon-3.30pm daily Sept, otherwise noon-3.30pm Sat & Sun)* and the geometrical baroque gardens were both designed by the great architect Nicodemus Tessin the Elder. Construction began in 1662, about the same time as Versailles and the palace is now home for the Swedish royal family. You're advised to walk around yourself, since the tedious one-hour guided tour (at 11am, noon, 1pm and 3pm daily in summer; included in the admission fee) assumes an in-depth knowledge of Swedish royalty and 18th-century Swedish history.

The **Lower North Corps de Garde** was originally a guardroom but it's now replete with gilt leather wall hangings, which used to feature in many palace rooms during the 17th century. The **Karl X Gustav Gallery**, in baroque style, depicts the militaristic endeavours of this monarch, but the ceiling shows battle scenes from classical times. The highly ornamented **State Bedchamber of Hedvig Eleonora** is the most expensive baroque interior in Sweden and it's decorated with paintings featuring the childhood of Karl XI. The painted ceiling shows Karl X and his queen, Hedvig Eleonora. Although Lovisa Ulrika's collection of

over 2000 books has been moved to the Royal Library in Stockholm, the **library** is still a bright and impressive room, complete with most of its original 18th-century fittings. The over elaborate **staircase**, with statues at every turn, was the work of both Nicodemus Tessin the Elder and the Younger. The circular **Drottningholm Palace Chapel** wasn't completed until the late 1720s.

The palace has a gift shop and there's an adjacent restaurant.

Drottningholms Slottsteater &Teatermuseum The Slottsteater *(Court Theatre; ☎ 759 0406; Skr50/free)* was completed in 1766 on the instructions of Queen Lovisa Ulrika. This is an extraordinary place, since it remained untouched from the time of Gustav III's death (1792) until 1922. It's the oldest theatre in the world still in its original state; performances are held here in summer still using the 18th-century machinery, such as ropes, pulleys and wagons. Scenes can be changed in less than seven seconds.

Illusion was the order of the day in here and there's fake marble, fake curtains and papier-mâché viewing boxes. Even the stage was designed to create illusions regarding size.

The interesting guided tour will also take you into some other rooms in the same building. You'll see hand-painted 18th-century wallpaper and an Italian-style room, the **salon de dejeuner**, with fake three-dimensional wall effects and a ceiling looking like the sky.

There are regular performances in the theatre every summer (see Theatre in the Entertainment chapter).

Tours in English run every hour from 12.30pm to 3.30pm daily in May. Tours are every hour 11.30am to 4.30pm daily (except midsummer) between June and August. They're at 1.30pm, 2.30pm and 3.30pm daily in September. Tours are also available in Swedish and German.

Kina Slott At the far end of the gardens is Kina Slott *(☎ 402 6270; Skr50/25;*

11am-4.30pm daily May-Aug & noon-3.30pm daily Sept), a lavishly decorated Chinese pavilion that was built by King Adolf Fredrik as a birthday gift to Queen Lovisa Ulrika (1753). It was restored between 1989 and 1996 and is now mostly in its original condition. There are 15 rooms, including the excellent **Mirrored Drawing Room** and the **Blue Drawing Room**. The **Octagonal Hall** has a magnificent mid-18th-century Swedish tiled stove. Guided tours (included in the admission fee) run at 11am, noon, 2pm and 3pm daily from 11 June to 31 August (also at noon and 2pm on weekends 1 May to 10 June, and at 2pm daily in September). There's a coffee shop on the premises.

On the slope below Kina Slott, the **Guards' Tent** *(free; open noon-4pm daily early June to mid-Aug)* was erected in 1781 as quarters for the dragoons of Gustav III, but it's not really a tent at all. The building now has displays about the gardens and Drottningholm's Royal Guard.

Evert Lundquists Ateljé The artist Evert Lundquist had his studio *(Skr50/25, pay at Kina Slott; open 5.30pm-7pm Wed & 11am-2pm Sun in summer)* in this converted power station between Kina Slott and the lake, but it was converted into a museum when he gave up painting. The museum shows Lundquist's studio exactly as he left it. Guided tours run on Wednesday at 4pm.

Ekerö & Munsö

These long and narrow islands in Mälaren are joined together and have a main road running most of their length; the ferry to Adelsö (see the following section) departs from the northern end of Munsö.

The two **churches** of Ekerö (also known as Ekerön) and Munsö date from the 12th century. Munsö kyrka (church) is an interesting structure with a round tower and a narrow steeple.

Bus Nos 311 and 312 run from the T-Brommaplan metro station in Stockholm roughly hourly (45 minutes to Munsö kyrka).

Adelsö

The medieval church **Adelsö kyrka**, which dates from the late 12th century, has a 14th-century **sacristy** but the distinctive square tower is somewhat younger. The interior, restored in 1832, contains a late 12th-century **font**, a 14th-century crucifix and a votive ship. The **pulpit** is also of significant interest. Just across the road, **Hovgården** features burial mounds (associated with nearby Birka and part of the Unesco World Heritage Site) and a spectacular **rune stone** with complex intertwined designs.

STF Vandrarhem Adelsögården (☎ 560 51450, fax 51400, ✉ adelsogarden@ alfa.telenordia.se) Dorm beds Skr120. Open 15 June-31 Aug. Located just south of the ferry pier, this hostel has a guest kitchen and a licensed restaurant. You can hire a bicycle or a canoe here. A walking trail from the hostel leads via some of the historic sites to the church, where there's a grocery store.

SL bus No 312 runs nine times daily (five times on Saturday and Sunday) to the Adelsö church from T-Brommaplan metro station via the medieval Ekerö and Munsö churches (one hour). Free car ferries run fairly frequently between Adelsö (also known as Adelsön) and Munsö.

Birka

The Viking trading centre of Birka, on Björkö in Mälaren, is now a Unesco World Heritage Site. It was founded around AD 760 with the intention of expanding and controlling trade in the region. The village attracted merchants and craft workers, and the population grew to about 700. A large defensive fort with thick drystone ramparts was constructed next to the village. In 830, the Benedictine monk Ansgar was sent to Birka by the Holy Roman Emperor to convert the heathen Vikings to Christianity and he lived in Birka for 18 months. Birka was abandoned in the late 10th century when Sigtuna took over the role of commercial centre.

The village site is surrounded by a vast graveyard. It's the largest Viking Age cemetery in Scandinavia, with around 3000

Vikings

The Viking Age, normally taken to have lasted from AD 800 to 1100, was the period when Scandinavians from Sweden, Norway and Denmark made their mark on the rest of Europe. Vikings travelled greater distances than the earlier Roman explorers and they established trading posts and an impressive communications network. Vikings settled in North America and Greenland, traded with eastern and southern Asia, fought for the Byzantine Empire and sacked and looted towns in southern Spain, among many other places.

The Vikings were not all warlike, but they were initially all pagans; all Scandinavian Vikings spoke the same language and worshipped the same gods. Burial of the dead usually included some possessions that would be required in the afterlife. In Sweden, it was popular to cremate the dead, then bury the remains in a clay pot under a mound. There are also a few impressive stone-ship settings, consisting of upright stones arranged in the plan of a ship, usually with larger prow and stern stones. Viking graves have yielded a large amount of information about their culture.

Rune stones were often erected as memorials, or markers for highways, graveyards or other important sites. Runic inscriptions were also carved on things such as metal and bone. Sweden has around 3000 such inscriptions, containing a wealth of information about the Viking world.

Applied art was important for decorative purposes, but some of the most spectacular art appears along with runic inscriptions and usually features dragons, horses or scenes from ancient sagas that bear little or no relevance to the attached runes.

graves. Most people were cremated, then mounds of earth were piled over the remains, but some Christian coffins and chambered tombs have been found. The fort and harbour have also been excavated. A cross to the memory of St Ansgar can be seen on top of a nearby hill.

The excellent **Birka Museum** (☎ 560 51445; Skr60/25, normally included in ferry tickets; open 10am-6.30pm daily 30 June-19 Aug, slightly shorter hours 28 Apr-23 Sept) includes finds from the excavations, which are still proceeding. There are also copies of the most magnificent objects and an interesting model showing the village as it was in Viking times. The museum has a restaurant.

On weekends from 28 April to 17 June and 20 August to 23 September, and daily between 18 June and 19 August, Mälarö skärgårdstrafik (☎ 711 1457) sails three times daily between Rastaholm (Ekerö) and Birka for Skr130/70 adult/child return (30 minutes). Tickets include guiding and admission to the Birka Museum. Bus Nos 311 and 312 from T-Brommaplan stop on the main road about 1.5km from Rastaholm (30 minutes).

Summer cruises to Birka depart from many places around Mälaren, including Västerås, Strängnäs, Mariefred, Södertälje and Stockholm. Between 28 April and 23 September, the return trip on Strömma Kanalbolaget's M/S *Victoria* from Stadshusbron, Stockholm, is a full day's outing (Skr220 including museum entry and a guided tour, six to 7¼ hours).

GRIPSHOLMS SLOTT
☎ 0159

Originally built in the 1370s, Gripsholms Slott (castle) passed into crown hands by the early 15th century. In 1526, Gustav Vasa took over and ordered the demolition of the adjacent monastery. A new castle with walls up to 5m thick was built at Gripsholm using materials from the monastery, but extensions, conversions and repairs continued for years. The oldest 'untouched' room is Karl IX's bedchamber, dating from the 1570s. The castle was abandoned in 1715, but it was renovated and extended during the reign of Gustav III (especially between 1773 and 1785). The moat was filled in and, in 1730 and 1827, two 11th-century **rune stones** were found. These stones stand by the access road and are well worth a look; one has a Christian cross, while the other describes an expedition against the Saracens. The castle was restored again in the 1890s, the moat was cleared and the drawbridge rebuilt.

Currently, Gripsholm *(☎ 10194; Skr50/ 25; open 10am-4pm daily May-Aug, 10am-3pm daily Tues-Sun Sept & noon-3pm Sat & Sun Oct-Apr)* is the epitome of castles with its round towers, spires and drawbridge. It contains some of the state portrait collection, which dates from the 16th century, and you can enjoy exploring the finely decorated rooms.

You can also visit the nearby *Grafikens Hus (☎ 23160; Skr40/free; open 11am-5pm daily May-Aug, Sat & Sun Sept-Apr)*, which is a centre for contemporary graphic art and classical prints.

Places to Stay & Eat
All places to stay and eat are in the small town of Mariefred, next to the castle.

STF Vandrarhem Mariefred (☎ 36100, fax 12350) Dorm beds Skr180. Open 11 Jun-12 Aug. This hostel, run by the Swedish Red Cross, is only 500m west of the castle. Some rooms have private bathrooms.

Gripsholms Värdshus & Hotel (☎ 347 50, fax 34777, ℮ info@gripsholms.vardshus .se, Kyrkogatan 1) Singles/doubles from Skr1300/1600. Gripsholms Värdshus & Hotel opened in 1609 and it's Sweden's oldest inn. There are great views of the castle and the excellent restaurant charges Skr235 to Skr245 for main courses.

Gripsholms Grill i Mariefred (☎ 21151, Gripsholmsvägen 1) Here you'll get fast food, including pizzas.

Getting There & Away
Mariefred isn't on the main railway line – the nearest station is at Läggesta, 3km west, with hourly trains from Stockholm (40 minutes). A museum railway (☎ 21000) from Läggesta to Mariefred runs on weekends from May to September (daily from 25 June to 12 August) once or twice an hour during the day (3rd/2nd class Skr40/56, children and railpass holders Skr20/28). Bus Nos

304 and 307 run hourly from Läggesta-Mariefred (five minutes).

The steamship S/S *Mariefred* (☎ 669 8850, Ⓦ www.gmaa.se) departs from Stadshusbron (Stockholm) for Gripsholm, daily except Monday from 13 June to 27 August, and weekends only from 20 May to 12 June and 2 to 12 September (single/return Skr120/ 180, 3½ hours one way). There's a cafe and restaurant on board. A return ticket from Stockholm including admission to the castle and Grafikens Hus, an SJ train, the museum railway and S/S *Mariefred* one-way costs Skr320.

SIGTUNA
☎ 08 • pop 34,766
Sigtuna, founded around AD 980, is the most pleasant and important historical town around Stockholm. It's also the oldest surviving town in Sweden and Stora gatan is probably Sweden's oldest main street. Around 1000, Olof Skötkonung ordered the minting of Sweden's first coins in the town. There are about 150 runic inscriptions in the area, most dating from the early 11th century and located beside ancient roads. Sigtuna has many quaint streets and wooden buildings still following the medieval town plan but, apart from the church, the original buildings didn't survive the devastating late-medieval town fires.

The tourist office (☎ 592 50020, fax 592 51244, ℮ turism@sigtuna.se) is in the 18th-century wooden house, Drakegården, at Stora gatan 33. It's open 10am to 6pm Monday to Saturday and 11am to 5pm Sunday from June to August, with shorter hours during the rest of the year. Nearby, and also on Stora gatan, there are two banks (with ATMs), a post office and a Pressbyrån newsagent. The hospital (Sigtuna läkarhus) can be reached at ☎ 592 51024.

Things to See
During medieval times, there were seven stone-built churches in Sigtuna, but most have now disappeared. Off Prästgatan, there's the ruin of the church of **St Per**, originally built in the 12th century, but with a

virtually intact tower. The ruin of **St Lars** is nearby. The **St Olof church** was built in the early 12th century, but became ruinous by the 17th century.

The adjacent **Mariakyrkan** *(Olofsgatan; free; open 9am-4pm daily)* is the oldest brick building in the area – it was a Dominican monastery church from around 1250, but became the parish church in 1529 after the monastery was demolished by Gustav Vasa. Inside, look for the excellent 14th- and 15th-century **murals and ceiling paintings** and the magnificent 5m-wide 15th-century German **reredos**. Free summer concerts are held once weekly.

Sigtuna Museum *(☎ 597 83870, Stora gatan 55; Skr20/free; open noon-4pm daily, except Mon, Sept-May)* looks after several attractions in the town, all of them on Stora gatan and near the tourist office. **Lundströmska gården** *(Skr10/5; open noon-4pm Sat & Sun May & Sept, daily June-Aug)* is an early 20th-century middle-class home and adjacent general store, complete with period furnishings and goods. **Sigtuna rådhus** *(free; open the same hours as Lundströmska gården)*, the smallest town hall in Scandinavia, dates from 1744 and was designed by the mayor himself. It's on the town square (opposite the tourist office). There's also an **exhibition hall** next to Systembolaget. The main museum building, at Stora gatan 55, has displays of artefacts (mostly from the 1988–90 excavations), including gold jewellery, runes, coins and loot brought home from abroad. The oddest find is the half-skeleton that turned out to be a mid-11th-century bishop of Sigtuna with a walrus ivory crozier! You can buy unique gold and silver jewellery in the museum shop.

Just 2km north of Sigtuna, the **Viby peasants township**, by the manor house Venngarns Slott, is a well-preserved group of 19th-century houses showing how agricultural workers lived before the era of land reforms. They're still in use as private homes and the area is not a museum.

The magnificent private palace **Steninge Slott** *(☎ 592 59500; Skr30/10; open 11am-4pm Sun-Fri & 11am-2pm Sat from 10 June-*

20 Aug, 11am-2pm Sat & 11am-3pm Sun from 2 Jan-9 Jun & 21 Aug-17 Nov), 7km east of Sigtuna, dates from 1705 and was designed by Nicodemus Tessin the Younger. You'll see luxuriously ornate interiors, but there's also a glassworks, ceramic works, candle factory, an **art gallery** (Skr40/10 extra) and a restaurant.

About 9km south-east of Sigtuna, **Rosersbergs Slott** *(☎ 590 35039; Skr50/25; guided tours every hour 11am-3pm daily May-August & Sat & Sun Sept)* is a large palace by Mälaren. It was constructed in the 1630s and used as a royal residence from 1762 to 1860; the interior has excellent furnishings from the Empire period (1790 to 1820) and **Queen Hedvig Elisabeth Charlotta's conversation room** is quite extraordinary.

Around 11km due north-west of Sigtuna (26km by road), there's the exceptionally fine whitewashed baroque palace **Skokloster Slott** *(☎ 018-386077, W www .skokloster.se; Skr65/20; guided tours 11am-4pm daily May-Aug, 1pm Mon-Fri & hourly noon-3pm Sat & Sun in Apr, Sept & Oct; tours in English on request)*, which was built between 1654 and 1671. The palace has impressive stucco ceilings and collections of furniture, textiles, art and arms. There's a small cafe on site. The adjacent **motor museum** *(☎ 386106; Skr40/10 adult/child age 7-14; open 11am-5pm daily May-Sept)* has a good collection of vintage cars and motorcycles. There's also a fire engine for kids to play in. The **Skokloster pageant** *(☎ 386725)* lasts five days in mid-July and includes around 350 performances (medieval tournaments, exhibitions, concerts, 18th-century activities etc).

Places to Stay

STF Vandrarhem Ansgarsliden (☎ 592 58200, fax 592 58384, e ansgarsliden@ svenskakyrkan.se, Manfred Björkquists allé 12) Dorm beds Skr110-125, hotel B&B from Skr285 per person. Open 25 June-5 Aug. The STF hostel is run by the Swedish church and lies about 1.6km west of the town centre.

Sigtunastiftelsens Gästhem (☎ 592 58900, fax 592 58999, e bokningen@

sigtunastiftelsen.se, Manfred Björkquists allé 2-4) Singles/doubles Skr800/930 (discounted Skr500/600). This hotel, run by a Christian Foundation, offers three-course dinners in the restaurant for only Skr210.

***Stora Brännbo** (☎ 592 57500, fax 592 57599, e contact@stora.brannbo.se, Stora Brännbovägen 2-6)* Singles/doubles Skr900/1000 (discounted Skr450/600). This hotel and conference centre is just north of the town centre.

There are also several hotels at Arlanda airport, only 17km east of Sigtuna.

Places to Eat

***Båthuset Krog & Bar** (☎ 592 56780, Strandpromenaden)* Mains Skr136-228, 2-course Sun dinner Skr245. Open 5pm-11pm Tues-Sun. The recommended place in town is a floating wooden house out on the lake, which serves fish, lamb and beef dishes.

***Farbror Blå Café & Kök** (☎ 592 56050, Storatorget 14)* Weekday lunch Skr65. Adjacent to the town hall, this cafe does baked potatoes with fillings for Skr65.

***Sigtuna Grillen**,* just across the street from the bus station, serves hot dogs and ice cream. Reasonable pizzas cost Skr37 to Skr55.

The ***Konsum*** and ***ICA*** supermarkets are on Stora gatan.

Getting There & Away

Getting to Sigtuna is easy and should take around an hour from Stockholm. Take an SJ or SL train to Märsta and change to bus No 570, 575 or 584 (frequent) just outside the Märsta train station (Skr40 from Stockholm, Skr16 from Märsta). Bus No 883 runs every hour or two from Uppsala to Sigtuna. The Märsta to Sigtuna bus passes 3km north of Steninge Slott. To get to Rosersbergs Slott, take the SL pendeltåg train to Rosersberg, then walk the final 2km to the palace (signposted). For Skokloster, take an hourly SJ train to Bålsta, then infrequent bus No 894.

Getting Around

Café Våfflan (☎ 592 50800), by the small boat harbour, offers bike and boat hire. Call Taxi 020 on ☎ 020 939393.

UPPSALA
☎ 018 • pop 135,608

Uppsala is 71km north of Stockholm. It's the fourth largest city in Sweden, and one of its oldest. Gamla (Old) Uppsala flourished as early as the 6th century; the cathedral was consecrated in 1435 after 175 years of building and the castle was first built in the 1540s, although today's edifice belongs to the 18th century. The city depends on the sprawling university, founded in 1477 and the oldest in Scandinavia.

Information

Uppsala Tourism (☎ 274800, fax 132895, e tb@uppsalatourism.se), at Fyris torg 8, is the main tourist office; it's open from 10am to 6pm on weekdays (and to 3pm Saturday) year-round, as well as from noon to 4pm on Sunday in summer. There's also a branch tourist office at Gamla Uppsala, open daily in July. Students in search of information can go to the student union on the corner of Åsgränd and Övre Slottsgatan.

Forex is on Fyris torg next to the main tourist office. You'll find banks with ATMs on Stora torget. The main post office is upstairs in the shopping arcade on the corner of Bredgränd and Dragabrunnsgatan

One of the best bookshops in Sweden, Akademibokhandeln Lundequistska, is upstairs in the Forum Gallerian Complex on the corner of Bredgränd and Dragarbrunnsgatan. For newspapers and magazines, go to Presscity, Drottninggatan 2. The public library, Svartbäcksgatan 17, is open from 11am Monday to Saturday in summer and offers free Internet access, but expect long waits or make an advance reservation for a one-hour slot. The city features on two Web sites: W www.res.till.uppland.nu and W www.uppsala.se. Expert, on Stora torget, has camera supplies.

The police station is at Salagatan 18. There's a pharmacy at Svartbäcksgatan 8 and for emergency treatment go to the university hospital (☎ 611 0000); enter from Sjukhusvägen. The pharmacy there (☎ 611 3455), at entrance No 70, is open until 9pm.

EXCURSIONS

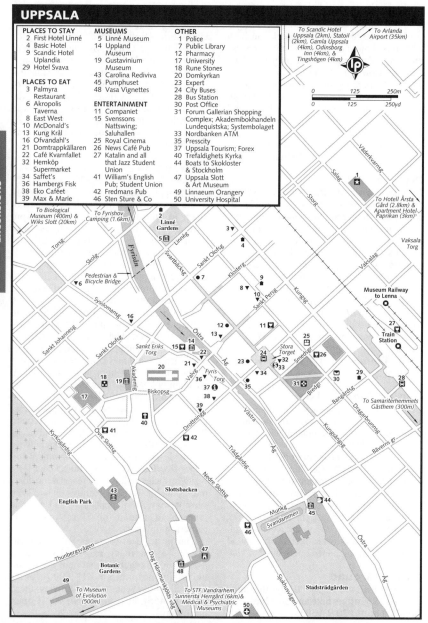

UPPSALA

PLACES TO STAY
2 First Hotel Linné
4 Basic Hotel
9 Scandic Hotel Uplandia
29 Hotel Svava

PLACES TO EAT
3 Palmyra Restaurant
6 Akropolis Taverna
8 East West
10 McDonald's
13 Kung Krål
16 Ofvandahl's
21 Domtrappkällaren
22 Café Kvarnfallet
32 Hemköp Supermarket
34 Saffet's
36 Hambergs Fisk
38 Eko Caféet
39 Max & Marie

MUSEUMS
5 Linné Museum
14 Uppland Museum
19 Gustavinium Museum
43 Carolina Rediviva
45 Pumphuset
48 Vasa Vignettes

ENTERTAINMENT
11 Companiet
15 Svenssons Nattswing; Saluhallen
25 Royal Cinema
26 News Café Pub
27 Katalin and all that Jazz Student Union
41 William's English Pub; Student Union
42 Fredmans Pub
46 Sten Sture & Co

OTHER
1 Police
7 Public Library
12 Pharmacy
17 University
18 Rune Stones
20 Domkyrkan
23 Expert
24 City Buses
28 Bus Station
30 Post Office
31 Forum Gallerian Shopping Complex; Akademibokhandeln Lundequistska; Systembolaget
33 Nordbanken ATM
35 Presscity
37 Uppsala Tourism; Forex
40 Trefaldighets Kyrka
44 Boats to Skokloster & Stockholm
47 Uppsala Slott & Art Museum
49 Linnaeum Orangery
50 University Hospital

To Scandic Hotel Uppsala (2km), Statoil (2km), Gamla Uppsala (4km), Odinsborg Inn (4km), & Tingshögen (4km)

To Arlanda Airport (35km)

0   125   250m
0   125   250yd

Gamla Uppsala

Uppsala began at the three great **grave mounds** at Gamla Uppsala, 4km north of the modern city centre. The mounds, said to be the graves of the legendary pre-Viking kings Aun, Egils and Adils, are part of a larger cemetery which includes about 300 small mounds and **boat graves**, dating from around 500 to 1100. A 10th-century boat grave in the Vicarage garden was excavated in the 1970s and a small oriental statue was found. Important chieftains were often buried in their boats, along with all necessary provisions for their final journey.

The new **Gamla Uppsala Historical Centre** (☎ 239300, Disavägen; Skr50/free; open 10am-5pm daily mid-Apr to mid-Aug & 10am-4pm mid-Aug to end Sept) exhibits artefacts excavated from Gamla Uppsala and nearby archaeological sites, including a king's **gilt helmet** and a **necklace** with an image of a Valkyrie.

Gamla Uppsala was supposedly the site of a great heathen temple where human and animal sacrifices took place, but there's no evidence to support this. However, Thor, Odin and the other Viking gods were certainly displaced when Christianity arrived in 1090. From 1164, the archbishop of Uppsala had his seat in a cathedral on the site of the present **church** (open 9am-6pm daily Apr-Sept), which, by the 15th century, was enlarged and painted with frescoes.

Next to the flat-topped mound **Tingshögen** is the **Odinsborg Inn** (☎ 323525), known for its horns of mead, although daintier refreshments are offered in summer. The farm museum village **Disagården** (☎ 169100, Disavägen; open 10am-7pm daily 20 May-3 Sept), a few minutes' walk from the church, is also worth a visit.

To get to Gamla Uppsala, take the direct bus No 2 departing from Stora torget (Skr21, four per hour).

Uppsala Slott

Construction of this castle (☎ 272482; Skr60/10 including entrance to Art Museum; guided tours in English 1pm & 3pm daily June-Aug) was ordered by Gustav Vasa in the 1550s and it features the state hall where kings were enthroned (and a queen abdicated). Nils Sture and his sons Erik and Svante were murdered in the castle in 1567 – Nils was stabbed by the crazed King Erik XIV, but others finished him off. The clothes Nils was wearing when he was killed are on display in the cathedral – they're the only 16th-century Swedish fashion clothes still in existence. The castle burnt down in 1702, but was rebuilt and took on its present form in 1757.

The **Vasa Vignettes** (☎ 272482; Skr40/10; open noon-4pm Mon-Fri & 11am-5pm Sat & Sun May-Aug) 'waxworks' museum in the death-stained dungeons shows the past intrigues of the castle. Uppsala Slott also houses an **Art Museum** (☎ 272482; Skr20/free; open noon-4pm Tues-Fri, 11am-5pm Sat & Sun), which features 16th- to 19th-century and contemporary art, including paintings of Martin Luther and his wife by Cranach.

Wiks Slott

This remarkable brick manor (☎ 561000; Skr30/20; tours 1pm & 3pm daily 1 June-20 Aug; tours in English on request), with an unusual clock tower and a magnificent park, is one of Sweden's best-preserved medieval houses and dates from the 15th century. The interior was reconstructed in the 1650s and again in the 1860s. B&B is available (see Places to Stay). The house is about 20km south-west of the city centre, next to an arm of Lake Mälaren; take bus No 847 (four to eight daily).

Other Attractions

The Gothic **Domkyrkan** (cathedral; ☎ 187 201; free; open 8am-6pm daily) dominates the city just as some of those buried here dominated their country: Gustav Vasa, Johan III, and Carl von Linné who established the system of scientific names for species. The **treasury** (Skr20/10; open 10am-5pm Mon-Sat & 12.30pm-5pm Sun May-Aug, Sat & Sun only in Sept, 12.30pm-3pm Sun rest of year) in the north tower has Gustav Vasa's sword and a great display of medieval clothing, including archbishops' vestments from 1200 onwards. The nearby **Trefaldighets Kyrka** isn't outwardly

EXCURSIONS

Norse Mythology

Some of the greatest gods of the Nordic world, Tyr, Odin, Thor and Frigg, live on in the English language as the days of the week – Tuesday, Wednesday, Thursday and Friday, respectively. Norse mythology is very complex, so we're restricted to a limited description here. A vast number of gods, wolves, serpents and other creatures are involved in the heroic Nordic tales of chaos and death.

The one-handed Tyr was the god of justice, including war-treaties, contracts and oaths. The principal myth regarding Tyr involves the giant wolf, Fenrir. The gods decided Fenrir had to be chained up, but nothing could hold him. Dwarfs made an unbreakable chain and the gods challenged Fenrir to break it. He was suspicious, but agreed on condition that one of the gods place his hand in his mouth. Tyr was the only one to agree. The gods succeeded in fettering Fenrir, but he retaliated by biting off Tyr's right hand.

The most eminent of the Nordic gods was the one-eyed Odin (the father of most of the other gods), whose eight-legged flying horse, Sleipnir, had runes etched on its teeth. As a god of war, Odin sent his 12 Valkyries (battle maidens) to select 'heroic dead' killed in battle to join him in everlasting feasting at the palace of Valhalla. Odin carried a spear called Gungnir, which never missed when thrown, and his bow could fire 10 arrows at once. Odin was also the god of poets, a magician and master of runes. Odin's great wisdom had been granted in exchange for his missing eye, but he also gained wisdom from his two ravens Hugin and Munin, who flew every day in search of knowledge.

Thor is usually depicted as an immensely strong god who protected humans from the malevolent giants with his magic hammer Mjolnir, which would return to the thrower like a boomerang. Thor represented thunder and the hammer was the thunderbolt. Thor's greatest enemy was the evil snake Jörmungand and they were destined to kill each other at Ragnarök, the end of the world, when the wolf Fenrir would devour Odin. At Ragnarök, the other gods and humans would also die in cataclysmic battle, the sky would collapse in raging fire and the earth would subside into the sea.

Frigg was Odin's wife and she's also known as a fertility goddess and the goddess of marriage.

---

as impressive, but has beautiful painted ceilings.

The **Gustavianum Museum** (☎ 471 7571, Akademigatan 3; Skr40/free under 12; open 11am-4pm daily 17 May-19 Sept, otherwise 11am-4pm Wed-Sun) has exhibits about the university and the history of science, an excellent antiquities collection and an old 'anatomical theatre'. The **Uppland Museum** (☎ 169100, St Eriks gränd 6; Skr30/free; open noon-5pm Tues-Sun), in a university water mill from the 1860s, houses county collections from the Middle Ages.

At the old university library **Carolina Rediviva** (☎ 471 3900, Dag Hammarskjölds väg 1; Skr10/free 15 May-17 Sept; open variable hours, daily 21 May-17 Sept) you'll see a display hall with maps and historical and scientific literature. The pride of the museum is Sweden's most precious book, the surviving half of the **Codex Argentus**, a holy bible written with silver ink on purple vellum in the now extinct Gothic language in Ravenna in 520.

The excellent **Botanical Gardens** (☎ *471 2838, Villavägen 6-8; free; open 7am-8.30pm daily May-Sept, 7am-7pm daily Oct-Apr*) which include the **Linnaeum Orangery** and a **tropical greenhouse** (*Skr20/ free for both; variable hours*), are below the castle hill. The gardens aren't to be confused with the **Linné Museum** (☎ *136540, Svartbäcksgatan 27; Skr30/free; open noon-4pm Tues-Sun 1 June-10 Sept*) and its **garden** (☎ *109 490, Svartbäcksgatan 27; Skr20; open 9am-9pm daily May-Aug & 9am-7pm daily Sept*). The museum keeps memorabilia of Linné's work in Uppsala. The garden (Sweden's oldest botanical garden), with more than 1000 herbs, was designed according to an 18th-century plan.

Take sandwiches and sit by the main **Uppsala University** building (which is imposing enough to demand a glance inside) and absorb the ambience of an historic university. On the lawn in front are nine typical Uppland **rune stones**. On 30 April, the students gather dressed in white to celebrate the Walpurgis Festival in procession and song. There's also a raft race on the river at 10am and a 'run' (starting at the University Library) at 3pm, on the same day.

The old waterworks **Pumphuset** (☎ *274 224, Munkgatan 2; Skr5/free under 12; open noon-4pm on selected dates*) has a museum covering all public utilities. The **Museum of Evolution** (☎ *471 2739, Norbyvägen 22; Skr20/10; open 1pm-4pm Tues-Thur & 11am-3pm Sun, Sept-May*) includes dinosaur fossils and a mineral display. It's also open on weekdays June to August by arrangement.

There's also the more obscure **Museum of Medical History** (☎ *611 2610, Eva Lagerwalls väg 8; Skr20; open 1pm-5pm Thur & last Sun of every month, closed July-Aug*) and the **Psychiatric Museum** (☎ *611 2948, Eva Lagerwalls väg 10; open 10am-2pm Thur & noon-3pm 1st Sun of every month, closed mid-June-Aug*). Both museums are south of the city centre and deal with the historical and development aspects of their respective topics.

Carl von Linné

Carl von Linné (1707–78), born Linnaeus and usually called the latter in English, is known for his classification of minerals, plants and animals, as described in his work *Systema Naturae*. Linnaeus journeyed throughout Sweden to make his observations – his most famous journeys were to Lappland (1732), Dalarna (1734) and Skåne (1749). His pupils and colleagues also gathered information worldwide, from Australia (with Cook's expedition) to Central Asia and South America. Linnaeus insisted on hard physical evidence before drawing any conclusions and his methods were thereafter absorbed by all the natural sciences. His theories of plant reproduction still hold today.

In 1739, Linnaeus was one of the founders of the Swedish Academy of Sciences, in Stockholm. Among other achievements, he took Celsius' temperature scale and turned it upside down, giving us 0°C for freezing point and 100°C for boiling point, rather than the other way around.

Activities

You can ride the steam train *Lennakatten* (☎ 130500) on a narrow-gauge museum railway into the Uppland countryside on Sunday, up to seven times daily, from early June to late August (one-way/return Skr65/ 100). Trips depart from the Uppsala Östra museum station, located behind the main station.

Old steamers depart from Östra Ågatan for the baroque castle Skokloster (one-way/ return from Skr75/115). You can ask at Strömma Kanalbolaget (☎ 58 14000, ℮ strommakanalbolaget@stromma.se) if there are connecting boats to Stockholm.

Places to Stay

There's more than enough to see in Uppsala to justify spending at least one night here.

Fyrishov Camping (☎ *274960, Idrottsgatan 2,* Ⓦ *www.fyrishov.se*) Tents from Skr85, cabins Skr445-680. Open year-round.

Located 2km north of the city and beside the river at Fyrisfjädern; take bus No 4, 24, 50 or 54.

STF Vandrarhem Sunnersta Herrgård *(☎ 324220, fax 324068, Sunnerstavägen 24)* Hostel beds Skr175, hotel singles/doubles B&B Skr540/640. Open 8 Jan-21 Dec. The hostel, with two- or three-bed rooms, is at an early 19th-century manor house some 6km south of the centre. Hostellers can buy the excellent breakfast for Skr60. Take bus No 20 or 50.

Private Room Agency *(☎ 109533, fax 128242)* Singles/doubles Skr250/350. This agency organises B&B accommodation around Uppsala.

Basic Hotel *(☎ 480 5000, fax 480 5050, Kungsgatan 27)* Singles/doubles from Skr690/790 (discounted from Skr600 per room). This central option has a range of rooms (all with private bathroom, some with self-catering facilities) and charges Skr60 extra for breakfast.

Hotell Årsta Gård *(☎/fax 253500, [w] www.hotellet.just.nu, Jordgubbsgatan 14)* Singles/doubles Skr475/595 (discounted Skr395/525), with shared bathroom. There's an art gallery at this pleasant hotel, which is a 15-minute bus ride (No 7 or 56) from Stora torget. There's free parking.

Apartment Hotel Paprikan *(☎ 262929, Paprikagatan 14)* Singles/doubles Skr300/400 with shared bathroom. Kitchen facilities are available.

Samariterhemmets Gästhem *(☎ 103400, fax 108375, Samaritergränd 2)* Singles/doubles Skr430/670 with shared bathroom, Skr510/770 with private bathroom (discounted Skr390/590 & Skr450/690 respectively). Run by a Christian community, this place is recommended.

Hotel Svava *(☎ 130030, fax 132230, [e] info.svava@swedenhotels.se, Bangårdsgatan 24)* Singles/doubles Skr1245/1450 (discounted Skr690/850). Hotel Svava is a modern hotel which offers high-standard facilities.

Scandic Hotel Uplandia *(☎ 102160, fax 696132, [e] upplandia@scandic-hotels.com, Dragarbrunnsgatan 32)* Singles/doubles Skr1069/1375 (discounted Skr690/790).

A recently refurbished modern hotel, with parquet floors throughout.

First Hotel Linné *(☎ 102000, fax 137597, Skolgatan 45)* Singles/doubles Skr1199/1449 (discounted Skr699/799). This excellent place is next to the gardens at the Linné Museum.

Scandic Hotel Uppsala *(☎ 495 2300, fax 495 2311, [e] uppsala@scandic-hotels.com, Gamla Uppsalagatan 50)* Singles/doubles Skr1069/1375 (discounted to Skr680 per room). Located 2.5km from the city centre on the road to Gamla Uppsala, with pleasant rooms, a bistro and restaurant.

Wiks Slott *(☎ 561000, fax 561006, [e] ingmarie.eriksson@service.lsu.lul.se)* Singles/doubles Skr275/450. Wiks Slott, an atmospheric manor house 20km south-west of the city, offers rooms from early June to mid-August.

Places to Eat

Domtrappkällaren *(☎ 130955, St Eriks gränd 15)* Weekday lunch Skr65 inclusive, 3-course business lunch Skr145-165. Open daily. Previously a prison, you can now dine in style either in the atmospheric basement or the more ordinary upstairs section.

Hambergs Fisk *(☎ 710050, Fyris torg 8)* Mains Skr135-220. Closed Mon. Hambergs Fisk is an excellent fish restaurant.

Akropolis Taverna *(☎ 105959, Sysslomansgatan 13)* Mains Skr85-125, pasta dishes Skr69-79. Open daily. This Greek restaurant offers takeaways and a kids' menu.

East West *(☎ 152890, Dragarbrunnsgatan 25)* Mains Skr58-128. You'll get burgers, tortillas and salads in this modern bistro/restaurant. Try the Toblerone fondue for dessert (Skr75).

Kung Kråi *(☎ 125090, Gamla torget)* Mains Skr69-175. Closed Sun Sept-Mar. Just the place for good filling Swedish and international food.

Ofvandahl's *(☎ 134204, Sysslomansgatan 3-5)* Cakes & desserts Skr14-22. Closed Sun. Ofvandahl's is the oldest and classiest cafe in town, with coffee and a baguette for Skr50.

Café Kvarnfallet *(☎ 150333, Fyris torg 4)* For more old-world romance go to this

13th-century cellar next to the river, where you can sit and sip in small vaulted rooms or at outdoor tables set up right beside the rapids.

Eko Caféet (☎ 121845, Drottninggatan 5) Weekday lunch Skr60. The best coffee in town and Italian-style organic food such as pasta and panini (Skr35-40) can be found here. There's also live music, from jazz to tango and Indian, at lunchtimes and evenings (free to Skr40).

Max & Marie (☎ 121216, Drottninggatan 7) Weekday lunch Skr60. This popular vegetarian restaurant serves great lunches with a large salad buffet. Takeaways and student discounts are available.

Palmyra Restaurant (☎ 100903, Kungsgatan 25) Weekday lunch Skr49. Palmyra Restaurant serves good, cheap felafels (from Skr15) and vegetarian pasta or chicken kebabs and rice costs Skr49.

There are several places to eat on the pedestrian mall and Stora torget. *Saffet's* on Stora torget specialises in Tex-Mex fast food but also serves kebabs, burgers and fish and chips (only Skr32). *McDonald's* is on St Persgatan.

There's a *Hemköp* supermarket on Stora torget. *Saluhallen*, the indoor produce market, is at St Eriks torg between the cathedral and the river, and a small open market is at Vaksala torg, behind the train station (both closed on Sunday). For alcohol, visit *Systembolaget (Dragarbrunnsgatan 50)*, on the first floor of the Svava shopping centre.

Entertainment
In the evenings, local university students and others converge on the popular *krog* (pub) restaurants.

Katalin and all that Jazz (☎ 140680, ⓦ www.katalin.com, Godsmagasinet) This excellent place, in a former warehouse, has regular live jazz and blues, with occasional pop and rock bands.

Sten Sture & Co (☎ 124030, Nedre Slottsgatan 3) This is a good upmarket pub, disco and club with live music.

Svenssons Nattswing (☎ 150150, Saluhallen, St Eriks torg) Admission free. Open

11pm-2am Fri & Sat. This nightclub imposes a minimum age of 30 years.

Companiet (☎ 105660, Påvel Snickares gränd) Swedish *dansband* music on the entrance level, but the downstairs disco appeals to those aged 25 to 35.

William's (☎ 140920, Åsgränd 5) Located in the university quarter, William's is an English-style pub.

Fredmans Pub (☎ 124212, Drottninggatan 12) Open 5pm-midnight Sun-Mon & 5pm-2am Wed-Sat. Fredmans is a pleasant pub/restaurant with occasional and varied live music.

News Café Pub (☎ 184560, Dragarbrunnsgatan 46) Open Sat & Sun. News Café Pub, at Folkets Hus, is really a restaurant with free discos on two floors.

Royal (☎ 135007, Dragarbrunnsgatan 44) This multiscreen cinema shows Hollywood films regularly.

Getting There & Away
The bus station is outside the train station. Bus No 802 departs once or twice each hour from 3.25am to 12.10am for the nearby Arlanda airport (Skr75/40 adult/child). Swebus Express runs to Stockholm (Skr40, one hour, once or twice an hour but fewer on weekends), Sala (Skr90, one hour, two or three daily) and other neighbouring cities.

There are frequent SJ trains from Stockholm (Skr85, 40 minutes), but X2000 trains require a supplement. Trains to Sala (Skr75, 35 minutes) run roughly once an hour. All SJ services between Stockholm and Gävle, Östersund and Mora, stop in Uppsala. SL coupons take you (and your bicycle) only as far as Märsta from Stockholm.

For car rental, contact Statoil (☎ 209100) at Gamla Uppsalagatan 48, next to the Scandic Hotel Uppsala.

Getting Around
Catch a city bus from near Stora torget; tickets cost a hefty Skr21 and give unlimited travel for 1½ hours.

Ask at the tourist office for information on bike hire. Upplands Lokaltrafik county buses take up to two bikes (Skr20 each) but local trains don't.

VÄSTERÅS
☎ 021 • pop 125,136

Both an old and a modern city, Västerås is now a centre of Asea Brown Boweri (ABB) industrial technology. The heavy industry, modern shopping malls and sprawling suburbs contrast with the old town centre and the wooden buildings along the Svartån River. You can relax on Lake Mälaren's shores or visit several historical sites nearby.

Västerås is the sixth largest city in Sweden and it has an international feel – over 7% of its inhabitants are immigrants.

Information
The tourist office (☎ 103830, fax 103850, ⓔ info@vastmanland.se), Stora Gatan 40, is open 9am to 7pm weekdays mid-June to mid-August, until 3pm Saturday and 10am to 2pm Sunday (shorter hours, and closed Sunday, for the rest of the year).

There's a Forex exchange office at Stora Gatan 18, Nordbanken ATMs (and Expert camera supplies) at Stora Gatan 23, and the main post office is at Sturegatan 18. The Akademibokhandeln bookshop is in the Gallerian Shopping Centre on Sturegatan, Pressbyrån is at Vasagatan 15, and the public library (☎ 164600), Biskopsgatan 2, has Internet access. The hospital, Centrallasarettet (☎ 173000) is just off the E18 motorway, towards Stockholm.

Things to See
Västmanlands länsmuseum *(☎ 156100, Slottsgatan; free; open noon-4pm Tues-Sun)*, in Västerås Slottet manor house, has a strong general historical collection including Iron Age gold jewellery, but it diverts into peculiarities such as dolls houses and Swedish porcelain. The neighbouring **Turbinhuset** (Turbine House), part of the same complex, was the inducement for ABB to move to Västerås from Arboga.

The nearby **Konstmuseum** *(Art Museum; ☎ 161300, Fiskartorget 2; free; open 10am-5pm Tues-Fri, 11am-4pm Sat & noon-4pm Sun)*, in the old city hall, has temporary exhibitions of Swedish painters and the permanent collections get an occasional airing. There's a cafe in the vaulted cellar.

The fine late 14th-century brick-built **Domkyrkan** *(cathedral; ☎ 161006, Biskopsgatan; free; open 8am-5pm Mon-Sat, until 7pm in summer, 9.30am-5pm Sun)*, has carved floor slabs, six altarpieces, the black marble sarcophagus of King Erik XIV and a **museum** *(Skr5)*.

Vallby Friluftsmuseum *(☎ 161670; open 7am-10pm daily June-Aug, otherwise 8am-sunset)*, off Vallbyleden near the E18 interchange 2km north-west of the city, is an extensive open-air collection assembled by the county museum. Among the 40-odd buildings, there's an interesting **farmyard** but the highlight is **Anunds Hus** *(Skr20; open 1pm-4pm daily mid-June-mid-Aug)*, a reconstructed 11th-century farm, which is 40m long. Take bus No 12 or 92 from Vasagatan.

The city is surrounded by ancient religious sites and the most interesting and extensive is the excellent **Anundshög**, the largest tumulus in Sweden, 6km north-east of the city. It has a full complement of prehistoric curiosities such as mounds, stone ship settings and a large 11th-century rune stone. The two main stone ship settings date from around the 1st century and the row of stones beside the modern road presumably mark the ancient royal ceremonial road Eriksgata. The area is part of the Badelunda Ridge, which includes the 13th-century **Badelunda kyrka** (1km north) and the odd 16m-wide **Tibble Labyrinth** (1km south). Ask the tourist office for the handy map *Badelunda Forntids Bygd*. Take bus No 12 or 92 to the Bjurhovda terminus, then walk 2km east.

Places to Stay
Johannisbergs Camping *(☎ 140279, Johannisbergsvägen)* Tents/cabins from Skr85/280. The closest camping ground is Johannisbergs Camping, 5km south of the city.

STF Vandrarhem Lövudden *(☎ 185230, fax 123036, Johannisbergsvägen)* Hostel beds Skr140, hotel singles/doubles B&B Skr450/650. About 4km south of the centre, this pleasant hostel and hotel is in former factory workers' lodgings. Hostellers can buy breakfast for Skr50 and there's also a daily special (available until 8.30pm) for Skr65. Take infrequent bus No 25.

Aabrin Lågprishotell (☎ 143980, fax 145701, Kopparbergsvägen 47) Singles/doubles Skr495/595 (discounted Skr345/445). This budget hotel is beside the E18 motorway. **Ta Inn Hotel** (☎ 139600, fax 139 690, Ängsgärdsgatan 19) Singles/doubles Skr695/850 (discounted Skr395/550). Also near the E18, this is a pleasant modern hotel.

Raka Vägen (☎ 300400, fax 300490, Hallsta Gårdsgata 1) Singles/doubles Skr749/849 (discounted Skr550/650). Raka Vägen is about 4km west of the city centre.

Stadshotellet (☎ 102800, fax 102810, ⒺⒺ stadshotellet.vaesteraas@elite.se, Stora Torget) Singles/doubles from Skr985/1295 (discounted Skr595/725). Stadshotellet is a flash, modern place with marble floors, mirrors and an indoor fountain.

Scandic Hotel Västerås (☎ 495 5800, fax 145709, Pilgatan 17) Singles/doubles Skr1090/1402 (discounted to Skr695 per room). This is another modern hotel with very nice rooms.

Radisson SAS Hotel Plaza (☎ 101010, fax 101091, ⒺⒺ mailbox@vasterasplaza.se, Karlsgatan 9A) Singles/doubles from Skr1210/1410 (discounted Skr625/790). Easily the most impressive hotel in town,

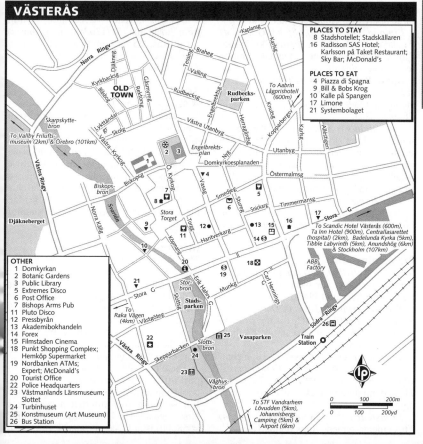

VÄSTERÅS

PLACES TO STAY
8 Stadshotellet; Stadskällaren
16 Radisson SAS Hotel;
   Karlsson på Taket Restaurant;
   Sky Bar; McDonald's

PLACES TO EAT
4 Piazza di Spagna
9 Bill & Bobs Krog
10 Kalle på Spangen
17 Limone
21 Systembolaget

OTHER
1 Domkyrkan
2 Botanic Gardens
3 Public Library
5 Extremes Disco
6 Post Office
7 Bishops Arms Pub
11 Pluto Disco
12 Pressbyrån
13 Akademibokhandeln
14 Forex
15 Filmstaden Cinema
18 Punkt Shopping Complex;
   Hemköp Supermarket
19 Nordbanken ATMs;
   Expert; McDonald's
20 Tourist Office
22 Police Headquarters
23 Västmanlands Länsmuseum;
   Slottet
24 Turbinhuset
25 Konstmuseum (Art Museum)
26 Bus Station

EXCURSIONS

the 'glass skyscraper' has superb modern accommodation.

Places to Eat

Stadskällaren (☎ 102800, Stora Torget) Mains Skr165-195. A pleasant brick-walled restaurant, but not really a cellar.

Karlsson på Taket (☎ 101010, Karls-gatan 9A) Mains Skr89-215. Enjoy a magnificent view and a fine meal from this restaurant on the 23rd floor of the Radisson SAS Hotel Plaza.

Piazza di Spagna (☎ 124210, Vasagatan 26) Mains Skr157-202, pizza/pasta from Skr66/74. You'll get a good, well-presented meal in this restaurant. Try the fried camembert with cloudberry jam (Skr76).

Limone (☎ 417560, Stora Gatan 4) Weekday lunch Skr55, mains Skr67-195. Closed Sun. The recommended Limone serves fine Italian food.

Bill & Bobs Krog (☎ 419921, Stora Torget 5) Mains Skr85-195. The 'classics' menu includes burgers, pork fillet and Chicken Thai.

McDonald's is at the base of the Radisson SAS Hotel skyscraper on Stora Gatan and there's another one on Vasagatan. *Kalle på Spangen*, beside the river, is a nice place which serves coffee, soup and sandwiches and you can buy the furniture too.

The *Hemköp* supermarket is in the Punkt Shopping Centre, off Stora Gatan. For alcohol, visit *Systembolaget (Stora Gatan 48)*.

Entertainment

Sky Bar (☎ 101010, Karlsgatan 9A) There's a great view from the bar at the top of the Radisson SAS Hotel Plaza.

Bishops Arms (☎ 102800, Östra Kyrko-gatan) Open until late. This is the place to go for a drink, but it also serves English-style pub food.

There are a couple of good discos, including *Extremes (☎ 122330, Kopparbergs-vägen 27B)* and *Pluto (☎ 189193, Torggatan 1)*, and minimum ages and charges vary nightly.

Filmstaden (☎ 128500, Gallerian 34) This cinema screens films regularly.

Getting There & Around

The airport (☎ 805600) is 6km east of the city centre; a taxi will cost around Skr140 but connecting buses (Skr12) run from the airport to the city centre. Skyways/SAS flies regularly on weekdays to Oslo, Malmö and Gothenburg. Ryanair now flies to Västerås from London Stansted (see the Getting There & Away chapter for details).

The bus and train stations are adjacent, on the southern edge of the city centre. Regional buses and trains to Sala cost Skr48 (some buses cost Skr42). Swebus Express runs daily to Stockholm (Skr55, 1¾ hours, four to six daily). Upplands Lokaltrafik bus No 804 runs to Uppsala via Enköping.

Västerås is readily accessible by train from Stockholm (Skr130, one hour, hourly).

Call Taxi Västerås on ☎ 185000. You can hire a bicycle at the tourist office for Skr75/450 per day/week.

SALA
☎ 0224 • pop 12,250
The sleepy town of Sala, 120km from Stockholm, is well worth a visit. The silver mine here was considered the treasury of Sweden in the 16th and 17th centuries and its importance changed the face of the town. Channels and ponds, the source of power for the mines, weave through and around the central area. The little wooden bridges that cross them are now the proud symbols of Sala.

Information

The tourist office (☎ 13145, fax 77322, [e] tur istbyran@sala.se) at Norrmanska Gården, just off Stora Torget, is open 10am to 6pm mid-June to mid-August (closing at 2pm weekends), otherwise 10am to 2pm weekdays. The town's Web site is at [w] www .sala.se. Though the town centre is compact, the free town map is useful if you want to use the walking paths.

There's a bank on Stora Torget and the post office is at Norrbygatan 14. There's a bookshop at Norrbygatan 5 and the public library (with free Internet access) is at Norra Esplanaden 5. Sala Lasarett (hospital; ☎ 58000) is at Lasarettsgatan 1.

Svenska Turistföreningen

Svenska Turistföreningen (STF; the Swedish Touring Club), has around 300,000 members and is among the largest nonprofit-making organisations in Sweden, with an annual turnover of Skr220 million. It was founded in 1885 with the aim of encouraging outdoor activities and travel. The founding members were scientists who worked in the mountains and the STF commenced operations by building a chain of mountain huts in northern Sweden.

Once the hut network was established, the STF expanded into youth hostels, with the first at Gränna, on Lake Vättern, opening in 1933. The hostel network expanded rapidly after WWII and soon passed the 300 mark. In the 1950s, Dag Hammarskjöld was an active vice president of the STF – even while he was in New York working as Secretary General to the UN. STF joined the IYHF, which later became HI (Hostelling International).

Nowadays, all hostels except *af Chapman*, Skeppsholmen, Torrekulla and Tjarö are franchise operations; the STF gets a cut from overnight fees at franchises in exchange for advertising and other promotions. The STF umbrella currently covers 316 hostels, eight mountain lodges and around 90 mountain huts. There are 87 local associations around the country that organise activities for members and there's also a travel section and publishing department at STF head office in Stockholm.

SVENSKA TURISTFÖRENINGEN

Things to See & Do

A stroll along the **Gröna Gången** path takes you south-west through the parks to the **Mellandammen** pond at Sofielund.

About 1km further south there's **Sala Silvergruva** (☎ 19541; 60m-level mine tour Skr80/40; open 10am-5pm daily May-Aug), the old silver mine area which was worked from the 15th century. The extensive mine area includes chimneys, holes, channels, mineheads, spoil heaps, touristy shops, an art gallery and a cafe. There are several different (but all fascinating) mine tours; tickets for the tour down to the 60m level include entry to the **museum** and the information centre, with a superb working **model mine** and films in **Skrädhuset**. Also have a wander around the museum village (free), whose centrepiece is the **Drottning Christinas Schakt** minehead. The village and mine area are off the Västerås road (take the Silverlinjen bus from the train station to Styrars, two to six daily except Sunday).

In town, next to the main park around the pond **Ekebydamm**, is **Väsby Kungsgård** (☎ 10637, Museigatan 2; Skr20/free under 12; open 1pm-4pm Sun-Fri June-Aug, otherwise 1pm-4pm Mon-Fri), a 16th-century royal farm where Gustav II Adolf reputedly met his mistress. Excitement for the traveller is limited to the beautifully preserved interiors and the comprehensive **weapons** collection of the sort wielded by the mighty Swedish armies of the 17th century. The vaulted cellars and wine benches have been restored. Included in the ticket price are the small **textile museum** (with manufacturing equipment) and **agricultural museum** (old farm tools).

Aguélimuseet (☎ 13820, Norra Esplanaden 7; Skr30; open 11am-4pm Tues-Fri, 10am-3pm Sat & Sun) houses a large, impressive collection by local artist Ivan Aguéli.

The rebuilt 17th-century **Kristina Kyrka** on Gruvgatan is impressive enough today, but it once had an 83m spire! The pulpit and the altar screen are 18th century. Older is the 14th-century **Sala Sockenkyrka**, off Hyttvägen, with the remains of frescoes signed by the esteemed Albertus Pictor in the 1460s. There are also two **rune stones**, a 13th-century **sandstone font** and an altar screen from around 1500.

The houses and courtyard **Norrmanska Gården** were built in 1736 and now the tourist office, shops and a cafe are here.

Places to Stay & Eat

STF Vandrarhem & Camping Sofielund (☎ 12730, Mellandammen) Dorm beds Skr110, camping Skr50. Open mid-May to Sept. The rustic hostel, west of the town centre and next to the Mellandammen pond, has a sauna and breakfast is available. It's a 25-minute walk along Gröna Gången from the bus station or take the Silverlinjen bus to the water tower.

Hotell Svea (☎/fax 10510, Väsbygatan 19) Hostel beds Skr150 (July only), hotel singles/doubles Skr495/595 (discounted Skr395/495), most with shared bathroom. You'll find this place diagonally right from the train station. Breakfast costs Skr50 extra for hostellers.

Sala Stadshotell (☎ 13030, fax 10980, ⓔ info@salastatt.se, Bråstagatan 5) Singles/doubles Skr895/995 (discounted Skr595/740) with private bathroom. Sala Stadshotell has a restaurant that serves typical Swedish fare (weekday lunch Skr55, mains Skr135 to Skr195) and there's also live music on some weekends.

LB's (☎ 17418, Rådhusgatan 1) Mains Skr95-162. Open daily for lunch & dinner. LB's serves good weekday lunches with a vegetarian option, baked potatoes and salads for Skr55.

Panini (☎ 10020, Esplanaden Shopping Centre, Stora Torget) Pasta & pizzas from Skr55, meat dishes Skr69-75. Panini serves excellent burgers and pizzas; fish and chips is Skr35.

Bergmästaren (☎ 86836, Fredsgatan 23) Weekday lunch Skr45, pizzas from Skr40. Bergmästaren also offers kebabs and salads. The pub/restaurant here serves a range of sit-down meals.

Stadsträdgården (☎ 18880, Hyttgatan 5) Mains Skr98-154. This reasonable restaurant also does pasta and omelettes for Skr75 to Skr85.

The *Konsum* supermarket is situated on Stora Torget, in the Esplanaden shopping centre, while *Systembolaget* is located on Rådmansgatan.

Getting There & Around

Swebus Express No 890 runs two or three times daily from Stockholm to Falun via Uppsala and Sala. The regional train or bus from Västerås (Skr48, some buses Skr42) is convenient. Regional and SJ trains to Uppsala (Skr75, 35 minutes) run roughly once an hour. Sala is on the main Stockholm to Mora line (via Uppsala), with trains to/from Stockholm every two or three hours (from Skr120, 1¾ hours).

For a taxi, call ☎ 83000.

Language

Swedish grammar follows the pattern of the Germanic languages. Verbs are the same regardless of person or number: 'I am, you are' etc are, in Swedish, *Jag är*, *du är* and so on. Definite articles ('the' in English) are determined by the ending of a noun: *-en* and *-et* for singular nouns and *-na* and *-n* for plural. Determining whether it's *-en* or *-et* as an ending can be difficult and has to be learnt word by word.

Pronunciation

Sweden is a large country and there's considerable dialectal variety. There are sounds in Swedish that don't exist in English, so in the following pronunciation guide we've tried to give the closest possible English equivalents.

Vowels

Vowels are long except when followed by double consonants, in which case they're short. Sometimes the distinction between the vowels **o/å** and **e/ä** can be blurred. There are, however, not as many exceptions to the rules of pronunciation as there are in English.

a	short, as the 'u' in 'cut' or long, as in 'father'
e	short, as in 'bet' or long, as in 'beer'
i	short, as in 'it' or long, as in 'marine'
o	short, as in 'pot' or long, as in 'pool'
u	short, as in 'pull' or long, as in 'ooze'
y	as the 'ee' in 'feet' but with pursed lips
å	short, as the 'o' in 'pot' or long, as the 'oo' in 'poor'
ä	as the 'e' in 'bet' or as the 'a' in 'act'
ö	similar to the 'er' in 'fern'

Consonants

Most consonants have similar pronunciation to their English counterparts. The following letter combinations and sounds are specific to Swedish:

c	as the 's' in 'sit'
ck	like a double 'k'; shortens preceding vowels
dj	as the 'y' in 'yes'
g	as in 'go'; sometimes as the 'i' in 'onion' before certain vowels and after **r**
sj, ch	similar to the 'ch' in Scottish *loch*
tj, rs	as the 'sh' in 'ship'

Basics

Hello.	*Hej.*
Goodbye.	*Adjö/Hej då.*
Yes.	*Ja.*
No.	*Nej.*
Please.	*Snälla/Vänligen.*
Thank you.	*Tack.*
That's fine.	*Det är bra.*
You're welcome.	*Varsågod.*
Excuse me. (Sorry)	*Ursäkta mig/Förlåt.*

Do you speak English?	*Talar du engelska?*
I don't understand.	*Jag förstår inte.*
How much is it?	*Hur mycket kostar den?*
What's your name?	*Vad heter du?*
My name is ...	*Jag heter ...*

Getting Around

Where is the ...?	*När avgår/kommer ...?*
bus stop	*busshållplatsen*
train station	*tågstationen*
tramstop	*spårvagnshållplatsen*

What time does the ... leave/arrive?	*När avgår/kommer ...?*
boat	*båten*
bus (city)	*stadsbussen*
bus (intercity)	*landsortsbussen*
tram	*spårvagnen*
train	*tåget*

I'd like ...	*Jag skulle vilja ha ...*
a one-way ticket	*en enkelbiljett*
a return ticket	*en returbiljett*

Signs

Ingång	Entrance
Utgång	Exit
Fullt	No Vacancies
Information	Information
Öppen	Open
Stängd	Closed
Förbjuden	Prohibited
Polisstation	Police Station
Lediga rum	Rooms Available
Toalett	Toilets
Herrer	Men
Damer	Women

1st class	*första klass*
2nd class	*andra klass*
left luggage	*effektförvaring*
timetable	*tidtabell*

Where can I hire a car/bicycle?	*Var kan jag hyra en bil/cykel?*

Where is ...?	*Var är ...?*
Go straight ahead.	*Gå rakt fram.*
Turn left.	*Sväng till vänster.*
Turn right.	*Sväng till höger.*
near	*nära*
far	*långt*

Around Town
bank	*bank*
city centre	*centrum*
... embassy	*... ambassaden*
my hotel	*mitt hotell*
market	*marknaden*
newsagency/ stationers	*nyhetsbyrå/ pappers handel*
post office	*postkontoret*
public telephone	*offentlig telefon*
public toilet	*offentlig toalett*
tourist office	*turistinformation*

What time does it open/close?	*När öppnar/ stänger de?*

Accommodation
hotel	*hotell*
guesthouse	*gästhus*
youth hostel	*vandrarhem*
camping ground	*campingplats*

Where is a cheap/ good hotel?	*Var det ett billigt/ bra hotell?*
What's the address?	*Vilken adress är det?*
Do you have any rooms available?	*Finns det några lediga rum?*

I'd like ...	*Jag skulle vilja ha ...*
a single room	*ett enkelrum*
a double room	*ett dubbelrum*

How much is it ...?	*Hur mycket kostar det*
per night/ per person	*per natt/ per person*
for one night	*en natt*
for two nights	*två nätter*

Does it include breakfast?	*Inkluderas frukost?*

Health
Where is the ...?	*Var är ...?*
chemist/ pharmacy	*apoteket*
dentist	*tandläkaren*
doctor	*läkaren*
hospital	*sjukhus*

I'm ...	*Jag är ...*
asthmatic	*astmatiker*
diabetic	*diabetiker*
epileptic	*epileptiker*

antiseptic	*antiseptisk*
aspirin	*magnecyl*
condoms	*kondomer*
contraceptive	*preventivmedel*
diarrhoea	*diarré*
medicine	*medicin*
nausea	*illamående*
sanitary napkins	*dambindor*
syringe	*spruta*
tampons	*tamponger*

Time, Days & Numbers
What time is it?	*Vad är klockan?*
today	*idag*
tomorrow	*imorgon*
yesterday	*igår*
morning	*morgonen*
afternoon	*efter middagen*
night	*natt*

Monday	*måndag*
Tuesday	*tisdag*
Wednesday	*onsdag*
Thursday	*torsdag*
Friday	*fredag*
Saturday	*lördag*
Sunday	*söndag*

Emergencies

Help!	*Hjälp!*
Call a doctor!	*Ring efter en doktor!*
Call the police!	*Ring polisen!*
Call an ambulance!	*Ring efter en ambulans!*
Go away!	*Försvinn!*
I'm lost.	*Jag år vilse.*

0	*noll*
1	*ett*
2	*två*
3	*tre*
4	*fyra*
5	*fem*
6	*sex*
7	*sju*
8	*åtta*
9	*nio*
10	*tio*
11	*elva*
12	*tolv*
13	*tretton*
14	*fjorton*
15	*femton*
16	*sexton*
17	*sjutton*

18	*arton*
19	*nitton*
20	*tjugo*
21	*tjugoett*
30	*trettio*
40	*fyrtio*
50	*femtio*
60	*sextio*
70	*sjuttio*
80	*åttio*
90	*nittio*
100	*ett hundra*
1000	*ett tusen*

one million	*en miljon*

Glossary

You may encounter some of the following terms and abbreviations during your travels in and around Stockholm. See also the Language chapter and the Food section in the Places to Eat chapter. Note that the letters å, ä and ö fall at the end of the Swedish alphabet.

AB – 'aktiebolag'; company
allemansrätt – 'every man's right'; a tradition allowing universal access to private property (with some restrictions), public land and wilderness areas
apotek – pharmacy
atelje – gallery
aventyrs bad – see *bad*
avhämtning – takeaways

bad – swimming pool, bathing place (usually *aventyrs bad*)
bakfickan – literally 'back pocket', an ordinary low profile eating place associated with a gourmet restaurant
bankautomat – cash machine, ATM
barn – child
berg – mountain
bibliotek – library
bil – car
billet – ticket
billetautomat – automatic ticket machines for street parking
biluthyrning – car hire
bio, **biograf** – cinema
björn – bear
black & white – steak with mashed potato
bokhandel – bookshop
bro – bridge
bruk – factory
bryggeri – brewery
buss – bus
båt – boat
bäver – beaver

centrum – town centre
cykel – bicycle

dagens rätt – daily special, usually only on lunchtime menus

dal – valley
dansbana – stage for dancing
domkyrka – cathedral
drottning – queen
dygnskort – 'day card', a daily bus pass

ej (or *inte*) – not
ekonomibrev – economy post
etage – floor, storey
expedition – office

fabrik – factory
fjäll – mountain
fjärd – fjord, drowned glacial valley
flod – large river
flygplats – airport
folkdräkt – folk dress
folkhemmet – welfare state
frukost – breakfast
fyr – lighthouse
fågel – bird
färja – ferry
färjeläge – ferry quay
fästning – fort, fortress
förening – club, association
förlag – company

galleria – shopping mall
gamla – old
gamla staden, gamla stan – the 'old town', the historical part of a city or town
gatan – street (often abbreviated to just **g**)
gatukök – literally 'street kitchen'; street kiosk/stall/grill selling greasy fast food
glögg – spicy mulled wine
grotta – grotto, cave
grundskolan – comprehensive school
gruva – mine
gränsen – border
gymnasieskolan – upper secondary school
gångrift – dolmen or passage tomb
gård – farm
gästhamn – 'guest harbour', where visiting yachts can berth; cooking and washing facilities usually available
gästhem – guesthouse

hamn – harbour
hembygdsgård – open-air museum, usually old farmhouse buildings
hjortron – cloudberries
hund – dog
hus – house, but sometimes also means 'castle'
husmanskost – traditional Swedish fare of the type you would expect to be cooked at home when you were a (Swedish) kid
hytt – cabin on a boat
hälsocentral – clinic

i – in
inte – not (or *ej*)
is – ice
ishall – ice-hockey stadium

jul – Christmas
järnvägsstation – train station

kaj – quay
kalkmålningar – lime paintings (as found in medieval churches)
kanotuthyrning – canoe hire
kart – map
Kartförlaget – State Mapping Agency (sales division)
klockan – o'clock, the time
klocktorn – bell tower
kommun – municipality
konditori – baker and confectioner (often with an attached cafe)
konst – art
kort – card
KRAV – this organisation sets standards for organic foods in Sweden
krog – pub or restaurant (or both)
krona (s), **kronor** (pl) – Swedish currency unit
kullar – hills
kulle – hill
kung – king
kust – coast
kyrka – church
kyrkogård – graveyard
kåta – tepee-shaped Sami hut
källare – cellar, vault
kött – meat
köttbullar och potatis – meatballs and potatoes

landskap – region, province, landscape
lasarett – hospital
lilla – lesser, little
lo – lynx
loppis – second-hand goods (usually junk)
lufsa – pork dumpling and smoked salmon (in the one dish)
län – county
lättmjölk – low-fat milk
lövbiff – thinly sliced fried meat

mat – food
midsommar – midsummer; first Friday after 21 June
MOMS – value-added tax
M/S – motorised sailing vessel
museum, museet – museum
mynt tvätt – coin-operated laundry
målning – painting, artwork

nattclub – nightclub
naturcamping – camping ground with pleasant environment
naturreservat – nature reserve
Naturum – national park or nature reserve visitor centre
Naturvårdsverket – Swedish Environmental Protection Agency (National Parks Authority)
nedre – lower
norr – north
norrsken – aurora borealis (northern lights)
ny – new
nyheter – news
näs – headland

och – and

palats – palace
pendeltåg – local train
pensionat – pension or guesthouse
P-hus – multistorey car park
polarcirkeln – Arctic Circle, 66° 33' north latitude
polis – police
post – post office
pytt i panna – Swedish dish; a mix of diced sausage, beef or pork fried with onion and potato
på – on, in

pålagg – toppings (for either sandwiches or pizzas)
påsk – Easter
påtår – free refill (coffee)

resebyrå – travel agent
restaurang – restaurant
RFSL – Riksförbundet för Sexuellt Lik-aberättigande; national gay organisation
riksdag – parliament
rådhus – town hall
räkor – shrimps
rökning förbjuden – no smoking

simhall – swimming pool
SJ – Statens Järnväg (Swedish Railways)
sjukhus – hospital
sjö – lake or sea
skog – forest
skål! – cheers!
skärgård – archipelago
slott – castle
smörgåsbord – Swedish buffet (lunch or dinner)
snabbtvätt – quick wash (at laundry)
snö – snow
spark – kicksledge, popular in winter
stark – strong, hot (spicy)
statsminister – Prime Minister
STF – Svenska Turistföreningen (Swedish Touring Association)
stora – big, large
strand – beach
stuga (s), **stugor/na** (pl) – hut or chalet
stugby – chalet park; a little village of chalets for tourists ('by' means town or village)
sund – sound
Sverige – Sweden
Sverigehuset – Sweden House (tourist office)
Svensk – Swedish
Systembolaget – state-owned liquor store
söder – south

tandläkare – dentist
teater – theatre
telefon kort – telephone card

toalett – toilet
torg, torget – town square
torn – tower
trädgård – garden open to the public
tull – customs
tunnelbana – underground railway or metro
turistbyrå – tourist office
tåg – train
tågplus – combined train and bus ticket
tält – tent

uthyrningsfirma – hire company, eg, *bi-luthyrning* (car hire) and *kanotuthyrning* (canoe hire)

vandrarhem – hostel
vattenfall – waterfall
vik – bay or other inlet
vuxen – adult
vårdcentral – hospital
väg – road
vänthall, väntrum, väntsal – waiting room
värdekort – value card, a travel pass that can be topped up at any time
värdshus (or *wärdshus*) – inn
väst – west (abbreviated to **v**)
västra – western
växel – switchboard, money exchange

wärdshus – see *värdshus*

å – stream, creek, river

älg – elk
älv – river

ö – island
öl – beer
öst – east (abbreviated to **ö**)
östra – eastern
övre – upper

Date abbreviations:

f.Kr. – Före Kristus – BC
e.Kr. – Efter Kristus – AD

LONELY PLANET

You already know that Lonely Planet produces more than this one guidebook, but you might not be aware of the other products we have on this region. Here is a selection of titles that you may want to check out as well:

Scandinavian & Baltic Europe
ISBN 1 86450 156 1
US$21.99 • UK£13.99

Scandinavian phrasebook
ISBN 1 86450 225 8
US$7.99 • UK£4.50

Europe on a shoestring
ISBN 1 86450 150 2
US$24.99 • UK£14.99

Read this First: Europe
ISBN 1 86450 136 7
US$14.99 • UK£8.99

Sweden
ISBN 0 86442 721 2
US$17.99 • UK£11.99

Available wherever books are sold

LONELY PLANET

ON THE ROAD

Travel Guides explore cities, regions and countries, and supply information on transport, restaurants and accommodation, covering all budgets. They come with reliable, easy-to-use maps, practical advice, cultural and historical facts and a rundown on attractions both on and off the beaten track. There are over 200 titles in this classic series, covering nearly every country in the world.

 Lonely Planet Upgrades extend the shelf life of existing travel guides by detailing any changes that may affect travel in a region since a book has been published. Upgrades can be downloaded for free from **www.lonelyplanet.com/upgrades**

For travellers with more time than money, **Shoestring** guides offer dependable, first-hand information with hundreds of detailed maps, plus insider tips for stretching money as far as possible. Covering entire continents in most cases, the six-volume shoestring guides are known around the world as 'backpackers bibles'.

For the discerning short-term visitor, **Condensed** guides highlight the best a destination has to offer in a full-colour, pocket-sized format designed for quick access. They include everything from top sights and walking tours to opinionated reviews of where to eat, stay, shop and have fun.

CitySync lets travellers use their Palm™ or Visor™ hand-held computers to guide them through a city with handy tips on transport, history, cultural life, major sights, and shopping and entertainment options. It can also quickly search and sort hundreds of reviews of hotels, restaurants and attractions, and pinpoint their location on scrollable street maps. CitySync can be downloaded from **www.citysync.com**

MAPS & ATLASES

Lonely Planet's **City Maps** feature downtown and metropolitan maps, as well as transit routes and walking tours. The maps come complete with an index of streets, a listing of sights and a plastic coat for extra durability.

Road Atlases are an essential navigation tool for serious travellers. Cross-referenced with the guidebooks, they also feature distance and climate charts and a complete site index.

LONELY PLANET

ESSENTIALS

Read This First books help new travellers to hit the road with confidence. These invaluable predeparture guides give step-by-step advice on preparing for a trip, budgeting, arranging a visa, planning an itinerary and staying safe while still getting off the beaten track.

Healthy Travel pocket guides offer a regional rundown on disease hot spots and practical advice on predeparture health measures, staying well on the road and what to do in emergencies. The guides come with a user-friendly design and helpful diagrams and tables.

Lonely Planet's **Phrasebooks** cover the essential words and phrases travellers need when they're strangers in a strange land. They come in a pocket-sized format with colour tabs for quick reference, extensive vocabulary lists, easy-to-follow pronunciation keys and two-way dictionaries.

Miffed by blurry photos of the Taj Mahal? Tired of the classic 'top of the head cut off' shot? **Travel Photography: A Guide to Taking Better Pictures** will help you turn ordinary holiday snaps into striking images and give you the know-how to capture every scene, from frenetic festivals to peaceful beach sunrises.

Lonely Planet's **Travel Journal** is a lightweight but sturdy travel diary for jotting down all those on-the-road observations and significant travel moments. It comes with a handy time-zone wheel, a world map and useful travel information.

Lonely Planet's eKno is an all-in-one communication service developed especially for travellers. It offers low-cost international calls and free email and voicemail so that you can keep in touch while on the road. Check it out on **www.ekno.lonelyplanet.com**

FOOD & RESTAURANT GUIDES

Lonely Planet's **Out to Eat** guides recommend the brightest and best places to eat and drink in top international cities. These gourmet companions are arranged by neighbourhood, packed with dependable maps, garnished with scene-setting photos and served with quirky features.

For people who live to eat, drink and travel, **World Food** guides explore the culinary culture of each country. Entertaining and adventurous, each guide is packed with detail on staples and specialities, regional cuisine and local markets, as well as sumptuous recipes, comprehensive culinary dictionaries and lavish photos good enough to eat.

OUTDOOR GUIDES

For those who believe the best way to see the world is on foot, Lonely Planet's **Walking Guides** detail everything from family strolls to difficult treks, with 'when to go and how to do it' advice supplemented by reliable maps and essential travel information.

Cycling Guides map a destination's best bike tours, long and short, in day-by-day detail. They contain all the information a cyclist needs, including advice on bike maintenance, places to eat and stay, innovative maps with detailed cues to the rides, and elevation charts.

The **Watching Wildlife** series is perfect for travellers who want authoritative information but don't want to tote a heavy field guide. Packed with advice on where, when and how to view a region's wildlife, each title features photos of over 300 species and contains engaging comments on the local flora and fauna.

With underwater colour photos throughout, **Pisces Books** explore the world's best diving and snorkelling areas. Each book contains listings of diving services and dive resorts, detailed information on depth, visibility and difficulty of dives, and a roundup of the marine life you're likely to see through your mask.

LONELY PLANET

OFF THE ROAD

Journeys, the travel literature series written by renowned travel authors, capture the spirit of a place or illuminate a culture with a journalist's attention to detail and a novelist's flair for words. These are tales to soak up while you're actually on the road or dip into as an at-home armchair indulgence.

The range of lavishly illustrated **Pictorial** books is just the ticket for both travellers and dreamers. Off-beat tales and vivid photographs bring the adventure of travel to your doorstep long before the journey begins and long after it is over.

Lonely Planet **Videos** encourage the same independent, tough-minded approach as the guidebooks. Currently airing throughout the world, this award-winning series features innovative footage and an original soundtrack.

Yes, we know, work is tough, so do a little bit of deskside dreaming with the spiral-bound Lonely Planet **Diary** or a Lonely Planet **Wall Calendar**, filled with great photos from around the world.

TRAVELLERS NETWORK

Lonely Planet Online. Lonely Planet's award-winning Web site has insider information on hundreds of destinations, from Amsterdam to Zimbabwe, complete with interactive maps and relevant links. The site also offers the latest travel news, recent reports from travellers on the road, guidebook upgrades, a travel links site, an online book-buying option and a lively traveller's bulletin board. It can be viewed at **www.lonelyplanet.com** or AOL keyword: lp.

Planet Talk is a quarterly print newsletter, full of gossip, advice, anecdotes and author articles. It provides an antidote to the being-at-home blues and lets you plan and dream for the next trip. Contact the nearest Lonely Planet office for your free copy.

Comet, the free Lonely Planet newsletter, comes via email once a month. It's loaded with travel news, advice, dispatches from authors, travel competitions and letters from readers. To subscribe, click on the Comet subscription link on the front page of the Web site.

Lonely Planet Guides by Region

Lonely Planet is known worldwide for publishing practical, reliable and no-nonsense travel information in our guides and on our Web site. The Lonely Planet list covers just about every accessible part of the world. Currently there are 16 series: Travel guides, Shoestring guides, Condensed guides, Phrasebooks, Read This First, Healthy Travel, Walking guides, Cycling guides, Watching Wildlife guides, Pisces Diving & Snorkeling guides, City Maps, Road Atlases, Out to Eat, World Food, Journeys travel literature and Pictorials.

AFRICA Africa on a shoestring • Botswana • Cairo • Cairo City Map • Cape Town • Cape Town City Map • East Africa • Egypt • Egyptian Arabic phrasebook • Ethiopia, Eritrea & Djibouti • Ethiopian Amharic phrasebook • The Gambia & Senegal • Healthy Travel Africa • Kenya • Malawi • Morocco • Moroccan Arabic phrasebook • Mozambique • Namibia • Read This First: Africa • South Africa, Lesotho & Swaziland • Southern Africa • Southern Africa Road Atlas • Swahili phrasebook • Tanzania, Zanzibar & Pemba • Trekking in East Africa • Tunisia • Watching Wildlife East Africa • Watching Wildlife Southern Africa • West Africa • World Food Morocco • Zambia • Zimbabwe, Botswana & Namibia
Travel Literature: Mali Blues: Traveling to an African Beat • The Rainbird: A Central African Journey • Songs to an African Sunset: A Zimbabwean Story

AUSTRALIA & THE PACIFIC Aboriginal Australia & the Torres Strait Islands •Auckland • Australia • Australian phrasebook • Australia Road Atlas • Cycling Australia • Cycling New Zealand • Fiji • Fijian phrasebook • Healthy Travel Australia, NZ & the Pacific • Islands of Australia's Great Barrier Reef • Melbourne • Melbourne City Map • Micronesia • New Caledonia • New South Wales • New Zealand • Northern Territory • Outback Australia • Out to Eat – Melbourne • Out to Eat – Sydney • Papua New Guinea • Pidgin phrasebook • Queensland • Rarotonga & the Cook Islands • Samoa • Solomon Islands • South Australia • South Pacific • South Pacific phrasebook • Sydney • Sydney City Map • Sydney Condensed • Tahiti & French Polynesia • Tasmania • Tonga • Tramping in New Zealand • Vanuatu • Victoria • Walking in Australia • Watching Wildlife Australia • Western Australia
Travel Literature: Islands in the Clouds: Travels in the Highlands of New Guinea • Kiwi Tracks: A New Zealand Journey • Sean & David's Long Drive

CENTRAL AMERICA & THE CARIBBEAN Bahamas, Turks & Caicos • Baja California • Belize, Guatemala & Yucatán • Bermuda • Central America on a shoestring • Costa Rica • Costa Rica Spanish phrasebook • Cuba • Cycling Cuba • Dominican Republic & Haiti • Eastern Caribbean • Guatemala • Havana • Healthy Travel Central & South America • Jamaica • Mexico • Mexico City • Panama • Puerto Rico • Read This First: Central & South America • Virgin Islands • World Food Caribbean • World Food Mexico • Yucatán
Travel Literature: Green Dreams: Travels in Central America

EUROPE Amsterdam • Amsterdam City Map • Amsterdam Condensed • Andalucía • Athens • Austria • Baltic States phrasebook • Barcelona • Barcelona City Map • Belgium & Luxembourg • Berlin • Berlin City Map • Britain • British phrasebook • Brussels, Bruges & Antwerp • Brussels City Map • Budapest • Budapest City Map • Canary Islands • Catalunya & the Costa Brava • Central Europe • Central Europe phrasebook • Copenhagen • Corfu & the Ionians • Corsica • Crete • Crete Condensed • Croatia • Cycling Britain • Cycling France • Cyprus • Czech & Slovak Republics • Czech phrasebook • Denmark • Dublin • Dublin City Map • Dublin Condensed • Eastern Europe • Eastern Europe phrasebook • Edinburgh • Edinburgh City Map • England • Estonia, Latvia & Lithuania • Europe on a shoestring • Europe phrasebook • Finland • Florence • Florence City Map • France • Frankfurt City Map • Frankfurt Condensed • French phrasebook • Georgia, Armenia & Azerbaijan • Germany • German phrasebook • Greece • Greek Islands • Greek phrasebook • Hungary • Iceland, Greenland & the Faroe Islands • Ireland • Italian phrasebook • Italy • Kraków • Lisbon • The Loire • London • London City Map • London Condensed • Madrid • Madrid City Map • Malta • Mediterranean Europe • Milan, Turin & Genoa • Moscow • Munich • Netherlands • Normandy • Norway • Out to Eat – London • Out to Eat – Paris • Paris • Paris City Map • Paris Condensed • Poland • Polish phrasebook • Portugal • Portuguese phrasebook • Prague • Prague City Map • Provence & the Côte d'Azur • Read This First: Europe • Rhodes & the Dodecanese • Romania & Moldova • Rome • Rome City Map • Rome Condensed • Russia, Ukraine & Belarus • Russian phrasebook • Scandinavian & Baltic Europe • Scandinavian phrasebook • Scotland • Sicily • Slovenia • South-West France • Spain • Spanish phrasebook • Stockholm • St Petersburg • St Petersburg City Map • Sweden • Switzerland • Tuscany • Ukrainian phrasebook • Venice • Vienna • Wales • Walking in Britain • Walking in France • Walking in Ireland • Walking in Italy • Walking in Scotland • Walking in Spain • Walking in Switzerland • Western Europe • World Food France • World Food Greece • World Food Ireland • World Food Italy • World Food Spain **Travel Literature:** After Yugoslavia • Love and War in the Apennines • The Olive Grove: Travels in Greece • On the Shores of the Mediterranean • Round Ireland in Low Gear • A Small Place in Italy

Lonely Planet Mail Order

Lonely Planet products are distributed worldwide.They are also available by mail order from Lonely Planet, so if you have difficulty finding a title please write to us. North and South American residents should write to 150 Linden St, Oakland, CA 94607, USA; European and African residents should write to 10a Spring Place, London NW5 3BH, UK; and residents of other countries to Locked Bag 1, Footscray, Victoria 3011, Australia.

INDIAN SUBCONTINENT & THE INDIAN OCEAN Bangladesh • Bengali phrasebook • Bhutan • Delhi • Goa • Healthy Travel Asia & India • Hindi & Urdu phrasebook • India • India & Bangladesh City Map • Indian Himalaya • Karakoram Highway • Kathmandu City Map • Kerala • Madagascar • Maldives • Mauritius, Réunion & Seychelles • Mumbai (Bombay) • Nepal • Nepali phrasebook • North India • Pakistan • Rajasthan • Read This First: Asia & India • South India • Sri Lanka • Sri Lanka phrasebook • Tibet • Tibetan phrasebook • Trekking in the Indian Himalaya • Trekking in the Karakoram & Hindukush • Trekking in the Nepal Himalaya • World Food India **Travel Literature:** The Age of Kali: Indian Travels and Encounters • Hello Goodnight: A Life of Goa • In Rajasthan • Maverick in Madagascar • A Season in Heaven: True Tales from the Road to Kathmandu • Shopping for Buddhas • A Short Walk in the Hindu Kush • Slowly Down the Ganges

MIDDLE EAST & CENTRAL ASIA Bahrain, Kuwait & Qatar • Central Asia • Central Asia phrasebook • Dubai • Farsi (Persian) phrasebook • Hebrew phrasebook • Iran • Israel & the Palestinian Territories • Istanbul • Istanbul City Map • Istanbul to Cairo • Istanbul to Kathmandu • Jerusalem • Jerusalem City Map • Jordan • Lebanon • Middle East • Oman & the United Arab Emirates • Syria • Turkey • Turkish phrasebook • World Food Turkey • Yemen **Travel Literature:** Black on Black: Iran Revisited • Breaking Ranks: Turbulent Travels in the Promised Land • The Gates of Damascus • Kingdom of the Film Stars: Journey into Jordan

NORTH AMERICA Alaska • Boston • Boston City Map • Boston Condensed • British Columbia • California & Nevada • California Condensed • Canada • Chicago • Chicago City Map • Chicago Condensed • Florida • Georgia & the Carolinas • Great Lakes • Hawaii • Hiking in Alaska • Hiking in the USA • Honolulu & Oahu City Map • Las Vegas • Los Angeles • Los Angeles City Map • Louisiana & the Deep South • Miami • Miami City Map • Montreal • New England • New Orleans • New Orleans City Map • New York City • New York City City Map • New York City Condensed • New York, New Jersey & Pennsylvania • Oahu • Out to Eat – San Francisco • Pacific Northwest • Rocky Mountains • San Diego & Tijuana • San Francisco • San Francisco City Map • Seattle • Seattle City Map • Southwest • Texas • Toronto • USA • USA phrasebook • Vancouver • Vancouver City Map • Virginia & the Capital Region • Washington, DC • Washington, DC City Map • World Food New Orleans **Travel Literature**: Caught Inside: A Surfer's Year on the California Coast • Drive Thru America

NORTH-EAST ASIA Beijing • Beijing City Map • Cantonese phrasebook • China • Hiking in Japan • Hong Kong & Macau • Hong Kong City Map • Hong Kong Condensed • Japan • Japanese phrasebook • Korea • Korean phrasebook • Kyoto • Mandarin phrasebook • Mongolia • Mongolian phrasebook • Seoul • Shanghai • South-West China • Taiwan • Tokyo • Tokyo Condensed • World Food Hong Kong • World Food Japan **Travel Literature:** In Xanadu: A Quest • Lost Japan

SOUTH AMERICA Argentina, Uruguay & Paraguay • Bolivia • Brazil • Brazilian phrasebook • Buenos Aires • Buenos Aires City Map • Chile & Easter Island • Colombia • Ecuador & the Galapagos Islands • Healthy Travel Central & South America • Latin American Spanish phrasebook • Peru • Quechua phrasebook • Read This First: Central & South America • Rio de Janeiro • Rio de Janeiro City Map • Santiago de Chile • South America on a shoestring • Trekking in the Patagonian Andes • Venezuela **Travel Literature**: Full Circle: A South American Journey

SOUTH-EAST ASIA Bali & Lombok • Bangkok • Bangkok City Map • Burmese phrasebook • Cambodia • Cycling Vietnam, Laos & Cambodia • East Timor phrasebook • Hanoi • Healthy Travel Asia & India • Hill Tribes phrasebook • Ho Chi Minh City (Saigon) • Indonesia • Indonesian phrasebook • Indonesia's Eastern Islands • Java • Lao phrasebook • Laos • Malay phrasebook • Malaysia, Singapore & Brunei • Myanmar (Burma) • Philippines • Pilipino (Tagalog) phrasebook • Read This First: Asia & India • Singapore • Singapore City Map • South-East Asia on a shoestring • South-East Asia phrasebook • Thailand • Thailand's Islands & Beaches • Thailand, Vietnam, Laos & Cambodia Road Atlas • Thai phrasebook • Vietnam • Vietnamese phrasebook • World Food Indonesia • World Food Thailand • World Food Vietnam

ALSO AVAILABLE: Antarctica • The Arctic • The Blue Man: Tales of Travel, Love and Coffee • Brief Encounters: Stories of Love, Sex & Travel • Buddhist Stupas in Asia: The Shape of Perfection • Chasing Rickshaws • The Last Grain Race • Lonely Planet ... On the Edge: Adventurous Escapades from Around the World • Lonely Planet Unpacked • Lonely Planet Unpacked Again • Not the Only Planet: Science Fiction Travel Stories • Ports of Call: A Journey by Sea • Sacred India • Travel Photography: A Guide to Taking Better Pictures • Travel with Children • Tuvalu: Portrait of an Island Nation

Index

Text

Note that the Swedish letters å, ä and ö fall at the end of the alphabet.

Bold indicates maps.

Bold indicates maps.

Places to Stay

Places to Eat

Boxed Text

MAP 1 – TRANSPORT SYSTEM

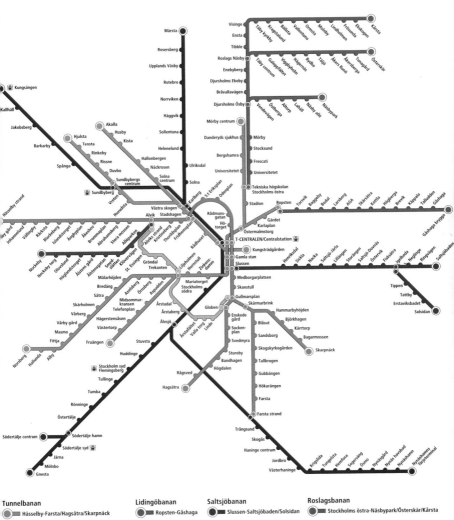

Tunnelbanan
- Hässelby-Farsta/Hagsätra/Skarpnäck
- Mörby centrum/Ropsten-Fruängen/Norsborg
- Akalla/Hjulsta-Kungsträdgården

Lidingöbanan
- Ropsten-Gåshaga

Nockebybanan
- Alvik-Nockeby

Saltsjöbanan
- Slussen-Saltsjöbaden/Solsidan

Tvärbanan
- Gullmarsplan-Alvik

Roslagsbanan
- Stockholms östra-Näsbypark/Österskär/Kårsta

Pendeltåg
- Kungsängen/Märsta-Nynäshamn/Södertälje/Gnesta

MAP 2

Barkarby

Skälby

To Västerås (E18)

Kista

To Sigtuna & Uppsala

Nationalstadsparken

To Vaxholm & Norrtälje

Klingsta

Hjulsta

Skälby-vägen

Lunda

Tensta

Hjulstavägen

279

3

Skälbyvägen

Avestagatan

1

2

Spånga Kyrkväg

Rinkeby

E4

4

Dandeeryd Sjukhus

A

Kälvesta

Solhem

Kymlingelänken

Bergshamra

E18

Bergslagsvägen

275

Vinsta

Flysta

Rissne

Enköpingsvägen

6

Ulriksdal

E18

Bergsham

Löfstavägen

Rissne

Hallonbergen

Sundbyberg

Brunns

viken

B

Hässelby Gård

Johannelund

Nälsta

Duvbo

Näckrosen

Solna

Uppsalavägen

16

15

Hässelby Strand

Vällingby

Vällingby

Eneby

7

Duvbo

Solna

14

Hag

par

Råcksta

Spångavägen

Ballstavägen

Sundbybergs

Centrum

12

13

Solna

Centrum

Hagalund

Blackeberg

Islandstorget

Bergslagsvägen

Norra

Ängby

8

Bromma

279

Vreten

Huvudsta

Västra

Skogen

MAP 3

E4

9

Södra

Ängby

Ängbyplan

Åkeshov

Bromma

Airport

Huvudsta

Karlberg

Sankt

Eriks

C

11

Brommaplan

261

275

Traneberg

Stadshagen

Fridhems

Abrahamsberg

Stora Mossen

Åkeslund

Alvik

Kristineberg

Thorildsplan

Nockeby

Torg

Alléparken

Alvik Strand

Nockeby

Olovslund

Älstensgatan

Klövervägen

Stora

Essingen

Lilla

Essingen

Långholmen

D

Lovö Kyrkallé

Höglandstorget

Appelviken

Horns

Nöckeby

10

Kärsön

Älstens Gård

Smedslätten

Stora

Essingen

Gröndal

Trekanten

Lovön

Ekerövägen

Fågelön

27

Gröndal

Liljeholmen

E

261

26

Hägersten

Aspudden

Essingeleden

Årstadal

Kungshatt

Mälarhöjden

Axelsberg

Örnsberg

Midsommar

kransen

Årstab

Mälarhöjden

Telefonplan

28

Bredäng

Hägerstensåsen

30

Västberga

F

Sätra

Bredäng

29

Västertorp

E4

E20

Solberga

Liseberg

Fiskarfjärden

Sätra

Södertäljevägen

Fruängen

Älvsjövägen

Älvsjö

Vårberg

Fruängen

226

Vårberg

Skärholmen

Herrängen

Älvsjö

Örby

G

E4

E20

Sergeltorp

Långsjön

Magelungsvägen

Högdale

Vårby Gård

Snättringe

Hagsätra

Vårby

Rågsved

To Södertälje & Nyköping

0 1 2km

0 0.5 1mi

allunda

Fittja

Masmo

Milsten

Stuvsta

Stuvsta

1 2 3 4 5

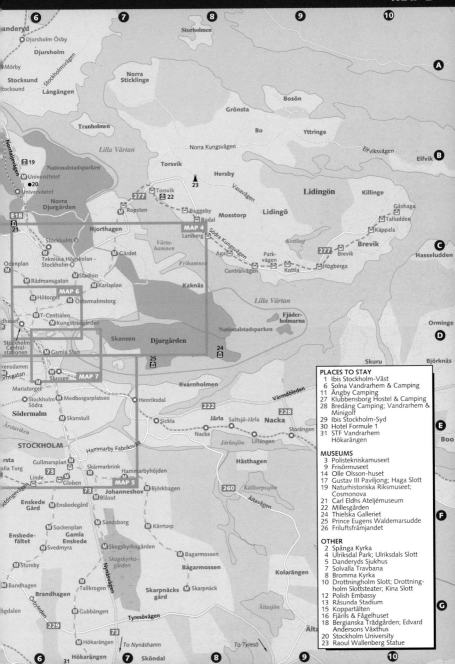

MAP 2

PLACES TO STAY
1 Ibis Stockholm-Väst
6 Solna Vandrarhem & Camping
11 Ängby Camping
27 Klubbensborg Hostel & Camping
28 Bredäng Camping; Vandrarhem & Minigolf
29 Ibis Stockholm-Syd
30 Hotel Formule 1
31 STF Vandrarhem Hökarängen

MUSEUMS
3 Polistekniskamuseet
9 Frisörmuseet
14 Olle Olsson-huset
17 Gustav III Paviljong; Haga Slott
19 Naturhistoriska Riksmuseet; Cosmonova
21 Carl Eldhs Ateljémuseum
22 Millesgården
24 Thielska Galleriet
25 Prince Eugens Waldemarsudde
26 Friluftsfrämjandet

OTHER
2 Spånga Kyrka
4 Ulriksdal Park; Ulriksdals Slott
5 Danderyds Sjukhus
7 Solvalla Travbana
8 Bromma Kyrka
10 Drottningholm Slott; Drottningholm Slottsteater; Kina Slott
12 Polish Embassy
13 Råsunda Stadium
15 Koppartälten
16 Fjärils & Fågelhuset
18 Bergianska Trädgården; Edvard Andersons Växthus
20 Stockholm University
23 Raoul Wallenberg Statue

A view from Djurgårdsbron bridge

One of the spires rising from Stadshuset

Some of the buildings lining Stockholm harbour

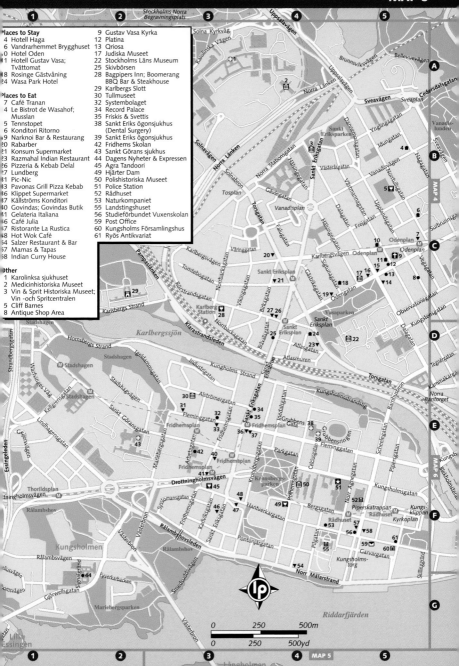

MAP 3

Stockholms Norra
Begravningsplats

Places to Stay
4 Hotell Haga
6 Vandrarhemmet Brygghuset
10 Hotel Oden
11 Hotell Gustav Vasa;
   Tvättomat
18 Rosinge Gästvåning
24 Wasa Park Hotel

Places to Eat
7 Café Tranan
14 Le Bistrot de Wasahof;
   Musslan
15 Tennstopet
16 Konditori Ritorno
19 Narknoi Bar & Restaurang
20 Rabarber
21 Konsum Supermarket
23 Razmahal Indian Restaurant
26 Pizzeria & Kebab Delal
27 Lundberg
31 Pic-Nic
33 Pavonas Grill Pizza Kebab
36 Klippet Supermarket
37 Källströms Konditori
40 Govindas; Govindas Butik
41 Gelateria Italiana
46 Café Julia
47 Ristorante La Rustica
48 Hot Wok Café
54 Salzer Restaurant & Bar
57 Mamas & Tapas
58 Indian Curry House

Other
1 Karolinksa sjukhuset
2 Medicinhistoriska Museet
3 Vin & Sprit Historiska Museet;
   Vin -och Spritcentralen
5 Cliff Barnes
8 Antique Shop Area

9 Gustav Vasa Kyrka
12 Platina
13 Qriosa
17 Judiska Museet
22 Stockholms Läns Museum
25 Skivbörsen
28 Bagpipers Inn; Boomerang
   BBQ Bar & Steakhouse
29 Karlbergs Slott
30 Tullmuseet
32 Systembolaget
34 Record Palace
35 Friskis & Svettis
38 Sankt Eriks ögonsjukhus
   (Dental Surgery)
39 Sankt Eriks ögonsjukhus
42 Fridhems Skolan
43 Sankt Görans sjukhus
44 Dagens Nyheter & Expressen
45 Agra Tandoori
49 Hjärter Dam
50 Polishistoriska Museet
51 Police Station
52 Rådhuset
53 Naturkompaniet
55 Landstingshuset
56 Studieförbundet Vuxenskolan
59 Post Office
60 Kungsholms Församlingshus
61 Ryös Antikvariat

MAP 4

Roslagsvägen
Brinellvägen
Ruddammsvägen
Brunbärsvägen
Nalnallavägen
Drottning Kristinas Väg
Norra Djurgården
Ugglevägen
Uggleviksvägen
Fiskartorpsvägen
Sörbyvägen

A
Cedersdalsgatan
Sveaplan
Roslagsgatan
1

Vanadislunden
2
Vanadisvägen
Sveavägen
Freigatan
Dalagatan
Birger Jarlsgatan
Valhallavägen
Kräpplundsvägen

B
Vanadisvägen
3
Teknika Högskolan - Stockholm
Teknika Högskolan - Stockholm
Östra Station
41
Odengatan
Östermalmsgatan
Karlavägen
Jarlaplan
Danderyds-plan
Valhallavägen
Drottning Sofias Väg
42
52
51
Lidingövägen
Starängsringen
Sandelsgatan
Strindbergsgatan

C
16
17
Spelbomskans Torg
15
13
9
10
14
18
Markvardsgatan
Tulegatan
Rehnsgatan
Kungstensgatan
Runebergs-plan
Engelbrektsgatan
Villagatan
Floragatan
43
Stadion
Östermalmsgatan
48
Valhallavägen
Jungfrugatan
Artillerigatan
49
50
Karlaplan
Oden-plan
Observatorielunden
12
11
Rådmansgatan
27
Rådmansgatan
40
44
Humlegården
47
Sturegatan
Karlavägen
46
45
Stadion
Kommendörsgatan

D
19
22
20
21
23
24
26
25
Rådmansgatan
31
32
30
29
36
35
28
37
33
34
38
39
Tegnérgatan
Luntmakargatan
Johannesgatan
Plutas-Backe
Engelbrekts-plan
David Bagares Gata
Humlegårdsgatan
Nybrogatan
Sibyllegatan
Skeppargatan
Grev Turegatan
Karlaplan
Vasavägen
Drottninggatan
Kungstensgatan
Dalagatan
Tegnérgatan
Uplandsgatan
Irgnerlunden
Kammakargatan
Wallingatan
Barnhusgatan
Olof Palmes Gata
Apelbergsgatan
Hötorget
Hötorget
Brunnsgatan
Kungsgatan
Oxtorget
Oxtorgsgatan
Jakobsbergsgatan
Östermalmstorg
Sture-plan
Östermalms-torg
Östermalmstorg
Linnégatan
Storgatan
66
65
Grevgatan

E
Torsgatan
Norra Bantorget
Östra Järnvägen
Kungsbron
Vasagatan
Gamla
Kungsbron
Klara Norra Kyrkogata
Brogatan
Drottninggatan
Sveavägen
Olofsgatan
Malmskillnadsgatan
Regeringsgatan
Mäster Samuelsgatan
Normalmstorg
Normalm-storg
Hamngatan
Berzelii Park
Raoul Wallenbergs Torg
Nybroplan
Strandvägen
Nybroviken
Ladugårdslandsviken
Styrmansgatan
67
Galärpa.
95

F
T-Centralen
Sergels Torg
T-Centralen
Klarabergsgatan
Brunke-bergstorg
Vattugatan
Herkulesgatan
Jakobsgatan
Gustav Adolfs Torg
Strömgatan
Kungsträd-gården
Kungsträdgården
Karl XII:s Torg
Stallgatan
Nybroviken
Klarabergsviadukten
Central-plan
Stockholm Central-stationen
Blekholmsterrassen
Kungsholmen
Hantverkargatan
Ragnar Ostbergs Plan
Blekholmstaren
Fredsgatan
Helgeandsholmen
Skeppsholmen
MAP 7
Tegelbacken
Rödbodtorget
Centralbron
Vasabron
Norbro
Slottskajen
Skeppsbron
Amiralitets-parken
Svensbundsvägen
Långa Raden

G
Riddarfjärden
Riddarholmen
Evert Taubes Terrass
Birger Jarls Torg
Stora Nygatan
Lilla Nygatan
Munkbroleden
Myntorget
Slottsbacken
Gamla Stan
Österlanggatan
Strömmen
Kastellholmen

MAP 5
Gamla Stan

MAP 4

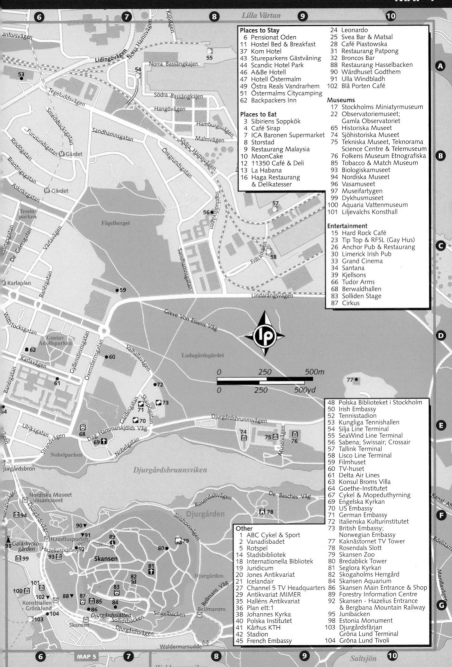

Lilla Värtan

Places to Stay
6 Pensionat Oden
11 Hostel Bed & Breakfast
37 Kom Hotel
43 Stureparkens Gästvåning
44 Scandic Hotel Park
46 A&Be Hotell
47 Hotell Östermalm
49 Östra Reals Vandrarhem
51 Östermalms Citycamping
62 Backpackers Inn

Places to Eat
3 Sibiriens Soppkök
4 Café Sirap
7 ICA Baronen Supermarket
8 Storstad
9 Restaurang Malaysia
10 MoonCake
12 11350 Café & Deli
13 La Habana
16 Haga Restaurang
   & Delikatesser

24 Leonardo
25 Svea Bar & Matsal
28 Café Piastowska
31 Restaurang Patpong
32 Broncos Bar
88 Restaurang Hasselbacken
90 Wärdshuset Godthem
91 Ulla Windbladh
102 Blå Porten Café

Museums
17 Stockholms Miniatyrmuseum
22 Observatoriemuseet;
   Gamla Observatoriet
65 Historiska Museet
74 Sjöhistoriska Museet
75 Tekniska Museet, Teknorama
   Science Centre & Telemuseum
76 Folkens Museum Etnografiska
85 Tobacco & Match Museum
93 Biologiskamuseet
94 Nordiska Museet
96 Vasamuseet
97 Museifartygen
99 Dykhusmuseet
100 Aquaria Vattenmuseum
101 Liljevalchs Konsthall

Entertainment
15 Hard Rock Café
23 Tip Top & RFSL (Gay Hus)
26 Anchor Pub & Restaurang
30 Limerick Irish Pub
33 Grand Cinema
34 Santana
39 Kjellsons
66 Tudor Arms
68 Berwaldhallen
83 Solliden Stage
87 Cirkus

Other
1 ABC Cykel & Sport
2 Vanadisbadet
5 Rotspel
14 Stadsbibliotek
18 Internationella Bibliotek
19 Juridicum
20 Jones Antikvariat
21 Icelandair
27 Channel 5 TV Headquarters
29 Antikvariat MIMER
35 Halléns Antikvariat
36 Plan ett:1
38 Johannes Kyrka
40 Polska Institutet
41 Kårhus KTH
42 Stadion
45 French Embassy

48 Polska Biblioteket i Stockholm
50 Irish Embassy
52 Tennisstadion
53 Kungliga Tennishallen
54 Silja Line Terminal
55 SeaWind Line Terminal
56 Sabena; Swissair; Crossair
57 Tallink Terminal
58 Lisco Line Terminal
59 Filmhuset
60 TV-huset
61 Delta Air Lines
63 Konsul Broms Villa
64 Goethe-Institutet
67 Cykel & Mopeduthyrning
69 Engelska Kyrkan
70 US Embassy
71 German Embassy
72 Italienska Kulturinstitutet
73 British Embassy;
   Norwegian Embassy
77 Kaknästornet TV Tower
78 Rosendals Slott
79 Skansen Zoo
80 Bredablick Tower
81 Seglora Kyrkan
82 Skogaholms Herrgård
84 Skansen Aquarium
86 Skansen Main Entrance & Shop
89 Forestry Information Centre
92 Skansen - Hazelius Entrance
   & Bergbana Mountain Railway
95 Junibacken
98 Estonia Monument
103 Djurgårdsfärjan
   Gröna Lund Terminal
104 Gröna Lund Tivoli

MAP 5

Waldemarsviken

Saltsjön

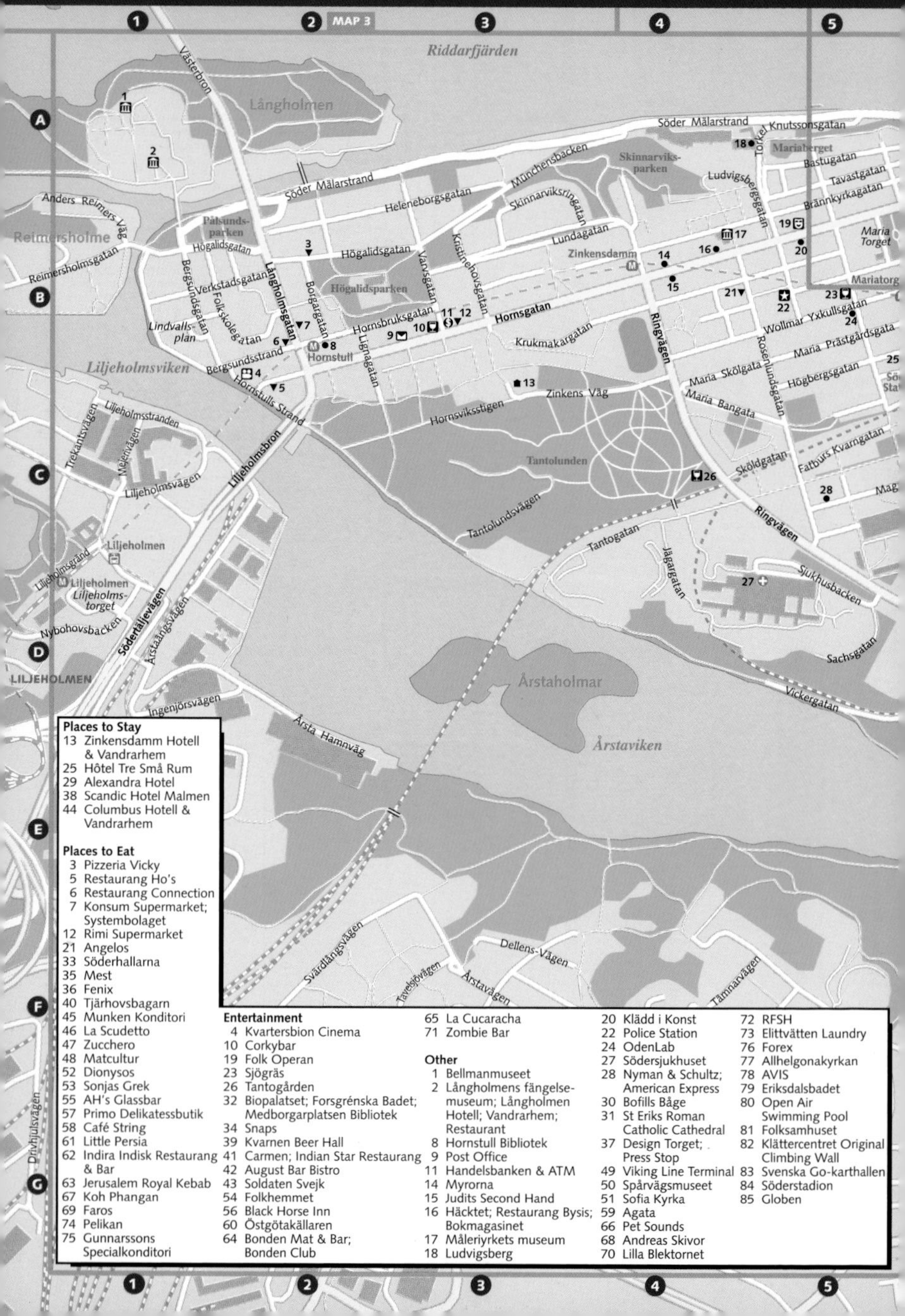

MAP 5

Riddarfjärden

Långholmen

Söder Mälarstrand
Knutssonsgatan

A

Skinnarviks-parken
18 Mariaberget
Bastugatan
Ludvigsbergsg. Tavastgatan
Bränkyrkagatan

Anders Reimers Väg
Påhlunds-parken
Heleneborgsgatan
Münchenbacken
Skinnarviksringen

Reimersholme
Högalidsgatan
Lundagatan
Zinkensdamm 19 Maria Torget

Reimersholmsgatan
Bergsundsgatan
Verkstadsgatan
3 Högalidsgatan
Högalidsparken
Kristinehovsgatan
14 16 17 20

B
Lindvallsgatan
Folkskolegatan
Långholmsgatan
Borgargatan
Hornsbruksgatan
Varvsgatan
Hornsgatan
15 21 22 23 Mariatorg
Mariatorget 24

Lindvalls plan
6 7
Hornstull
11 12
Krukmakargatan
Ringvägen
Wollmar Yxkullsgatan
Rosenlundsgatan

Liljeholmsviken
9 10 8
Maria Prästgårdsgatan
Maria Skolgata
Högbergsgatan 25
Sö Sta

Liljeholmsstranden
4 5
Bergsundsstrand
Hornstulls Strand
Zinkens Väg 13
Hornsvikssstigen
Maria Bangata

C
Liljeholmsvägen
Liljeholmsbron
Tantolunden
Skjöldgatan
Fatbur Kvarngatan
28 Mag

Trekantsvägen
Mejerivägen
Tantolundsvägen
26
Ringvägen
Sjukhusbacken

Liljeholmen
Liljeholmstorget
Tantogatan
Jägargatan
27
Sachsgatan

D
Nybohovsbacken
Södertäljevägen
Årstalundsvägen
Ingenjörsvägen
Årsta Hamnväg
LILJEHOLMEN
Årstaholmar
Årstaviken
Vickergatan

Dellens-Vägen

E
Svärdlångsvägen
Tarbyvägen
Årstavägen
Tämnarvägen

F

Dirihusvägen

G

Places to Stay
- 13 Zinkensdamm Hotell & Vandrarhem
- 25 Hôtel Tre Små Rum
- 29 Alexandra Hotel
- 38 Scandic Hotel Malmen
- 44 Columbus Hotell & Vandrarhem

Places to Eat
- 3 Pizzeria Vicky
- 5 Restaurang Ho's
- 6 Restaurang Connection
- 7 Konsum Supermarket; Systembolaget
- 12 Rimi Supermarket
- 21 Angelos
- 33 Söderhallarna
- 36 Mest
- 36 Fenix
- 40 Tjärhovsbagarn
- 45 Munken Konditori
- 46 La Scudetto
- 47 Zucchero
- 48 Matcultur
- 52 Dionysos
- 53 Sonjas Grek
- 55 AH's Glassbar
- 57 Primo Delikatessbutik
- 58 Café String
- 61 Little Persia
- 62 Indira Indisk Restaurang & Bar
- 63 Jerusalem Royal Kebab
- 67 Koh Phangan
- 69 Faros
- 74 Pelikan
- 75 Gunnarssons Specialkonditori

Entertainment
- 4 Kvartersbion Cinema
- 10 Corkybar
- 19 Folk Operan
- 23 Sjögräs
- 26 Tantogården
- 32 Biopalatset; Forsgrénska Badet; Medborgarplatsen Bibliotek
- 34 Snaps
- 39 Kvarnen Beer Hall
- 41 Carmen; Indian Star Restaurang
- 42 August Bar Bistro
- 43 Soldaten Svejk
- 54 Folkhemmet
- 56 Black Horse Inn
- 60 Östgötakällaren
- 64 Bonden Mat & Bar; Bonden Club
- 65 La Cucaracha
- 71 Zombie Bar

Other
- 1 Bellmanmuseet
- 2 Långholmens fängelse-museum; Långholmen Hotell; Vandrarhem; Restaurant
- 8 Hornstull Bibliotek
- 9 Post Office
- 11 Handelsbanken & ATM
- 14 Myrorna
- 15 Judits Second Hand
- 16 Häcktet; Restaurang Bysis; Bokmagasinet
- 17 Måleriyrkets museum
- 18 Ludvigsberg
- 20 Klädd i Konst
- 22 Police Station
- 24 OdenLab
- 27 Södersjukhuset
- 28 Nyman & Schultz; American Express
- 30 Bofills Båge
- 31 St Eriks Roman Catholic Cathedral
- 37 Design Torget; Press Stop
- 49 Viking Line Terminal
- 50 Spårvägsmuseet
- 51 Sofia Kyrka
- 59 Agata
- 66 Pet Sounds
- 68 Andreas Skivor
- 70 Lilla Blektornet
- 72 RFSH
- 73 Elittvätten Laundry
- 76 Forex
- 77 Allhelgonakyrkan
- 78 AVIS
- 79 Eriksdalsbadet
- 80 Open Air Swimming Pool
- 81 Folksamhuset
- 82 Klättercentret Original Climbing Wall
- 83 Svenska Go-karthallen
- 84 Söderstadion
- 85 Globen

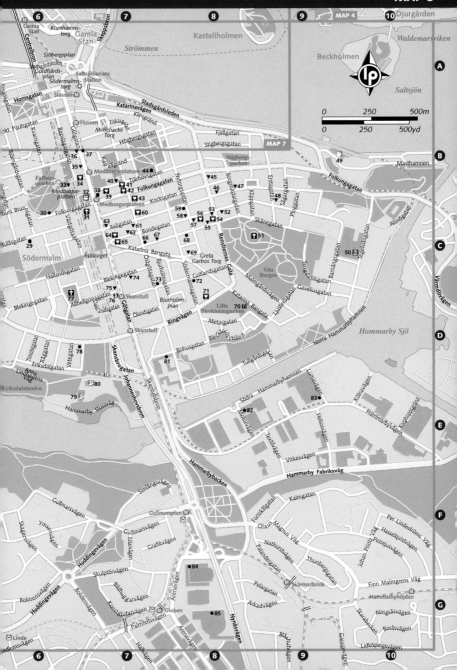

MAP 5

MAP 6

MAP 4
MAP 3
MAP 3
MAP 7

Jutas Backe

Rådmansgatan
Uplandsgatan
Västmannagatan
Teknologatan
Tegnérgatan
Drottninggatan
Tegnérgatan
Saltmätargatan
Sveavägen
Döbelnsgatan
Johannesgatan
Malmskillnadsgatan

Tegnerlunden

Kammakargatan
Hollandergatan
Adolf Fredriks Kyrkogata
Luntmakargatan

Tegnérgatan
Dalagatan
Wallingatan
Wallingatan

Olofsgatan
Hötorget
Malmskillnadsgatan

Barnhusgatan
Apelbergsgatan

Wallingatan
Västmannagatan

Olof Palmes Gata
Hötorget
Hötorgsfaret

Norra
Bantorget

Östra Järnvägsgatan
Vasagatan
Kungsgatan
Klara Norra Kyrkogatan
Gamla Brogatan
Hötorget
Sveavägen

Klarastrandsleden
Kungsbron

Mäster Samuelsgatan
T-Centralen
Sergels Torg
Brunkebergs torg

Kungsbron
Bryggargatan
T-Centralen
Klarabergsgatan
Klara Östra Kyrkogatan
Malmtorg

Blekholmsterrassen
Terminalslingan

Kungsbron
Klarabergsviadukten
Centralplan
Klara Västra Kyrkogatan
Vattugatan
Herkulesgatan
Drottninggatan

Kaplans-
trappan
Kungsholms Strand

Stockholm Central-
stationen
Vasagatan
Klarabergs Rödbodgatan
Jakobsgatan

Kungsholmen

Serafimerstranden
Blekholmsfaret

Rödbod-
torget
Fredsgatan

Tegelbacken

Kaplansbacken
Hantverkargatan
Stadhusbron

Ragnar
Ostbergs
Plan

Hantverkargatan
Vasabron

Samuel Owens Gata

Strömsborg

Norr Mälarstrand
Centralbron

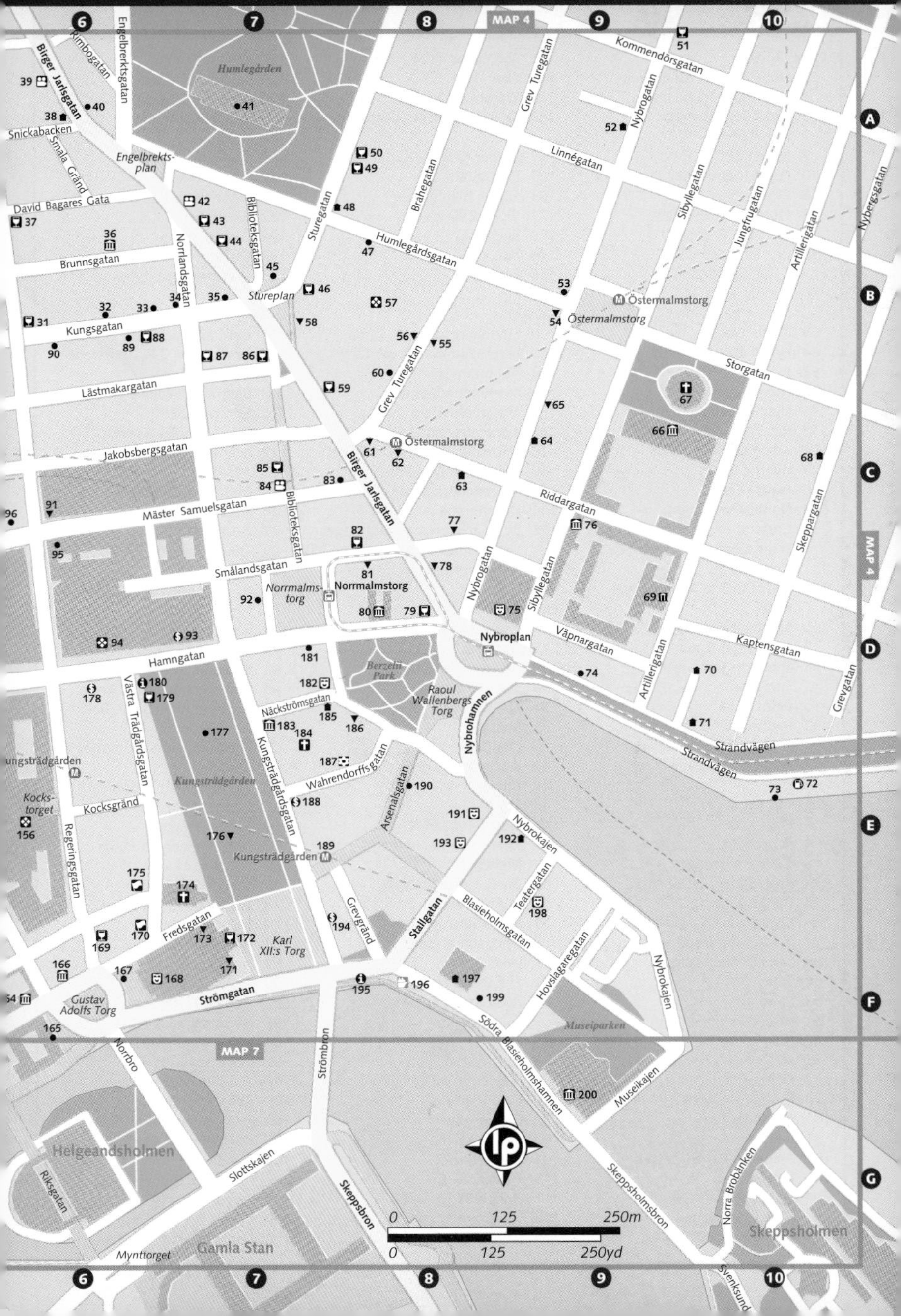

MAP 6

Humlegården

Birger Jarlsgatan
Engelbrektsgatan
Kommendörsgatan
Grev Turegatan
Nybrogatan
Sibyllegatan
Jungfrugatan
Artillerigatan
Nybergsgatan
Linnégatan
Engelbrekts-plan
David Bagares Gata
Brunnsgatan
Norrlandsgatan
Bibliotksgatan
Sturegatan
Brahegatan
Humlegårdsgatan
Östermalmstorg
Storgatan
Skeppargatan
Kungsgatan
Stureplan
Grev Turegatan
Birger Jarlsgatan
Lästmakargatan
Jakobsbergsgatan
Riddargatan
Mäster Samuelsgatan
Bibliotksgatan
Smålandsgatan
Sibyllegatan
Norrmalms-torg
Norrmalmstorg
Väpnargatan
Kaptensgatan
Nybroplan
Hamngatan
Berzelii Park
Raoul Wallenbergs Torg
Nybrohamnen
Strandvägen
Västra Trädgårdsgatan
Näckströmsgatan
Kungsträdgårdsgatan
Wahrendorffsgatan
Arsenalsgatan
Nybrokajen
Kungsträdgården
Kungsträdgården
Kocks-torget
Kocksgränd
Regeringsgatan
Grevgatan
Stallgatan
Blasieholmsgatan
Teatergatan
Hovslagaregatan
Nybrokajen
Fredsgatan
Karl XII:s Torg
Strömgatan
Gustav Adolfs Torg
Södra Blasieholmshamnen
Museiparken
Norrbro
Strömbron
Museikajen
Skeppsholmsbron
Helgeandsholmen
Riksgatan
Slottskajen
Skeppsbron
Norra Brobänken
Mynttorget
Gamla Stan
Skeppsholmen
Svensksund

0   125   250m
0   125   250yd

MAP 6

Places to Stay
1 Hotell August Strindberg
2 Hotell Lilla Rådmannen
3 Hotel Tegnérlunden
7 Hotell Bema
9 Hostel Mitt i City
10 Good Night Hotell Danielsson
16 City Backpackers
18 Queen's Hotel; Bistro
Boheme; Regina
38 Crystal Plaza Hotel;
Finlandsinstitutet
48 Lydmar Hotel
52 Mornington Hotel
63 Castle Hotel
64 Hotell Örnskjöld
68 Pärlan
70 Hotel Esplanade
71 Hotel Diplomat
112 Rica City Hotel
124 Adlon Hotel
125 Central Hotel
126 Freys Hotel
127 Nordic Hotel Light
131 Comfort Hotel Prize; World
Trade Center & City Office
132 Nordic Hotel Sea
136 Radisson SAS Royal Viking
Hotel
155 Scandic Hotel Sergel Plaza;
Restaurant Anna Rella
158 Sheraton Stockholm;
Europcar
185 Berns Hotel
192 Radisson SAS Strand Hotel
197 Grand Hôtel Stockholm;
Franska Matsalen

Places to Eat
4 Rolfs Kök
6 Sabai Sabai
8 Carinas Pizzeria
12 Restaurang Spice House
25 Djingis Khan
54 Östermalms Saluhall;
Tysta Mari; Depå Sushi
55 Grodan Grev Ture
56 Tures
58 Sturehof
61 Vivo T-Jarlen Supermarket
62 Sturekatten
65 McDonald's Nybrogatan
77 Collage
78 Restaurant Riche
81 Restaurant KB
91 Rooster
97 Allemans Bar & Matsal
103 Kungshallen
104 Hötorgshallen;
Filmstaden Sergel
123 Vetekatten

135 McDonald's (24 Hours)
142 Eken
143 Stadshuskällaren
145 Orientexpressen Restaurang
& Bar
153 Burger King
160 Fredsgatan 12
163 Sibylla Klaragrillen
171 Operakällaren
173 Bakfickan
176 Piccolino
186 Berns

Museums
5 Strindbergsmuseet; Strindbergs; Antikvariat Blå Tårnet
13 Apoteksmuseet
36 Marionettmuseet;
Marionetteatern
66 Armémuseum
76 Musikmuseet; Kronobagariet
80 Hallwylska Museet
164 Medelhavsmuseet
166 Dansmuseet
183 Bolagsmuseet; Systembolaget
Head Office
200 National Museum

Entertainment
11 Phukets Oslag Bar
15 Dansens Hus
28 Glenn Miller Café
30 Saga Cinema
31 The Loft; Tiger Rum & Bar
37 Nalen
39 Zita Cinema
42 Biografen Sture Cinema
43 Chiaro
44 Spy Bar
46 Sturecompagniet
49 Kharma Restaurant &
Nightclub
50 Crazy Horse Saloon
51 St Andrews Inn
59 Bull & Bear Inn
75 Dramatiska Teatern
79 Level
82 The Dubliner
84 Röda Kvarn Cinema;
Sophies Bar
85 Biblos
86 East; Nanso
87 Norrlands Bar & Grill
88 Café Vivels
99 Golden Hits
100 Royal Cinema
101 Konserthuset
115 Karlsson & Co
117 Holger Bar & Mat
118 Torsgatan 1
120 Vasa Teatern

128 Oscars Teatern
129 Jazzclub Fasching
130 Heaven; Sargasso
152 Stadsteatern
168 Operan
169 Naglo Vodka Bar
172 Café Opera
179 Daily News Café
182 China Teatern
191 Nybrokajen 11
193 Stallet
198 Wallmans Salonger

Other
14 Centralantikvariatet
17 Norra Latin City Conference
Center
19 Biografen Skandia
20 Centralbadet
21 Adolf Fredriks Kyrka
22 Svensk Hemslöjd
23 Aeroflot
24 Exchange Center
26 Telia Phoneshop
27 X-Change; STA Travel
29 Friluftsbolaget
32 Stadium
33 Kilroy Travels
34 Naturkompaniet
35 Silja Line
40 Rönnells Antikvariat
41 Kungliga Biblioteket
45 SAS; Skyways; Lufthansa;
Austrian Airlines; Air Baltic
47 DIS Inredning
53 English Theatre Company
Office
57 Sturegallerian Shopping
Centre; Sturebadet
60 Systembolaget
67 Hedvig Eleonora Kyrka
69 Kungliga Hovstallet
72 Shell Petrol Station
73 Tvillingarnas Boat Hire
74 Svenskt Tenn
83 Konsthantverkarna
89 Nordiska Kristall
90 Aer Lingus; Alitalia
92 Finnair; Hotel Stockholm
93 Nordbanken & ATM
94 NK Department Store
95 Systembolaget
96 Akademibokhandeln
98 Rese Varuhuset
102 Svala & Söderlund; Duka
105 Kodak Image Center
106 Good Food
107 Australian Embassy
108 Sergel Foto
109 Expert
110 Central Post Office

MAP 6

Moorings on Stockholm harbour

MAP 7

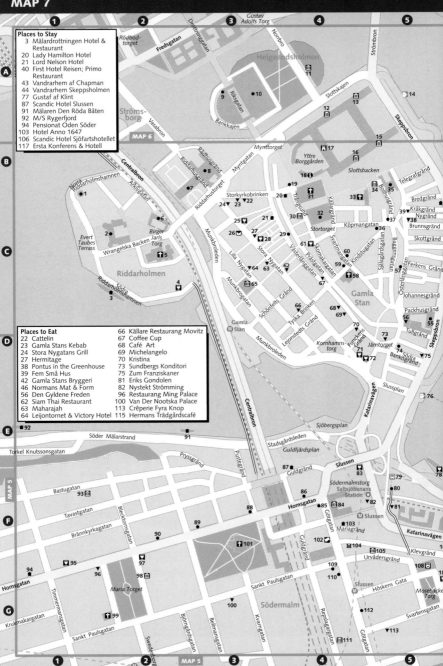

Places to Stay
- 3 Mälardrottningen Hotel & Restaurant
- 20 Lady Hamilton Hotel
- 21 Lord Nelson Hotel
- 40 First Hotel Reisen; Primo Restaurant
- 43 Vandrarhem af Chapman
- 44 Vandrarhem Skeppsholmen
- 77 Gustaf af Klint
- 87 Scandic Hotel Slussen
- 91 Mälaren Den Röda Båten
- 92 M/S Rygerfjord
- 94 Pensionat Oden Söder
- 103 Hotel Anno 1647
- 106 Scandic Hotel Sjöfartshotellet
- 117 Ersta Konferens & Hotell

Places to Eat
- 22 Cattelin
- 23 Gamla Stans Kebab
- 24 Stora Nygatans Grill
- 27 Hermitage
- 38 Pontus in the Greenhouse
- 39 Fem Små Hus
- 42 Gamla Stans Bryggeri
- 46 Normans Mat & Form
- 56 Den Gyldene Freden
- 62 Siam Thai Restaurant
- 63 Maharajah
- 64 Leijontornet & Victory Hotel
- 66 Källare Restaurang Movitz
- 67 Coffee Cup
- 68 Café Art
- 69 Michelangelo
- 70 Kristina
- 73 Sundbergs Konditori
- 75 Zum Franziskaner
- 81 Eriks Gondolen
- 82 Nystekt Strömming
- 96 Restaurang Ming Palace
- 100 Van Der Nootska Palace
- 113 Crêperie Fyra Knop
- 115 Hermans Trädgårdscafé

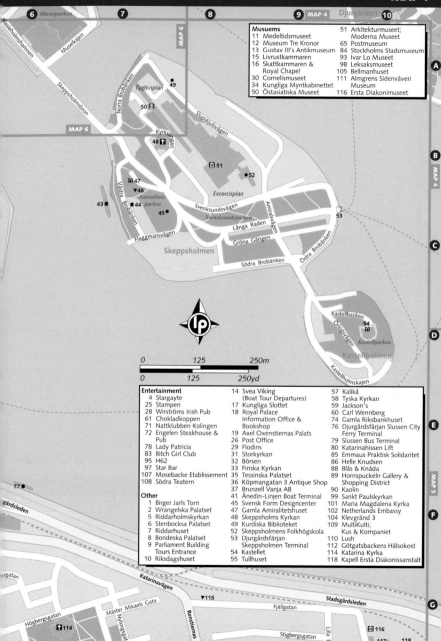

MAP 7

Museums
- 11 Medeltidsmuseet
- 12 Museum Tre Kronor
- 13 Gustav III's Antikmuseum
- 15 Livrustkammaren
- 16 Skattkammaren & Royal Chapel
- 30 Cornelismuseet
- 34 Kungliga Myntkabinettet
- 50 Östasiatiska Museet
- 51 Arkitekturmuseet; Moderna Museet
- 65 Postmuseum
- 84 Stockholms Stadsmuseum
- 93 Ivar Lo Museet
- 98 Leksaksmuseet
- 105 Bellmanhuset
- 111 Almgrens Sidenväveri Museum
- 116 Ersta Diakonimuseet

Entertainment
- 4 Stargayte
- 25 Stampen
- 28 Wirströms Irish Pub
- 61 Chokladkoppen
- 71 Nattklubben Kolingen
- 72 Engelen Steakhouse & Pub
- 78 Lady Patricia
- 83 Bitch Girl Club
- 95 H62
- 97 Star Bar
- 107 Mosebacke Etablissement
- 108 Södra Teatern

Other
- 1 Birger Jarls Torn
- 2 Wrangelska Palatset
- 5 Riddarholmskyrkan
- 6 Stenbocksa Palatset
- 7 Riddarhuset
- 8 Bondeska Palatset
- 9 Parliament Building Tours Entrance
- 10 Riksdagshuset
- 14 Svea Viking (Boat Tour Departures)
- 17 Kungliga Slottet
- 18 Royal Palace Information Office & Bookshop
- 19 Axel Oxenstiernas Palats
- 26 Post Office
- 29 Flodins
- 31 Storkyrkan
- 32 Börsen
- 33 Finska Kyrkan
- 35 Tessinska Palatset
- 36 Köpmangatan 3 Antique Shop
- 37 Brunzell Vanja AB
- 41 Ånedin-Linjen Boat Terminal
- 45 Svensk Form Designcenter
- 47 Gamla Amiralitetshuset
- 48 Skeppsholms Kyrkan
- 52 Skeppsholmens Folkhögskola
- 53 Djurgårdsfärjan Skeppsholmen Terminal
- 54 Kastellet
- 55 Tullhuset
- 57 Kalikå
- 58 Tyska Kyrkan
- 59 Jackson's
- 60 Carl Wennberg
- 74 Gamla Riksbankhuset
- 76 Djurgårdsfärjan Slussen City Ferry Terminal
- 79 Slussen Bus Terminal
- 80 Katarinahissen Lift
- 85 Emmaus Praktisk Solidaritet
- 86 Helle Knudsen
- 88 Blås & Knåda
- 89 Hornspuckeln Gallery & Shopping District
- 90 Kaolin
- 99 Sankt Paulskyrkan
- 101 Maria Magdalena Kyrka
- 102 Netherlands Embassy
- 104 Klevgränd 3
- 109 MultiKulti; Kus & Kompaniet
- 110 Lush
- 112 Götgatsbackens Hälsokost
- 114 Katarina Kyrka
- 118 Kapell Ersta Diakonissanstalt

MAP LEGEND

CITY ROUTES

Freeway	Freeway		Unsealed Road
Highway	Primary Road		One Way Street
Road	Secondary Road		Pedestrian Street
Street	Street		Stepped Street
Lane	Lane		Tunnel
	On/Off Ramp		Footbridge

REGIONAL ROUTES

	Tollway, Freeway
	Primary Road
	Secondary Road
	Minor Road

BOUNDARIES

	International
	State
	Disputed
	Fortified Wall

HYDROGRAPHY

	River, Creek		Dry Lake; Salt Lake
	Canal		Spring; Rapids
	Lake		Waterfalls

TRANSPORT ROUTES & STATIONS

	Train		Ferry
	Metro		Walking Trail
	Tram		Walking Tour
	Underground Metro		Path
	Funicular		Pier or Jetty

AREA FEATURES

	Building		Market		Beach
	Park, Gardens		Sports Ground		Cemetery
	Campus		Plaza		

POPULATION SYMBOLS

CAPITAL	National Capital	CITY	City	Village	Village
CAPITAL	State Capital	Town	Town		Urban Area

MAP SYMBOLS

	Place to Stay		Place to Eat	Point of Interest

	Airport		Cycling		Museum		Swimming Pool
	Bank		Embassy, Consulate		Parking		Synagogue
	Bus Terminal		Fountain		Police Station		Theatre
	Camping		Hospital		Post Office		Tomb
	Castle		Internet Cafe		Pub or Bar		Tourist Information
	Church		Jazz Location		Shopping Centre		Transport
	Cinema		Monument		Stately Home		Zoo

Note: not all symbols displayed above appear in this book

LONELY PLANET OFFICES

Australia
Locked Bag 1, Footscray, Victoria 3011
☎ 03 8379 8000 fax 03 8379 8111
email: talk2us@lonelyplanet.com.au

UK
10a Spring Place, London NW5 3BH
☎ 020 7428 4800 fax 020 7428 4828
email: go@lonelyplanet.co.uk

USA
150 Linden St, Oakland, CA 94607
☎ 510 893 8555 TOLL FREE: 800 275 8555
fax 510 893 8572
email: info@lonelyplanet.com

France
1 rue du Dahomey, 75011 Paris
☎ 01 55 25 33 00 fax 01 55 25 33 01
email: bip@lonelyplanet.fr
www.lonelyplanet.fr

World Wide Web: www.lonelyplanet.com or AOL keyword: lp
Lonely Planet Images: lpi@lonelyplanet.com.au